The Evaluation and Measurement of Library Services

Joseph R. Matthews

LIBRARIES
UNLIMITED
A Member of the Greenwood Publishing Group

Westport, Connecticut • London

Library of Congress Cataloging-in-Publication Data

Matthews, Joseph R.
  The evaluation and measurement of library services / Joseph R. Matthews.
    p. cm.
  Includes bibliographical references and index.
  ISBN-13: 978-1-59158-532-9 (alk. paper)
  1. Libraries—United States—Evaluation. 2. Public services (Libraries)—
United States—Evaluation. 3. Libraries—Evaluation. 4. Public services
(Libraries)—Evaluation. I. Title.
  Z678.85.M37 2007
  025.10973—dc22   2007017726

British Library Cataloguing in Publication Data is available.

Library of Congress Catalog Card Number: 2007017726
ISBN-13: 978-1-59158-532-9

First published in 2007

Libraries Unlimited, 88 Post Road West, Westport, CT 06881
A Member of the Greenwood Publishing Group, Inc.
www.lu.com

Printed in the United States of America

The paper used in this book complies with the
Permanent Paper Standard issued by the National
Information Standards Organization (Z39.48–1984).

10 9 8 7 6 5 4 3

This book is dedicated to all types of librarians who are inquisitive and enthusiastic about the variety and quality of services they provide. They formulate an evaluation study, research ways the study can be done, collect and analyze the data, and write a report. More important, they also prepare an article for publication. It is because of this cadre of dedicated professionals that librarians have a literature they can draw on to improve services for the library's customers. And to the librarians who conducted research and have been "published," on behalf of the profession, thanks so much!

Even a cursory examination of this book will reveal the wide variety of methods that librarians have applied to evaluate library services and the contributions of the library in the lives of their customers. It is my hope that you will feel empowered to apply some of these methods in the evaluation of services in your library. If you do, the end result will be beneficial to your library's customers.

If I have missed an evaluation topic you feel should have been included or omitted a cite to favorite article, research report, or book you feel should be included, please do let me know, so perhaps I can include it in the next edition of this book.

Contents

Part III
Evaluation of Library Services

Chapter 8: Evaluation of the Physical Collection (*Cont.*)

Chapter 9: Evaluation of Electronic Resources 149

Chapter 10: Evaluation of Reference Services..165

Chapter 11: Evaluation of Technical Services 183

Part IV
Evaluation of the Library

Foreword

James G. Neal, vice president for information services and university librarian at Columbia University, surmises that in academic libraries "decisions are routinely not supported by the evidence of well-designed investigations" and that "research in the field is poorly communicated, understood, and applied." He concludes that "it is imperative that academic librarians and higher education libraries develop and carry out systematic research and development programs."[1] More than likely, his speculation is applicable to many other types of libraries around the globe. Compounding the situation, many graduate programs of library and information science, especially in the United States, do not require students to take a course in research methods and evaluation. The graduates of those programs probably have not even taken an elective course on the topic.

As a result, they are ill prepared to make informed judgments based on a view of evaluation as a systematic inquiry process, the purpose of which is to collect data useful for documenting the quality and effectiveness of existing programs and services, and to use that information for service improvement, demonstrating best practices, or providing evidence of accountability. Evaluation is part of a research process: collecting and interpreting evidence and using those results to meet the institutional or organizational missions effectively and efficiently.

In the libraries of today and tomorrow, there will be greater focus on leadership and the accomplishment of a shared vision, one that transforms libraries. Successful change management aimed at transforming library roles, values, and vision involves creating an organizational culture that supports and rewards change. The culture of the organization is one of the most critical factors in determining an organization's capacity to change and maintain effectiveness. Evaluation research will have to become more of a regular part of that culture.

As is evident, evaluation is not an end unto itself and it might be combined with assessment. Neither evaluation nor assessment will go away; rather, they are embedded in the feedback loop of an open systems environment. Any judgments rendered impact the planning process and the relationship of a library to the communities it serves and those to whom the library director reports, the value of the library to its parent organization, and the expectations of stakeholders. Evaluation also involves internal efficiencies for an organization.

Joe Matthews provides a good introduction to evaluation and measurement, guiding those unfamiliar with evaluation research in how to gather data upon which to render judgments about library collections and services. The book does not require prior knowledge about the research process and how to gather reliable and valid data. He introduces concepts and the evaluation research process in a clear and concise manner, with references to some excellent writings.

As librarians new to the research process engage in collecting data to make those judgment calls, they might view *The Evaluation and Measurement of Library Services* as a guide to inform them better about the process and how to conduct a study that can withstand external scrutiny while producing data useful to rendering judgments about ongoing programs and services.

Peter Hernon
Professor
Simmons College, Boston

NOTES

1. James G. Neal. The Research and Development Imperative in the Academic Library: Path to the Future. *portal: Libraries and the Academy*, 6 (1), 2006, 1.

Acknowledgments

No effort to prepare the manuscript for a book could be accomplished by a single individual. Thus, it is important to acknowledge those who reviewed drafts of chapters and provided helpful comments and suggestions. This book is much improved as a result of the care and dedication of these friends and colleagues who gave of their time to suggest improvements. I would like especially to thank Peter Hernon, professor at the Simmons Graduate School of Library and Information Science, and Karen Markey, professor at the University of Michigan Library School, who provided insightful comments and thought-provoking suggestions on the complete manuscript.

In addition, I thank Jo Bell Whitlach, a recently retired librarian from the San Jose State University who provided comments on the reference services chapter; Christie Koontz, professor at the College of Information at Florida State University, who reviewed the chapter on users; Michael Buckland, Emeritus Professor, School of Information, University of California, Berkeley, for his review of two chapters; Bob Molyneux for his review of the two chapters on statistics and the analysis of data; and Neal Kaske, chief, Public Services at NOAA library, for his review of several chapters.

The book has also been improved by comments from Ken Haycock, dean of the School of Library & Information Science at San Jose University; Mary Somerville, associate dean at San Jose State University Library; and Leigh Estabrook, professor at the Graduate School of Library and Information Science, University of Illinois, Champaign Urbana.

And thanks also to Teri Roudenbush, head of the interlibrary loan department at the California State University San Marcos Library. Teri and her staff always manage to find required books and articles while remaining cheerful in the face of a daunting workload. I also appreciate the cooperation of a large number of libraries that supplied the needed materials through interlibrary loan.

Thanks also to Sharon DeJohn for her careful and thoughtful editing of the manuscript. Sharon is able to take my ramblings and make them much more readable.

Joe Matthews
Joe@JoeMatthews.Org
Carlsbad, CA

Introduction

The evaluation and measurement of library services is an important part of the management of any library. In concept, evaluation is fairly simple. In the best of all possible worlds, an evaluation project would start out with clear and specific objectives that would in turn lead to the selection of the most appropriate measurement tools. However, in many cases an evaluation starts out without real clear objectives and just a nagging feeling that something needs to be explored. John Tukey called this latter process exploratory data analysis, a form of detective work.[1] Comparing a variety of performance measures with a group of peer libraries may reveal some anomalies that deserve a closer look. This exploration has been called "noodling around in the numbers" by Bob Molyneux.

The individual or team involved with the evaluation determines

- whether there has been a change in performance over a selected period of time,
- whether the change is in the preferred direction, and
- the extent of the change.

Evaluation is a part of the feedback loop on how well the library is performing. In order for evaluation to be particularly meaningful, the process requires objectives as criteria.

Most librarians are content to continue what libraries have traditionally done to provide services to customers. Occasionally a library will introduce a new service, but rarely does a library embrace the concept of using evaluation as a part of its day-to-day activities. The vast majority of performance measures and statistics historically gathered and used by libraries are focused on inputs and outputs. Yet these measures and statistics do little to reveal the impact the library has on the lives of its customers.

The intended audience for this book is library directors and managers in all types of libraries who are interested in evaluating one or more library services. The book is also intended for library school students, who, it is hoped, will find the content to be valuable in a number of courses as they prepare for a wonderful career in librarianship.

The purpose of this book is to suggest that the concerns identified by Don Revill many years ago about research in librarianship can be overcome. These concerns follow:

1. You can't do research in librarianship.
2. And if you can:
    a. It shouldn't be called research, and
    b. It can't be generalized to any other library or situation.
3. But if research can be done, no one does so because he or she can't understand the research.
4. And if someone did understand the research, he or she wouldn't accept it.
5. And if someone did, he or she would be deluding himself or herself, because the research wouldn't work.[2]

The purpose of this book is to provide a set of tools that will assist any library in evaluating a particular library service, whether covered in this book or not. The goal is to remove some of the mysteries surrounding the process of evaluation so that many librarians will see the value of performing evaluation in their libraries.

This book is divided into four parts. Part I introduces the concept of evaluation, explores a number of evaluation models that might be used, and discusses a number of issues surrounding the process of evaluation.

Part II is concerned with methodological issues. A number of different tools are discussed so that the librarian will know more about the strengths and limitations of any particular tool or methodology. Each tool is explained so that it can be used in a particular evaluation project.

Part III presents a number of chapters that are focused on evaluating a specific library service. Each chapter includes a definition of the service, a discussion of possible methods that can be or have been used to evaluate a service, and a summary of the available research pertaining to a particular topic.

Some obvious areas of library services have purposely been excluded because they would require substantial discussion. These include, among other topics, evaluation of the information retrieval process, evaluation of automated systems (due in part to the very high reliability of systems today), catalog use studies, and the evaluation of library buildings.

Part IV presents an overview of the models with which the value of all the services and functions of a library can be determined. Chapters pertaining to the accomplishments of an individual, as well as the economic and social impacts of the library, are presented. Frameworks that have been used for a librarywide evaluation can be particularly helpful when communicating with the library's funding stakeholders.

NOTES

1. John W. Tukey. *Exploratory Data Analysis*. Reading, MA: Addison-Wesley, 1970.

2. Don Revill. You Can't Do Research in Librarianship. *Library Management News*, 11, February 1980, 10–25.

Part I

Evaluation: Process and Models

1

Evaluation Issues

I think there's an increasing awareness that the role of evaluation is not to prove, but to improve.

—Amy Owen[1]

What distinguishes evaluation is not planning, methodology, or subject matter, but *intent*—the purpose for which it is done. Unlike research, with its concern about rigorous methodology and publication, an evaluation employs standard research methods for evaluative purposes. As Thomas Childers and Nancy Van House have noted:

> Evaluation is the assessment of goodness. It consists of comparing the organization's current performance against some standard or set of expectations. Evaluation has two parts: the collection of information . . . about the organization's performance; and the comparison of this information to some set of criteria. The collection of information is not itself evaluation: a critical component of evaluation is the exercise of judgment in which criteria are applied to the organization's current reality.[2]

Clearly the library profession has wrestled with and not found a good definition for "goodness." So how is "goodness" defined for a library? Is it possible to compare the library with an ideal or a set of standards? These are important issues for anyone who is involved with the preparation of an evaluation study.

Evaluation can be characterized from several different perspectives, among them the following:

- In most cases, evaluation is concerned with *service-derived questions*—the quality, cost, or effectiveness of a service or program. Typically an evaluation study represents matters of administrative and programmatic interest.

- Evaluation compares "what is" with "what should (could) be." The element of *judgment* against criteria (implicit or explicit) is basic for all evaluations.

- Acknowledging that an evaluation study can take on a life of its own, it is important to remember the service or program is *serving* people—the library's customers.

- The focus of evaluation is *improvement,* and many of the reports of evaluation studies sit in file folders. In some cases, a library may post an evaluation study report on its Web site, but those involved in the project will not take the next step to produce a journal article. Alternatively, the underlying concern of most research is publication and the dissemination of results.

- Evaluation has been called "action research" due to its direct application to the real world, while basic research focuses on explanation or prediction.

- An evaluation may generate *conflict.* Often professionals believe strongly in a program or service they are providing and thus see little need for evaluation. In a sense, they may view an evaluation project as being "on trial." Those involved in the evaluation effort should communicate often and share the message that the focus of the evaluation is about the process, program, or service and not people.

- An evaluation project may be designed to provide *feedback* to and evaluate a commercial vendor such as a book vendor or serial subscription service.

- Communicating the results of an evaluation closes the feedback loop and shows the library staff and interested stakeholders that the library is improving its services.

- An evaluation project may be designed to enhance the visibility of library services, describe their impact, and strengthen the library's political position among stakeholders.

- In the academic environment, evaluation is often referred to as *assessment.*[3]

Evaluation should be an essential tool for any manager. Richard Orr suggested that a manager has four major responsibilities:

- to define the goals of the organization;

- to obtain the resources needed to reach these goals;

- to identify the programs and services required to achieve those goals, and to optimize the allocation of resources among these programs and services; and

- to see that the resource allocations for a particular activity are used wisely (cost efficiency).[4]

Clearly the latter two responsibilities imply the use of evaluation methods. The third responsibility focuses on evaluating the outcomes of a program or service; this is sometimes called effectiveness. The fourth responsibility must of necessity focus on how efficient a library program or service is.

José-Marie Griffiths and Don King identified some principles for good evaluation research:

- Evaluation must have a purpose, rather than be an end in itself.

- There is no need to evaluate without the potential for some action.

- Evaluation must go beyond description and understand the relationships among operational performance, users, and organizations.

- Evaluation can be a tool for communication among staff and users.

- Evaluation should be ongoing rather than sporadic.

- Ongoing evaluation provides a means for monitoring, diagnosis, and improvement.

- Evaluation should be dynamic, reflecting new knowledge and changes in the environment.[5]

WHO DECIDES

The types of individuals involved depends on the focus of the evaluation effort. As shown in Table 1.1, an evaluation can have an internal orientation (library-centric view) or an external perspective (customer-centric view), or be a combination of the two. Each of these perspectives answers a different "how" question.

Table 1.1. Answering the "How" Questions

Library-centric View	Combination View	Customer-centric View
How much?	How reliable?	How well?
How many?	How accurate?	How courteous?
How economical?	How valuable?	How responsive?
How prompt?		How satisfied?

The *library-centric view* has an internal or operations viewpoint. The focus of evaluation efforts is on processes, functions, and services. The things that are measured in this type of evaluation are typically transactions, context, and the performance of the library. In order to provide a comparison, a group of "peer" libraries is selected. Telltale signs of when the library is not performing well include errors, higher costs than peer libraries, delays, customer complaints, and staff complaints about other staff members or activities (or lack of activity) in another department.

Evaluating the internal operations of a library requires those involved to answer some important questions:

- How do our costs compare to our peers'?

- How do our service delivery times compare to our peers'? To customer expectations?

- Will an alternate resource mix produce better results? Should we consider outsourcing a process?

- Does the library have the needed resources?

- Do the library's staff have the necessary mix of skills?

- What criteria will be used to select "peer" libraries? Should libraries from outside the state be included in developing a set of peer libraries? When considering a group of peer libraries, how many should be in the group?

The *combination view* requires both the library and the customer to answer service quality questions. Here the expectations of customers are an important part of the assessment process (it is also possible to identify and quantify the gaps in service). The evaluation examines the differences that may exist between customer expectations and the quality of service actually delivered. And the only standard that counts is the customer's! If poor service is provided, then the customer will be dissatisfied and will not likely return to the library—as well as tell others about his or her "bad" experiences.

Notice that this view will not rely on traditional library *output* measures, which include such performance measures as annual circulation and number of reference transactions. Rather, it may require the library to start exploring the use of *outcome* measures to answer the question of "how valuable" the library is. *Outcome* is defined as a change in attitude, behavior, knowledge, skill, status, or condition. Thus, outcome-based evaluation is a systematic way to assess the extent to which a program or a service has achieved its intended results. Among the key questions that might be addressed are the following:

- What are the impacts or consequences for those who utilize a service?
- What are the real results rather than the rhetoric of intent?
- How has this program or service made a difference?
- What do stakeholders expect this service or program to deliver?
- What outcome measures should be used to measure impacts?
- Can the library develop a cause-and-effect relationship between a service or program and the intended outcomes?

The *customer-centric view* requires some effort to prepare an evaluation that will produce meaningful and valuable results. Customers form expectations based on their experiences in other competitive environments—bookstores, video rental stores, used bookstores, music stores. And these expectations are created based on prior visits by the customer to physical and virtual (Web site) stores. Libraries are increasingly turning to customer surveys to determine the extent to which the library is or is not meeting the customer's expectations.

Libraries have developed a range of collections and services to meet the needs of their customers. Special libraries typically have a specific focus and a limited set of customers to serve, such as hospital, medical, legal, business, or technical organizations. School libraries serve children and their teachers up through high school. Academic libraries, which are a part of a college or university, serve students, faculty, and researchers, who are engaged in teaching, learning, and research. Public libraries usually serve their communities from one or more locations. Any evaluation should start with a clear understanding of the needs of those served by the library.

In some cases, an evaluation may be a requirement for receiving grant funding. A more extensive list of "how" questions was developed by Peter Hernon and Ellen Altman (see Table 1.2).[6]

Table 1.2. Components of the "How" Questions

Library Control				Library and Customers Decide				Customers Decide		
How much?	**How many?**	**How economical?**	**How prompt?**	**How valuable?**	**How reliable?**	**How accurate?**	**How well?**	**How courteous?**	**How responsive?**	**How satisfied?**
Magnitude	Magnitude	Resources used	Cyrcle times	Effort expanded	Dependability	Completeness	Accuracy	Attentive	Anticipatory	Expectations met
Percent of change last year	Change	Units processed	Turnaround time	Cost	Access	Comprehensiveness	Promptness	Welcoming	Helpful	Materials obtained
Percent of overall change			Anticipatory	Benefit obtained	Accuracy	Currency	Courtesy		Empathetic	Personal interaction
Cost							Expertise			Ease of use
										Equipment used
										Environment
										Comfort
										Willingness to return

What the library thinks its customer wants
Is not necessarily the same as
What the library thinks it has to offer
Is not necessarily the same as
How the customer experiences a library service
Is not necessarily the same as
What the customer really wants.

AN EVALUATION ACTION PLAN

Preparing an evaluation involves a number of discrete activities, including the following:

- Identifying the problem
- Determining the scope of the analysis
- Determining whether the answer already exists
- Determining the kind of analysis to do
- Deciding what data will be needed
- Conducting the analysis and preparing a report
- Using the results for service improvement: the feedback loop

Identifying the Problem

Selecting a topic or area as a candidate for evaluation is, in most cases, fairly straightforward. The library should pay attention to the following:

- **Production bottlenecks.** Are there any backlogs? Bottlenecks may be symptomatic of staffing shortages, poor supervision, cumbersome procedures, or inadequate training. It is important to note that bottlenecks are rarely the fault of staff.

- **Tasks that are performed frequently.** The more frequently a task is performed, the better a candidate it becomes for evaluation. Some obvious candidates are circulation, reference, interlibrary loan, and technical services.

- **Activities that require frequent movement.** The movement may be people, forms, equipment, book trucks, and so forth. Even frequent movement involving short distances can translate into high costs. An evaluation in this area will need to consider and identify optimum physical arrangements.

- **Declining budgets.** Every library will face this challenge sooner or later. Consider activities or services that consume large portions of the budget. The evaluation will have to identify what alternatives exist for accomplishing the same tasks, along with the associated costs for each alternative.

A brief statement of the evaluation project or a problem statement should be prepared. This statement should not suggest any solutions or attempt to identify the causes for the problem. It should answer the following:

- What is the problem or perceived problem? What is the current performance of the process or activity (if known or can be quantified) that it is proposed to evaluate?
- What are the symptoms pointing to the problem?
- What is problematic or unacceptable about this performance?
- When and where do problems occur?
- What is the impact of the problem from the perspective of our customers?

Following are examples of a problem statement or proposed evaluation:

> The acquisitions budget is likely to be reduced. We are unsure of the amount of use our librarians and customers make of our fairly extensive print reference collection. We should determine the extent of and type of actual use, especially in light of our fairly large expenditures for licensing electronic databases. We may be able to reduce our expenditures for reference print materials without compromising the quality of service.

> Determine why ILL is taking longer than our customers expect. Currently our turnaround time for borrowing interlibrary loan books is averaging X days for 80 percent of our transactions. Our customers are requesting materials in Y days, based on a recent ILL customer survey. We need to gather data about the time it takes to place requested materials in the hands of our customers. Will we be able to reduce the time?

Determining the Scope of the Analysis

It is important to determine what will and will not be evaluated. Will the evaluation take an internal perspective that focuses on library operations, or will an external focus be included and customers be involved in some manner? Perhaps both perspectives might be included in the evaluation.

A number of other important issues have to be addressed as the planning for the evaluation takes place:

- Are the current patterns of use cause for concern? Has demand for a service dropped off? Has demand suddenly peaked?
- Will costs have to be determined? If so, does the budget provide sufficient details to identify all of the cost components for providing the service?
- Should customers of the library be involved? If so, what will be the manner of their participation?
- What evaluation methodology and design will be used? How will the data be collected? If a survey is going to be used, is it possible to use one that has been employed by other libraries?
- What is the purpose for doing the evaluation? Is the library attempting to improve its operational efficiencies (an internal focus), or is the study being done to better understand the effectiveness of a library service (an outward focus)?

Determining Whether the Answer Already Exists

Prior to actually starting to collect data, it is important to learn what your colleagues have done in the area. Your might chat with or send an e-mail to a colleague in a similar type of library or someone whom you know has completed a similar evaluation project. Other resources are available, including checking with a professor at a library school or a consultant or posting a query on a listserv. Discovering the experiences of others will help the library avoid some of the pitfalls that others have encountered the hard way—through trial and error.

One of the most important activities is to conduct a literature review. Conducting a search of the literature, especially of recently published articles, will help the library to better shape the evaluation study and, ultimately, improve the results of the project. A content analysis has shown that research on evaluation ranges from 15 to 57 percent of the published literature, depending upon the year.[7]

When preparing a literature review, a serious challenge arises since the literature will often present a confusing and contradictory picture. Thus it is necessary to assess and prioritize the results of the literature and the studies discussed in various articles and books. It is particularly important to identify whether any systematic review articles have been prepared that summarize the research in a particular subject area. Systematic reviews are typically written by two or more authors, in order to minimize possible bias, using orderly and explicit methods to identify, select, and appraise relevant research. Such an article will summarize a number of prior studies that meet specific criteria for inclusion in the analysis. Once a review article has been prepared in draft form, it is subjected to a rigorous peer review process involving individuals knowledgeable in the field. One of the by-products of the systematic review article is that it will identify "best practices."

Systematic reviews are useful for a number of reasons:

- *Too much information is available,* and the summary produced by the review will mean that less research and reading is required.

- *Too little information is available* for some topics.

- *They resolve discrepancies* and may help more clearly define the issues in a hotly debated issue.

- *To plan for new research,* a systematic review may be produced to identify fruitful methods.

- *They provide teaching or training materials,* since a review provides significant depth of analysis.[8]

Recently the practice of evidence-based evaluation has emerged from within the library community. Building on the tradition and history of evidence-based medicine, evidence-based librarianship provides a method for categorizing or rating the various research and evaluation studies reported in the literature, in order to determine a set of recommendations that is based on sound research rather than feeling and experience. In some ways, this is reflective of the call for developing a "culture of assessment."[9]

Andrew Booth and Anne Brice, both involved in the development of evidence-based librarianship, suggest that more weight should be given to the findings of research studies that are more rigorous from a methodological point of view.[10] They suggest prioritizing the research in the following manner (from best to worst):

- **I. Experimental study using randomized controlled trials.** In clinical medicine, randomized controlled trials are considered the "gold standard" to assess the effectiveness of a treatment, since the trial can provide the strongest evidence for (or against) the effectiveness of an intervention. Very few randomized controlled trials have been conducted in the library environment.

- **II. Experimental study without randomization.** This includes cohort studies and case-control studies. In the medical environment, cohorts are identified prior to the appearance of the disease under investigation. The study groups, so defined, are observed over a period of time to determine the frequency of disease among them. Again, in the library environment, no cohort studies have been conducted.

  The case control study begins with the identification by researchers of an outcome or effect (e.g., lung cancer, heart disease, or even longevity), and a number of potential causative factors. A group of cases is selected that exhibit the outcome under investigation. A number of control subjects (or controls) are then chosen who do not exhibit the outcome or effect under investigation; there may be one or more per case subject. These controls should match the cases as closely as possible with respect to the nonrisk variables; this allows the proposed nonrisk variables to be ignored in the analysis. The case and control groups are then compared on the proposed causal factors, and statistical analysis is used to estimate the strength of association of each factor with the studied outcome. In the library environment, only a few studies have been conducted that used the case control methodology.

- **III. Observational study without a control group.** This includes cross-sectional studies, before-and-after study designs, and case studies. Rather than using large samples and following a rigid protocol to examine a limited number of variables, the case study method involves an in-depth examination of a single instance or event—a case. They provide a systematic way of looking at events, collecting data, analyzing information, and reporting the results. As a result the researcher may gain a sharpened understanding of why the instance happened as it did, and what might become important to look at more extensively in future research.

- **IV. Case reports.** In medicine, a case report is a detailed report of the diagnosis, treatment, and follow-up of an individual patient. Case reports may contain a demographic profile of the patient, but usually they describe an unusual or novel occurrence. The library literature is replete with case reports—or "how I done it good in my library."

  This category also includes ideas, editorials, and opinions. This category is for ideas that as yet are unsupported by any data or research and thus have little or no value when trying to reach a conclusion supported by research and evaluation studies.

The majority of library research employs case studies or case control studies. In addition, it should be noted that qualitative research, which is prevalent in the library and information science field, is not addressed by the categories of research listed above. Future library research and evaluation studies would be much improved through the use of cohort studies and controlled trials or at least the use of a control group, especially when attempting to measure the outcomes of the use of library resources and services. The increased use of experimental designs would also be beneficial.

The result of the literature review typically is a section in the evaluation report or in an article that documents the results of the evaluation project. It should also be noted that the literature review may reveal "best practices," which will suggest a course of action that does not require further study.

Determining the Kind of Analysis to Do

In general, there are two broad methodologies that can be used to gather information about a library service: quantitative and qualitative. Each method is discussed in some detail in subsequent chapters of this book.

Library research has been for the most part pragmatically oriented, yet it appears to be so closely tied to professionally acceptable solutions that it seldom contemplates alternatives which might cause pronounced upheaval in the existing order.
—P. Wasserman and M. Bundy[11]

Quantitative methods gather data using a variety of techniques. The resulting data can then be subjected to data analysis, ranging from simple descriptive statistics to more complex statistical analysis.

Qualitative methods gather information about a library service that is not numerical in nature. The purpose of a qualitative method is insight. Insight is, roughly, the recognition of connections or patterns. Typical qualitative methods include observations, in-depth interviews, and focus groups. Insight studies can often point to the reasons behind the results of a study that a quantitative study cannot identify.

The literature review will have identified several methods other libraries have used to conduct an evaluation study. These methods obviously are prime candidates for a library to follow, since it is easier to replicate a study done elsewhere (and compare and contrast the results) than to pioneer a new method.

The specific procedures that will be used in the evaluation project should be decided upon and documented. It may be necessary for some staff members to be trained so that they can assist in the data collection process. The individual or individuals who will be responsible for collecting the data and their analysis should be specified in the project plan. In addition, the project plan should include a time frame for the completion of the project and any intermediate milestones.

A review of the procedures may indicate the need for some resources to be allocated to the project or for some volunteers to be recruited and trained. It may be necessary to develop a budget for the evaluation project.

Deciding What Data Will Be Needed

The choice of evaluation method will determine, in large part, what data will be needed. Having a clear picture of the evaluation objectives will ensure that unnecessary data are not collected and, even more important, that needed data are actually gathered.

If a survey is being distributed, then the responses will have to be gathered and analyzed. Depending on the complexity of planned data analysis, it may be necessary to have the information in a format that can be imported into a data analysis software package.

One suggestion is to run a prototype of the study, including the collection and analysis of a limited amount of data. This "dry run" will often expose some unanticipated problems that can be resolved before the library incurs the time and costs associated with a much larger data collection effort.

However, it is important to note that

[p]erfect data are impossible to obtain. Near-perfect data can take so long to obtain that the opportunity will pass you by or the problem will engulf you. Settle for good enough data to get the job done.[12]

If data are to be collected from individuals in an academic setting, then most likely permission will be required from the campus institutional review board, which exists to protect people's privacy and rights. Typically there is a specific and detailed process that the library will have to follow to gain the approval of this board.

Conducting the Analysis and Preparing a Report

After the quantitative data collection process or the qualitative information-gathering process is completed, the resulting information must be analyzed. After all, the purpose of analysis is insight! This is especially important since the library has gone to considerable efforts to prepare for and conduct the evaluation.

The function of the evaluation report is to document the purpose and focus of the evaluation, how the project was conducted, what the quantitative data or qualitative information has to say, and what results and recommendations are being made.

The audience for the report may be the library's top management team, the library's funding decision makers, or those involved in a program review, as in the case of an academic library. For the latter audience, it is important not to use library jargon (if any jargon is used, make sure it is the jargon of the decision makers). And since this audience is normally fairly busy, the report should include a one- or two-page executive summary of the evaluation project.

Using the Results for Service Improvement: The Feedback Loop

With the results of the evaluation known, the library will most likely need to make changes in processes or procedures to implement the recommendations of the evaluation study. Communicating with staff during the evaluation about the project and its findings will assist in getting the cooperation and enthusiasm needed to make the changes occur smoothly.

OBSTACLES TO EVALUATION

The commonsense and intuitive approaches to managing a library ignore the reality that today a library, any library, is more complex and involves many variables that prevent a library from delivering high-quality services. Without objective information about a service, provided by an evaluation, a library will simply continue to muddle along—confident in its belief that all is well.

It is also important to acknowledge that an evaluation might be misused. For example, an evaluation might

- have a political agenda that is hidden (despite the quality and use of a service, it might be scheduled for termination);
- only examine those components of a program that generate positive results, without looking at the total program;

- cover up program failures or limited use;
- be used to delay taking action in the short term (An evaluation project will require time to design the study, gather and analyze the data, and prepare the report.);
- be sabotaged by staff who refuse to gather data in the prescribed manner, thus skewing the results;
- strike fear in the management team, who are concerned that an evaluation will show resources are being wasted or misapplied; or
- be flawed because those involved in the evaluation project have not received the training to correctly complete the tasks needed for the project.

As Peter Hernon and Ellen Altman have observed, "Evaluation, after all, is most productive in an open organization truly interested in planning and self-improvement, and in demonstrating its *worth* and *value*."[13]

ETHICS OF EVALUATION

The Joint Committee on Standards for Educational Evaluation created standards in four areas to help guide evaluators:

- **Utility.** The goal of evaluation is to ensure that the information needs of intended users are met. This may include stakeholder identification; scope and selection of the evaluation; and report clarity, timeliness, and dissemination.
- **Feasibility.** The focus is to ensure that the evaluation will be realistic, follow accepted research methods, and not be too costly.
- **Propriety.** The evaluation should be conducted legally, ethically, and with due regard for the welfare of those involved with the evaluation. This might include rights of human subjects, disclosure of findings, and complete and firm assessment.
- **Accuracy.** The evaluation should reveal accurate information about the program or service being evaluated. Thus, the source of the data, methods for collecting the data, and analysis of the data must be included in the evaluation report.[14]

NOTES

1. Amy Owen. So Go Figure: Measuring Library Effectiveness. *Public Libraries*, 26, Spring 1987, 23.

2. Thomas A. Childers and Nancy A. Van House. *What's Good? Describing Your Public Library's Effectiveness*. Chicago: American Library Association, 1993.

3. See Joseph R. Matthews. *Library Assessment in Higher Education*. Westport, CT: Libraries Unlimited, 2007.

4. Richard H. Orr. Measuring the Goodness of Library Services: A General Framework for Considering Quantitative Measures. *Journal of Documentation*, 29, 1973, 315–32.

5. José-Marie Griffiths and Donald W. King. *A Manual on the Evaluation of Information Centers and Services*. New York: American Institute of Aeronautics and Astronautics Technical Information Service, 1991.

6. Peter Hernon and Ellen Altman. *Assessing Service Quality: Satisfying the Expectation of Library Customers*. Chicago: American Library Association, 1998, 56.

7. Denise Koufogiannakis and Ellen Crumley. Research in Librarianship: Issues to Consider. *Library Hi Tech*, 24 (3), 2006, 324–40.

8. K. Ann McKibbon. Systematic Reviews and Librarians. *Library Trends*, 55 (1), Summer 2006, 202–15.

9. Amos Lakos. Opinion Piece. The Missing Ingredient—Culture of Assessment in Libraries. *Performance Measurement and Metrics*, August 1999, Sample Issue, 3–7; and Amos Lakos and Shelley Phipps. Creating a Culture of Assessment: A Catalyst for Organizational Change. *portal: Libraries and the Academy*, 4 (3), July 2004, 345–61.

10. Andrew Booth and Anne Brice. *Evidence-Based Practice for Information Professionals: A Handbook.* London: Facet, 2004. A new Internet-based journal called *Evidence Based Library and Information Practice* is available. Visit http://ejournals.library.ualberta.ca/index.php/EBLIP/issue/current for all of the issues.

11. P. Wasserman and M. Bundy. *Reader in Research Methods in Librarianship.* NCR Microcard Editions, 1970, 257.

12. Denise Troll Covey. Using Data to Persuade: State Your Case and Prove It. *Library Administration & Management*, 19 (2), Spring 2005, 84.

13. Peter Hernon and Ellen Altman. *Service Quality in Academic Libraries.* Norwood, NJ: Ablex, 1996, 18.

14. Joint Committee on Standards for Educational Evaluation. *The Program Evaluation Standards.* 2nd ed. Thousand Oaks, CA: Sage, 1994.

2

Evaluation Models

Evaluation is the process of determining the worth, merit, or value of something. It consists of comparing "what is" to "what ought to be." Implicit in the comparison is the need to select one or more measures, often called performance measures, to use as the basis for comparison. Measurement is the precursor for evaluation in order to fully understand a system, service, or process. Measurement entails the quantification of a service or process or is a qualitative assessment of a service or process.

An evaluation can be done using one of these four broad levels of analysis:

- **Individual.** An individual library customer's experience could be the basis for an evaluation, but it is difficult to generalize based on a single observation or interaction. Thus, most evaluations are done at a higher level. The evaluation of a library staff member is usually called a personnel evaluation, and this topic is not addressed in this book.

- **Service.** A program or service is the focus of a majority of library evaluation projects. In this case, the experience of a group of library customers is evaluated in order to draw some conclusions.

- **Organizational.** Another option would evaluate all of the library's services. However, the perspective is internally focused. That is, the evaluation would compare one library to a group of peer libraries.

- **Societal.** The final level of analysis examines the impact of the library on the local community (community would mean a city or county for a pubic library; the students, faculty, and researchers in a university setting; the parent organization of a special library; or the students and teachers of a school library).

Having a clear understanding of the level of analysis that a library will be performing is important because it will affect which methodology will be used and the tools that can be used to analyze the resulting data.

17

EVALUATION MODELS

Evaluation models are used to assist in our understanding of the functions and services provided by a library. A number of models have been developed, and several are presented here. The use of a particular model may be helpful for a specific library depending on the characteristics of the larger organization.

Several models have adopted the use of a matrix in an effort to convey the different types of evaluation studies. A broad and generic evaluation model has been suggested by Blaise Cronin.[1] He developed the evaluation matrix shown in Figure 2.1 and suggested that a library could focus its evaluation efforts on costs, benefits, and effectiveness, while acknowledging that three different perspectives would influence the type of evaluation that would be prepared. The choice of a particular perspective will influence the expectations of library staff members as well as those of the library's stakeholders. Typically, an evaluation will focus on a single cell within the matrix.

	User	**Management**	**Sponsor**
Cost			
Effectiveness			
Benefits			

Figure 2.1. Cronin's Evaluation Matrix

José-Marie Griffiths and Donald King developed a similar evaluation matrix, which suggested that five evaluation perspectives were possible (the library, user, organization that the library is a part of, industry, and society at large) as well as what could be evaluated, as shown in Figure 2.2.[2] This particular model is most often applied in the corporate environment.

	Library	**User**	**Organization**	**Industry**	**Society**
Entire library					
Functions					
Services/Products					
Activities					
Resources					

Figure 2.2. Griffiths's and King's Evaluation Matrix

Scot Nicholson suggested a slightly more simplified evaluation matrix, shown in Figure 2.3.[3] Nicholson employed an internal-focus (the library) or an external-focus (the customer) perspective. Similarly, the evaluation effort could look at the library or its use. Comparing the library's efficiency with its benefits is a way to prepare a cost-benefit analysis. Similarly, examining the quality and effectiveness from the customer's perspective is a way to determine the relevance of the library.

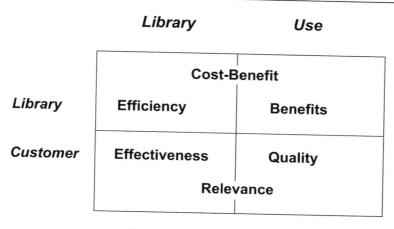

Figure 2.3. Nicholson's Evaluation Matrix

One model that has been used for some time in the academic environment was developed by Alexander Astin (see Figure 2.4).[4] This is a fairly straightforward model that suggests a progression moving from inputs to the environmental setting of the university, to the outcomes generated by the university. Examples of the factors that comprise each component of the model are shown in the figure.

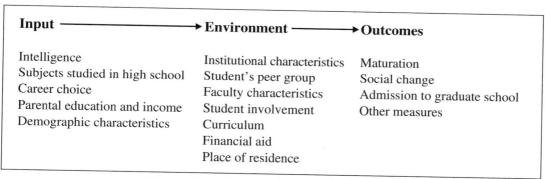

Figure 2.4. Academic (Astin's) Evaluation Model

One of the oldest, and certainly the most frequently cited, evaluation model in library literature was developed by Richard Orr in 1973. His Input-Process-Output-Outcomes model, shown in Figure 2.5, has value since its structure is clearly applicable in a library setting.[5] Astin's Input-Environment-Outcome model is very similar to Orr's and reflects a process orientation for evaluation.

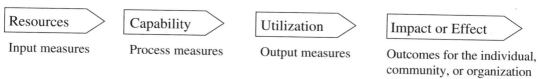

Figure 2.5. Orr's Evaluation Model

When a library is established, it is provided with a set of *resources*. Those resources are organized and directed so that they become transformed and have the *capability* to provide a set of services. These capabilities are then *utilized*. Once used, the information and service that have been provided have the potential to make a positive, beneficial *impact or effect* on the community or organization.

Input measures are the easiest to quantify and gather and have been used by librarians for a long time. Typically input measures are grouped into five broad categories: budget, staff, collections, facilities, and technology. Input measures are usually counts or a numerical value.

Process measures or *productivity measures* are focused on the activities that transform resources into services offered by the library and as such are internally directed. Process measures are reflected in an analysis that will quantify the cost or time to perform a specific task or activity. Process measures are ultimately about efficiency and thus answer the question, "Are we doing *things right*?" Usually a library will compare its process measures with a group of peer libraries in order to make an assessment of how efficient the library is.

Output measures are used to indicate the degree to which the library and its services are being utilized. More often than not, output measures are simply counts to indicate volume of activity. Historically, use of output measures has been regarded as a measure of goodness—after all, the library's collection (physical and electronic) and its services were being used, often intensively so! Therefore, the library was doing "good." A multiplicity of measures exist to demonstrate use of services, use of the collection (physical and electronic), use of facilities (gate count, program attendance), visits to the library's Web site, and so forth.

Broadly speaking, *outcomes* indicate the effect of this exposure to services on the customer. It is also important to note that outcomes can be planned (sometimes called goals) or unintended, and that the actual outcomes may be less than, equal to, or greater than what was intended. Outcomes occur first in an individual and then in the larger context—the organization or community. Outcomes allow a library to assess its effectiveness and to answer a very important question, "Are we doing the *right things*?"

Assessment of outcomes, sometimes called impact analysis or impact evaluation, is typically done to determine which outcome changes occur as a result of natural forces such as experience or maturation and which occur as a result of the interventions provided by a program or service. In some cases, these positive outcomes from a service or program are called benefits.

An extension of Orr's model answers the "how, who, what, and why" questions, as shown in Figure 2.6.

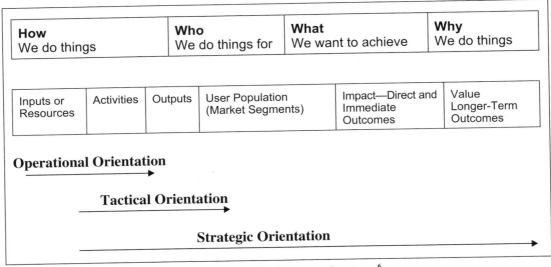

Figure 2.6. The Performance Spectrum[6]

A focus on operations is reflected in the use of input and process performance measures. A tactical orientation will find a library using process and output measures. A strategic orientation requires the use of output measures to demonstrate use of the library (an implied value) as well as use of outcome measures.

The outcomes that may occur in an individual include changes in

attitude,

skill,

knowledge,

behavior, and

status or condition.

Table 2.1 (p. 22) provides a number of generic outcomes that a library could consider using as part of an evaluation plan to demonstrate the value of the library in the lives of its users. Also, Rhea Rubin has suggested that focusing on outcomes is beneficial for many reasons, including the following:

- Assumptions are made explicit.

- It is good for collaboration with users and stakeholders.

- Milestones can be identified as the library selects interim and long-range outcomes.

- It focuses staff and stakeholders on the goals of a program or service.

- Improvements and innovations can result from an examination of outcomes.

- It provides insights into how and why a program or service is being used by some and not by others.

- Outcomes become a vehicle for determining the contributions a library makes to the lives of its customers.[7]

Peter Hernon and Robert Duggan have noted that an output is institutionally or organizationally based, whereas some outcomes, such as a student's learning outcomes, occur within an individual. Further, there need not be a progression from outputs to outcomes, although this can occur in some cases.[8] Outputs are measurable and are typically compiled, counted, or gathered, while outcomes or impacts are often not so easily measured.

Outcomes or impacts may be what was intended or a surprise, positive or negative, short-term or long-term, and be significant or trivial. To be considered meaningful, an outcome must be identified as being sensitive to change and intervention.

Combining the Griffiths and King model described above with Orr's Input-Process-Output-Outcomes model results in a conceptual framework for library metrics, as shown in Figure 2.7 (p. 23).

Table 2.1. Generic Outcomes*

Knowledge and Understanding	Knowing about something Learning facts/information Making sense of something Learning how libraries operate Giving specific information—naming things, people or places Making links and relationships between things Using prior knowledge in new ways
Skills	Knowing how to do something Being able to do new things Intellectual skills—reading, thinking critically and analytically, making judgments Key skills—numbers and statistics, literacy, use of IT, learning how to learn Information management skills—finding, assessing and using Social skills Communication skills
Attitudes and Values	Feelings Perceptions Opinions about ourselves, e.g., self-esteem Opinions or attitudes towards other people Increased capacity for tolerance Empathy Increased motivation Attitudes towards the library Positive and negative attitudes in relation to experience
Enjoyment, Inspiration, and Creativity	Having fun Being surprised Innovative thoughts Creativity Exploration and experimentation Being inspired
Activity, Behavior, and Progression	What people do What people intend to do (intention to act) What people have done A change in the way people manage their time Reported or observed actions

*Adapted from Jennifer Cram and Valerie Shine. *Performance Measurement as Promotion: Demonstrating Benefit to Your Significant Others.* Paper presented at the School Library Association of Queensland Biennial Conference, 29 June–1 July 2004, Gold Coast, Queensland. Available at http://www.alia.org.au/~jcram/PMasPromotion.pdf

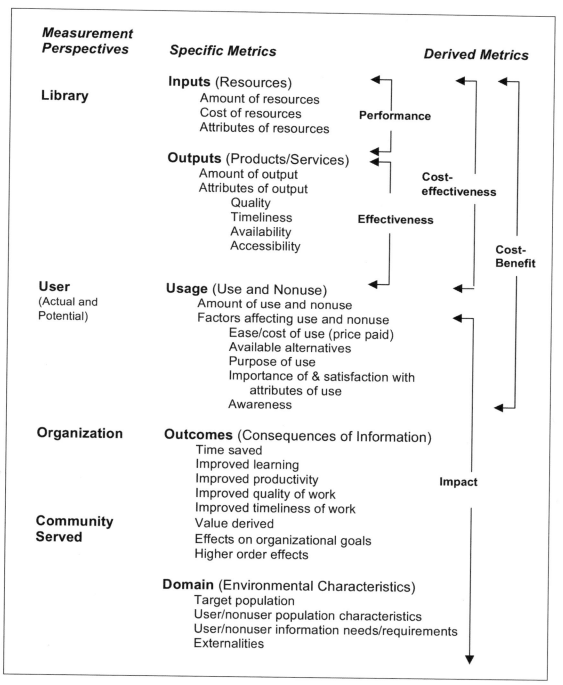

Figure 2.7. Conceptual Framework for Library Metrics. Adapted from Donald W. King and Peter B. Boyce. Library Economic Metrics: Examples of the Comparison of Electronic and Print Journal Collections and Collection Services. *Library Trends*, 51 (3), Winter 2003, 379.

Peter Brophy has suggested that it might be useful to also consider the magnitude of outcomes in a Levels of Impact Model, as shown in Table 2.2.

Table 2.2. Levels of Impact Model*

−2	Hostility	A user may be so disappointed with the service that he or she decides that it is a total waste of money. Perhaps the result is a letter of condemnation to an influential third party, such as a city council person or senior manager.
−1	Dismissive	The user is not hostile, but simply feels that the service is not worthwhile. It is a waste of personal effort to get involved, even if no attempt is made to undermine the service. There is a barrier to future engagement.
0	None	The user has neither positive nor negative feelings nor views about the service. It is almost as if it didn't exist.
1	Awareness raised	The service has a positive impact but the user is made aware of something she or he was not aware of before. He or she knows the service exists, does not dismiss it out of hand, and might turn to it in the future if he or she feels a need. He or she might also mention, or possibly even recommend, it positively to friends and colleagues.
2	Better informed	As a result of coming into contact with the service, the user has better information than before.
3	Improved knowledge	The information obtained has been considered, and the user is now more knowledgeable about the subject.
4	Changed perception and/or ability	The knowledge gained has resulted in a change to the way that the user looks at a subject. Real learning has taken place and/or a new skill has been acquired.
5	Changed worldview	The user is transformed by the service. His or her view of the world has shifted significantly, and constructive learning has taken place, which will have long-term effects. Transferable skills have been acquired.
6	Changed action	The new worldview has led to the user acting in a way he or she would not have before. Learning has turned into action, so that the encounter with the service has changed not just that user, but—in some way—the broader world.

*Adapted from Peter Brophy. The Development of a Model for Assessing the Level of Impact of Information and Library Service. *Library & Information Research*, 29 (93), Winter 2005, 43–49.

Additional problems that may arise when attempting to identify the outcomes or impacts of the library on the lives of its customers include the following:

- A library service can have a different value and outcome for different user groups.

- Data that might be relevant for demonstrating impact are not available (or are only available with considerable effort) due to considerations of protecting the privacy of individuals.

- Since various methods have been used in different libraries to identify impacts, the results are difficult to compare and synthesize.

- Long-term effects cannot be assessed if the library customer is not available for tests or surveys.

- It is difficult to isolate the contribution of the library from the contributions of others—friends, teachers, family, the Internet, and so forth.

- Rarely is the impact the result of a single encounter with the library's collection or service, and this makes attempting to determine the impact in an individual's life even more challenging.[9]

Since Congress passed the Government Performance and Results Act (GPRA), federal government agencies have been encouraged (read mandated) to embrace outcome-based evaluation. Outcome-based evaluation (OBE) is a systematic way to assess the extent to which a program or service has achieved its goals. OBE is designed to answer two key questions: (1) How has this program or service made a difference? and (2) How are the lives of the program or service recipients better?

A program or service is developed as a result of assumptions about people's needs. Thus, outcome-based evaluation focuses on the following:

- **Need.** A condition, want, or deficit common to a group of individuals.

- **Solution.** A program or service that will change attitudes, skills, knowledge, behaviors, status, or condition.

- **Desired results.** The change or improvement that is expected.

Outcome-based evaluation is designed to get an organization, such as a library, to answer a crucial question:

We do *what*, for *whom*, for what *outcomes* or *benefits*?

Figure 2.8 (p. 26) presents the same information found in Orr's model (see Figure 2.5) from a slightly different perspective, in order to indicate the relationship between quality and value and the fact that the library (the organization or community) is influenced and constrained by its external environment. Such outside environmental factors include the characteristics of its service population, dependence on an outside organization for financial and other resources, and so forth.

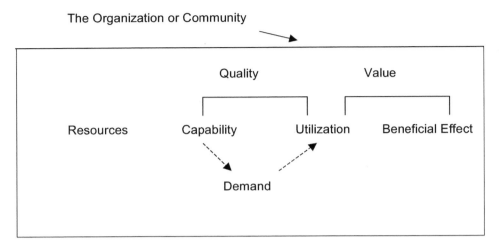

The Organization or Community

Quality   Value

Resources   Capability   Utilization   Beneficial Effect

Demand

Figure 2.8. Variation on Orr's Evaluation Model

Note that an evaluation of quality occurs between the capability of the library and its staff members and the use of the collection and library services by the library's customers. The perception of the customer is much more important than any objective measure of the quality of the service being delivered. That is, if a library delivers a high-quality service and yet the customers view the service as so-so, then the service is only so-so in the eyes of the most important stakeholders—the customers of the library! The value of library services can only be determined after the service or product is used by the customer and its value has been ascertained by the customer.

LIMITATIONS

One of the disappointments of the library profession is that it has been unable to develop a predictive model of library service. That is, the cause-and-effect relationships among inputs, outputs, and outcomes are not understood. Consider, for example, the following facts.

- Two public libraries from different communities are of similar size and socioeconomic characteristics. Yet the budgetary support for each library will vary, often significantly. And use of each library will also vary, as evidenced by in-library use of materials and annual circulation numbers, attendance at programs, use of reference services, and so forth.

- Two academic libraries serving a similar size faculty and number of students will have quite different size library buildings, size of collections, and use of library resources.

- Two school libraries, often in the same school district, will have different budgets and support from other teachers and the school principal.

- Two special libraries, for example, in law firms, will have different budgets and number of staff. In one law firm, the library is viewed as helping the firm meet its objective of providing high-quality service to its clients and contributing to the bottom line. In the other firm, the library is viewed as administrative overhead, which drags down the bottom line.

PROCESS MODEL

One important model that has been used by many organizations to improve the quality of the processes used to make a product or deliver a service is called the Plan-Do-Check-Act (PDCA) Model (see Figure 2.9). The PDCA Model was developed by Walter Shewhart, an engineer who worked at Bell Labs, who is referred to as the creator of statistical quality control. PDCA is sometimes referred to as the Deming cycle or Deming wheel, in honor of Dr. W. Edwards Deming, the father of modern quality control. PDCA should be repeatedly implemented, as quickly as possible, in order to move to an environment of continuous improvement.[10]

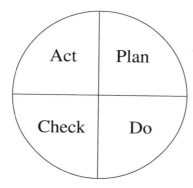

Figure 2.9. The PDCA Model

The power of Deming's concept is in its simplicity. While easy to understand, it is often difficult to accomplish on an ongoing basis due to complacency, distractions, loss of focus, lack of commitment, reassigned priorities, lack of resources, and so forth. In order to derive real benefits from using PDCA, an organization must instill its use in staff until it becomes second nature. PDCA is not something that should be used for one project and then abandoned.

Six Sigma is a methodology to manage process variations that cause defects and to systematically work toward managing variations to eliminate those defects. Defects are defined as unacceptable deviations from the mean or target. The objective of Six Sigma is to deliver high performance, reliability, and value to the end customer. The process is designed to reduce defect levels to below 3.4 defects per (one) million opportunities, or a methodology of controlling a process to the point of ± six sigma (standard deviations) from a centerline.

The key methodology is called DMAIC (Define, Measure, Analyze, Improve, Control). The methodology consists of the following five phases:

- **Define.** Formally define the goals of the design activity that are consistent with customer demands and enterprise strategy.

- **Measure.** Identify service capabilities, production process capability, risk assessment, etc.

- **Analyze.** Develop and design alternatives, create high-level design, and evaluate design capability to select the best design.

- **Design.** Develop a detailed design, optimize the design, and plan for design verification.

- **Verify.** Design, set up pilot runs, implement a production process, and hand it over to the process owners.

A team at the University of Arizona used the Six Sigma process to substantially improve the timeliness of interlibrary loan service while reducing costs.[11]

Evaluation is the assessment of goodness. It consists of comparing the organization's current performance against some standard or set of expectations. Evaluation has two parts: the collection of information . . . about the organization's performance; and the comparison of this information to set of criteria. The collection of information is not itself evaluation: a critical component of evaluation is the exercise of judgment in which criteria are applied to the organization's current reality.
—Thomas A. Childers and Nancy A. Van House[12]

SUMMARY

Choosing an evaluation model can assist the library in better understanding the relationships between the resources it is provided and the outputs and outcomes it achieves. In most cases, unless otherwise stated, libraries will implicitly choose Orr's Input-Process-Output-Outcomes model. The reason for this is the relation of the model to the reality experienced by the library. Most libraries are accustomed to reporting inputs and outputs to a variety of agencies. Thus, expanding these measures to include process and outcome measures does not require a big leap.

NOTES

1. Blaise Cronin. Taking the Measure of Service. *ASLIB Proceedings*, 34 (6/7), 1982, 273–94.

2. José-Marie Griffiths and Donald King. *Special Libraries: Increasing the Information Edge.* Washington, DC: SLA, 1993.

3. Scot Nicholson. A Conceptual Framework for the Holistic Measurement and Cumulative Evaluation of Library Services. *Journal of Documentation*, 60 (2), 2004, 164–82.

4. Alexander Astin. *What Matters in College?* San Francisco: Jossey-Bass, 1993.

5. Richard Orr. Measuring the Goodness of Library Services. *Journal of Documentation*, 29 (3), 1973, 315–52.

6. Adapted from Jennifer Cram and Valerie Shine. Performance Measurement as Promotion: Demonstrating Benefit to Your Significant Others. Paper presented at the School Library Association of Queensland Biennial Conference, 29 June–1 July 2004, Gold Coast, Queensland. Available at http://www.alia.org.au/~jcram/PMasPromotion.pdf.

7. Rhea Joyce Rubin. *Demonstrating Results: Using Outcome Measurement in Your Library*. Chicago: American Library Association, 2006.

8. Peter Hernon and Robert E. Duggan. Continued Development of Assorted Measures, in *Outcomes Assessment in Higher Education: Views and Perspectives*. Westport, CT: Libraries Unlimited, 2004, 309–18.

9. Roswitha Poll and Phillip Payne. Impact Measures for Libraries and Information Services. *Library HiTech*, 24 (4), 2006, 547–62.

10. Masaaki Imai. *Kaizen: The Key to Japan's Competitive Success.* New York: Random House, 1986, 60–65. See also Daniel Seymour. *On Q, Causing Quality in Higher Education.* Phoenix: Oryx Press, 1992, 77–78.

11. Jeanne Voyles and Ellen Knight. You Want Your ILL When? Right *Now*? Presentation at the Living the Future '06 Conference held 6–8 April 2006 in Tucson, Arizona. PowerPoint™ presentation available at http://www.library.arizona.edu/conferences/ltf/2006/proceedings.html.

12. Thomas A. Childers and Nancy A. Van House. *What's Good? Describing Your Library's Effectiveness*. Chicago: American Library Association, 1993, 9.

Part II

Methodology Concerns

3

The Right Tools for the Job

Understanding the context of the problem and the service objectives that have been established by the library is a foundation for selecting the evaluation method and the tools to use. Selecting the right tools or methodology is crucial, because the analysis that the tool facilitates will determine a particular view of the library service. This chapter discusses activity based costing along with several other tools that can be used to better understand an existing process within the library. The goal of this chapter is to create a toolbox that will assist the librarian in analyzing a library service.

The following two chapters discuss the strengths and limitations of qualitative and quantitative methods that can be used in the evaluation and measurement of library services. These methods will increase the set of available tools in the librarian's toolbox.

One important tool is acknowledging that one's view of the world can affect how one perceives potential problems. For example, an organizational perspective reflecting an organizational chart—the vertical view—does not really show how the work is done. A horizontal or systems or process perspective provides a different focus for how problems are analyzed, resources are allocated, and so forth. James Harrington has suggested that these different perspectives lead to the comparisons shown in Table 3.1 (p. 34).[1] The process perspective acknowledges that processes are not self-sustaining and thus get better or worse over time; they rarely stay the same. Processes that are not monitored will deteriorate and begin to produce waste.

Table 3.1. View of the World Perspectives

Organizational Focus	Process Focus
Employees are the problem	The process is the problem
Do my job	Help to get things done
Measure individuals	Measure the process
Change the person	Change the process
Can always find a better employee	Can always improve the process
Motivate people	Remove barriers
Control employees	Develop people
Don't trust anyone	We are all in this together
Who made the error?	Reduce variation
Understand my job	Know how my job fits into the total process

ACTIVITY BASED COSTING

The vast majority of libraries, and their parent organizations, use a line-item budget. Using broad categories—personnel, equipment, materials, supplies, utilities, travel, and so forth—every individual and item is accounted for in the budget. A line-item budget is unable to determine the costs for providing a service.

Originally developed by Robin Cooper and Robert Kaplan, activity based costing collects costs into functional cost pools and then allocates them on the basis of activity cost drivers.[2] The generators of costs are called cost drivers, and variations in a cost driver will cause costs to vary. Activity based costing (ABC) can be used to identify the costs for almost all activities in a library. The library can control the level of analysis, but allocating all costs to a service that is too broad—for example, public services—will do little to assist in understanding the library's cost structure. As librarians gain awareness of the true costs of providing a service, they can make choices to better utilize limited resources. Snyder and Davenport provide a lucid description of some of the issues involved with activity based costing.[3]

There is a four-step approach to implement activity based costing:

- Identify the key activities and relevant cost drivers.

- Allocate staff time to activities.

- Attribute staff salaries and other costs to activity cost pools.

- Determine a cost per cost driver.

Step 1—Identify Key Activities and Relevant Cost Drivers

Identifying Key Activities

Ascertaining the key activities in the library is a relatively straightforward task. The process may involve engaging in conversations with staff and the library's management team. In some cases, the library may find that preparing a flow chart of a process can be helpful because it may reveal hidden cost categories such as information technology.

The activities within technical services may be broken up into several smaller activities, which will assist in better understanding the cost structure within this broad activity. For example, ordering, receiving materials, handling invoices, cataloging, processing, and so forth can be a useful group of activities to analyze. Similarly, circulation services might be broken down into patron registration, checkout, placing holds, check in, handling overdues, returning items to the shelf, and so forth.

Identifying Cost Drivers

Discovering the cost driver for each activity is the next step. It is important to determine the underlying cause-and-effect relationship so that the cost driver selected by the library will control the costs associated with a key activity. Table 3.2 provides some examples of key activities (the cost pool) and their associated cost drivers.

Table 3.2. Cost Pools and Associated Cost Drivers

Cost Pool	Cost Driver
Borrowing an item	Number of checkouts
Returning an item	Number of returns
Renewing an item	Number of renewals
Overdue items	Number of overdue items
Shelving an item	Number of returns
Interlibrary loan requests	Number of items requested
Interlibrary loan supplied	Number of items supplied
Computer maintenance	Computer use
Reference desk	Number of inquiries
Copy cataloging	Number of records available
Original cataloging	Number of items with no records
Physical processing	Number of items added
Programs	Number of programs offered
Public computers	Number of public use computers

Step 2—Allocate Staff Time to Activities

This step will apportion library costs to the activity cost pools. Depending on the size of the library, some staff members will work full-time on a particular task or activity—for example, physical processing of materials. However, most staff members will spend a portion of their time working on two or more activities. Asking staff to estimate the time spent on each activity is one frequently used method, but this approach has the potential for a large margin of error. Another approach is to ask staff to complete a small survey over the course of a week or two in which they track how much time they spend accomplishing each activity. This latter approach will increase the costs of the process slightly but will significantly improve the reliability of the information. In some cases, a library will have a duty roster that indicates time spent on various activities.

Once all of the staff members' hours have been accounted for, the results are tallied by activity, as a percentage of the total hours worked by each staff member. Table 3.3 provides a simplified illustration of the percent of staff time allocated to activities.

Table 3.3. Staff Time Allocated to Activities

Employee	Check Out (%)	Check In (%)	Overdues (%)	Shelving (%)	ILL (%)	Total (%)
A	50	50				100
B	25	25	50			100
C	50	50				100
D	25	25		50		100
E	25	25		50		100
F	25			75		100
G	25	25			50	100

Step 3—Allocate Staff Salaries and Other Costs to Activity Cost Pools

Typically staff salaries will constitute the largest cost category for each cost pool. Salary costs are allocated by multiplying the individual salary costs for each employee by the proportion of time spent on each activity. Usually the actual costs for each employee are used because there are not that many employees. For large libraries, it may be easier to use the average salary for each employee classification than attempting to use each employee's actual salary. Library managers' and administrative staff's time will have to be allocated to each cost pool using a proportional basis to distribute their costs. One basis is to apportion the costs based on the percent of employee hours within the cost pool.

In addition, it will be necessary to add in the costs associated with the overhead of fringe benefits: vacation pay, health benefits, sick leave, and so forth. In most cases, a different fringe benefit overhead rate is used for different employee classifications—for example, 27 percent, 43 percent. Table 3.4 identifies the costs for the activity cost pools. The amounts in the activity columns were then added to arrive at the total cost per activity.

Table 3.4. Allocation of Staff Costs to Activity Cost Pools

Employee	Check Out ($)	Check In ($)	Overdues ($)	Shelving ($)	ILL ($)	Total ($)
A	15,360	15,360				30,720
B	8,740	8,740	17,480			34,960
C	17,120	17,120				34,240
D	6,550	6,550		13,100		26,200
E	6,550	6,550		13,100		26,200
F	6,550			19,650		26,200
G	9,470	9,470			18,940	37,880
Totals	70,340	63,790	17,480	45,850	18,940	216,400

Accounting for Other Indirect and Direct Costs

Other costs found in the library's line-item budget will have to be allocated in a proportional manner to all the activity cost pools. Among these other costs are utilities, maintenance, information technology overhead (maintenance of the servers, software, local area network, Internet connection, and IT staff costs), equipment replacement, insurance, travel, supplies, and so forth. Some libraries have allocated IT costs using the proportion of computers for each activity.

The method for the proportional allocation of the other costs is not particularly important, but the method should be rational and justifiable.

Step 4—Determine Cost Per Cost Driver

Having determined the total cost for each activity, the next step calculates the cost per cost driver. This is accomplished by dividing the total activity cost pool by the cost driver volume, as illustrated in Table 3.5 (p. 38). The result is the cost per activity (the driver), which can be used in a number of ways.

Table 3.5. Activity Cost Driver Table

Activity	Cost Driver	Total Cost ($)	Driver Volume	Cost per Driver ($)
Borrowing an item	no. of checkouts	70,340	42,789	1.64
Returning an item	no. of returns	63,790	42,600	1.50
Overdue items	no. of overdue items	17,480	4,500	3.88
Shelving an item	no. of returns	45,850	42,600	1.08
ILL requests	no. of items requested	14,205	4,125	3.44
ILL supplied	no. of items supplied	4,735	650	7.28
Reference desk	no. of inquiries	194,620	36,940	5.27
Copy cataloging	no. of records available	60,613	4,100	1.48
Original cataloging	no. of items	32,642	895	36.47
Physical processing	no. of items added	116,350	4,995	23.29
Programs	no. of programs offered	46,200	250	184.80
Public computers	no. of public use computers	112,420	48	2,633.75

Increased demands for accountability, plus the desire to provide quality services, often in the face of declining or stable budgets, mean the library will have to do more with less. Having a clear understanding of the costs to provide a service will allow the library to make comparisons with a set of peer libraries to ensure that the local library is operating in an efficient manner. The comparison with peer libraries can be done in a formal way, such as participating with a group of libraries in a benchmarking study. Alternatively, the cost information can be used in preparing an internal evaluation report. In addition, knowing the cost of the various activities needed to provide a service is the foundation for greater understanding of existing procedures and processes so that changes can be made.

Activity based costing has been used in higher education libraries in the United States, England, and Australia.[4] Madeline Daubert provides a thorough review of various methods to analyze library costs, including activity based costing.[5] The topic of managerial accounting and activity based costing is thoroughly discussed in a book by Stevenson Smith.[6]

Once the library has a clear understanding of the costs associated with providing each service, it should also consider the *opportunity costs*. Key to understanding opportunity costs is that the use of resources in one way prevents their use in other ways. Thus, the opportunity costs are the benefits lost because the next best alternative was not selected. For example, if a library staff member is involved with providing programming in a library, the library is forfeiting the time of that staff member spent performing other activities.

STATISTICAL PROCESS CONTROL

In addition to its role as a means of communicating a variety of statistics about the library, a line chart is an important tool when a library is attempting to understand and improve any process using a method called *statistical process control*. The basic tool of this method is to plot the data using a line chart. For example, Figure 3.1 shows the amount of time (in number of days) it takes to fill a request (the average number of days to fill the requests completed each day). Clearly there is variability in the process—the average is 15.5 days.

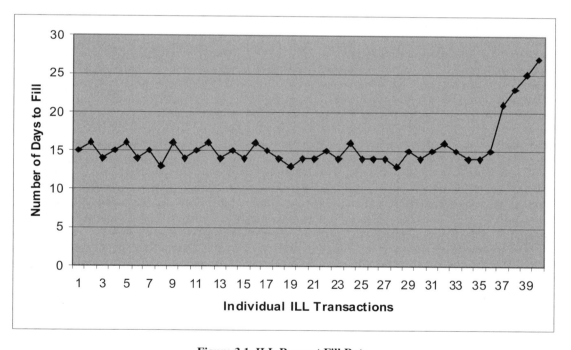

Figure 3.1. ILL Request Fill Rate

An important factor in understanding the statistical process control methodology is to recognize that every process will have variability. The issue is whether the process under control and the variability is within normal limits or the process is out of control. To determine the normal limits of variability, take the following steps.

Step 1

Calculate the moving ranges between each value (determine the difference in successive daily values) and create a Moving Ranges Graph (see Figure 3.2). In this example, the moving range average is 1.4 days.

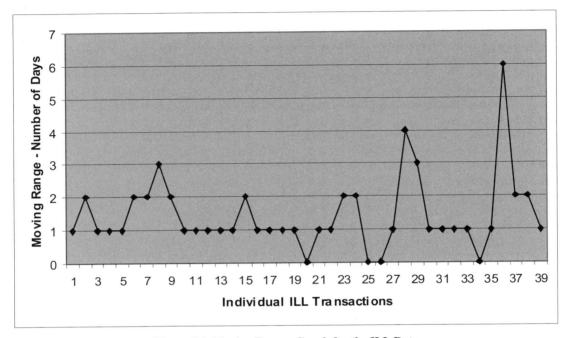

Figure 3.2. Moving Ranges Graph for the ILL Data

Step 2

Calculate the Upper Natural Process Limit by multiplying the Average Moving Range by 2.66 (1.4 days X 2.66 = 3.7 days) and add the result to the average processing time of 15.5. The result is 19.2 days.

Step 3

Calculate the Lower Natural Process Limit by multiplying the Average Moving Range by 2.66 (1.9 days X 2.66 = 3.7 days) and subtract the result from the average processing time of 15.5 (see Figure 3.3). The result is 11.8 days.

Step 4

The Upper Natural Process Limit and the Lower Natural Process Limit are then added to the line chart, as shown in Figure 3.3. Thus, the existing ILL processes that are being used to fill requests for journal articles will operate in a range from 11.8 to 19.2. The process is neutral as to whether or not the library likes the upper and lower limits. The procedures and activities that compose the existing process will determine the results—sometimes this is called the

"Voice of the Process." When a request is filled in a time period that exceeds the upper limit, that is a signal that something is not operating correctly.

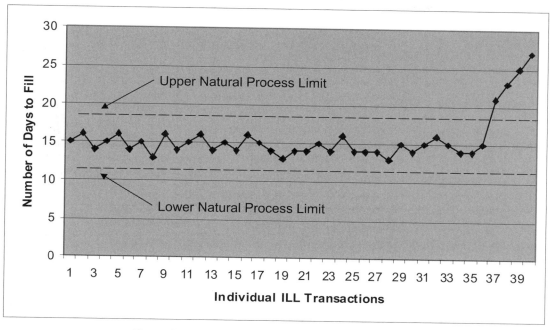

Figure 3.3. Fill Rate for ILL Transactions with Limits

Converting the raw data into a chart with its associated upper and lower limits helps the library better understand the data and begin to ask interesting and important questions. A library wishing to gain a deeper understanding of the statistical process control techniques should consult one of the many books published in this area.

The existing performance of a process may or may not be acceptable. The library should initiate a dialogue with its customers to better understand their expectations, using focus groups, analysis of complaints, and so forth. The customer's expectations have been referred to as the "Voice of the Customer."[7]

OTHER TOOLS

It is important to note that staff frustrations and quality issues are usually related. Involving staff in the process by discussing their frustrations allows them to vent, after which they can then be involved in offering possible suggestions for improvements.

A host of other tools are available to assist a library in better understanding its internal operations and processing. Several of the more useful tools are presented here.

The Flow Chart

Creating a flow chart allows the library to better understand the steps and activities associated with a particular process. A wealth of resources in most libraries explain how to create a flow chart. Two common types are the functional-activity flow chart (includes the job titles of those involved in a process—not department names) and task-procedure flow chart.[8]

The Five Whys

Assume that there are areas in the library that should be improved. Start with a simple descriptive statement of the problem, such as, "On average, it takes us X days to fill an ILL request." Then ask, "Why is this happening?" five times.[9] With each iteration of the question, the possible reasons for the problem will begin to emerge. This helps everyone step back from the "this is how we do it" view of the functional area within the library to discover the strengths and limitations of the processes that are contributing to the existing level of service.

Fishbone Diagram

Dr. Kaoru Ishikawa, a Japanese quality control statistician, invented the fishbone diagram. (Therefore it may be referred to also as the Ishikawa diagram.) The design of the diagram looks much like the skeleton of a fish (see Figure 3.4), which is why it has acquired its name. The fishbone diagram is an analysis tool that provides a systematic way of looking at effects and the causes that create or contribute to those effects. Therefore the fishbone diagram may be referred to as a cause-and-effect diagram. Whatever its name, the value of the fishbone diagram is that it assists teams in categorizing the many potential causes of problems or issues in an orderly way, as well as in identifying root causes.

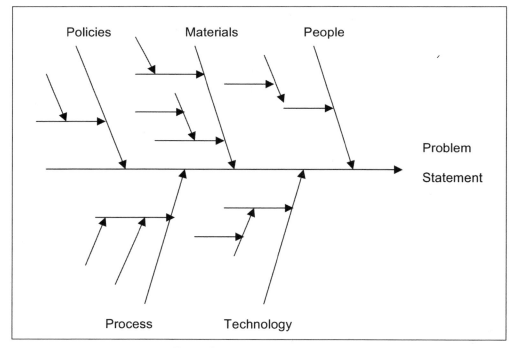

Figure 3.4. The Fishbone Diagram

A fishbone diagram should be used by a library in the following situations:

1. The library needs to study a problem or issue to determine the root cause.

2. The library wants to study all the possible reasons why a process is beginning to have difficulties, problems, or breakdowns.

3. The library needs to identify areas for data collection.

4. The library wants to study why a process is not performing properly or producing the desired results.

A fishbone diagram is constructed as follows:

1. Draw the fishbone diagram.

2. List the problem or issue to be studied in the "head" of the "fish."

3. Label each "bone" of the fish. The major categories typically used are

    - policies, people, process, materials, and technology;

    - the four Ms: methods, machines, materials, and manpower;

    - the four Ps: place, procedure, people, and policies; and

    - the four Ss: surroundings, suppliers, systems, and skills.

    Note: You may use one of the four categories suggested, combining them in any fashion, or make up your own. The categories are to help you organize your ideas.

4. Use an idea-generating technique—such as the five whys or brainstorming—to identify the factors within each category that may be affecting the problem or issue or effect being studied. The team should ask, "What are the technology issues affecting or causing . . . ?" Responses might be "the system does not do . . . ." "These data elements are not found in the system." "The equipment is unreliable when . . . ."

5. Repeat this procedure with each factor under the category to produce subfactors. Continue asking, "Why is this happening?" and put additional bone segments in the diagram for each response.

6. Continue until you no longer get useful information when you ask, "Why is this happening?"

7. Analyze the results of the fishbone after team members agree that an adequate amount of detail has been provided under each major category. Do this by looking for those items that appear in more than one category. These become the "most likely causes."

8. For those items identified as the "most likely causes," the team should reach consensus on those items, listing them with the most probable cause first. A fishbone diagram showing the issues surrounding the problem of reshelving items that have been used (or have been returned to the library but not checked in by the customer) is shown in Figure 3.5 (p. 44).

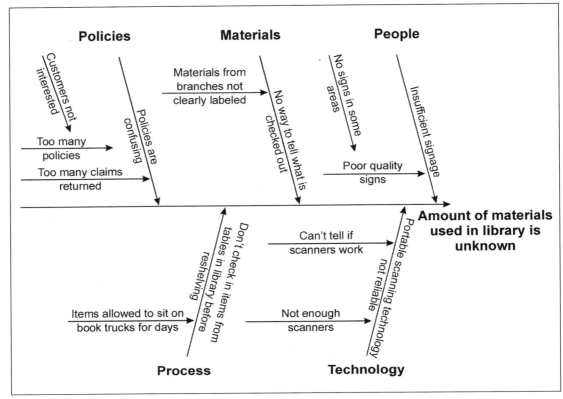

Figure 3.5. Fishbone Diagram for Items Needing Reshelving

Pareto Chart

A Pareto chart is used to graphically summarize and display the relative importance of the differences between groups of data. A Pareto chart can be constructed by segmenting the range of the data into groups (also called segments, bins, or categories). For example, 80 percent of the problems can be accounted for by 20 percent of the problem categories.

The left-side vertical axis of the Pareto chart is labeled Frequency (the number of counts for each category), the right-side vertical axis of the Pareto chart is the cumulative percentage, and the horizontal axis of the Pareto chart is labeled with the group names of your response variables. The Pareto chart is ordered in descending frequency magnitude, as shown in Figure 3.6, which illustrates the problems of receiving materials from acquisitions vendors.

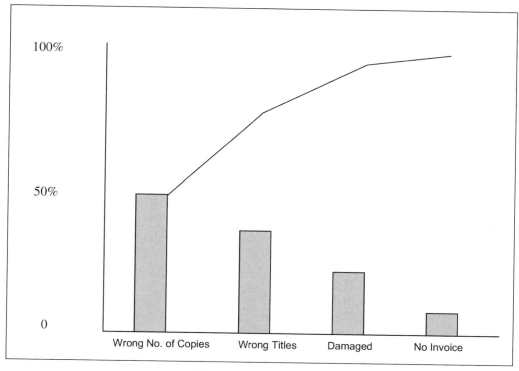

Figure 3.6. Pareto Chart

PRINCIPLES FOR PROCESS REDESIGN

Attempting to improve an existing process can be significantly facilitated by considering a number of design principles during the development of the new process. Among the more important principles are the following:

- Design the process around value-adding activities.
- Reduce waiting, moving, and rework time.
- Reduce batch sizes.
- Perform activities in their natural order.
- Reduce checks and reviews.
- Build quality in to reduce inspection and rework.
- Simplify steps.
- Capture information once and share it widely.
- Reduce the number of people performing a process.
- Eliminate bottlenecks.
- Redesign the process, then automate it.
- Install performance measures and analyze the data regularly.
- Involve staff in analyzing, designing, and implementing improvements.[10]

ADDITIONAL TOOLS

To explore the use of additional tools that can assist in problem solving and improving processes within a library, see Sara Laughlin et al., *The Library's Continuous Improvement Fieldbook.*[11]

SUMMARY

This chapter has identified and discussed a number of tools that any library will find to be of value as it seeks to evaluate a specific library service or implements changes in its processes in order to improve productivity.

NOTES

1. H. James Harrington. *Business Process Improvement*. New York: McGraw-Hill, 1991, 5.

2. Robin Cooper and Robert S. Kaplan. Measure Costs Right: Make the Right Decisions. *Harvard Business Review*, 66 (5), September/October 1988, 96–103.

3. Herbert Snyder and Elisabeth Davenport. What Does It Really Cost? Allocating Indirect Costs. *The Bottom Line*, 10 (4), 1997, 158–64.

4. L. Tatikonda and R. Tatikonda. Activity-Based Costing for Higher Education Institutions. *Management Accounting Quarterly*, Winter 2001, 16–27; James R. Montgomery and Julie K. Snyder. Costing a Library: A Generic Approach. *Research in Higher Education*, 30, 1989, 48–54; Jennifer Ellis-Newman. Activity-Based Costing in User Services of an Academic Library. *Library Trends,* 51 (3), Winter 2003, 333–48; Jennifer Ellis-Newman and P. Robinson. The Cost of Library Services: Activity-Based Costing in an Australian Academic Library. *The Journal of Academic Librarianship*, 24, 1998, 373–79; Michael Heaney. Easy as ABC? Activity-Based Costing in Oxford University Library Services. *The Bottom Line*, 17 (3), 2004, 93–97.

5. Madeline J. Daubert. *Analyzing Library Costs for Decision-Making and Cost Recovery*. Washington, DC: Special Libraries Association, 1997.

6. G. Stevenson Smith. *Managerial Accounting for Libraries & Other Not-for-Profit Organizations*. Chicago: American Library Association, 2002.

7. Donald J. Wheeler. *Understanding Variation: The Key to Managing Chaos*. Knoxville, TN: SPC Press, 2000.

8. Dan Madison. *Process Mapping, Process Improvement, and Process Management: A Practical Guide for Enhancing Work and Information Flow*. Chico, CA: Paton Press, 2005. See chapter 2.

9. James C. Collins and Jerry I. Porras. Building Your Company's Vision. *Harvard Business Review*, 74 (5), September-October 1996, 65–77.

10. Dan Madison. *Process Mapping, Process Improvement, and Process Management: A Practical Guide for Enhancing Work and Information Flow*. Chico, CA: Paton Press, 2005. See chapter 10.

11. *The Library's Continuous Improvement Fieldbook: 29 Ready-to-Use Tools*. Chicago: American Library Association, 2003.

4

Qualitative Tools

Qualitative research methods are particularly helpful when attempting to better understand complex relationships among and between variables. Qualitative methods have been called "naturalistic research" since it is possible to develop multiple interpretations of reality. Qualitative methods use smaller samples, which means that making generalizations is much more difficult. Qualitative data can include interactions among individuals, groups, and organizations as well as describing phenomena. Qualitative methods are used to define the "why," while quantitative tools are used to define the "what" and "how many." While qualitative methods have been used in some evaluation of library services projects, more often quantitative methods are employed.

Rather than attempting to quantify a library service or activity, qualitative methods are seeking to document the complexities of what is experienced or observed. The strength of qualitative data is their rich descriptions. In short, it is an attempt to better understand the "why" and "how" of a particular topic or activity by capturing the thoughts, feelings, and behaviors of individuals. Qualitative analysis techniques were developed in the social sciences, where researchers are unable to control many of the variables relevant to the topic under investigation. Within the field of library and information science, researchers have been using qualitative methods to better understand information seeking and information retrieval, among many other topics. One of the keys to quality qualitative research is the use of multiple methods, often called triangulation. Not surprisingly, the qualitative research field has evolved its own terminology, which addresses important research-related topics, as shown in Table 4.1 (p. 48).

Table 4.1. A Comparison of Conventional and Naturalistic Inquiry*

Criterion	Conventional Term	Naturalistic Term	Naturalistic Techniques
Truth value	Internal validity	Credibility	Prolonged engagement Persistent observation Triangulation Referential adequacy: use of content rich materials Peer debriefing Member checks Reflexive journal
Applicability	External validity	Transferability	Thick description Purposive sampling Reflexive journal
Consistency	Reliability	Dependability	Dependability audit Reflexive journal
Neutrality	Objectivity	Confirmability	Confirmability audit Reflexive journal

*Adapted from Yvonna S. Lincoln and Egon G. Guba. *Naturalistic Inquiry*. Newbury Park, CA: Sage Publications, 1985, 79.

A central concept of qualitative methods is the idea of a "case study," which attempts to provide a depth of understanding about a particular topic, activity, process, and so forth. David Silverman provides an overview of qualitative methods that includes exploring meanings rather than behaviors, to craft studies that are hypothesis generating rather than the testing of hypotheses.[1]

The strength of qualitative methods is that they can provide

- greater sensitivity to the needs of and the impact of a library service on the life of a user,
- an understanding of how responsive a library service is to a changing environment and various user groups,
- awareness of time and history,
- a better understanding of the context of a library program or service,
- an opportunity to immerse an observer without preconceptions to better understand what is happening, and
- greater flexibility of perspective.[2]

In almost all cases, multiple qualitative methods are employed rather than simply relying on a single method. These methods can be subdivided into three groups: no contact with an individual, one-to-one interaction, and interacting with a group. These three groupings are outlined below.

- No contact
  - Examining documents
  - Diaries
- One-to one
  - Observation
  - Interviewing
  - Grounded theory
  - Think aloud/think after verbal protocol
  - Ethnographic methods
- Group interaction
  - Focus groups
  - Delphi method
  - Critical incident technique
  - Concept mapping

EXAMINING DOCUMENTS

This methodology is rarely used because there are few "documents" in a library that are not much more susceptible to quantitative analysis. For example, examining the paper copies of the patron registration forms would reveal information about the registered library card holders. However, since the same information is stored in the library's automated system, quantitative reports can be quickly generated.

Some libraries have found it helpful to analyze the customer complaint forms submitted to the library. This analysis might reveal some patterns of reported problems that should be addressed. It is also possible to analyze the responses to open-ended questions when a survey is completed.

Other documents that can be analyzed are the library's policy manual and the memos that are periodically distributed throughout the organization. Some have studied job announcements in an attempt to understand the changing competency requirements for librarians and other staff members. Others have examined reference interviews (person-to-person or virtual conversations).

In some cases, the analysis of text is called *hermeneutics,* which relates to the development and study of theories of the interpretation and understanding of texts.

Content analysis involves the researcher using analytical constructs or rules to draw inferences about recurring identifiable aspects of text content. The key is making the analytical construct explicit.[3] For example, Danuta Nitecki examined phrases that contained the word stem "librar."[4] Green performed a similar study analyzing the use of the word "information" in the *Library and Information Science Abstracts* (LISA) database.[5]

DIARIES

Some evaluation studies and research projects have asked respondents to keep a diary of their activities, thoughts, motivations, and emotions throughout the life of the project. For example, Carol Kuhlthau asked a group of high school students to use diaries in an information-seeking study.[6] If a group of respondents faithfully record all that they are experiencing, the result is a deep and rich repository of ideas and thoughts that can be mined to extract nuggets of insight. Participants need some instruction about how much detail to provide, how often they should make an entry, and so forth.

A variation of this approach is to ask a group of respondents to carry a timer that will go off at random intervals during the day. Each time the timer alerts the respondents, they are asked to record what activity they are engaged in at that moment—talking on the telephone, reading, in a meeting, and so forth.

Another variation asks respondents to use an audiotape recorder and to record their comments as they complete a task or activity.

OBSERVATION

Observation is a method for learning about the activities of a library customer. While it is possible to observe how a collection is used, this approach has so many problems—e.g., exactly which item is being used—that it is rarely used in evaluation studies.

Activity sampling can provide accurate estimates of time spent on various activities. Having two observers simultaneously recording the activities of customers in the library will improve the consistency and accuracy of the results. One study that employed two observers noted that consistency ranged from 80 to 92 percent.[7]

Another variation of this method is to approach customers while they are in the library and either conduct a brief interview (if they agree) or ask them to complete a questionnaire about their activities.

Another form of observation has been used in unobtrusive evaluations of reference service by using volunteers or paid observers to approach a reference desk seeking assistance. The approach can be made in person or via the telephone. A variation of this approach that some libraries have employed is to use "mystery shoppers" to observe and evaluate a library facility and its services during a visit.[8]

One of the most significant challenges facing those who would be observers in an evaluation study is to decide ahead of time the role they will play. That is, is the observation technique to be used complete observer, observer and participant (with some interaction with the participant), or participant with the individual being observed? Each approach has obvious positive and negative attributes, and the bias of the observer will creep in unless the method is carefully chosen. Note that some librarians may have difficulty in not assisting the participant, even if asked not to do so.

Those involved in an observation study must decide the number of participants, whether the participants will be staff or library customers, the setting or activities that will be observed, and how broad or narrow the focus of the inquiry will be.

INTERVIEWING

An interview offers the opportunity of gaining a better and more in-depth understanding of a situation from the point of view of the library customer. The interview format can vary from formal or structured—an orally administered questionnaire—to semi-structured, from a loose framework for the questions to a completely unstructured discussion. The strength of the interview method is that it allows the questioner to probe and ask clarifying questions in order to gain a better understanding.

The semi-structured and unstructured interviews are more appropriate for use in an exploratory study, where the researcher is attempting to better understand a situation or subject —what is not known is not known. This type of interview has been called "river-and-channel" and provides great depth on a relatively narrow topic while the questions follow the current of conversation no matter where it leads.[9]

Structured interviews are more reliable because the same questions will be asked of a group of people. The questioner has some knowledge of the topic, even though that knowledge is not complete. This interviewing approach has been called the "tree-and-branch"; the questions are designed to explore each branch of the tree to the same extent.[10]

Although most one-on-one interviews occur face-to-face, it is also possible to conduct one-on-one interviews using the telephone. Typically an interview will start off with some "icebreaker" questions, which allow the respondent to feel safe in answering. As the respondent becomes more comfortable, the interviewer can move to more difficult questions.

The different types of questions that can be asked depend on the type of study. Among these are the following:

- **Experience and behavior questions** probe what a person does or has done, with the intent of eliciting descriptions of behaviors, actions, and activities that are observable.

- **Feeling questions** seek to elicit the emotional responses of people based on their experiences and thoughts. The researcher is looking for adjectives that describe feelings, words such as happy, frustrated, upset, and anxious.

- **Opinion and value questions** are aimed at understanding the cognitive processes of the respondent. The researcher is seeking information pertaining to goals, desires, values, and intentions.

- **Knowledge questions** are asked to determine the level of knowledge and information the respondent has about a particular topic.

- **Sensory questions** ask about what is seen, heard, touched, tasted, and smelled. For example, "When you walk into the library, what do you see?"

- **Demographic questions** identify the characteristics of the respondent.

Lokman Meho summarized a number of studies that examined the use of e-mail as a means for conducting interviews and found the approach to be a viable alternative to face-to-face and telephone interviewing, but there are problems with this as with any methodology.[11]

If the interviews are recorded and then transcribed, hundreds of pages of transcripts can be the result. This may require the use of a software tool to analyze the transcripts to assist in identifying themes, frequently occurring phrases, and so forth.

Tips for conducting a successful interview include the following:

- DO'S

    - Divide the interview into major sections.

    - Provide transition between major topics.

    - Develop rapport with the participant prior to asking sensitive questions.

    - Be alert to your biases and remain neutral.

    - Know when to stop probing for more detail.

    - Keep the participant focused on the topic.

- DON'TS

    - Interrupt the participant.

    - Attempt to fill every silence.

    - Insert your own observations.

    - Disagree with the participant.

    - Allow the discussion to ramble.

Often the results of one or more interviews and observations will be written up in the form of a case study. The case study approach has been used in the field of library and information science to investigate a wide range of topics. A case study is an exploration of a specific program, event, or activity that has clearly delineated boundaries. The concept of the case study arises from law schools, in which a single case before a court is carefully examined. The use of the case study in law school was popularized by the movie and TV show *The Paper Chase*. The case study is also used in other professions, most notably by the Harvard Business School and other MBA programs.

First used in the library arena in 1984 by Fidel, and subsequently by many others, the case study methodology must ameliorate a number of shortcomings:

- Study effect—the very act of studying something may change it

- Participant bias
- Observer bias.[12]

GROUNDED THEORY

Grounded theory was developed as a systematic methodology, and its name underscores the generation of theory from data. When the principles of grounded theory are followed, the researcher will formulate a theory about the phenomena being studied that can be evaluated. In some cases the observer will have prepared a data coding sheet to assist in gathering data. Others suggest that a coding sheet will prevent the researcher from really understanding what is happening.[13]

THINK ALOUD/THINK AFTER VERBAL PROTOCOL

Another kind of interview asks the library customer to perform a prescribed task or activity. The respondent is asked to verbalize what he or she is thinking while doing this activity —the think aloud protocol, sometimes called the protocol analysis. Using this methodology requires that the respondents be highly verbal in nature. Caution should be used with this methodology because it will likely affect people's cognitive processes, as well as their behavior.[14]

A variation of this is to ask the respondent to describe his or her thoughts after completing the task. Respondents using the think after method will likely "forget" steps they may have taken in the middle of their tasks.

In most cases when this method is used, the respondents are asked for their permission to record their comments with an audio- or videotape recorder. The resulting comments are then transcribed for analysis. Computer software programs are available that can be used to analyze the text.[15] Such software is particularly helpful if the evaluation project is going to involve a fair number of participants, with the resulting transcriptions being quite voluminous and difficult to analyze manually.

The amount of data generated using the think aloud or think after method depends on the complexity of the task to be performed and the number of nonproductive "dead ends" encountered by the respondent.

This approach has been applied to studies of library online catalogs and library Web sites. For example, Jennifer Branch used both methods to study the information-seeking processes of adolescents.[16]

ETHNOGRAPHIC METHODS

Tools have been developed by cultural anthropologists to better understand people in different cultural settings. Cultural data assume the form of directly observable material items (tools, cultivated fields, houses, statues, clothing), individual behaviors and performances (ceremonies, fights, games, meals), and ideas and arrangements that exist only in people's heads. From the perspective of the culture concept, anthropologists must first treat all these elements as is and must record observations with due attention to the cultural context and the meanings assigned by the culture's practitioners. These demands are met through two major research techniques: participant observation and key informant interviewing. The more interesting methods include

- drawing a picture,
- taking photographs,
- using a map to track activities, and
- videotaping environments.

FOCUS GROUPS

A focus group is a group interview designed to learn about the beliefs and attitudes people hold and how those beliefs influence behavior. Typically such a discussion starts broadly and then narrows to focus more specifically on the topic being studied, hence the name focus group. The value of a focus group is that the comments of one individual will often trigger really valuable comments from others.

Libraries have used focus groups to address a number of topics, including customer information needs analysis, community analysis, marketing studies, learning more about how a promotion might affect use of a planned or existing library service, value and utility of the library's collections, assessing existing or planned library facilities, and much more.

Focus groups typically have from seven to twelve people as participants. Volunteers are recruited who are representative of a particular group. (Some participants may be compensated in a small way.) In some cases, multiple focus group sessions are held with participants from different groups of the population served by the library. Typically, an outside trained moderator is used to facilitate the discussion and keep the comments on track. Thus, depending upon the number of focus group sessions, the costs can mount up quickly.

Focus groups usually run from one to two hours in length and should be held in a comfortable room that is free from outside distractions. Refreshments help keep the atmosphere comfortable. The library should work with the moderator to develop a list of topics that will be discussed. It is the moderator's responsibility to ensure that the conversation is not monopolized by one or two individuals and to encourage the participation of all attendees. The moderator is there to provide some guidance in order to keep the discussion flowing but is not to judge or edit the discussion.

In addition to recording the session—with audio- or videotape equipment—the library should have one or two staff members in attendance to take notes and record pertinent comments and observations. The text of the recording is usually transcribed (it may take three to four hours to transcribe one hour of conversation) and is usually subjected to content analysis using a software package. In general the software will produce a summary of the text and identify recurring themes. Some text mining software will summarize the text, identify and extract entities, and produce theme "maps" showing the relationships or links among the themes.[17]

Having two or more people review the transcripts of the focus group sessions will assist in producing a summary of what the groups had to "say." This will help reduce any bias that may creep in. Focus groups have been used in libraries to explore a number of topics, including services to youth[18] and the reliability of services.[19]

DELPHI METHOD

The Delphi method is a systematic interactive forecasting method based on the independent contributions of selected experts who answer a series of questionnaires. The name "Delphi" derives from the Oracle of Delphi. The Delphi method recognizes the value of expert opinion, experience, and intuition. The selection of well-informed leading authorities in a particular field is crucial to the success of the Delphi method.

Questions are usually formulated as hypotheses, and experts react to each of these. Each round of questioning is followed with feedback on the preceding round of replies, usually presented anonymously. Thus the experts are encouraged to revise their earlier answers in light of the replies of other members of the group. It is believed that during this process the range of the answers will decrease and the group will converge toward "consensus." The following key characteristics of the Delphi method help the participants focus on the issues at hand and separate Delphi from other methodologies:

- Structuring of information flow

- Regular feedback

- Anonymity of the participants

The panel director controls interactions among the participants by processing the information and filtering out irrelevant content. This prevents the negative effects of face-to-face panel discussions and solves the usual problems of group dynamics.

The Delphi method has been used for a number of studies within the library community. For example, recent Delphi studies have considered the library as place, the future of the academic library, the future of library school instruction, the future of the electronic journal, and the importance of the stakeholder in performance measurement.[20]

CRITICAL INCIDENT TECHNIQUE

The critical incident technique is a method for analyzing critical incidents—any observable human activity that is sufficiently complete in itself to permit inferences and predictions to be made about the persons performing the act. Typically the critical incident is used to gather and analyze data pertaining to the most memorable experience, not necessarily the most recent. The critical incident technique was developed by John Flanagan and others in the 1950s.[21]

The technique is used to evaluate and identify ways to increase effectiveness of service in a variety of fields, including libraries. The critical incident technique has been shown to be a reliable and valid explanatory method as well as useful for gathering information about human behavior in a survey.

The procedures typically used in a critical incident evaluation include the following:

- **General aims.** A brief statement of the focus of evaluation is prepared.

- **Plans and specifications.** If observations are going to be made, the groups and behaviors to be observed are identified and data collection forms are prepared. If a survey is to be used, the survey is designed and pretested.

- **Data collection.** The data are recorded by the observer, or the surveys are distributed and then collected.

- **Data analysis.** The data are described and summarized. In some cases, the text of transcripts might be analyzed using a software program, or survey data might be input into a statistical package.
- **Interpretation and reporting.** In addition to presenting the data, the possible limitations to the data collection and analysis should be identified.

Marie Radford applied the critical incident technique in a study of the reference process. Radford analyzed not only the content of the message but also the manner in which the message was delivered—interpersonal skills.[22]

Marie Radford also used the critical incident technique as part of a qualitative evaluation of the Connecting Libraries and Schools Project in New York City. In this project 2,416 fifth- and seventh-grade students shared their perceptions of interactions with urban public librarians and library staff.[23]

CONCEPT MAPPING

Concept mapping is any process that represents ideas in pictures of maps. The process provides a structured methodology for organizing ideas of a group or to form a common framework that can be used for planning and evaluation. It integrates structured group processes such as brainstorming, unstructured idea sorting, and rating tasks with statistical methods to produce maps.[24]

Generally concept mapping involves six steps:

- **Preparation**
    - **Focus.** The desired outcomes for the use of concept mapping must be articulated. What is the question(s) that should be addressed?
    - **Who will participate?** The number and types of stakeholders to be involved in the process should be identified. In some cases, the names of specific individuals will be identified.
    - **Scheduling.** The time frame in which group interaction will occur must be identified. The group may meet physically or virtually.

- **Generating ideas**
    - **Generating statements.** The process might involve brainstorming or another idea-generating process.
    - **Ideas analysis.** The idea statements are sorted and modified into a large set.

- **Structuring the statements.** This activity might involve several steps, including
    - **unstructured idea sorting**—asking each individual to sort the ideas into groups and labeling each group;
    - **sorting by stakeholder groups**—organizing the ideas by the group that generated the ideas; and
    - **ratings**—assigning values to each idea (ratings might be obtained for feasibility, value or importance, and so forth).

- **Concept mapping analysis.** This step can involve a number of statistical analysis techniques that are used to generate the concept maps. Among the maps that can be produced using a computer software program are a point map, point cluster map, cluster map, point rating map, and cluster rating map. A sample point cluster map is shown in Figure 4.1.

- **Interpreting the maps.** Once prepared, the maps are shared with the stakeholders to obtain their understanding, and to develop ownership of the results.

- **Utilization.** For evaluation purposes, the concept maps will identify the types of performance measures that should be used so that the measures are linked to the desired outcomes.

Concept mapping has also been applied to analyzing the open-ended responses to survey questions if the number of responses is quite high.

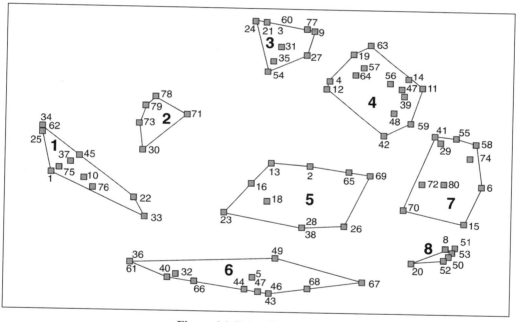

Figure 4.1. Point Cluster Map

SUMMARY

As noted above, a number of different qualitative methods might be employed in an evaluation project. A sample of 12 to 20 can generate useful data for thoughtful reflection and analysis. All of these methods consume a fair amount of time and generate a considerable amount of rich data that must be analyzed. This analysis process can, in and of itself, be time consuming. While the analysis can be done manually, usually a text analysis tool is used to assist in the process. A number of software packages can be downloaded for free or purchased for a modest amount.[25]

The amount of data in raw form, as well as the output from a text analysis software program, can be considerable—hundreds of pages of transcripts from a few hours of interviews.

The usefulness of a qualitative method depends on the researcher thinking carefully about what is being said and done. The goal is to identify the patterns and themes that are present in the data and to develop meaningful categories in an effort to understand what is being evaluated. In some cases, qualitative data analysis is called *content analysis* or *thematic analysis*. The conclusions being drawn must be supported by the data.

NOTES

1. David Silverman. *Doing Qualitative Research: A Practical Handbook*. London: Sage, 2000.

2. Carol H. Weiss. *Evaluation: Methods for Studying Prgorams and Policies*. Upper Saddle River, NJ: Prentice Hall, 1998.

3. Marilyn Domas White and Emily E. Marsh. Content Analysis: A Flexible Methodology. *Library Trends*, 55 (1), Summer 2006, 22–45.

4. Danuta A. Nitecki. Conceptual Models of Libraries Held by Faculty, Administrators and Librarians: An Exploration of Communications in the Chronicle of Higher Education. *Journal of Documentation*, 49 (3), 1993, 255–77.

5. R. Green. The Profession's Models of Information: A Cognitive Linguistic Analysis. *Journal of Documentation*, 47, 1991, 130–48.

6. Carol Kuhlthau. *Seeking Meaning: A Process Approach to Library and Information Services*. 2nd ed. Norwood, NJ: Ablex, 2004.

7. D. E. Campbell and T. M. Shlecter. Library Design Influences on User Behavior and Satisfaction. *Library Quarterly*, 49 (1), January 1979, 26–41.

8. For example, the Chula Vista (CA) Public Library, the Newport Beach (CA) Public Library, and the Cerritos (CA) Library have used mystery shoppers.

9. Herbert J. Rubin and Irene S. Rubin. *Qualitative Interviewing: The Art of Hearing Data*. Thousand Oaks, CA: Sage, 1995.

10. Rubin and Rubin, *Qualitative Interviewing*.

11. Lokman Meho. E-Mail Interviewing in Qualitative Research: A Methodological Discussion. *Journal of the American Society for Information Science and Technology*, 57 (10), 2006, 1284–95.

12. Lisl Zach. Using a Multiple-Case Studies Design to Investigate the Information-Seeking Behavior of Arts Administrators. *Library Trends*, 55 (1), Summer 2006, 4–21.

13. A. Strauss. *Qualitative Analysis for Social Scientists*. Cambridge, England: Cambridge University Press, 1987; B. Glaser. *Basics of Grounded Theory Analysis*. Mill Valley, CA: Sociology Press, 1992; K. Charmaz. *Constructing Grounded Theory: A Practical Guide Through Qualitative Analysis*. Thousand Oaks, CA: Sage, 2006.

14. Timothy D. Wilson. The Proper Protocol: Validity and Completeness of Verbal Reports. *Psychological Science*, 5, 1994, 249–52.

15. Among the software packages are ATLAS.ti, Code-A-Text, The Ethnograph, Kwalitan, MAXqda,Qualrus, TAMS Analyzer, and Transana. Some of the software can be downloaded for free.

16. Jennifer L. Branch. Investigating the Information-Seeking Processes of Adolescents: The Value of Using Think Alouds and Think Afters. *Library & Information Science Research*, 22 (4), 2000, 371–92.

17. Kimberly Neuendorf. *The Content Analysis Guidebook*. Thousand Oaks, CA: Sage, 2001.

18. S. Hughes-Hassell and K. Bishop. Using Focus Group Interviews to Improve Library Services for Youth. *Teacher Librarian*, 32 (1), 2004, 8–12.

19. J. Ho and G. H. Crowley. User Perceptions of the "Reliability" of Library Services at Texas A&M University: A Focus Group Study. *The Journal of Academic Librarianship*, 29 (2), 2003, 82–87.

20. L. Ludwig et. al. Library as Place: Results of a Delphi Study. *Journal of the Medical Library Association*, 93 (3), July 2005, 315–26; B. Feret et. al. The Future of the Academic Library and the Academic Librarian. A Delphi Study. *IATUL Proceedings*, 15, 2005, 1–23; P. C. Howze et. al. Consensus Without All the Meetings: Using the Delphi Method to Determine Course Content for Library Instruction. *Reference Services Review*, 32 (2), 2004, 174–84; S. Baruchson-Arbib, et. al. A View to the Future of the Library and Information Science Profession: a Delphi Study. *Journal of the American Society for Information Science and Technology*, 53 (5), March 2002, 397–408; A. Keller, Future Development of Electronic Journals: A Delphi Survey. *The Electronic Library*, 19 (6), 2001, 383–96; and John B. Harer and Bryan R. Cole. The Importance of the Stakeholder in Performance Measurement: Critical Processes and Performance Measures for Assessing and Improving Academic Library Services and Programs. *College & Research Libraries*, 66, March 2005, 149–70.

21. John C. Flanagan. The Critical Incident Technique. *Psychological Bulletin*, 51 (4), July 1954, 327–58.

22. Marie L. Radford. Communication Theory Applied to the Reference Encounter: An Analysis of Critical Incidents. *Library Quarterly*, 66 (2), 1996, 123–37.

23. Marie L. Radford. The Critical Incident Technique and the Qualitative Evaluation of the Connecting Libraries and Schools Project. *Library Trends*, 55 (1), Summer 2006, 46–64.

24. Mary Kane and William M. K. Trochim. *Concept Mapping for Planning and Evaluation.* Thousand Oaks, CA: Sage, 2007.

25. Text analysis software uses several different programming languages and runs on different operating systems. Among the many software programs are AnnoTape; Aquad Five; ATLAS.ti; Automap—Extract, Analyze and Represent Individual Mental Models; C-I-SAID—Code-A-Text Integrated System for the Analysis of Interviews and Dialogues; ESA—Event Structure Analysis; Ethno; The Ethnograph; EZ-TEXT; HyperResearch; KEDS—Kansas Event Data System; Kwalitan; MaxQDA; QSR NUD*IST—Non-numerical Unstructured Data Indexing Searching and Theorizing; QSR NVivo; Prospero; QDA-Miner; QMA—Qualitative Media Analysis; Qualrus; SuperHyperqual; TABARI—Text Analysis By Augmented Replacement Instructions; and Weft QDA.

5

Quantitative Tools

The people involved with conducting an evaluation study gather data using one and sometimes several data collection methods. The resulting data are then subjected to analysis. The data collection tools discussed in this chapter are categorized as quantitative methods. Quantitative research is usually used to estimate or predict a future outcome or to diagnose the existing or current state of a subject.

In general, numerical data can be gathered using a variety of methods. It should be noted that these categories are not mutually exclusive. They include

- counting,
- measuring,
- surveys,
- conjoint analysis,
- transaction log analysis, and
- experiments.

COUNTING

Libraries have been counting things for a long time, perhaps as long as they have been around. Whether the counts are reflected as input measures—budget, number of staff, number of workstations, size of the library's collection, size of the buildings, and so forth—or as output measures—counts of circulation, number of reference questions answered, number of people walking into the library—the results are a variety of numbers that are usually found in library directories, the library's annual report, and so forth.

A variety of means may be used to capture the counts: Reports may be generated by an automated library system, a physical counter may be located in a gate, or staff members may make tick marks on a form. Clearly some methods will result in higher accuracy and consistency than others.

Aside from reporting of the counts, the library may wish to plot the count information to discover any patterns or use the counts to improve control of the various processes found in the library. This latter use of the count information, sometimes called statistical process control, is discussed in the next section.

MEASURING

When attempting to understand and improve a process, a method known as DMAIC (Define, Measure, Analyze, Improve, and Control) is recommended. A process is a series of activities that produce a result. Examples of processes are cataloging and the physical preparation of new materials, reshelving items returned from circulation, the loaning of materials, and so forth.

The heart of DMAIC—pronounced "die–maic"—is measurement. Measurement assists the library in understanding a problem or potential problem. The goal is to collect and display data that will help narrow the range of potential causes of a problem.

It is important to identify the key measures that will reflect the performance of the process. It is important to verify that each performance measure or metric is actually measuring what it purports to be and is therefore "valid." If the same value for the measure occurs when an identical activity is performed, it is said to be "reliable."

In addition to measuring the time to complete a particular subtask or activity, it is also important to measure the waiting time between activities. Often a greater awareness of the process will be achieved if a flow chart of the "as is" process is prepared; that is, what are the sequences of activities required to complete a process?

In some cases it may be necessary to calculate the costs associated with various tasks and activities. Chapter 3 addresses this topic in greater detail.

SURVEYS

Whenever a survey is used in a library setting, it almost certainly is a descriptive one. A descriptive survey is used to explain the characteristics of a population of interest, estimate proportions in a population, make specific predictions, and test for possible relationships in the data.

> *[Surveys] are like bikinis. What they reveal is interesting, but what they conceal is essential.*
>
> —Kenneth Boulding[1]

The respondents' answers to the questions in the survey may reflect their perceptions, expectations, intentions, and imperfect memories rather than their actual experiences. Thus, great care must be exercised both in developing and administering the survey and also in analyzing the resulting data.

Other types of surveys exist. Among these are the following:[2]

- **Trend study:** Uses almost all the same questions repeatedly over time so as to identify trends, patterns, and change.

- **Cohort study:** Collects data from the same population group more than once. The same people may not be surveyed, but all of the people in the group are selected from the same population.

- **Panel study:** Collects data from the same people over time. The trend study and panel study are sometimes referred to as a longitudinal study.

- **Parallel samples study:** Covers a specific topic, but data are collected from two or more groups, for example, student and faculty in an academic library setting.

- **Contextual study:** Surveys the environment of a single individual, gathering data from multiple perspectives to better understand a task or problem.

- **Cross-sectional study:** Examines phenomena across a representative sample of the population; is large in scale (e.g., Gallup poll).

The library then has to create a descriptive survey instrument or questionnaire. Designing comprehensive, clear questions is difficult. At this point, it is important to try to adhere to the old adage of "not reinventing the wheel." A number of state libraries maintain a list of survey instruments that have been used in one or more libraries. Other resources are also available.[3] Not surprisingly, questionnaires have both strengths and weaknesses, as noted in Table 5.1.

A survey is only as good as the wording.
—Carol Tenopir[4]

Table 5.1. Advantages and Disadvantages of Questionnaires

Advantages	Disadvantages
Frank answers are encouraged due to the anonymity of the respondent.	They eliminate personal contact between the respondent and the observer.
They eliminate possible interviewer bias.	Answers cannot be qualified easily.
Quantitative data are easy to collect and analyze.	There is a general resistance to mail questionnaires.
They can be relatively inexpensive to administer.	Nonresponse rates for surveys can be high.

Types of Questions

The kind of information needed for a survey will usually dictate the types of questions to be asked. Among the types of questions are the following:

- **Factual questions:** Used to determine the respondent's age, gender, and so forth. The resulting data are objective in nature.

- **Opinion and attitude questions:** Used to ascertain inclinations, prejudices, ideas, and so forth. The resulting data are subjective in nature.

- **Self-perception questions:** Restricted to the respondents' opinions of themselves.

- **Information questions:** Designed to measure the respondent's knowledge of a topic.

- **Standards of action questions:** Used to determine how the respondent would act in a specific situation.

- **Past or present behavior questions:** Result in subjective information about the respondent's behavior. More accurate data are obtained when asking about present behavior than about past behavior.
- **Projective questions:** Allow respondents to answer indirectly by projecting their attitudes and beliefs onto others (peers, colleagues and so forth).

Form of Questions

A question may take two basic forms: fixed response or structured questions, and open-ended or unstructured questions. The types of structured questions are illustrated below.

Checklists

Each item may require a response. For example:

When visiting the library, do you (Circle one number on each line.)		
	Yes	No
Borrow a book?	1	2
Borrow an audio CD?	1	2
Borrow a video?	1	2

Items may require the selection of a "best" answer. For example:

What is the primary reason you visit a library? (Circle one number only.)	
Borrow materials	1
Use materials in the library	2
Make photocopies	3
Meet with friends to study	4
Use the computers	5

Items may have categories. For example:

What is the highest grade of school completed? (Circle one number only.)				
Grade school	08			
High school	09	10	11	12
College	13	14	15	16
Beyond college	17			

There may be grouped responses. For example:

> What is your age group? (Circle one group only).
>
> 1–12   13–18   19–39   40–59   60+

Fill in the Blank

In some cases more accurate information will result if questions ask the respondent to fill in the blank as a way of responding. For example:

> How many miles do you live or work from this library? _____ miles

Scaled Responses

There may be a specific category scale. For example:

> How important is each of the following? (Circle one number on each line.)
>
> | Item | Very Important | Of Some Importance | Of Little Importance | Not Important |
> |---|---|---|---|---|
> | More hours | 1 | 2 | 3 | 4 |
> | More parking | 1 | 2 | 3 | 4 |
> | Helpful staff | 1 | 2 | 3 | 4 |

There may be a graphic rating scale. The respondent can mark along a continuum. For example:

> Indicate your degree of agreement by marking along the continuum.
>
> *The library has a sufficient number of Internet workstations.*
>
> Strongly Disagree   Strongly Agree
>
> *The library needs to sell coffee and soft drinks.*
>
> Strongly Disagree   Strongly Agree

A rank-order scale may be used. For example:

Indicate the relative importance of library services on a scale of 1 to 5, with "1" being the most important and "5" being the least important.

Borrowing books   _____

Borrowing audios & videos   _____

Study facilities   _____

Internet computers   _____

Magazines & newspapers   _____

A differential scale may be used. Sometimes called a Thurston scale, it presents a series of statements with equal distances between them. This type of scale is very difficult to use to design questions that represent values equidistant from one another while avoiding bias on the part of those developing the questions. Use of this scale is not recommended.

A Likert scale uses questions that represent favorable or unfavorable positions. A Likert scale is also called a summated scale. For example:

Item	Disagree	Strongly Disagree	Agree	Strongly Agree
An acquisitions librarian should consider requests from customers as the top priority for ordering.	SD	D	A	SA
The library should purchase more copies of "best-seller" books to meet the demand.	SD	D	A	SA

Another way to present a Likert scale is to use numbers rather than letters for the response. For example:

Item	Disagree	Strongly Disagree	Agree	Strongly Agree
An acquisitions librarian should consider requests from customers as the top priority for ordering.	1	2	3	4
The library should purchase more copies of "best-seller" books to meet the demand.	1	2	3	4

A semantic differential scale provides pairs of synonyms and antonyms along with a five- or seven-option rating scale. For example:

For each pair below, circle the number that comes closest to describing service at the reference desk. (Circle one number on each line.)						
	Extremely	**Moderately**	**Neither**	**Moderately**	**Extremely**	
Helpful	1	2	3	4	5	Unhelpful
Friendly	1	2	3	4	5	Reserved
Active	1	2	3	4	5	Passive
Effective	1	2	3	4	5	Ineffective
Rapid	1	2	3	4	5	Slow

A cumulative scale consists of related statements with which the respondent can agree or disagree. Since the statements are related to one another, the respondent "should" respond to subsequent items in a similar manner.

Self-ratings do have limitations resulting from potential bias and the subjectivity of questions included in the survey instrument.

Open-ended Questions

These unstructured questions allow respondents to make whatever comments they wish and thus are much more difficult to analyze and categorize. Response rates to open-ended questions are typically lower because they require the respondent to take some time to formulate and write answers. The open-ended responses can be categorized, and there are software tools to assist in the process if the amount of text is large. Examples of such unstructured questions follow:

What I like best about this library is . . .

When I visit the library I . . .

The library service I use the most is . . .

Question Construction

The development of questions in a survey should be done carefully. This is not the time to become creative, as people have been exposed to many surveys. Usually survey questions proceed from the general to the specific. Demographic information is typically asked last because some respondents are not inclined to reveal personal information. If possible, use questions that have been used in other library surveys. Following are some recommendations about writing questions.

- Use simple language—one- or two-syllable words are better than three- and four-syllable words.

- Keep questions under 20 words in length.

- Be specific and clear about what is being asked.

- Only ask the question if you need to know the answer.
- Don't use library jargon, and if necessary, define a term in the question itself. Questions using such terms as "access tools," "electronic journals," "users," "service problems," and "information skills" are meaningless to respondents.
- Avoid "yes-no" questions.
- Avoid double negatives.
- Don't combine two or more categories. For example, "Did you attend a program and borrow materials while visiting the library?"
- Use wording normally found in surveys. Avoid slang.
- Avoid "gift" questions that most people would agree to.
- If necessary, include information to jog people's memories.
- Avoid shorthand or incomplete sentences.
- Ask respondents about their experiences, not the experiences of others.
- Be sensitive to cultural differences.
- Ask participants to discuss desired outcomes.
- Double check to ensure that each question is necessary and that the resulting data will be useful in the analysis.

One study asked two groups the same question but used two different words in a single question—"should" and "might." This slight change in wording of a question evoked very different responses from those taking the survey.[5] Abraham Bookstein also asked two groups about various library services and whether an individual using the service considered the use a "library use." Again, differences were noted but were not analyzed statistically.

Surveys that are short and focused are more likely to be answered and yield useful information. Write an introduction to the survey that will invite cooperation from the participants. Once the questionnaire has been developed, it should be pretested to discover any ambiguity in the wording of the questions or other problems that may arise. Pretesting should be done with a small sample of the intended participants, not library staff members or others who are handy. Once revised (and in some cases, pretested again), the questionnaire is ready to go. Well, you hope it is ready to go. Pretesting after revision is advisable.

Distributing the Survey

When a survey is distributed can have an effect on the results. For example, in the academic environment, surveys at the start of the semester will likely have different results than those distributed during the middle or at the end of the semester.

There are five ways to administer the survey questionnaire: through the mail (sometimes called a self-administered survey), through e-mail, on the telephone, in interviews, and on the Web.

Mail Survey

The mail survey has been long used by researchers in a variety of fields. It is sent to the desired group of respondents, only a portion of whom will complete the survey and return it. The number of returned questionnaires compared to the total number of distributed surveys is the response rate. In general, the higher the response rate, the more generalizable the results—assuming a representative sample responds to the survey. If the library wants to have a fairly large sample of respondents, it may be necessary to distribute a much larger number of questionnaires. In some cases, it may be necessary to send out a second round of surveys to improve the number of responses.

Research has shown that higher response rates will result if a stamped, self-addressed envelope is sent to the respondent with the questionnaire. Normally a library will ask that the complete questionnaires be returned within 10 to 14 days.

A variation of mailing the survey is to approach someone entering the library and ask if he or she would be willing to complete the survey. Keith Curry Lance and his colleagues used this approach in the Counting on Results project. Interestingly, the respondents had the choice of completing a paper-based survey or using a Palm Pilot to enter their responses to the survey questions.[6]

E-mail Survey

A questionnaire can be distributed by sending e-mail to potential respondents. The survey instrument can be contained within the body of the e-mail or be provided as an attachment. The respondents can use the e-mail reply feature or return the completed survey using e-mail or regular mail.

The difficulties in using an e-mail survey include the fact that it can only be distributed to those whose e-mail address is known. This may mean that it will be difficult to obtain a random sample of the population. Further, the response rate may be low because the e-mail may be viewed as spam.[7]

Telephone Survey

Telephone surveys are popular and can be an effective method for garnering the required data for a study. However, telephone surveys must be carefully constructed and cannot be too long, as the time required to complete the survey may be too much for respondents, sometimes called "responder burden." The final questions in a survey may not be answered if respondents reach their patience threshold and simply hang up before the survey is completed.

One important advantage of this method is that the responses are normally entered into a computer database, which makes the data analysis relatively simple. On the other hand, all across the United States, people are dropping the use of their regular "land line" telephones in favor of using their cell phones. This change in telephone technology is making it increasingly difficult to generate a truly representative sample for a survey.

The Interview

Administering the survey questions in a face-to-face meeting can be useful because it allows the person conducting the interview to follow up and ask clarifying questions. However, it is important to avoid rephrasing the questions, as this will lead to a different response to a seemingly different question and, in turn, lead to difficulties in comparing the responses among all the respondents. Showing emotions, such as surprise or shock, at any of the responses is to be avoided. Developing an answer sheet with codes for anticipated responses will improve the accuracy of the data collection effort. With the respondent's permission, tape recording open-ended questions will ensure accuracy when later transcribing notes taken during the interview.

Web-based Survey

The survey can be administered using the Internet. The respondent is asked to click on a link to complete the survey. The survey can be administered using the library's Web site, or the library can use one of several free Internet sites that provide free online surveys—with some restrictions on the length of the survey.[8]

Since survey fatigue is now a common problem, offering respondents a choice of formats should increase the response rate. All of the responses are stored in a database, which can then be accessed for the data analysis.

An analysis of surveys distributed in three ways showed that the Web-based survey had slightly lower response rates than the paper survey distributed by mail. The importance of carefully designed follow-up procedures to ensure an adequate response rate cannot be emphasized enough.[9] A comparison of a Web-based and a paper survey found small differences in the responses of library patrons.[10]

The strengths and limitations of each method of gathering the survey data are shown in Table 5.2.

Table 5.2. Comparison of Methods of Distributing a Survey

	Mail*	Telephone	In Person	Web-based
Turnaround time	Slow	Fast	Moderate	Moderate
Cooperation rate	Low	Moderate	Highest	Moderate
Geographic coverage	Excellent	Excellent	Difficult	Excellent
Interviewer bias	None	Moderate	Substantial	None
Interviewer supervision	None required	Excellent	Poor	Excellent
Quality of response	Poor	Better	Best	Better
Questionnaire structure	Simple	Complex	Complex	Complex
Who is in control?	Respondent	Interviewer	Interviewer	Interviewer
Obtrusiveness	Low	High	High	Low
Ability to cope with interruptions	Easy	Difficult	Difficult	Easy
Length of interview	Short	Medium	Long	Long
Cost	Low	Moderate	High	Low

*Snail mail or e-mail

Types of Sampling

There are two broad types of sampling methods: nonprobability and probability.

Probability Sampling

Probability sampling enhances the prospect that the sample used in a study will be reflective of the entire population and that the resulting data can be used with some assurance that the sample is representative of the total population. Each element in the sample has the same possibility of being included as the other elements in the total population.

- **Simple random sample.** Using this method means that every individual or item in the population list has an equal chance of being selected for the sample. In theory, after being selected the item should go back into the population list so that the probability of being selected remains constant. However, due to practical considerations, once selected an item is not returned.

  Selecting a sample usually involves use of a random number table, which is used to make selections from the population list—rather than choosing every nth item. A random number chart can be found on the Internet or in a research methods book.

- **Systematic sample.** This method selects every nth element in the population list—starting from a random point in the list—until the desired sample size has been achieved. For practical purposes, an alphabetical list can be considered a random list.

- **Stratified random sample.** This approach requires that the total population be divided into groups, and a random sample is then drawn from each group. One approach when using a stratified random sample is to ensure that the size of the sample for each group is proportional to the total size of the group in relation to the total population. Thus, in an academic environment, undergraduates might account for 70 percent of the population, graduate students make up another 20 percent, and faculty and staff the remaining 10 percent. The sample that is selected should have the same relative percentages for each group. This is the approach that many researchers normally use.

  The other alternative, called a disproportionate stratified sample, allows for over-representation of a group to ensure an adequate sample size to make comparisons across all groups.

  A variation of a stratified random sample is use of a cluster sample when the total population is very large and it would be difficult to create a population list. In this case, the population is divided into clusters (from which a list can be created), from which a random sample is drawn.

Nonprobability Sampling

Nonprobability sampling methods are used when it is not possible to determine the probability of any one unit being included in the sample. However, the primary problem is that statistical inferences cannot be made because the selection probabilities are unknown—the sample is not random. Yet nonprobability sampling may be appropriate because an evaluation study most likely will not be using sophisticated statistical analysis that requires a probability sample.

- **Accidental sampling.** With this method (sometimes called a convenient, opportunistic, or available sample), no attempt is made to generate a random sample. Rather, whatever is available is used. Thus, a library might choose participants on a first-come, first-asked basis until the desired sample size is reached.

- **Quota sampling.** This method is similar to an accident sample, but it is used to ensure that different groups within a population are included in the sample, hopefully in the same proportion that they occur in the overall population. A variation of the quota sample is the snowball sample, which asks members of a group for assistance in locating similar members of that group.

- **Purposive sampling.** An evaluation study might be exploring the use of a new service. This method samples other libraries that are already using the service, which might be appropriate to learn about the strengths and weaknesses of the proposed service. Clearly this method is susceptible to bias.

- **Self-selected sampling.** With this method, an evaluation team might publish a notice asking for volunteers to participate in a study. The data resulting from such an approach will only be reflective of those who participate, for whatever reasons.

- **Incomplete sampling.** An incomplete sample might be the result of a very low response rate or of a sample that was selected with incomplete or inaccurate information about the characteristics of the population. Obviously any data from such a sample must be used with great care or not be used at all.

- **Extreme case sampling.** In this method, a small sample focuses on cases or situations that are rich in information because they are unusual in some way.

- **Intensity sampling.** This method consists of a small to moderate-sized sample of information-rich cases that are unusual in some way—excellent service provider, low-cost service provider, and so forth.

- **Homogenous sampling.** A small, homogenous sample may be selected and then studied in some depth. Focus group interviews are an example of homogenous groups.

Determining Sample Size

In a library setting, sampling can be done for just about every activity or physical object. For example, libraries have done evaluation studies involving a sample of different locations, customers, items in the collection, activities or processes, and time.

Determining the size of a sample is a balancing act. And while the larger the sample the better, a sample that is too large is wasting money and other resources. A sample that is too small, say less than 100, will not be representative of the population. Criteria to determine the appropriate sample size include the following:

- **The degree of accuracy, sometimes called precision, between the sample and the population.** The need for more accuracy means a larger sample is needed.

- **The method of sampling to be used.**

- **The variability of the population.** The greater the variability, the higher the sample size.

- **The type of data analysis that is planned.** Some statistical analysis tools require larger sample sizes.

Although it is possible to use a formula to determine the necessary sample size, in most cases those involved with evaluations use a table to determine a random sample size, with precision of .05, as shown in Table 5.3.[11] Note that the sample size requirements are fairly large when the population is small, while the sample size grows quite slowly in proportion as the population increases rapidly.

Table 5.3. Table for Determining Sample Size*

Population Size	Sample Size	Population	Sample Size
100	80	2,000	322
200	132	3,000	341
300	169	4,000	351
400	196	5,000	357
500	217	10,000	370
750	254	20,000	377
1,000	278	50,000	381

*Reflects 95 percent confidence level and a ±5 standard deviation.

Survey Nonresponse

Jacquelyn Burkell examined the response rates of surveys published in three major library and information science journals over a six-year period and found that the average response rate was 63 percent. Almost three-fourths of the surveys had a response rate of less than 75 percent—the level generally held to be required for generalizability. Nonresponse always results in a biased sample. The question is whether the bias affects survey results or whether data from nonrespondents would have changed the survey conclusions.[12] And Peter Hernon has observed that it is more common for studies to report response rates below 50 percent—perhaps in the 20 to 40 percent range.[13]

Strategies to improve response rates include prenotification; personalized cover letters; the use of reminders; incentives with the invitation to participate (including small monetary incentives of $2 to $5 or returned surveys qualifying for the drawing of a prize); and the use of stamped, self-addressed envelopes for the return of mail surveys.

If nonresponse rates remain high despite efforts to boost completed surveys, then care must be exercised to limit survey conclusions appropriately.

Caveats

Problems can arise when using surveys. Assuming a reasonable response rate, the library is not sure that those who did respond to the survey have different characteristics than those who chose not to participate. Obviously they are different in at least one dimension, willingness to complete a survey.

A second problem is that most libraries will ask those who are physically present in the library to participate in a study. This approach to distributing a survey is based on convenience and excludes the views of those who visit the library infrequently or not at all.

Despite the fact that all statistical analyses have a margin of error or a level of confidence, plus or minus "x" percent, managers and decision makers tend to forget the limitations of the data and rely on them as a certainty. The size of the error is affected by four factors:

- Sample size—the larger the sample the smaller the error
- Sample size relative to population size
- Inherent variability of observations
- Choice of statistical sampling method

Other nonsampling errors may also occur. Sources of these errors include improper questionnaire design, choice of an inadequate sampling method, nonresponses, mistakes in responding to questions, clerical processing, and analyst error.

After the sample size and type of sample have been determined, selecting the sample is crucial. Rather than selecting every nth record in a file, for example, it is better to use a random number table (available from various Web sites) to select the sample. This will improve the reliability of the results.

Some of the biggest problems with library research and evaluation projects are unsatisfactory sampling techniques, primitive survey instruments, and studies conducted on too small a scale to permit generalizations.

CONJOINT ANALYSIS

Conjoint analysis, also called multi-attribute compositional models, is a statistical technique that was developed by Paul Green at the Wharton School of the University of Pennsylvania.[14] Today it is used in many of the social sciences and applied sciences, including marketing, product management, and operations research. The objective of conjoint analysis is to determine what combination of attributes is most preferred by respondents. It is used frequently in testing customer acceptance of new product designs and assessing the appeal of advertisements.

Respondents are shown a set of products, prototypes, mock-ups, or pictures. Examples are similar enough that consumers will see them as close substitutes, but they are dissimilar enough that respondents can clearly determine a preference. Each example is composed of a unique combination of product or service features. The data may consist of individual ratings, rank-orders, or preferences among alternative combinations. The two most frequently used variations of this tool are adaptive conjoint analysis and choice-based conjoint analysis.

Any number of algorithms may be used to estimate utility functions. These utility functions indicate the perceived value of the feature and how sensitive consumer perceptions and preferences are to changes in product features.

The advantages of conjoint analysis include that it

- measures preferences at the individual level and
- estimates psychological tradeoffs that consumers make when evaluating several attributes together.

The disadvantages include that

- only a limited set of features can be used because the number of combinations increases very quickly as more features are added,
- the information-gathering stage is complex, and

• respondents are unable to articulate attitudes toward new categories.

A research project in Germany, described by Reinhold Decker and Antonia Hermelbracht, used conjoint analysis in a study that reached almost 5,000 respondents to explore new academic library services. The Web-based survey used a combination of text and pictures to describe each alternative. A total of 118 services or service concepts were analyzed.[15] Another project used conjoint analysis to model public library use and choice behavior.[16]

TRANSACTION LOG ANALYSIS

Most computer systems will keep a log of all transactions—inputs from the user and system outputs. These transaction logs can then be analyzed, although it can be difficult to decide how to separate each of the data elements and to choose the most useful statistics, since most logs squeeze all the data together as a single string of characters. Transaction log analysis, also called log analysis, log file analysis, log tracking, Web logging, or Web log analysis, will most likely require a programmer to create a file in a prescribed format that can then be imported into a statistical data analysis software package such as Access or SPSS, two of the more frequently used statistical analysis tools. Lisa Goddard provides an excellent review of the challenges facing those who wish to use transaction log analysis and what information is available from shareware or commercial software analysis tools.[17]

While it is possible to select a sample of transactions for analysis, typically all transactions that occurred during a particular period of time—a day, a week, a month, a year—are used for the analysis because the computer can make quick work of calculating the data if dealing with thousands of transactions or hundreds of thousands of transactions. Logs can typically be generated by information retrieval systems, library online catalogs, Web sites, intranets, and Web-based database systems.

Transaction log analysis has been used to examine the actual behavior of users of an online catalog to compare their behavior to that anticipated by system designers.[18] In some cases, the analysis has been restricted to periodical title searching in an online catalog.[19] In other cases, the technique has been used to identify the actual content used in five different online health information systems.[20] Karen Markey used this method to examine spelling errors in online catalogs.[21] This method has also been used to examine a wide variety of Web sites.

However, it is important to note that transaction log analysis does have limitations:

• The log represents a snapshot in time.

• Various user characteristics and experience in searching cannot be identified.

• Users' linguistic skills are not revealed.

• Users' understanding of a domain of knowledge cannot be determined.

EXPERIMENTS

Experimental research is most likely the most rigorous of all research methods. If correctly designed, an experiment allows the testing of cause-and-effect relationships. Experimental research is most rigorous when one variable is being tested to determine the presence or absence of an effect or consequence. In the social sciences, a variety of factors are often tested to determine their contribution to a certain event happening. If X, the independent variable, is a necessary condition for Y, the independent variable, to occur, then Y will never occur unless X is present.

However, it is usually impossible to demonstrate that one variable causes another. Thus, cause-and-effect relationships are typically inferred based on an analysis of the available data. As with any methodology, care must be taken when planning and conducting an experiment to not compromise the results. Among the problems to avoid are having too small a sample, selecting a nonrepresentative sample, using poorly designed data collection instruments, not including all of the likely variables, and not using the most appropriate statistical tools.

Experiments have been designed by Pauline Atherton to test the impact of enhancing the bibliographic record with additional table-of-contents and back-of-the-book information[22]; by Karen Markey, who tested search systems with additional Dewey-related information included as part of one test system[23]; by Ray Larson, who used experiments in testing an online catalog system called Cheshire[24]; and by researchers in England, who tested various features of an online catalog called Okapi.[25]

In almost all cases an experimental design is not used to evaluate a library service because too many variables are outside the control of the researcher.

SUMMARY

This chapter has reviewed the strengths and limitations of a wide variety of quantitative tools that a library is likely to find useful as it plans for and conducts an evaluation of library services. The two broad methodologies available for an evaluation study—qualitative and quantitative—have strengths and limitations, which are summarized in Table 5.4.

Table 5.4. Comparison of Qualitative and Quantitative Methods

	Qualitative	Quantitative
Key Concept	Meaning	Statistical relationships
Design	Flexibility	Structured, predetermined
Data	People's own words, field notes, behavior	Counts, measures, numbers
Data Collection	Less structured	More structured
Sampling	Small, nonrepresentative	Large, random, stratified, representative of the population
Methods	Observations, interviews, review of documents	Survey instruments, data sets
Relationships with Subjects	Personal, emphasis on trust	Short term, distant, impersonal
Instruments	Researcher, tape recorder, video recorder, camera	Questionnaires, computer
Replication	Difficult	Easier to repeat and thus higher reliability
Data Analysis	Ongoing, evolving, inductive	Deductive, statistical, and objective
Advantages	Flexibility, goal is to gain understanding	Ease of use, high acceptance
Disadvantages	Time, hard to study groups, difficult to distill the data	Controlling other variables, oversimplification

NOTES

1. Quoted in Bruce Heterick and Roger C. Schonfeld. The Future Ain't What It Used to Be. *Serials,* 17 (3), November 2004, 226.

2. Gary Golden. *Survey Research Methods.* Chicago: Association of College & Research Libraries, 1982.

3. Several hundred surveys created by librarians are available at http://www.nsls.info/services/fastfacts/category.aspx.

4. Carol Tenopir. What User Studies Tell Us. *Library Journal,* 128 (14), September 1, 2003, 32.

5. Abraham Bookstein. Questionnaire Research in a Library Setting. *The Journal of Academic Librarianship*, 11 (1), March 1985, 24–28.

6. Keith Curry Lance, Marcia J. Rodney, Nicolle O. Steffen, Suzanne Kaller, Rochelle Logan, Kristie M. Koontz, and Dean K. Jue. *Counting on Results: New Tools for Outcome-Based Evaluation of Public Libraries.* Aurora, CO: Bibliographic Center for Research, 2002.

7. Peter Hernon and John R. Whitman. *Delivering Satisfaction and Service Quality: A Customer-Based Approach for Libraries.* Chicago: American Library Association, 2001, 125.

8. Among the many Web-based sites that offer free surveys are Zoomerang.com, FreeOnlineSurveys.com, SurveyConsole.com, SurveyMonkey.com, and QuestionPro.com. The data are displayed using some simple charts, and the data analysis tools are fairly limited. The number of respondents to a survey is typically limited (e.g., 100), and it is not possible to download the survey data into a spreadsheet or database for further analysis. A subscription generally costs about $20 per month, which provides a greater range of capabilities.

9. Michele M. Hayslett and Barbara M. Wildemuth. Pixels or Pencils? The Relative Effectiveness of Web-based Versus Paper Surveys. *Library & Information Science Research*, 26, 2004, 73–93.

10. Gay Helen Perkins and Haiwang Yuan. A Comparison of Web-based and Paper-and-Pencil Library Satisfaction Survey Results. *College & Research Libraries*, 62 (4), July 2001, 369–77.

11. More extensive tables that determine sample size can be found on the Internet.

12. Jacquelyn Burkell. The Dilemma of Survey Nonresponse. *Library & Information Science Research*, 25, 2003, 239–63.

13. Peter Hernon. Components of the Research Process: Where Do We Need to Focus Attention? *The Journal of Academic Librarianship*, 27 (2), March 2001, 81–89.

14. Paul Green and V. Srinivasan. Conjoint Analysis in Consumer Research: Issues and Outlook. *Journal of Consumer Research*, 5, September 1978, 103–23; and Paul Green, J. Carroll, and S. Goldberg. A General Approach to Product Design Optimization via Conjoint Analysis, *Journal of Marketing*, 43, Summer 1981, 17–35.

15. Reinhold Decker and Antonia Hermelbracht. Planning and Evaluation of New Academic Library Services by Means of Web-based Conjoint Analysis. *The Journal of Academic Librarianship*, 32 (6), November 2006, 558–72. See also Antonia Hermelbracht and Bettina Koeper. ProSeBiCA: Development of New Library Services by Means of Conjoint Analysis. *Library HiTech*, 24 (4), 2006, 595–603.

16. Akio Sone. An Application of Discrete Choice Analysis to the Modeling of Public Library Use and Choice Behavior. *Library & Information Science Research*, 10, 1988, 35–55.

17. Lisa Goddard. Getting to the Source: A Survey of Quantitative Data Sources Available to the Everyday Librarian: Part 1: Web Server Log Analysis. *Evidence Based Library and Information Practice*, 2 (1), 2007, 48–67.

18. Susan Jones, Mike Gatford, Thien Do, and Stephen Walker. Transaction Logging. *Journal of Documentation*, 53 (1), January 1997, 35–50.

19. Patricia M. Wallace. Periodical Title Searching in Online Catalogs. *Serials Review*, 23 (3), September 1997, 27–35.

20. David Nicholas, Paul Huntington, and Janet Homewood. Assessing Used Content Across Five Digital Health Information Services Using Transaction Log Files. *Journal of Information Science*, 29 (6), 2003, 499–515.

21. Karen M. Drabenstott and Marjorie S. Weller. Handling Spelling Errors in Online Catalog Searches. *LRTS*, 40 (2), April 1996, 113–32.

22. Pauline Atherton. *Books Are for Use: Final Report of the Subject Access Project to the Council on Library Resources*. Washington, DC: Council on Library Resources, 1978.

23. Karen M. Drabenstott et. al. Analysis of a Bibliographic Database Enhanced with a Library Classification [Online Catalog Incorporating DDC Subject Terms]. *Library Resources & Technical Services*, 34, April 1990, 179–98; Karen M. Drabenstott. Searching and Browsing the Dewey Decimal Classification in an Online Catalog. *Cataloging & Classification Quarterly*, 7, Spring 1987, 37–68; Karen M. Drabenstott et. al. Findings of the Dewey Decimal Classification On-line Project. *International Cataloguing*, 15, April 1986, 15–19; Karen M. Drabenstott. Class Number Searching in an Experimental Online Catalog. *International Classification*, 13 (3), 1986, 142–50.

24. Ray R. Larson. TREC Interactive with Cheshire II. *Information Processing & Management*, 37 (3), May 2001, 485–505; Ray R. Larson et. al. Cheshire II: Designing a Next-Generation Online Catalog. *Journal of the American Society for Information Science*, 47, July 1996, 555–67; Ray R. Larson. Evaluation of Advanced Retrieval Techniques in an Experimental Online Catalog [Probabilistic SMART Retrieval Methods in a Cheshire Catalog]. *Journal of the American Society for Information Science*, 43, January 1992, 34–53; and Ray R. Larson. Classification Clustering, Probabilistic Information Retrieval, and the Online Catalog [Experimental Cheshire System Employing SMART Principles]. *The Library Quarterly*, 61, April 1991, 133–73.

25. The Okapi Project produced a plethora of publications. See, for example, Edward M. Keen. The Okapi Projects. *Journal of Documentation*, 53, January 1997, 84–87; Stephen E. Robertson. Overview of the Okapi Projects. *Journal of Documentation*, 53, January 1997, 3–7; Stephen E. Robertson, Stephen Walker, and Micheline Hancock-Beaulieu. Large Test Collection Experiments on an Operational, Interactive System: Okapi at TREC. *Information Processing & Management*, 31, May/June 1995, 345–60; and Micheline Hancock-Beaulieu. Query Expansion: Advances in Research in Online Catalogues. *Journal of Information Science*, 18 (2), 1992, 99–103.

6

Analysis of Data

Statistics can be used as the drunkard uses the lamp post—for support if not for illumination.

—Kendon Stubbs[1]

Data that are collected for an evaluation project will have to be analyzed. For most evaluations, the analysis of data is relatively simple and will not involve the dreaded "S" word—statistics. Regardless of the method selected to assist in the analysis of data, it is important to remember:

The purpose of analysis is **insight**!

The analysis of data can be divided into two broad groups:

- **Descriptive methods for organizing, summarizing, and presenting information**; in short, making sense of the data. Using these tools, the librarian can identify trends, perform comparisons, and make better informed decisions. Descriptive statistics are normally applied to population data rather than sample data.

- **Inferential statistics allow the librarian to make generalizations using sample data.** From the sample it is possible to infer the characteristics of the whole population—if it could be analyzed. Inferential statistics have a probabilistic component since the analysis might be wrong. Thus, if .05 level is associated with a statistic, this indicates there is a 1 in 20 probability the analysis is wrong.

It is helpful to understand the meaning of a number of frequently used terms when talking about the analysis of data. Some of these important terms are defined here:

- **Population** is a group of items having at least one shared characteristic. Items may be objects (such as materials found in the library's collection), people, measurements, or observations.

- An **attribute** may be used to define or place limits around a population. For example, a population may be limited to the residents in a specific city or county.

- A **target population** is the population that is the focus of the evaluation study.

- A **variable** is any characteristic of the population that may vary. For example, a collection of books can vary by age, size, author, subject, and so forth.

- A **score** is the value of the variable. For example, the number of years since a book has been published is the score for the variable "age."

- **Attribute data** can be described by a word—author, subject headings, place of publication, and so forth. Attribute data can also be numerical—library card bar code number, Social Security number, or driver's license number.

- A variable can be placed into **categories**, in which case the scores of the variables must be mutually exclusive. For example, materials in a library's collection can be placed in material type categories—books, audio, video, microforms, and so forth.

Some data are better than other data depending on how they have been measured and categorized. There are four different ways of measuring data:

- **Nominal scale measurement** gives a variable meaning by assigning a name or label to the score; it reflects only equality or inequality. For example, a nominal scale might include type of library, type of college or university, book publisher names, and so forth. The library customer's bar code identifies a specific individual.

- **Ordinal scale measurement** reflects categories that have some associated order—be it hierarchical or some other manner of organizing the data. Thus, the order of the categories is important. For example, the amount of education a person has received is typically reflected in the categories "grade completed"—1 through 8 for elementary school, 9 through 12 for high school, 13 through 16 for college, and 17+ for graduate school. Also, ordinal scale measurement does not reflect the distance between categories.

- **Interval scale measurement** is used to rank variables that have equal intervals between values. The purpose of this type of measurement is to compare values, and it is permissible to add and subtract values. A thermometer is an example of an interval scale measurement.

- **Ratio scale measurement** is anchored by true zero. For example, this type of scale can be used to identify the number of children in a family—from zero on up. Absolute zero exists for measuring such units as temperature, weight, time, area, and volume. Using a ratio scale, it is possible to make such statements as "three times as many" or "twice as fast."

In order to be assured that decision makers are using the appropriate data, two additional characteristics of data must be discussed—reliability and validity.

- **Reliability** is concerned with consistency, stability, and predictability of the data. That is, each time a data variable is measured using the same device, the same result should be obtained if the circumstances are identical. For example, one library might treat the renewal of an item as a check in and then a checkout, while another library would only extend the due date and not adjust (increase) the statistical counts. Cronbach's alpha, a statistical analysis test, is often performed to determine the reliability of specific questions.

- Data **validity** is concerned with the relationship between the evidence and the argument, that is, determining whether the correct variable is being used for the evaluation project. Validity focuses on the meaning that is being attributed to the data. Consider a library trying to understand customer complaints about the time it takes to get materials reshelved. The library collects data about the length of the time people wait in the queue at the circulation desk. While these data might be interesting, they are not germane to what is being evaluated: how long it takes to get a recently returned item back on the shelf.

    Bias is the enemy of validity. It can be introduced through poor sampling, faulty wording, and sloppy administration of the data collection instrument (survey or interview); inaccurate data recording; and inappropriate interpretation of the results. Pretesting may alert the participants or educate them about the topic under study and thus introduce bias.

DESCRIPTIVE STATISTICS TECHNIQUES

Typically, the analysis of data will begin with a count of the scores for each variable. These *frequency distributions* can be reported in a table and include simple, cumulative, percentage, and grouped distributions. However, it does not take too much data before a table full of numbers becomes fairly meaningless. It is interesting to note that most library monthly management reports use tables to report their statistics. It would be much more helpful to convert some, but not all, of these tabular data into charts or graphs, because they help reveal interesting structures present in the data.

Converting tables of data into charts or graphs will make the data much more understandable. The widespread availability of spreadsheet programs makes the production of charts and graphs a simple task. The greatest value of any chart or diagram is that it *forces* the observer to notice the unexpected.

Thermometer Chart

Responses to a unidimensional scale can be shown effectively using a "thermometer" chart. Figure 6.1 (p. 82) shows a typical thermometer chart, with the ratings library customers assign to various service attributes.

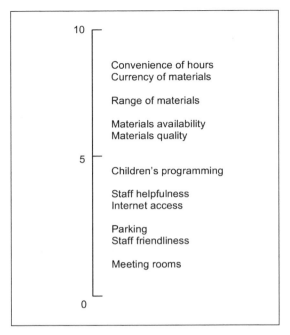

Figure 6.1. Thermometer Chart Showing Customer Preferences

Histogram

A histogram is a graph composed of a series of rectangles with their base on the horizontal or X-axis. Figure 6.2 shows the copyright dates of books in a hypothetical library.

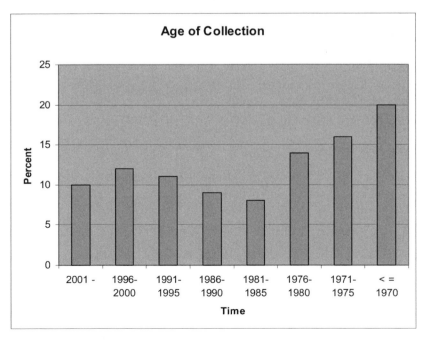

Figure 6.2. Age of Library Book Collection

Frequency Polygon

A frequency polygon is a graph that plots category frequency with the category mid-points. The number of values or observations in a category is assumed to be concentrated at the midpoint. Figure 6.3 presents a sample frequency showing the distribution of a hypothetical library's nonfiction book collection using call number range. Each category midpoint is connected with a line to adjacent midpoints. The relative frequency information, when expressed as a percent, must total 100 percent.

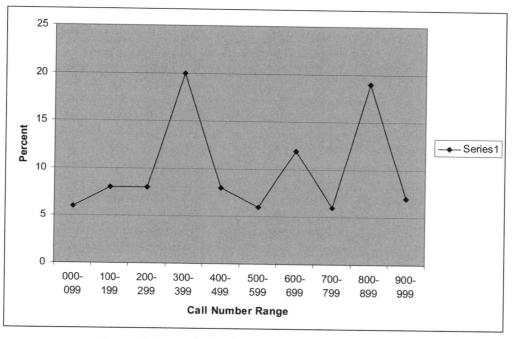

Figure 6.3. Library's Nonfiction Book Collection Distribution

A cumulative frequency distribution is constructed by adding the distribution frequencies of successive classes together. Figure 6.4 (p. 84) shows the histogram in Figure 6.2 with a cumulative frequency distribution line added.

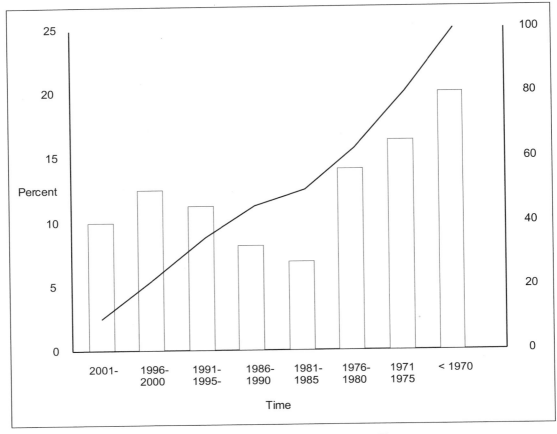

Figure 6.4. Age of Collection with a Cumulative Frequency

Bar Charts

Both horizontal and vertical bar charts effectively compare related items. Since one chart can accommodate many bars, a fair amount of information can be presented and understood by the reader. The bar chart can be organized to reflect numerical order, decreasing values, chronology, and so forth. Bar charts can be arranged in a variety of ways, and the bars can be subdivided, paired, or grouped. Figure 6.5 presents a bar chart that compares circulation with holdings for a public library.

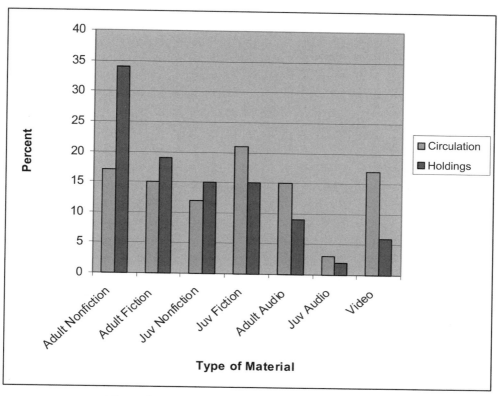

Figure 6.5. A Comparison of Circulation and Holdings

Line Charts

A line chart or line graph is especially effective at showing trends—that is, the rise and fall of a variable. A line chart is particularly useful when comparing this year's performance with that achieved last year, as shown in Figure 6.6 (p. 86). A quick look at this figure indicates that circulation has increased for almost every month compared to the previous year's circulation numbers.

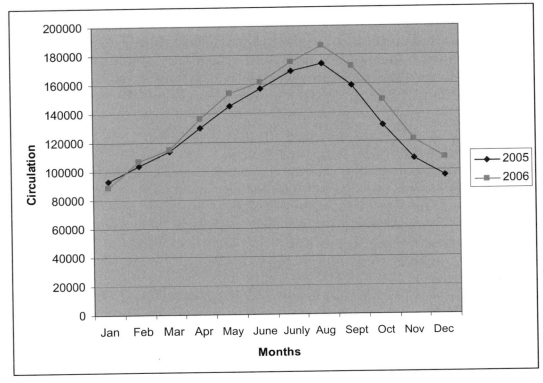

Figure 6.6. Annual Circulation by Month

Pie Charts

A pie chart or circle graph segregates and identifies the components of the whole, such as budgets, portions of the collection, segments of the population who actively use the library's services, and so forth. Each component is identified as a wedge-shaped portion of a circle. A pie chart illustrating the components of a library's budget is shown in Figure 6.7. In general, pie charts should not contain more than five segments.

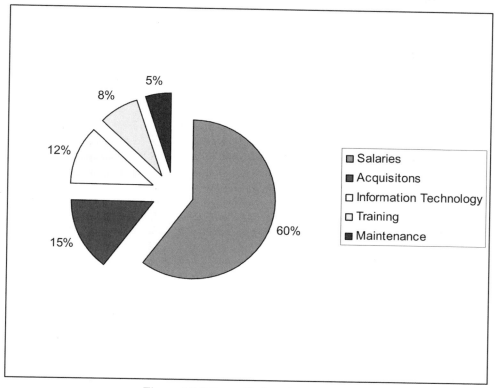

Figure 6.7. Library Budget Components

MEASURES OF CENTRAL TENDENCY

As previously noted, the data collected as a part of an evaluation project can be organized into tables, frequency distributions, and charts. However, the characteristics of a distribution are important to understand and include the spread or width of a distribution, the middle value of the distribution, and the general shape of the distribution. In addition, the measures of central tendency allow for the side-by-side comparison of two or more distributions.

The Mode

The distribution's center, called the mode, is the data score or data point that occurs most frequently in the distribution. While most distributions will have a single mode, in some cases a distribution will have two modes. The latter situation is described as bimodal.

For example, in the data set [3, 3, 4, 5, 5, 5, 6], the mode is 5, since 5 occurs most frequently. However, it should be noted that a data set may not contain a mode.

The Median

The median divides the distribution in half. Arranging the scores in a distribution from smallest to largest will assist in identifying the midpoint value of the data set. Thus, half the scores of the distribution will be less than the median and the remaining half will be greater than the median value.

For example, in the data set [1, 1, 2, 2, 3, 4, 4, 5, 5], the median is 3—the midpoint score. When the data point contains an even number of scores, the median is the value between the two scores closest to the middle. For example, in the data set [1, 2, 3, 4, 5, 6, 7, 8], the median is the number that lies between the fourth and fifth scores, or 4.5. In this case, the median is rounded because it must be a discrete value: 5.

A box-and-whisker diagram illustrates the spread of a set of data. It also displays the upper and lower quartile. For example, consider the data set [14, 13, 3, 7, 9, 12, 17, 4, 9, 10, 18, 18]. The upper and lower values are 3 and 18, so the range is 15 and the median (the midpoint) has the value of 11. The upper quartile is the median value for 12, 13, 14, 16, 17, 18, or midway between 14 and 16: 15. The lower quartile is the median value for 3, 4, 7, 9, 9, 10, or midway between 7 and 9: 8.

The box in the box-and-whiskers diagram is composed of the upper and lower quartiles, while the whiskers connect the upper and lower quartiles, and the median is also shown in the middle, as illustrated in Figure 6.8.

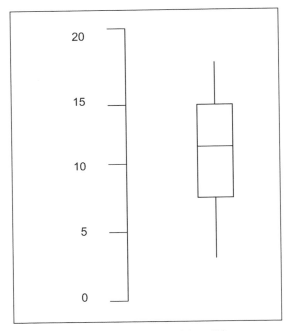

Figure 6.8. Box-and-Whiskers Diagram

The Mean

The arithmetical mean or average is determined by adding all the scores in the data set and dividing by the number of scores. For example, in the data set [1, 2, 3, 4, 5, 6, 7, 8], the mean is 4.5. Since the mean is sensitive to extreme values, it may be helpful to calculate two means—one that includes the extreme value(s) and one that does not.

What Is an Average?

Consider the 9,206 public libraries in the United States. They serve populations ranging in size from 19 to 3,912,200, but the vast majority of libraries serve populations that are quite small, as shown in Chart 1.

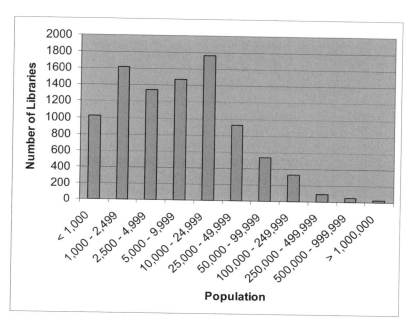

Chart 1. Number of Public Libraries by Population Served

So what could be considered an average population served for a public library?

The *mean* population served is 30,788.

The *median* population served is 6,598.

The *mode* of the population served is 5,387.

And given the extremely wide range of population size, it is not surprising that the *standard deviation* is also large: 123,165.

A Distribution's Shape

The distribution of data can be separated into two broad categories: the scores in the data set clustering at the center of the distribution and the scores tending to cluster toward the higher or lower values of the distribution.

A *symmetric distribution* occurs when the median and mean are equal. The most well-known symmetric distribution is the *normal distribution,* also called the Gaussian distribution, illustrated by the bell-shaped distribution shown in Figure 6.9 (p. 90) (more about the bell-shaped curve when inferential statistics are discussed later). Another variation of a symmetric distribution, called a *unimodal distribution,* is also illustrated in the same figure.

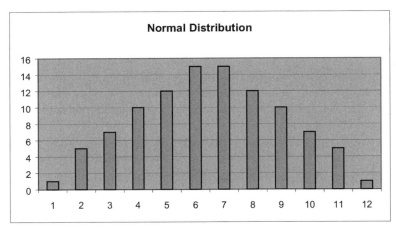

Figure 6.9. Normal Distribution

Distributions are said to be *skewed* when the median and mean are not the same. Since the bulk of the scores in the data set are located at either the low or the high end of the distribution, the resulting curve representing the data seems to have a "tail," as shown in Figure 6.10. Note that a great deal of library-related data is skewed and does not reflect a bell-shaped distribution!

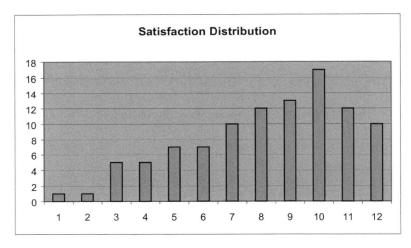

Figure 6.10. Skewed Distribution

When the highest frequency occurs in the first or last category in a data set, it is called a J-Distribution, because graphically the curve resembles the letter J (or a reversed letter J), as shown in Figure 6.11. The J-Distribution has recently been popularized by Chris Anderson, who wrote about the "long tail" in *Wired* magazine and a book, in which he suggested that there are an infinite number of niche markets that are economically viable due to falling distribution costs of the Internet, and in the aggregate they represent sizeable sales.[2]

Vilfredo Pareto, a nineteenth-century economist, developed the 80/20 rule after examining the distribution of wealth in Italy. This is another example of the J-curve. A Pareto distribution has been observed in the library environment in a number of different contexts. For example, 80 percent of a library's circulation is typically accounted for by about 20 percent of the library's customers.

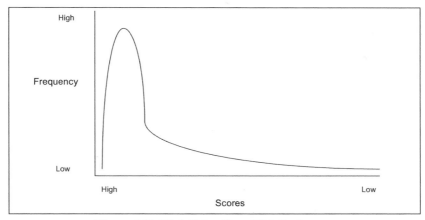

Figure 6.11. High Value Skew Distribution

MEASURES OF VARIABILITY

To better understand a specific data set, measures of central tendency (mean, median, mode) should be augmented by measures of variability, sometimes called *measures of dispersion*. Such measures will assist in judging the reliability of the central tendency measures.

Range

Range is the difference between the two extreme values in a data set. The greater the range of data, the more spread out or dispersed are the scores. While helpful, range does not indicate the dispersion of data within the data set. For example, the range in this data set [1, 2, 3, 4, 5, 6, 7, 8, 9, 10] is 9 (10 – 1), while a different data set with the same range could be entirely different [1, 8, 8, 8, 9, 9, 9, 10, 10, 10].

Percentiles

Percentiles divide a large data set that is in rank order (lowest to highest) into 100 equal parts. For anyone who has taken one of the many standardized tests—GRE, SAT, ACT, and so forth—the results provide two numbers to indicate performance. The first is the individual's test score as reflected in the point score (questions answered correctly compared to the total possible points). The second number reflects the individual's test score as compared to all who took the test (percentile). Consider someone who is in the 75th percentile—25 percent of all test takers scored higher than this individual.

Note that the median is the 50th percentile—the median divides the distribution into two equal data sets. Dividing the distribution into four equal parts will produce *quartiles*.

Standard Deviation

One of the most readily recognized measures of a data set is the standard deviation, which tells how far the typical score is from the mean of the distribution. It is called *standard* because it applies uniformly to all scores in the distribution, and *deviation* refers to the differences in the scores. In other words, standard deviation refers to the spread or dispersion of the data away from the distribution's mean. The Greek character sigma is used to refer to the standard deviation. A large standard deviation means that the data points are far from the mean, while a small standard deviation means that they are clustered about the mean.

Calculating the standard deviation can be accomplished in four steps:

1. Determine the mean of the data set.

2. Subtract the mean from each score in the data set and double the resulting value—this is called a squared deviation.

3. Add all the squared deviations together—this is called the sum of the squares—and divide the result by (n-1), where n = the number of scores in the data set.

4. Calculate the square root of the quotient found in step 3.

To spare you the tedious task of manually calculating the standard deviation, most spreadsheets and statistical software packages will do this for you.

The Russian mathematician P. L. Chebyshev noticed that for any set of data, the formula $1 - (1/k^2)$ would predict the proportion of data that lies within k standard deviations of the mean. For a normal distribution of data, the interval within 1 standard deviation on either side of the mean contains 68 percent of all scores, and within 1.5 standard deviations, 86.6 percent of all scores can be found.

Within the quality movement, the goal for really high quality is often expressed as achieving six sigma: three standard deviations to the left of the mean and three to the right of the mean, or virtually all scores within a data set. To achieve six sigma, a process must not produce more than 3.4 defects per million opportunities.

INFERENTIAL STATISTICS

In some cases, a research project or evaluation study will formulate a hypothesis. A variety of definitions of *hypothesis* exist, but for our purposes a hypothesis can be thought of as the proposition guiding the investigation of a problem. Generally a hypothesis will involve attempting to understand the relationship between two or more variables.

Inferential statistics are used to test hypotheses using tests of statistical significance to determine if observed differences between variables are "real" or merely due to chance. Inferential statistics are usually divided into two groups, parametric and nonparametric. Parametric statistics assume a normal population or distribution. Nonparametric statistics are regarded as distribution free.

The use of inferential statistics simply does not happen in most evaluation studies. Thus, a detailed description of the various inferential statistical tests and methods is not provided here but can be found elsewhere.[3]

Among some of the better known inferential parametric statistical tests encountered in the literature are Pearson's correlation coefficient, student's t-test, analysis of variance (ANOVA), and regression analysis. An example of a nonparametric test is the Chi-square test.

- A **correlation** is the extent to which two variables are related, and a *correlation coefficient* is the mathematical expression of the relationship. A correlation coefficient can take on values that range from –1.0 to +1.0 and not surprisingly, the plus sign indicates that relationship is positive and the negative sign that the relationship is negative. When there is no relationship between the two variables, the value of the correlation coefficient is zero. However, it is important to note that the correlation coefficient does not imply cause and effect between the two variables.

  Greater understanding is gained by calculating the *coefficient of determination* by squaring the coefficient correlation, which explains the proportion of the variability of scores in one variable that can be associated with another variable. For example, if the coefficient correlation between college grades and the GRE is .60, then 36 percent (.60 squared) of the variability in GRE scores and college GPA can be explained by achievement. Or, 74 percent of the variability of GPA is unrelated to academic achievement. Note that correlation coefficients of .40 and lower should not be used to explain any relationships!

- The **student's t-test** is used to determine whether a relation exists between a two-group nominal or ordinal variable—gender, full-time versus part-time variable—and a second variable measured on an interval or ratio scale. This test evaluates the difference between two groups' mean scores on the ratio or interval variable. For example, the t-test could be used to determine whether women had higher grade point averages than men.

- **Analysis of variance (ANOVA)** is a multigroup extension of the t-test that compares means. When the grouping variable has more than two categories, the ANOVA test must be used. The ANOVA test will indicate only that no less than one of the possible pairs of the group means is statistically significant—and it will not reveal which one(s).

  Pauline Atherton's Books Project created two different databases for searching (one with enhanced bibliographic records and one without enhanced records). Participants then searched one of the systems, and the retrieved records were analyzed for relevance and precision and recall scores were calculated. ANOVA was then used to determine if the differences between the two average recall and two average precision scores were significant. They were![4]

  The word "significant" should only be applied to inferential data, since "statistical significance" is a measure that the conclusion can be applied to the entire population. Statistical significance between two means depends on four factors: the absolute difference in size, the variance of responses around the mean, the size of the sample, and the level of precision at which the difference is being considered. Given a large enough sample, virtually all differences will be determined statistically significant.

  Statistical significance does not equate to importance. A finding may be true, however, without being important.

- **Regression analysis** models the relationship between one or more response variables, sometimes called dependent variables, explained variables, or predicted variables—and the predictors, also called independent variables, explanatory variables, or control variables. Simple linear regression and multiple linear regression are related statistical methods for modeling the relationship between two or more random variables using a linear equation. Simple linear regression refers to a regression on two variables, while multiple regression refers to a regression on more than two variables. Linear regression assumes the best estimate of the response is a linear function of some parameters. If the predictors are all quantitative, the multiple regression method is used.

  Path analysis is a technique that uses linear regression techniques to test the causal relations among variables. A drawing is created based on a theory or a set of hypotheses, and the direct and indirect effects are noted by calculating the path coefficients.

- The **Chi-square test** of association or goodness-of-fit evaluates whether two variables are related, but this test provides no information about the strength of the relationship. The test indicates whether a relationship is real as opposed to being a chance occurrence.

PRESENTATION OF DATA

After the analysis of data has been completed, it is necessary to prepare a report that describes the evaluation project and the results that have been achieved. The writing must be logical and lucid, and the data must be presented in a manner that enhances the understanding of the reader.

Howard Wainer has suggested some "rules" for displaying data badly.[5] Reflecting Wainer's rules in a more positive manner results in the following suggestions:

1. Show as much data as necessary to convey real meaning.

2. Reveal the characteristics of data you do show—scale, range, distribution.

3. Graph data in a clear context.

4. Never change scales in mid-axis.

5. Provide data labels that are legible, complete, and correct.

6. Less leads to clarity—fewer decimal places and dimensions.

THE EVALUATION REPORT

The results of an evaluation effort should be documented in a report. The ready availability of such tools as MS Word™ and Excel™ makes the production of an appealing report fairly straightforward. A table of contents for a typical evaluation report should contain:

- an executive summary;
- an introduction to the focus of the evaluation;
- a literature review;
- the data collection methodology;
- analysis of the data;
- conclusions and recommendations;
- limitations of the study;
- appendixes, which might contain a copy of the data collection instruments; and
- a bibliography.

If the report is made available to a broader audience on a library Web site, for example, it might be "published" using the PDF format, for portability and security reasons.

NOTES

1. Kendon L. Stubbs. On the ARL Library Index, in *Research Libraries: Measurement, Management, Marketing: Minutes of the 108th Meeting*. Washington, DC: Association of Research Libraries, 1986, 18–20.

2. Chris Anderson. *The Long Tail: Why the Future of Business Is Selling Less of More*. New York: Hyperion, 2006.

3. See, for example, Arthur W. Hafner. *Descriptive Statistical Techniques for Librarians*. Chicago: American Library Association, 1998.

4. Pauline Atherton. Books Are for Use: Final Report of the Subject Access Project to the Council on Library Resources. Syracuse, NY: School of Information Studies, 1978.

5. Howard Wainer. How to Display Data Badly. *The American Statistician*, 38 (2), May 1984, 137–47.

Part III

Evaluation of Library Services

7

Library Users and Nonusers

SERVICE DEFINITION

Having a clear understanding of potential customers and actual customers in a community or academic environment can assist the library in better understanding their needs. This information is often assembled when the library is involved in a planning process.[1]

EVALUATION QUESTIONS

An analysis of who uses and does not use the library can be helpful in addressing the following types of evaluation questions:

- What are the characteristics of those who use the library occasionally and those who use it more frequently?
- What services are used by which different segments of library customers?
- What are the characteristics of those who do not use the library?
- Why do nonusers not visit the library (physically or virtually)?
- How does the geographic location of the library influence use of the library?
- What services, if offered, might attract more people to use the library?

EVALUATION METHODS

A variety of evaluation methods have been used to gain a better understanding of library users and nonusers. Each of the methods reveals different information about the various segments of a population. These methods include

- desk work analysis,
- focus groups, and
- surveys of library users and of the community.

DISCUSSION OF PRIOR EVALUATIONS AND RESEARCH

It is possible to segment a population using five different methods or techniques:

- Demographics
- Lifestyles
- Geography
- Volume of use
- Benefits or purpose

This segmentation process can involve a population of citizens living in a specific community (city or county), a college or university, or employees of a company or government agency. The real value occurs when two or more segmentation techniques are applied simultaneously, for example, combining demographics information with geographic information or combining several variables to obtain a better understanding of the community characteristics: age, income, and ethnicity. In addition, combining demographics with lifestyle information can reveal a great deal about a community.

Demographics

Historically, public libraries have used census information to build a profile of the citizens of their community. This allowed the library to segment citizens according to age, education, sex, ethnicity, marital status, family income, number of children, and so forth. For example, age-related information assists a library in identifying the possible need for preschool programs or large print materials for seniors.

In almost all cases, census information is manually extracted at the city or county levels, although it is possible to present the information at the census track or census block level (about 1,000 people in a block).

Lifestyles

Market researchers have also identified consumers according to their lifestyles. The lifestyles approach combines demographics with how people decide to spend their time and money. Although a choice of lifestyle relates in large part to income, it is influenced only slightly by education.[2]

One study analyzed more than eight million circulation transactions in 10 communities of different types and found that lifestyles had little to do with circulation patterns—the patterns were remarkably similar across the communities.[3] Fiction and audiovisual materials accounted for about two-thirds of all circulations regardless of the community and its characteristics or lifestyles. Another study analyzed adult circulation patterns among 21 branches of the Indianapolis-Marion County (Indiana) Public Library and found that people tended to read very similar types of materials regardless of the characteristics of the populations served by each branch.[4]

Geography

Using geographic-based computer software, sometimes called geographic information system (GIS) software, it is possible to create a map of the city or county (or a combination of counties) and present the census information in a map-based form. This is a particularly effective tool for libraries that have branches because they can assign each census track to a service area for each branch location. This allows the decision makers the opportunity to visually see the demographic differences among the citizens of the jurisdiction. Many local government agencies use GIS for planning the location of facilities: police and fire stations, police patrol areas, and much more.

Christie Koontz at Florida State University has developed the Public Library Geographic Database (the GeoLib database), which is accessible via the Internet.[5] The GeoLib database pulls together the census information, public library use data, and other publicly available information for all 16,000+ public library locations in the United States. The library can adjust the service area boundaries for each branch location.

America's shifting demographics require that public libraries shift their tactics to better respond to the needs of a changing population. The flexibility of the mapping software allows a library to explore different scenarios for service delivery.[6] The resulting maps can be helpful at the time of budget hearings, for exploring alternative branch site locations, and for general reporting to the library's stakeholders. The GeoLib system can help libraries answer questions such as the following:

- What are the population characteristics within one mile of each library location? Do the population characteristics differ as the distance increases to two miles, three miles, and so forth?

- What percent of the senior population lives within three miles of each library location?

- What percent of an ethnic population (pick a group) who live within three miles of a library location are under the age of 18? Under the age of 10?

- What impact do topographical boundaries such as major highways or rivers have on demand for services?[7]

The importance of branch library location cannot be overemphasized. People *choose* to spend time and resources traveling from home or a workplace to visit the library. The average library customer will not travel more than two to three miles to visit a library. So, just as for a retail store or a fast-food restaurant, the old real estate maxim holds true: location, location, location.[8]

One of the most compelling reasons for using a geographic information system is that it will visually display how different segments of the population "cluster" within a community—especially in regard to the location of library facilities.

Methods that have been used in the past to understand how people are drawn to a location include using the experience of the library staff, assigning census tracts to a branch library location (5,000 to 8,000 people in a tract), drawing a radius around each location to determine what proportion of the population lives within the radius, or plotting library card holder address information on a map.

Christie Koontz mapped demographic and library use data for several public libraries with branches and found that branch libraries serving primarily minority populations had higher in-library use, higher reference transactions, and greater program attendance, while at the same time having lower circulation figures.[9] This is significant because most public library systems will use circulation as the sole indicator of a branch library's performance.

Another study found that large bookstores reduce the probability of household public library use for some, but not all, uses of the library. While children's programming is found to be immune to competition, job-related and informational uses of the library are reduced.[10]

Several studies used multivariate analysis (multiple regression analysis) in modeling public library use and postulated that a resident's library use is a function of his or her socioeconomic and locational characteristics.[11] Demographic variables alone do not accurately predict library use, but topographical features, hours of operation, size of the building, and unique population characteristics will affect library use.[12]

Volume of Use

It is also possible to segment the population by use, which results in the classic split of users and nonusers. The more optimistic prefer to call nonusers "potential users." With today's automated systems, it is fairly easy to obtain a set of reports that will sort the registered borrowers into several groups:

- Customers are "card-carrying individuals" who use the library. They can be subdivided into three groups:

  - *Frequent users* are those who use the library on a monthly or more frequent basis.

  - *Moderate users* will use the library at least quarterly.

  - *Infrequent users* are those who will use the library at least once a year.

- "Lost customers" are people who visited the library, completed an application form, and received a library card. However, they have not used the library for more than a year. So, while they "found" the library once, they are now "lost." Depending on how often library user records are purged from an automated system, as much as 30 to 40 percent of registered library users will fall into the lost category.

- Nonusers are people within a community who may or may not be aware of the location of libraries and the range of services they offer. It is interesting to note that even though these individuals do not have library cards, they are generally very supportive of the concept of the public library and will support the library, as evidenced by their willingness to vote for library bonds and so forth. Note that nonusers can be divided into two groups: those who can be enticed into the library and those who will never, under any circumstances, use the library.

  Identifying the number of nonusers is a straightforward calculation. Subtracting the number of registered library borrowers from the total population of the jurisdiction will provide the number of nonusers. Note that the total number of registered borrowers may exceed the total population of a jurisdiction due to nonresidents becoming registered library card holders.

Discrete choice analysis links the microeconomic consumer theory with the statistical analysis of categorical data (users, lost users, and nonusers). A study that applied a discrete choice analysis in a public library setting found that lost users and nonusers alike did not use the library primarily due to distance, inconvenience of hours, and their preference to purchase their own materials. Further analysis revealed that adding to the collection in each location would entice lost customers to return, while building more locations and adding more hours would attract nonusers to the library.[13]

Benefit Segmentation

Another relatively new segmentation technique is to identify the reasons why people visit a library—that is, what benefits they receive from a physical or virtual visit to the library. A pilot study at the Dover Public Library (a convenience sample size of 113 one-on-one interviews) identified eight identity-related reasons for a visit to the library.[14] The eight types of users identified follow:

- **Experience seekers** look to the library as a venue for entertainment or social connection. Thy like being around people and may be seeking an activity to occupy their time. Selected by 36 percent of the respondents.

- **Explorers** are individuals who are curious and love to learn but do not have a content or subject agenda prior to the visit. Selected by 35 percent of the respondents.

- **Problem solvers** have a specific question or problem they want to solve. They might be looking for health information or investment information, be planning a trip, and so forth. Selected by 23 percent of the respondents.

- **Facilitators** are users who are there to support someone else in their use of the library—their children or a friend. Selected by 16 percent of the respondents.

- **Patrons** are individuals with a strong sense of belonging to the library. They belong to the Friends group and will often volunteer at the library. Selected by 16 percent of the respondents.

- **Scholars** are those with a deep interest in and a history of research work in one topic area, such as genealogy or religion. Selected by 9 percent of the respondents.

- **Spiritual pilgrims** will focus on the library as a place of reflection or rejuvenation. Selected by 8 percent of the respondents.

- **Hobbyists** are individuals looking to further their interest in a particular area. Selected by 4 percent of the respondents.

"Others" are those individuals who do not fit into any of the above groups; they are there to drop something off or pick up something.

The benefit segmentation approach has the possibility of improving library services. How would (could) a library organize its services (other than as they are currently organized) to better meet the needs of each benefit segment?

In Singapore, the data collected from a survey were subjected to a cluster analysis, and seven segments with distinct learning- and reading-related lifestyles were identified.[15] These seven types of users follow:

- **Career-minded people** hold strong beliefs about education and family and turn to the library first for their reading.

- **Active information seekers** possess a moderate education, have an entrepreneurial spirit, and place greater importance on social status and material well-being.

- **Self-suppliers** prefer to purchase their own books, are better educated, and hold managerial or executive positions.

- **Group readers** have an avid appetite for reading and are heavy library users.

- **Narrowly focused learners** are students who read to fulfill a course requirement.

- **Low motivators** have little interest in reading.

- **Facilitators** are females with lower education levels who value highly the importance of the library for their children.

As shown in Figure 7.1, identification of the reasons for possible use of the library leads to insights about reading habits and visits to the library.

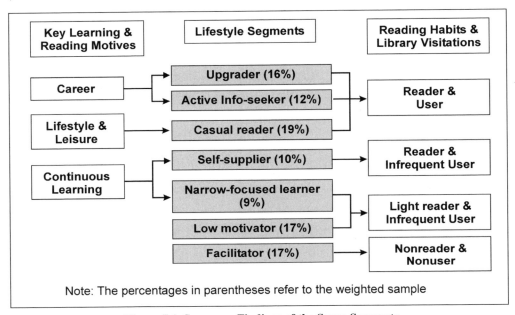

Figure 7.1. Summary Findings of the Seven Segments

Joan Durrance and Karen Fisher did a series of interviews with users of specific library services to better understand the impact of the service on the lives of each participant. The interviews were recorded and transcribed and carefully analyzed to determine the outcomes of the library service.[16]

USERS

The analysis of library users typically involves a user's survey. Such surveys, and there have been many, help develop a profile of real users and how they use the library. Studies have been conducted in all types of libraries—academic, public, and special. An individual chooses to visit the library—physically or virtually—when the utility gain for using the library is greater than going to the next-best alternative, for example, the bookstore. The individual compares the value of the item minus the price and waiting costs at each source, choosing the source with the highest net value.[17]

Surveys range from those designed to improve services in a specific library to those designed to lead to broad conclusions and support for theory. In addition to the quantitative data that result from surveys, libraries have also used interviews (one-on-one and focus groups) as well as observation to understand how people use the library. More recently, libraries have been using a customer satisfaction survey as another tool in providing quality library services. (The topic of customer satisfaction surveys is discussed in chapter 15.) The characteristics most frequently examined in these studies are sex, age, education, family income, marital status, and the number of small children living at home.

Carol Kronus prepared an analysis that determined what variables explained some part of the use of the public library.[18] Her analysis suggested that education, urban residence, and family life cycle factors predicted rate of library use. The commonly used factors of age, sex, and race had no independent influence on library use.

Attempting to better understand the relationships between library use and user characteristics, George D'Elia developed a model with a hierarchy of variables that included such items as individual characteristics, patron awareness of library services, perceived accessibility, and ease of library use.[19] He concluded that users of the public library perceived the library as more accessible than did nonusers, and that frequency and intensity of use were related to awareness of the range of available library services.

Ronald Powell, looking for a more predictive answer concerning library use, examined the personality of the user. He found no link between personality type and use of the library.[20]

A survey conducted on behalf of the American Library Association indicated that about 62 percent of Americans have a library card.[21] Thus, demographics partially predict who will use the library and who will not. Other nondemographic factors such as life style, social roles, and travel distance also influence library use.

A nationwide Australian survey of library nonusers (725 telephone survey respondents) and users of the state libraries and public libraries (868 interviews) found that the libraries had been used in the last year by only 30 percent of the population. The study recommended more imaginative promotional efforts and forming partnerships with various organizations to reach out to community members to remind them of the value of their local libraries.[22]

A combination of demographic factors is often more important than a single characteristic. Characteristics of the public library user that have been discussed and analyzed in a large number of user studies include the following:

- **Education.** The more education an individual has, the more likely he or she is to use the public library. Education is the single most important predictor of library use, and it is not unusual for more than half of library users to have some college, a college degree, or postgraduate work.[23] While it is true that income, occupation, and education are all intercorrelated, regression analysis demonstrates that everything disappears except education.

- **Age.** There is consistent evidence suggesting that those who use the library the most are young adults, and that use of the library declines with age. However, Kronus noted that the relationship between public library use and age was misleading and not statistically valid. Library users in 2002 were:[24]

18–24	14%
25–34	19%
35–44	23%
45–54	17%
55 +	21%

- **Number of small children.** Adults with small children are more likely to have a library card and to visit the library on a fairly regular basis (the greater the number of children, the more frequently the library is used). Households with children are much more likely to use the public library than those without children—61 percent compared to 35 percent.[25]

- **Family income.** Individuals with higher incomes will use the local library more frequently. However, use is greater among middle-income levels than among the poor or the rich. It may be that low use of the library by the poor is related to poor reading skills. In 2002, one-quarter of library user households earned from $25,000 to $49,999, while more than one-third earned $50,000 or more.[26] Similar results were noted in a 1991 survey, which showed that use of the public library was clearly correlated with family income.[27] With increased income comes discretionary time for reading and information-seeking activities.

  One study, using a "library activity" index composed on circulation, in-library use of materials, number of reference transactions, and annual program attendance, found that higher incomes tended to be associated with higher library usage rates per capita.[28] This study also noted that other factors will affect the use of library services, including the availability and location of branch libraries, number of hours open, size and scope of the library's collection, and so forth.

- **Sex.** Women are more likely to use the library than men, although Berelson noted that men would use reference services more frequently, while women will use circulation services more than men. Although women use the library more than men, taking employment status into consideration and holding education constant, the dominant use by women disappears.[29]

- **Marital status.** Single individuals use the library more than married people. This is likely the case because single adults are younger than married adults, and use declines with age. In addition, married adults probably have less leisure time than single adults due to domestic responsibilities.

- **Ethnicity.** Depending on the ethnic population within a community, use of the library will generally reflect the relative proportions of the population, although more use will likely occur among members of the white ethnic group. One national survey found that 56 percent of users were white, while 38 and 42 percent of the respondents were Hispanic and black, respectively.[30] Another national survey found that among households that had used a public library, 80 percent were white, 9 percent black, and 7 percent Hispanic, which is roughly the distribution of the U.S. population.[31]

  One study found that patrons of color use the library for educational support and for information gathering more than do their Caucasian counterparts.[32]

  Racial and ethnic minority groups are growing at a much faster pace than the general U.S. population. Thus, a public library should periodically review the demographic shifts that are occurring within its geographic and service area boundaries in order to better respond to changing demands for services.

Brenda Dervin has suggested that the traditional methods for categorizing users, predicting access and potential for contact using a "if . . . then" model, are not very helpful. Rather, Dervin suggests using an alternative set of categories that describe a person at a particular moment in time and space rather than across time and space.[33]

A survey of faculty members in a sample of community colleges, University of California campuses, and California liberal arts colleges found a broad spectrum of user types, ranging from the nonuser, to the inexperienced novice, to the highly proficient. Not surprisingly, the older instructors were the lightest users. Faculty used digital resources to integrate primary materials into their teaching, to include materials that would otherwise be unavailable, and to improve student learning.[34]

The Principle of Least Effort

This principle states that most people, even academic scholars and scientists, will choose easily available information sources, even if they are of low quality. Further, people tend to be satisfied with whatever can be found easily in preference to tracking down high-quality sources that would require a greater expenditure of effort.

The principle of least effort, sometimes called the "principle of information seeking parsimony," is also known as Zipf's Law of Least Effort.[35] The reality is that people tend to choose perceived ease of access over quality of content. And people will "satisfice"—a word first coined by Herb Simon to indicate that individuals will set modest goals and then stop searching when these goals are reached.

Evidence for the validity of this principle is substantial and covers many decades of study. Victor Rosenberg found in his investigation of information-seeking behavior that the guiding principle for the design of any information system should be the system's ease of use rather than the amount or quality of information provided.[36] Thomas Gerstberger and Thomas Allen arrived at a similar conclusion in their study of engineers and noted that there was a direct relationship between the perceived accessibility of an information channel and several objective measures of use. The observed behavior of engineers was that they minimized the effort involved to gain access to information.[37]

John Salasin and Toby Cedar, in their study of 1,666 mental health practitioners, researchers, and policymakers, found that an information source was chosen based on the perceived ease of use rather than other criteria.[38] Herbert Poole noted that 43 out of 51 studies that focused on the information behavior of scientists demonstrate the principle of least effort.[39] Similar results were observed in a study of social scientists that reported that study participants tended to rely on footnote chasing and forgo use of indexes to the literature.[40]

William Paisley noted that the level of frustration in using libraries is high for most people, and that people "are conditioned to feeling that the library is a place . . . [they] almost have to drag something out of."[41]

Thomas Mann challenged the library profession, observing that it was time to stop blaming library users for being "lazy":

> Ironically, disregarding the Principle of Least Effort is itself a result of the same principle at work: it is easier for many library managers and information scientists to concentrate on "hard" problems of technology than to do the difficult library research on "soft" human behavior.[42]

And one does not have to look too far for similar findings in a more recent study. OCLC's survey of 3,348 respondents in several countries found that 84 percent start their search for electronic information using a search engine, and only 1 percent visit a library Web site. And among a list of sources of information identified as "trusted," the library was last.[43]

The implications of this principle are serious indeed and have been ignored by the library profession for far too long! It is time to focus on usability of the library's physical and virtual collections. Hoping that library users will recognize that the library contains quality resources and start using the library in increasing numbers is simply delusional thinking.

NONUSERS

Public libraries are reluctant to admit that they will never serve 100 percent of their citizens. Some people, for a variety of reasons, don't know what or where the library is, wouldn't know how to find information once they arrived at a library, or place little emphasis on reading or on other information services normally found at the local public library, and thus they will never obtain a public library card. Part of the planning process should be to recognize what proportion of the population "might" be interested in public library services and then determine how the library is doing in terms of meeting the needs of "prospective users."

Interestingly, most public libraries do very little to figure out why someone will come once to the library, obtain a library card, and then never return. A library could use a brief mail survey, a focus group, or other means to identify the reasons for this failure to return to the library. A survey of former library users in Jefferson County, Colorado (located just west of Denver) who had not used the library in more than a year revealed that the typical "once but no-longer a user" was an employed (one-third were retired), well-educated Caucasian over the age of 50.[44] In short, the typical "lost customer" was an "empty nester" who either was too busy or would rather buy books than visit the local public library.

Another more comprehensive survey of nonusers in a community found that the reasons for nonuse included the following:

- Not enough time to read (46 percent of the respondents).
- I get books elsewhere (39 percent of the respondents).
- Library hours don't suit me (17 percent of the respondents).
- Don't like reading (16 percent of the respondents).
- Unsure of services offered (14 percent of the respondents).
- Library too far from home (11 percent of the respondents).
- Library doesn't provide anything I require (7 percent of the respondents).
- I can't ever find anything I want (6 percent of the respondents).
- I don't drive/can't get around (6 percent of the respondents).
- Did not know I could use the library (5 percent of the respondents).
- I need more help with the computer (5 percent of the respondents).[45]

Almost all undergraduate students procrastinate about academic activities such as studying for an examination or writing a term paper.[46] And almost two-thirds of graduate students procrastinate due to fear of failure and task aversiveness.[47] One study found that task aversiveness was related to barriers with library staff, affective barriers, comfort with the library, and knowledge of the library.[48] These findings are similar to those in other studies pertaining to procrastination.[49]

SUMMARY

This chapter has presented information about a variety of tools that can be used to learn more about the characteristics of library users and nonusers. Having a clear understanding of the actual and potential users of a library is critical to any evaluation activity.

NOTES

1. Jennifer Rowley. Focusing on Customers. *Library Review*, 46 (2), 1997, 81–89; Ana Reyes Pacios Lozano. A Customer Orientation Checklist: A Model. *Library Review*, 49 (4), 2000, 173–78; Jennifer Rowley. Managing Branding and Corporate Image for Library and Information Services. *Library Review*, 46 (4), 1997, 244–50; Jennifer Rowley and Jillian Dawes. Customer Loyalty—A Relevant Concept for Libraries? *Library Management*, 20 (6), 1999, 345–51.

2. Michael J. Weiss. *The Clustering of America*. New York: Harper, 1988; and Michael J. Weiss. Clustered America: The Communities We Serve. *Public Libraries*, 28 (3), June 1989, 161–65.

3. Hazel M. Davis and Ellen Altman. The Relationship Between Community Lifestyles and Circulation Patterns in Public Libraries. *Public Libraries*, 36 (1), January/February 1997, 40–45.

4. John R. Ottensmann, Raymond E. Gnat, and Michael E. Gleeson. Similarities in Circulation Patterns Among Public Library Branches Serving Diverse Populations. *Library Quarterly*, 65, January 1995, 89–118.

5. Accessible at www.geolib.org/PLGDB.cfm.

6. Christie Koontz and Dean Jue. Unlock Your Demographics. *Library Journal*, 129 (4), March 1, 2004, 32–33.

7. Christie Koontz, Dean Jue, Charles R. McClure, and John Carlo Bertot. The Public Library Geographical Database: What Can It Do for Your Library? *Public Libraries*, 43 (2), March/April 2004, 113–18.

8. Christie M. Koontz. Public Library Site Evaluation and Location: Past and Present Market-Based Modeling Tools for the Future. *Library & Information Science Research*, 14 (4), 1992, 379–409; and Christie M. Koontz. *Library Facility Siting and Location Handbook*. Westport, CT: Greenwood, 1991.

9. Christie M. Koontz. Technology—Pied Piper or Playground Bully, or Creating Meaningful Measures Using Emerging Technologies: Separating the Reality from the Myths. *Proceedings of the 4th Northumbria International Conference on Performance Measurement & Libraries & Information Services*. New Castle, England: University of Northumbria, 2001.

10. Jeffrey A. Hemmeter. Household Use of Public Libraries and Large Bookstores. *Library and Information Science Research*, 28, 2006, 595–616.

11. George D'Elia. The Development and Testing of a Conceptual Model of Public Library Use Behavior. *Library Quarterly*, 50, 1980, 410–30; Janet M. Lange. Public Library Users, Nonusers and Type of Library Use. Ph.D. dissertation, Claremont Graduate University, California, 1984; and Douglas L. Zweizig. Predicting Amount of Library Use: An Empirical Study of the Role of the Public Library in the Life of the Adult Public. Ph.D. dissertation, Syracuse University, New York, 1973.

12. Christie M. Koontz. Public Library Site Evaluation and Location: Past and Present Market-Based Modeling Tools for the Future. *Library and Information Science Research*, 14 (4), 1992, 379–409.

13. Akio Sone. An Application of Discrete Choice Analysis to the Modeling of Public Library Use and Choice Behavior. *Library & Information Science Research*, 10, 1988, 35–55.

14. Institute for Learning Innovation. *Dover, DE Library User Identity—Motivation Pilot Study*. Dover: Delaware Division of Libraries, December 2005.

15. Kau Ah Keng, Kwon Jung, and Jochen Wirtz. Segmentation of Library Visitors in Singapore: Learning and Reading Related Lifestyles. *Library Management*, 24 (1/2), 2003, 20–33.

16. Joan C. Durrance, and Karen E. Fisher. *How Libraries and Librarians Help: A Guide to Identifying User-Centered Outcomes*. Chicago: American Library Association, 2005.

17. Nancy A. Van House. A Time Allocation Theory of Public Library Use. *Library and Information Science Research*, 5, 1983, 356–84; and Nancy A. Van House. *Public Library User Fees: The Use and Finance of Public Libraries*. Westport, CT: Greenwood Press, 1983.

18. Carol I. Kronus. Patterns of Adult Library Use: A Regression and Path Analysis. *Adult Education*, 23, 1973, 115–31.

19. George D'Elia. The Development and Testing of a Conceptual Model of Public Library User Behavior. *Library Quarterly*, 50, 1980, 410–30.

20. Ronald R. Powell. Library Use and Personality: The Relationship Locus of Control and Frequency of Use. *Library and Information Science Research*, 6, 1984, 179–90.

21. KRC Research & Consulting. *@ Your Library: Attitudes Toward Public Libraries Survey*. June 2002. Available at http://www.ala.org/pio/presskits/nlw2002kit/krc_data.pdf.

22. Colin Mercer and Tony Bennett. *Navigating the Economy of Knowledge: A National Survey of Users and Non-Users of State and Public Libraries*. Brisbane: Institute for Cultural Policy Studies Griffith University, 1995.

23. Unless otherwise noted, this summary of the user characteristics is based on a review of the work of Berelson, Kronus, and D'Elia in Ronald R. Powell. *The Relationship of Library User Studies to Performance Measures: A Review of the Literature*. Occasional Paper Number 181. Champaign: University of Illinois, Graduate School of Library and Information Science, 1988.

24. KRC Research, *@ Your Library*.

25. Mary Jo Lynch. Using Public Libraries: What Makes a Difference? *American Libraries*, 28 (10), November 1997, 64–65.

26. KRC Research, *@ Your Library*.

27. Jim Scheppke. Who's Using the Public Library. *Library Journal*, 119, October 15, 1994, 35–37.

28. Mary Kopczynski and Michael Lombardo. Comparative Performance Measurement: Insights and Lessons Learned from a Consortium Effort. *Public Administration Review*, 59 (2), March/April 1999, 124–34.

29. Kronus, Patterns of Adult Library Use.

30. Jim Scheppke. Who's Using the Public Library. *Library Journal*, 119, October 15, 1994, 35–37.

31. Lynch. Using Public Libraries, 64–65.

32. George D'Elia and Eleanor J. Rodger. Public Library Roles and Patron Use: Why Patrons Use the Library. *Public Libraries*, 33 (3), 1994, 135–44.

33. Brenda Dervin. Users as Research Inventions: How Research Categories Perpetuate Inequities. *Journal of Communication*, 39 (3), Summer 1989, 216–32.

34. Diane Harley et al. *Use and Users of Digital Resources: A Focus on Undergraduate Education in the Humanities and Social Sciences*. Available at http://digitalresourcesstudy.berkeley.edu.

35. George K. Zipf. *Human Behavior and the Principle of Least Effort*. Cambridge, MA: Addison-Wesley, 1949.

36. Victor Rosenberg. Factors Affecting the Preference of Industrial Personnel for Information Gathering Methods. *Information Storage and Retrieval*, 3 (3), July 1967, 119–27.

37. Peter G. Gerstberger and Thomas J. Allen. Criteria Used by Research and Development Engineers in the Selection of an Information Source. *Journal of Applied Psychology*, 52 (4), August 1968, 272–79; see also Thomas J. Allen and Peter G. Gerstberger. *Criteria for Selection of an Information Source*. Cambridge, MA: MIT Press, 1967.

38. John Salasin and Toby Cedar. Person-to-Person Communication in an Applied-Research Service Delivery Setting. *Journal of the American Society for Information Science*, 36 (2), March 1985, 103–15.

39. Herbert Poole. *Theories of the Middle Range*. Norwood, NJ: Ablex, 1985.

40. L. Uytterschaut. Literature Searching Methods in Social Science Research: A Pilot Inquiry. *American Behavioral Scientist*, 9 (9), May 1966, 14–26.

41. William J. Paisley. Information Needs and Uses. *Annual Review of Information Science and Technology*, 3, 1968, 18.

42. Thomas Mann. *Library Research Models: A Guide to Classification, Cataloging, and Computers*. Oxford: Oxford Press, 1993, 98.

43. Cathy De Rosa, Joanne Cantrell, Diane Cellentani, Janet Hawk, Lillie Jenkins, and Alane Wilson. *Perceptions of Libraries and Information Resources*. Dublin, OH: OCLC, 2006. See also Cathy De Rosa, Joanne Cantrell, Janet Hawk, and Alane Wilson. *College Students' Perceptions of Libraries and Information Resources*. Dublin, OH: OCLC, 2006.

44. Kathy L. Harris. Who Are They? In Search of the Elusive Non-User. *Colorado Libraries*, 27 (4), Winter 2001, 16–18.

45. Louise Flowers. Non-Users of the Upper Goulburn Library Service. *The Australian Library Journal,* 44, May 1995, 67–85.

46. Albert Ellis and William J. Knaus. *Overcoming Procrastination*. New York: Institute for Rational Living, 1977.

47. Mary B. Hill. A Survey of College Faculty and Student Procrastination. *College Student Journal*, 12 (2), Fall 1978, 256–62.

48. Anthony J. Onwuegbuzie and Qun G. Jiao. I'll Go to the Library Later: The Relationship Between Academic Procrastination and Library Anxiety. *College & Research Libraries*, 61 (1), January 2000, 45–54.

49. Laura J. Solomon and Esther D. Rothblum. Academic Procrastination: Frequency and Cognitive-Behavioral Correlates. *Journal of Counseling Psychology*, 31, October 1984, 503–9 and Joseph R. Ferrari, Johnson L. Judith, and William G. McCowan. *Procrastination and Task Avoidance: Theory, Research, and Treatment*. New York: Plenum, 1995.

8

Evaluation of the Physical Collection

*One problem with collecting everything to get the "good" is that we
are not sure of the impact of every "bad" volume on a "good" collection.*
—Elizabeth Futas and David Vidor[1]

SERVICE DEFINITION

Historically, the physical collection has been the raison d'être of any library. Perhaps due to the tangible nature of a library's physical collection, much literature exists about the evaluation of the extent and use of a library's collection.

EVALUATION QUESTIONS

Evaluations of library collections have been used for a number of purposes, including

- gaining a more accurate understanding of the nature, depth, and utility of the collection;
- assessing of the current collection development policy and acquisitions programs, methods, or sources;
- assessing the capacity of the collection to support research or the curriculum;
- providing a guide for collection planning and pruning (weeding);
- identifying possible gaps in library holdings;
- assessing how well the collection is able to meet demand;
- providing a more rational basis for allocating the acquisitions budget; and
- defending the materials acquisitions budget.

EVALUATION METHODS

A library's collection can be evaluated using both quantitative and qualitative methods as well as from the perspective of the library (inward-looking) or from the perspective of the customer (outward-looking), as shown in Figure 8.1.

When evaluating a library's physical collection, it is important to use several methods so as to obtain a more balanced perspective of how well the collection is meeting the needs of its customers. The difficulty that arises when evaluating a collection is that there is no definition for the term "good," so that the question "How *good* is the library's collection?" can be answered. And yet, collection evaluation should be an integral part of the library's collection development policy. Without a periodic review and assessment of the library's collection, the collection development policy will be operating in a vacuum, not being updated to meet the changing needs of its customers.

	Qualitative	Quantitative

Library Perspective	Expert opinion
	Checking lists
	Conspectus
		Size
		Analyzing use
		Comparison with peers
		    using bibliographic
		    records
		Overlap studies
		Citation studies
		Interlibrary loan analysis
		Loss rate analysis

Customer Perspective		User surveys Shelf availability studies Document delivery In-library use studies Formula approach Curriculum analysis Analysis of ILL stats Weeding Value

Figure 8.1. Collection Evaluation Methods

DISCUSSION OF PRIOR EVALUATIONS AND RESEARCH

Qualitative Methods

While it is acknowledged that quantitative data are not necessarily more objective than qualitative information, the qualitative approach to assessing a collection is subjective. Despite the fact that qualitative methods can be made less subjective through the use of appropriate tools, criteria, guidelines, and procedures, in the end the method relies on subjective judgment. Some would argue that the qualitative approach is also much more difficult to defend to the library's funding decision makers.

Expert Opinion

Examining the materials on the shelves, sometimes called shelf scanning, is an effective way to assess a collection, particularly smaller and more specialized collections. Such an approach obviously requires a knowledgeable and skilled professional who is a subject specialist. The expert performing the shelf scan might identify titles to be added to the collection, identify candidates for restoration or discard, and produce a written report of his or her findings. The examination can be completed in a relatively brief period of time.

There are obvious problems with this approach. A subject specialist is not necessarily an expert in the literature in that subject area. In addition, the subject specialist may not be familiar with the needs of the library's customers. And the subject specialist should not be the individual responsible for building the collection; there is an obvious conflict of interest. Attempting to use experts in a larger collection will require numerous evaluators, and the cost may mount quickly.

Core lists that are considered essential for teaching and research can be created by polling the faculty in an academic environment. One study compared the results of a faculty survey with data based on citation analysis and circulation transactions and found the core lists of journals almost identical.[2] In some cases, librarians have developed cancellation lists based on their "best judgment." One study found that the "subjective" judgments made by librarians to cancel specific journal subscriptions were almost identical to faculty recommendations.[3]

Checking Lists

Depending on the type of library, an individual or team can check its holdings against a published list or series of bibliographies. The list or bibliographies must be well chosen, a method decided upon (check the complete list or a sample—and if the latter, how large a sample?), an analysis performed, and a report prepared. Checking lists is one of the oldest forms of collection assessment. Typically list checking is combined with another form of collection assessment.

Several techniques are available that can be adapted to serve the needs of most types of libraries:

- **A check of a list of monographic titles that has been published for a particular type of library.** A variation of this approach is to compare the local library's holdings against those of several peer libraries.

- **A check of a list of journal titles that has been published for a particular type of library.**

- **Creating a list from the citations in selected journals.**

- **Creating a list and selecting a sample of citations from the first list to create a second list.** A sample of citations from the second list is used as a third list. This successive generation of lists is called "tiered" list checking. Each list is used to check the availability of holdings in the library.

- **A check of bibliographies or citation lists from works of significance to local users or programs.**

- **Checks of lists of most-used, most-cited titles**—from reading lists, subject reading lists, or departmental bibliographies.

Dennis Ridley and Joseph Weber completed a list checking study, which they then combined with an analysis of in-library study of customer browsing of the collection.[4] Harriet Lightman and Sabina Manilov used list checking in conjunction with citation analysis to evaluate Northwestern University's economics collection.[5] Russell Dennison used the tiered checklist approach to assess a library's collection.[6] Criticisms of this method include that the lists have a short life expectancy, and they do not identify the fact that comparable books owned by the library are not on the lists.

Conspectus

The development of the conspectus, popular in the 1980s and 1990s, allowed an academic library to assess the depth or comprehensiveness of its collection. The assessment (using a 1–5 rating, with 5 reflecting the greatest depth—a first-rate research collection) typically used a variety of tools to assist in the process, but ultimately the rating was a subjective judgment.[7] It was hoped that the conspectus would help facilitate cooperative collection development and work as a planning tool to upgrade portions of a library's collection. The use of the conspectus fell out of favor when its utility could not be squared with the high costs of development and maintenance. There is also a growing skepticism that measures of collection size or depth are inadequate measures of the collection's quality or its benefit to the university community.

A variation of the conspectus approach was developed by Howard White and is based on comparing short lists—what White calls brief tests—to a library's holdings. White's brief tests method is based on the premise that comparing a library's collection to another library does not reveal whether the library has the right mix of items for the subject area or the correct mix of levels for the college's curriculum.[8] A simplification of the brief tests method has been suggested by David Lesniaski.[9]

Quantitative Methods

The attractiveness of the quantitative approach to collection assessment is that it provides a relatively clear picture of the size of the problem (if any exists). In addition, the numbers are rather comforting: "compared to our peers, this library has 10 percent more holdings" or "our users find 70 percent of what they are looking for, while other libraries have availability rates that are lower." Despite the attractiveness of this approach, quantitative methods must be used judiciously because a statistic can be misinterpreted or lead to unsound conclusions.

Size

The absolute size of a collection is one characteristic that can be used for evaluation. In fact, counts of a library's materials are probably one of the oldest measures for assessing and comparing libraries. For many decades the size of a library's collection was compared to a standard. Standards existed for school, public, junior college, college, and special libraries of various types. During the 1980s the use of standards generally fell out of favor, although some states still use standards for public libraries. One of the principal problems of standards is that a "minimum" standard is often regarded by decision makers as a "maximum," thus inhibiting the growth of a given library.

Creating large "just-in-case" collections made sense in a print-only environment. If the collection contains what students and faculty are looking for, then it will be used (at least that was the hope!). Most academic libraries responded to the expressed needs of faculty and used the positive feelings engendered by faculty to get more money to build ever larger collections. This approach, of course, led to judging quality by size (as in the Association of Research Libraries or ARL rankings), and libraries, in good times and bad, were held captive to this standard. The end result, as Allan Pratt and Ellen Altman have wryly noted, is that the library will "live by the numbers, and die by the numbers."[10]

Johann Van Reenen confirmed that the ARL rankings are a measure of the relative size of university libraries and demonstrated that it is unrealistic to expect any particular library to move up more than five points, due to budgetary and other resource constraints.[11]

In addition to raw counts, there are numerous permutations of measures that reflect size: number of volumes per capita, volumes per student (FTE), counts of subdivisions of the collection (by type of material and call number range), growth of the collection, and so forth.

Analyzing Use

Preparing an analysis of use of the library's collection based on in-library use or borrowing of materials is another method to assess the adequacy of the collection. The analysis will reveal collection areas that receive little or no use as well as areas that are intensively used. The theory of use relative to holdings was developed by A. K. Jain[12] and George Bonn.[13] Bonn suggested creating a "use factor" by dividing the circulation percentage of a given subject by the holdings percentage of the same subject. Large use factors (e.g., 2.1) represent portions of the collection that are intensively used, and perhaps the acquisitions budget should be expanded in this area. Conversely, small use factors (e.g., .3) represent portions of the collection that are not used very much, and perhaps less of the acquisitions dollars should be spent in this area. A use factor of 1.0 indicates a balance between acquisitions and use. Paul Metz called the "use factor" a proportional use statistic.[14]

Terry Mills expanded this concept and suggested that Bonn's use factor should be multiplied by 100 to create the "percentage of expected use." If the expected use of a subject area is 100 percent, which sounds logical, then subject areas that are above 100 percent are overused, while those below 100 percent are underused.[15]

Rather than relying on subjective demarcation lines, Ken Dowlin and Lynn McGrath recommended using the standard deviation as a more objective way to define overuse and underuse.[16] William Aguilar suggested that such an analysis should be complemented by preparing a "ratio of interlibrary loan borrowings to holdings." The calculation would divide the percent of borrowing in a subject area by the holdings percentage in the same area.[17]

The availability of use information by title or copy is relatively simple given the reporting capabilities of almost all of today's automated library systems. One helpful analysis is to compare percent holdings (by type of material and call number range) with percent circulation using the categories shown in Figure 8.2A (p. 116). This analysis has been called the "circulation/holdings ratio," the "circulation/inventory ratio," "stock turnover ratio," "inventory use ratio," and "intensity of circulation."

The chart can be enhanced by plotting the current percent of the acquisitions budget for the same categories. Similar charts can be prepared for the nonfiction collection (no more than 20 categories should be included in the analysis)—see Figure 8.2B (p. 116); percent circulation to percent acquisitions budget—see Figure 8.2C (p. 117), and many other variations.

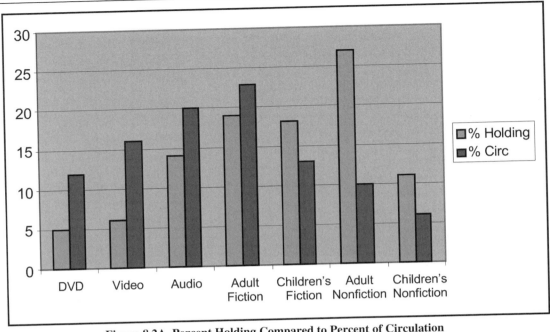

Figure 8.2A. Percent Holding Compared to Percent of Circulation

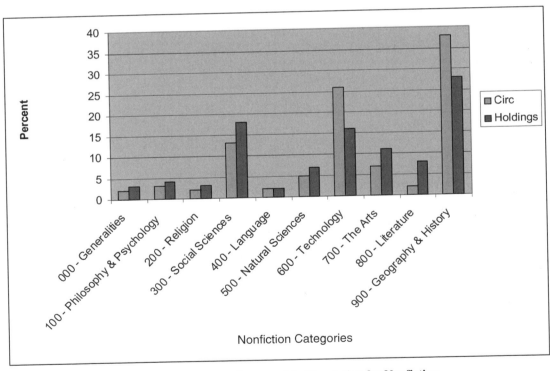

Figure 8.2B. Holdings Compared to Circulation for Nonfiction

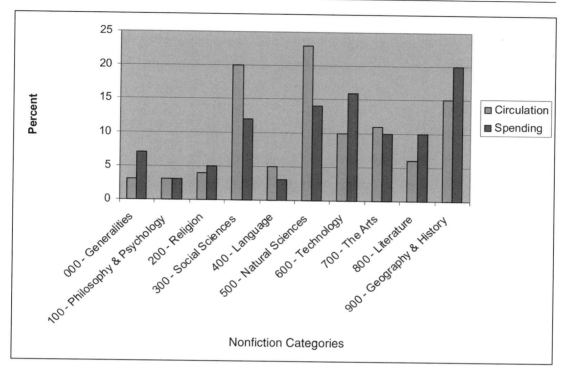

Figure 8.2C. Circulation and Spending for Nonfiction

Some types of libraries, such as those in academic institutions, will have relatively few duplicate titles, while in a public library, especially with a large number of branches, the number of volumes can be quite high compared to the number of unique titles. A majority of public libraries will routinely prepare a report indicating the number of holds to the number of copies of a title, so that additional copies of the title can be ordered if the hold/holdings ratio exceeds a certain threshold.

An analysis of circulating children's books found that

- award-winning books are found infrequently on best-seller lists;

- the best-seller lists contain many series books, such as the <u>Harry Potter</u> series or the <u>Series of Unfortunate Events</u> books;

- fewer prize-winning books than bestsellers are found on the shelves; and

- few books that stimulate children to read more are prize-winning books.[18]

Richard Trueswell introduced the 80/20 rule by showing that a small proportion of the print collection (about 20 percent) would account for 80 percent of the circulation.[19] As a corollary, 50 percent of holdings will be responsible for 90 percent of circulation, while 60 percent of holdings will correspond to 99 percent of circulation. The 80/20 rule, more popularly known as the Pareto effect, was developed by Italian economist Vilfredo Pareto in 1906. Dr. Joseph Juran recognized a universal principle he called the "vital few and trivial many" when he identified 20 percent of the defects causing 80 percent of the problems. The University of Tennessee, Knoxville library prepared an analysis that confirmed the applicability of the 80/20 rule for the entire collection—see Figure 8.3 (p. 118)—but the rule did not apply to various sections of the Library of Congress classification system (80 percent of the circulation within a class would require from 6 to 40 percent of the holdings).[20] Using such an analysis, a library might "reward" those areas of the collection that are intensively used with enlargement and scale back acquisitions in those segments of the collection that are not being used (holding numbers larger than the 20 percent).

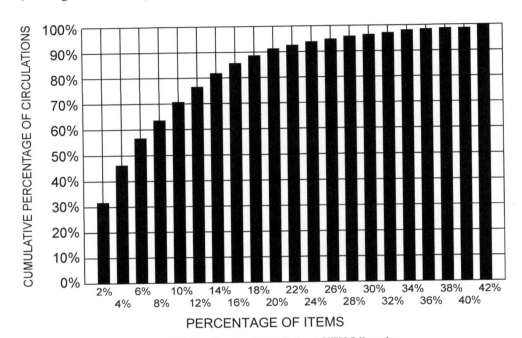

Figure 8.3. Testing the 80/20 Rule at UTK Libraries

Not surprisingly, the 80/20 rule prompted some discussion in the profession. Seymour Sargent reported on a study done at the University of Wisconsin—Oshkosh library. A sample of 1,200 books was examined to determine the amount of use, and owing in part to the relatively young age of the library's collection, a shelf time of only 7½ years could account for 99 percent of circulation, and only 12 percent of the sample had never circulated.[21]

Consider a portion of the collection. The more heavily used it is, the more likely it is that any particular item will not be on the shelf when looked for by a customer. This intensive use and its impact on the customer are called "shelf bias." An example will help illustrate this phenomenon. During the day one customer after another retrieves items from the shelf in a specific area of the collection and finds fewer choices. As the day wears on, the selection of available items becomes less and less interesting as shelf bias increases. The end result is that the shelves will contain items that nobody wants.[22]

Yvonne Jones examined the use of oversized materials in academic libraries and found that these materials were shelved in a separate area in almost half of the libraries that were surveyed, while 28 percent shelved oversized materials in a separate area but on the same floor. However, regardless of where they were shelved, oversized materials experienced significantly less circulation than the rest of the collection.[23]

Paul Kantor and Wonsik Shim analyzed circulation data from the Association of Research Libraries from 1995 to 1996 and formulated the "Square Root Law," which states that circulation is proportional to the square root of the product of reader population (number of FTE students) and the fractional power of the collection size.[24]

The University of Pittsburgh Study. A very important study was conducted by Allen Kent and his colleagues at the University of Pittsburgh. The team examined the 36,892 books cataloged in 1969 and found that 40 percent had never circulated by the end of 1975. The team also examined in-library use of materials and concluded that circulation data can be utilized with a high degree of confidence to measure total book use—in terms of books used at least once. An examination of journal use found that generally usage was low and what journals were used were primarily current ones. The study also calculated cost per use for books and journals.[25] Not surprisingly, the study generated extreme controversy.[26] Kent and his co-authors responded to the criticism, noting that the team was conservative in its analysis.[27]

The data collected by Kent and his colleagues suggest that after a book is added to the collection, there is only a one in two (1/2) chance that it will ever be used. After the first two years in the library, the chance that it will ever be used drops to one in four (1/4). And if it is not used after the first six years, the probability that it will ever be used drops to 1/50.

Larry Hardesty replicated the Pittsburgh Study at DePauw University in Indiana, examining the circulation history of 1,904 books acquired between 1972 and 1983. This study validated the Pittsburgh Study and noted that generally, books are used less than at Pittsburgh; 37 percent of books did not circulate during the five-year study, while 44 percent failed to circulate within the first three years of acquisition. In the case of DePauw, 30 percent of the books accounted for 80 percent of the circulation, roughly confirming Trueswell's 80/20 Rule.[28]

The Pittsburgh Study was replicated a second time by Hardesty at Eckerd College in Florida. The 1,398 books purchased during the fiscal year 1982–1983 were monitored, and approximately one-third of these books did not circulate once. A high correlation was found between in-library use of materials and borrowed materials.[29] Thus, it would seem that despite the size of the academic library, building a "just-in-case" collection will result in a large proportion of the materials never being used!

Materials selected by librarians were likely to circulate as much or more than those suggested by faculty, according to a study conducted by Debbi Dinkins.[30]

Finally, Robert Hayes analyzed the data from the Pittsburgh Study and asserted that circulation data do not adequately represent the total use of a research collection. He suggested that if circulation data were the only criterion to relegate material to remote storage, up to 25 percent of in-library use would be adversely affected.[31]

Also, in a classic study conducted at the University of Chicago, Herbert Fussler and Julian Simon found that past use is a good predictor of present use and, thus, present use is likely a good predictor of future use.[32]

Paul Metz and Charles Litchfield suggested that three days of circulation data was a minimum amount from which to draw a sample, provided the sample size was sufficiently large.[33] However, the automated systems installed in almost all libraries today allow for the analysis of circulation data for considerable periods of time using the same effort as would be required for shorter periods of time. In addition, using longer periods of time will even out any variations in use that may occur during the year or semester.

Illustrating the need to determine use patterns in a specific library, two studies reflecting monograph use at an academic health sciences library are of interest. Jonathan Eldridge at the University of New Mexico School of Medicine found that most monographs (84 percent) had circulated at least once in the four years following acquisition.[34] The second study found that of 1,674 monographs, 81 percent had circulated once during the first three years of shelf life—39 percent occurred in the first year, 32 percent in the second year, and 29 percent in the third year.[35] Both studies observed that a low monograph-to-user ratio might account for their atypical use pattern.

Comparing Bibliographic Records

Given the ready availability of machine-readable bibliographic records, it is possible to prepare an analysis that compares the holdings in a specific library with the holdings of a peer group of libraries.

OCLC provides a service called WorldCat Collection Analysis that allows a library to compare its collection with a group of peer libraries that the library selects. Comparisons can be made for specific subject areas or for the entire collection. The analysis will cover size, age, growth, title overlap, and uniqueness.[36] One of the reports is a list of titles held by the other libraries that are not owned by the "target" library. This list of titles does not indicate whether these titles have ever been circulated or used in the library. A useful extension of this OCLC service would automatically obtain the circulation history or simply the fact that the title had been circulated at least once during the prior five years at the peer libraries.

Overlap Studies

An overlap study will determine how materials are distributed among a number of libraries. Overlap studies are intended to provide information on overlap or duplication among collections while also revealing materials that are *not* duplicated. An overlap study is useful in planning cooperative or distributed programs among libraries.

Sampling methods that may be used to prepare an overlap analysis include

- comparing segments of the catalog to determine which material is held in common;

- sampling from external lists such as a national bibliography or subject bibliography;

- selecting random samples from each library and checking them against the other libraries involved (Each sample should be proportional to the size of the collection.); and

- comparing recent acquisitions, which may involve a degree of duplication among recently acquired titles.

One type of overlap study will determine the overlap of titles held by two or more libraries as well as identifying the distribution of unique titles. A study of overlap among the University of California libraries found that 75 percent of Berkeley's holdings were unique among the northern UC libraries, and 45 percent of UCLA's titles were unique among the southern UC libraries. Also, 53 percent of the Berkeley and UCLA holdings were duplicated in another UC library.[37]

During the late 1970s, 82 percent of all titles added in the University of Wisconsin system libraries were held by just one library, and only 18 percent were held by two libraries.[38] The SULAN libraries in Indiana found that 45 percent of titles were unique, and that another 26 percent were held by two libraries.[39] A higher rate of 52 percent was noted by Thomas Nisonger when he examined the holdings of 17 Texas libraries.[40] An even higher rate of original titles was found by William Potter when he examined the holdings of 21 academic libraries in Illinois.[41]

An analysis of the OhioLINK consortium's holdings was made to determine the amount of duplication of recently published materials as well as the number of copies available for patron-initiated borrowing.[42] Using a sample of 415 titles, it was found that there is a high level of duplication (70 percent of purchased copies were not being used), and that over time the level of duplication increases.

A study in two hospital health science libraries found an overlap that ranged from 20 to 26 percent for monographs and 45 to 58 percent for serial titles.[43] Although it is slightly dated, William Potter prepared an excellent review of collection overlap studies.[44]

William McGrath prepared a table showing the overlap between libraries, similar to a table showing distances between cities in a road atlas. McGrath's table is known as a multidimensional scaling technique. An analysis prepared by McGrath after examining data from 60 libraries showed a clustering by type of library and that regional location did not seem to affect overlap.[45]

Citation Studies

Bibliometrics, the term introduced by Alan Pritchard in 1969,[46] uses statistical data to analyze patterns pertaining to the use of documents and scholarly communication. The main branch of bibliometrics is citation studies—an analysis of references in and citations to documents such as books and articles. Among the uses of citation studies are

- identifying the core journals for a discipline, which will allow the library to satisfy the majority of demand;

- analyzing a discipline's structure in terms of language, age, and place of publication;

- identifying the most productive authors, departments, universities, and nations;

- identifying the growth, obsolescence, and scattering of a discipline;

- identifying little-cited serial publications as candidates for cancellation

- determining whether serial/monograph expenditure ratios are appropriate;

- checking textbook citations against a library's holdings; and

- evaluating university faculty's research productivity.

The value of a citation analysis is that citations are treated seriously by scholars and are used to look for additional materials related to a topic. Citation analysis is most frequently done in the academic environment, although it has been used in some special libraries. Citation analysis is attractive as a focus for study because the citations are readily available and unobtrusive. It can also be applied to the digital environment. Co-citation is the frequency with which two documents are cited together.

The *Journal Citation Reports* provides four types of citation data for thousands of scientific journals:

- *Total Citations* details the aggregate number of citations received by all issues of a journal during the year.

- *Impact Factor* provides the ratio of citations received to articles published by the journal. One study found little correlation between the Impact Factor and local journal use data.[47] These citation data are available for a specific institution for a fee through *Local Journal Utilization Reports,* a product offered by the Institute for Scientific Information (ISI).

- *Cited Half-Life* designates the median age of the articles cited from a specific journal.

- *Immediacy Index* reveals how quickly a journal's articles are cited.

Francis Narin reviewed a number of studies and concluded that bibliometric measures correlate highly with more subjective and survey-based measures of productivity, eminence, and quality of research.[48]

> *The impact factor may be a pox upon the land because of the abuse of that number.*
>
> —Robert H. Austin[49]

A number of studies that have examined journal impacts factors have produced decidedly mixed results. For example:

- Two studies found that global journal impact factors do not correlate with use of print journals in individual libraries.[50]

- Two studies found that when journals were grouped by subject, scope, and language, a positive correlation was noted between journal impact factor and use of print journals.[51]

- One study found no relationship between citation-based measures and holding counts, which suggests that using citation-based measures as an indicator of quality is problematic.[52]

- One study concluded that citation-based measures could be used without correcting for journal self-citation, although self-citations do exert a major effect on the rankings for a small number of journals.[53]

Other studies have had inconclusive results.[54]

Blecic found correlations between local citation and publication data and in-library use as measured by print journal reshelving data, circulation, and citation by faculty.[55] Joanna Duy and Liwen Vaughn found that local citation data are a valid reflection of total journal usage.[56] Robin Devin and Martha Kellogg, after reviewing a number of citation studies, developed a table that recommends a percent of the acquisitions budget that should be spent on serials, subdivided by subject.[57]

As disenchantment with impact factors has grown, some new tools have emerged to help evaluate scientists and their research. Among these are the following:

- **The Faculty of 1,000,** which uses 2,000 scientists to rate each paper they read each month from some 800 journals. This approach will identify important articles published in journals with high- or low-impact factors.

- **The h-index,** developed by a physics professor named Jorgu Hirsh, which identifies the highest number of papers each researcher has published that receive the same number of citations.[58] One study calculated the h-index for U.S. library and information science school faculty members (Nicholas Belkin had the highest score of 20) and there was a strong correlation between an individual's h-index and the total number of citations an individual received.[59] A similar study was conducted in the U.K.[60]

- **The Number Needed to Read (NNR),** which may be useful for health care libraries. It is an index of how many papers in a journal have to be read to find one of adequate clinical quality and relevance.[61]

Five basic bibliometric "laws" are often mentioned in the citation analysis literature:

- **Bradford's Law,** sometimes called the "law of scattering." It is based on the distribution of publications in a discipline or of articles in a set of journals. The "law" is concerned with the scatter of literature within a scientific discipline and states that there is a high degree of concentration of related papers in a relatively small number of "core" journals. Or, a small percentage of journals accounts for a large percentage of what articles are published, and an even smaller percentage accounts for what is cited. Beyond the small nucleus of "core" journals, Bradford identified "zones" of less-productive journals, each zone providing reduced yield as an increasing number of marginally productive journals are added.

The numbers of the groups of journals to produce nearly equal numbers of articles is roughly in proportion to $1: n: n^2 \ldots$, where n is called the Bradford multiplier.[62] When Bradford scattering data are plotted as a log-normal graph, the central portion becomes a straight line (see Figure 8.4). There are usually deviations from this straight line both for core journals and the most peripheral journals. The latter deviation is now referred to as "Groos droop."[63] A later analysis proved that this deviation is not caused by incomplete data.[64]

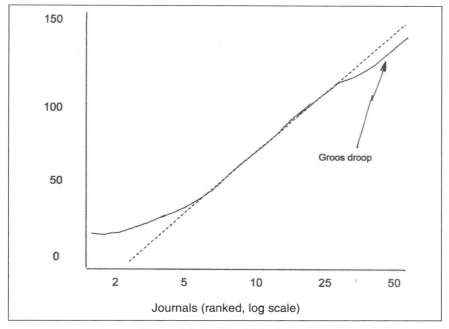

Figure 8.4. Bradford Distribution

- **Garfield's Law of Concentration** states that all disciplines combined produce a multidisciplinary literature core for all of science that consists of 500 to 1,000 journals.

- **Lotka's Law** is based on the number of authors publishing in a discipline or other defined field. The number of authors publishing a certain number of articles is a fixed ratio to the number of authors publishing a single article. As the number of articles published increases, authors producing that many publications become less frequent. There are one-quarter as many authors publishing two articles within a specified time period as there are single-publication authors, one-ninth as many publishing three articles, one-sixteenth as many publishing four articles, etc. Though the law itself covers many disciplines, the actual ratios involved are very discipline-specific.

- **Zipf's Law** is based on word-frequency rankings in a defined set of documents. The frequency of any word is roughly inversely proportional to its rank in the frequency table. The most frequent word will occur approximately twice as often as the second most frequent word, which occurs twice as often as the fourth most frequent word, etc. In other words, people are more likely to select and use familiar rather than unfamiliar words.

- **Half-Life Law.** The half-life of a literature is the time during which one-half of the currently active literature was published.[65] The half-life of a subject area can be determined and is sometimes used as a descriptive measure of a particular subject; for example, the physics literature has a half-life of 9.4 years. Charles Bourne demonstrated that although there are differences, they are not dramatic differences in various subject areas.[66] Depending on the method uses, either 400 or 580 items are needed to estimate the half-life within 10 percent.[67]

De Solla Price analyzed a large number of citations and found that in any given year, 35 percent of all existing papers are not cited at all, 49 percent are cited once, and the remaining 16 percent are cited an average of 3.2 times.[68] He further noted that only 1 percent of all papers are cited six or more times a year. Price then developed the "Price Index," which is the proportion of references to papers published in the last five years compared to the total volume of papers in a discipline (the value can range from 0 to 100 percent). Price also noted that recent papers tended to be cited more often than the amount of recent literature might suggest and called this difference the "immediacy factor." He suggested that the immediacy factor might vary among disciplines since some relied more on older literature than others.

Stern conducted a study of the characteristics of the literature of literary scholarship and found that monographic literature was heavily cited. Primary sources and older materials were heavily used; about 50 percent of the citations were 20 years old or older.[69] A citation analysis study of eight humanity fields found that monographs remain the dominant format of cited sources, and that French and German language materials are the most frequently cited foreign-language items.[70] An examination of 13,648 citations from six biological journals published in 1968 and 1998 found that authors included more citations for articles published in 1998 than in 1968. And while there is a clear bias toward citing the recent literature, that bias seems to be no greater now than it was in 1968, before the advent of computer databases.[71]

Undergraduate use of an academic library's collection will not be reflected in citation studies. Rose Mary Magrill and Gloriana St. Clair prepared a citation analysis of undergraduate papers at four academic institutions. They found that science students used twice as many references in their papers as humanities or social sciences students. Further, a clear majority (66 percent) of the citations used by the science undergraduates were to journal articles, while two-thirds of the citations used by the humanities undergraduates were to books.[72]

Analyzing the references contained in faculty publications or in doctoral dissertations is problematic. Several studies have shown that the principle of least effort has a significant impact on the information-seeking behavior of faculty and students—the more accessible an information source, the more likely it will be used.[73] A study at the University of Georgia Libraries compared 1,768 citations from 1991 theses and dissertations to 1,595 citations from 2001 and found that citations to Web sites went from 0 to 3.5 percent of all citations in 2001. Further, citations to ERIC microform documents sharply declined, while citations to monographs owned by the library increased during the 10-year period.[74]

And Soper has suggested that accessibility influences citation behavior—the more accessible a source, the more likely it will be cited.[75] Liu has suggested that a "normative theory of citing" exists—the more an electronic journal article is read, the more it is cited.[76] Supporting evidence for this theory was found on the Web-based NASA Astrophysics Data System.[77]

Lois Kuyper-Rushing examined music dissertation citations from across the United States and compared a composite list of journals to a single institution's list. She concluded that analysis of a single institution would likely result in a skewed list of journals and raised the issue of whether an analysis of doctoral dissertation citations as a basis for collection decision is justified.[78] A more recent study by Penny Beile and her colleagues also found that analysis of a single institution can result in a skewed list of core journals.[79]

Johanna Tuñón and Bruce Brydges developed a rubric for assessing the quality of citations that included currency, type of document, and other document-specific criteria. They also developed a second rubric for the subjective assessment of citations based on five criteria: number and variety of documents cited, depth of understanding through the inclusion of theoretical and background documents, scholarliness, currency, and relevance of the resources. The authors found that most students failed to include retrieval statements and thus the use of bibliometric information about students' use of electronic resources will be murky.[80]

An analysis of citations obtained from several sources found that the University of Illinois library owned some 77 percent of items found in monographs, 87 percent found in periodicals, and 91 percent found in dissertations. The study concluded that

- monographs used as sources of citations are best suited to assess the strength of a collection in terms of foreign language materials, general monographs, and older materials;

- periodicals used as sources of citations are best suited to assess the strength of a collection in relation to recently published materials, its own periodical coverage, and its comprehensiveness in terms of "other" types of materials; and

- dissertations used as sources of citations are best suited to assess the strength of a collection in relation to its holdings of conference proceedings, dissertations, and reports.[81]

Yet several cautions must be noted:

- Core journals can change rapidly due to editorial changes, a new title, or changes in emphasis in a field.

- Citation studies are useful to predict use of research and scholarly materials and not for other purposes.

- Citation analysis resources are readily available for the sciences and social sciences but less so for other subject areas.

- It is necessary to ensure that the citations used for analysis come from more than one institution to prevent bias.[82]

- It is easy to focus on the mathematical distributions without seeking the meaning behind the numbers.

- Citation analysis should be just one of several factors in the decision-making process.

Loss Rate Analysis

The library may want to identify the amount of material that is no longer in its collection due to theft. Typically a loss rate analysis is performed when a library is considering installing a theft detection system, but it also has value in identifying materials the library may wish to replace in its collection. Losses may be items that have been checked out to a customer but never returned as well as materials that are "borrowed" from the library but not checked out—often the latter is called theft. Clearly theft deprives all users except the thieves of access to library materials.

A library may generate a report from its automated library system identifying the titles of materials that have been borrowed but not returned in more than three to six months. This list can be used to identify titles that the library will order again to ensure that they are found in its collection. The total number of items that have not been returned after 12 months compared to total circulation will yield a percent loss rate.

Other libraries have selected a sample of titles from their shelf lists and then checked to see whether the items are on the shelf and have been borrowed by a customer. It is then possible to calculate a percent loss rate—number of items not "found" compared to the total number of items checked in the sample. One survey of a nonrepresentative sample of 74 libraries found that libraries "share consistent theft patterns."[83]

A library should also ensure that the theft or nonreturn of materials is addressed as part of its collection development policies, especially if theft is a persistent problem.

User Surveys

Some libraries have asked their customers to rate the library's collection in terms of how well it meets their needs and to suggest areas that are weak. In some cases, additional demographic information is obtained so that the results can be compared among different groups—young vs. old, student vs. faulty, and so forth. It should be noted that the focus of this type of survey is on the library's collection, and it is not a general customer satisfaction survey.

A number of studies have demonstrated that users of academic libraries select materials on the basis of subject matter and topicality.[84] Other studies have found that the most desirable sources were those that were accessible and easy to understand.[85] A study that examined undergraduate student selection criteria showed that the content, table of contents, and book organization were the most important factors. Noticeably absent from the student decision making were the author's credentials, date of publication, and publisher.[86]

Joan Bartram used a survey to determine faculty's expectations about the library's collection.[87] If a user survey is used, it should be complemented with other methods to evaluate the library's collection. Daniel Gore asked a group of students to keep a diary of their book searches over an academic semester. A total of 422 items were sought, and the library owned 90 percent of them. Of the items owned, 88 percent were found on the shelf—an availability rate of 88 percent.[88]

The Availability Study

An availability study examines the reasons customers are unable to find the items they are looking for when they visit the library. An availability study has also been called a "shelf availability study," a "frustration study," or "failure study." Such studies have been conducted chiefly at academic libraries. The reasons an item might not be available range from being it checked out, missing, or misplaced on the shelf, to the customer searching incorrectly or the item not being owned by the library. In general, these studies reveal that a library customer only has about a 60 percent chance of getting the item, as shown in Table 8.1.

Table 8.1 Summary of Availability Studies[89] in Academic Libraries

Study	Study Year	Sample Size	Availability Rate (Percent)
Coliberti	1985	401	.51
Ferl	1986	408	.61
Frohmberg	1980		.48
			.56
			.64
			.72
			.60
Kantor (a)	1973	211	.65
	1975	312	.56
Kantor (b)	1976	353	.53
Kochtanek	1979	203	.51
Kolner	1984	760	.59
Mansbridge	1984	421	.55
Palais	1981	1,097	.60
Radford	1983	2,497	.64
Rashid	1990	1,000	.60
Rinkel	1983	316	.72
Saracevic	1972	423	.48
	1974	437	.56
Schofield	1975	1,851	.63
Shaw	1980		.53
			.58
Smith	1981	2,375	.54
Whitlach	1978	1,441	.59
Wulff	1978	388	.63
Average		817	.58

Generally, more useful information can be obtained by using the customer as the source of the desired titles. This approach can be characterized as a customer-centric method. Other, library-centric, methods include

- obtaining a sample from the shelf list.

- using citations selected by experts in a subject field, and

- using indexes, abstracts, or general bibliographies.

A sample drawn from the shelf list of a library is unlikely to be a good one for use in studies of item availability because it will over-represent items that have low or very low levels of demand. Paul Kantor has suggested an approach that overcomes this bias.[90]

Involving the customers is a method that asks them to record on a form what they are looking for and whether the desired items are found. The forms are distributed as the customer enters the library. Alternatively, a staff member could interview customers as they begin their search. The completed forms are then analyzed by staff to determine the cause of failure, if any. A sample data collection form is shown in Figure 8.5.

We need your help!

Today we are studying availability of library books. Please use this form to report which books you are looking for in the library. We want to know whether or not you were able to find these books on the shelf. This study will help us analyze the reasons that books are not always readily available.

If you want the library to notify you if and when we find books that you cannot find today, please ask at the Circulation Desk as usual. We need this completed form in any case.

Thanks for your cooperation!

Author and Title	Call Number	Did Not Find Book (Check)	Found Book? (Check)

Please drop off this form on your way out.

Figure 8.5. Sample Book Availability Study Data Collection Form

The availability study is examining the success of the library's collection when the customer is looking for a known item. This approach, which can be easily adapted for use in any type of library, has studied both monograph and serials collections. A study conducted at the University of North Carolina at Chapel Hill noted that its customers found about 81 percent of the journal articles they were seeking (sample of 2,056 journal citations).[91]

The sample sizes of the availability studies summarized in this section ranged from slightly more than 200 to more than 2,300, with an average of 802. Clearly the library management team will have more confidence in the results of an analysis with a larger sample size, but this needs to be balanced with the costs associated with the data collection effort.

Kantor developed a branching technique to illustrate the relationship between the various categories (see Figure 8.6). Available items were seen as flowing through a pipeline, some being sidetracked along branches for various reasons and thus becoming unavailable. Those items emerging at the end of the pipe were available for use by the customer.[92] Probabilities are calculated using the number of items that made it past the branch divided by the number of items that approached the branch.

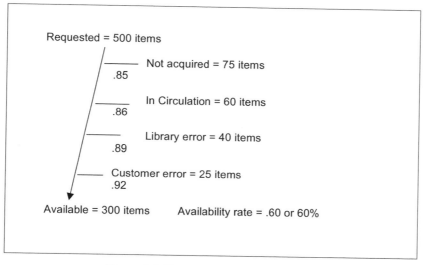

Figure 8.6. Kantor's Branching Diagram

Reasons an item might not be available include the following:

- **Collection Failure:** The library does not own the desired item. The availability studies have shown that a collection failure will occur about 10 percent of the time. An analysis of customer requests to purchase titles for the collection as well as of interlibrary loan requests will assist in reducing customer frustrations.

- **In Circulation:** The desired item has been checked out to another customer or is on the hold shelf waiting to be checked out. This happens, on average, for about 15 to 20 percent of the items.

- **Library Error:** The item should be on the shelf but it is waiting to be shelved (yet to be sorted, on a sorting shelf or a book truck), is missing, is reported lost, or is shelved incorrectly. While there is some variation reported in the studies, library error averages about 13 percent.

- **Catalog Error:** The customer cannot find the item in the catalog. This occurs about 7 percent of the time. Among the factors that might be examined are the complexity of the user interface with the library's online catalog, the clarity of information (information overload) displaced as the result of a search, the number of misspellings in the catalog, and so forth.

- **Customer Error:** The customer brings an incorrect citation, wrote down the call number incorrectly, or can't locate the item on the shelf. Customer error averages about 10 percent.

The Kantor branching diagram approach has been used in a number of academic libraries,[93] a specialized academic library,[94] a public library,[95] and a study of the availability of periodicals.[96] Haseeb Rashid suggested that a broader perspective that captured information about more categories of failure or disappointment would assist a library management team in understanding how they could make improvements. Rashid proposed 13 categories that should be tracked:[97]

- Quality of information brought to the library by the patron
- Whether the book title is owned by the library
- If the item is now owned by the library, whether the item meets the collection development policies of the library
- Whether the call number is recorded correctly
- Whether the item is located in a special collection/location identified in the library catalog
- Whether the item is located in a special collection/location *not* identified in the library catalog
- Whether the book has been properly shelved but not located by the patron
- Whether the book has been misshelved
- Whether the item is in use in the library
- Whether the book has been checked out
- Whether the book is in a preshelving area
- Whether the book is missing or reported lost
- Other factors

Anne Ciliberti expanded on the Kantor branching diagram by slightly revising the model for known-item searching and developing a parallel model for subject searching, shown in Figure 8.7.[98] She and her colleagues further elaborated the model by identifying the hurdles encountered in journal title searches.[99] This study revealed a number of problems that customers encountered that were unsuspected by library staff, including the need for better inventory control, better signage, and removing abbreviations from the catalog.

Another study, by Eugene Mitchell et al., successfully applied the Kantor branching diagram to subject searches and found the approach to be helpful in identifying needed improvements for the library's procedures.[100] Three primary factors affect availability of a particular item: the item's popularity (best-seller list, recommendation by a professor, and so forth), the number of copies available for loan, and the length of the loan period.[101]

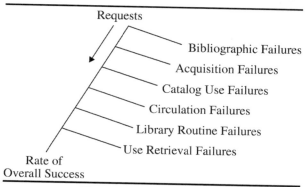

Known-Item Searches

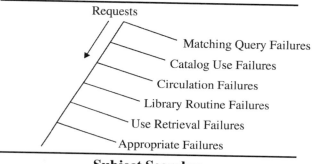

Subject Searches

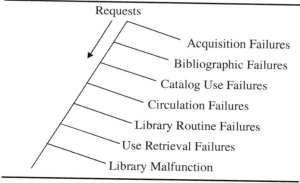

Journal Title Searches

Figure 8.7. Ciliberti Branching Diagrams

An alternative to the availability study is for the library to conduct a snapshot inventory. Topsy Smalley suggests sampling 3 percent of the library's circulating collection to determine the percent of the sample that is unavailable (neither on the shelf nor checked out).[102]

Thomas Nisonger prepared a thorough review of more than 50 studies and found availability rates for known-item searches by actual library users of about 61 percent, which was almost identical to an earlier review that Nisonger had prepared.[103]

Neal Kaske has suggested that as "just-in-case" collections are losing their utility, so too the availability study may no longer be useful. The traditional availability studies ignore the "just-in-time" efforts made by a library to meet a specific demand from a customer (purchasing the item with 24- to 48-hour delivery, recalling an item, interlibrary loan, document delivery, and so forth), as well as the increasing availability of print materials in electronic formats. Kaske argues the need for a new measure that focuses on the time the customer waits for the desired item.[104]

Document Delivery Tests

A document delivery test creates a pool of citations from a broad range of recently published literature. The degree of accessibility is then determined for each title in the pool of citations. It is assumed that the citation pool will represent the information needs of real users.

A major document delivery test was conducted by Richard Orr and his colleagues in biomedical libraries. The research team created a citation pool of 300 citations and assigned a speed code as an indication of the degree of accessibility; possibilities ranged from immediate shelf availability to loan using an interlibrary loan service.[105] The speed of delivery used a scale of 1–5:

1. Document available in less than 10 minutes

2. Document available in more than 10 minutes but less than 2 hours

3. Document available in more than 2 hours but less than 24 hours

4. Document available in more than 24 hours but less than 7 days

5. Document not available in less than 7 days.

The team also developed a Document Delivery Capability Index, with a maximal value of 100 only if all the sample documents were found "on the shelf" and available in less than 10 minutes. The Capability Index ranged from a low of 47 to a high of 88 in the participating biomedical libraries.

A similar study was conducted to determine the performance of 20 public libraries. The study team created three citation pools to test the availability of recently published books, current periodical literature, and other titles known to be in the libraries' collections. The goal was to determine the probability that an item was owned and, if owned, the probability that it was available for use—called the "Probability of Availability." Using a pool of 500 citations Ernest DeProspo and his colleagues checked the library catalogs to determine if something was owned and then checked the shelf to determine its availability. The Probability of Availability was then calculated for each library.[106]

In-Library Use

Documenting the in-library use of the collection is typically accomplished by recording items (manually or using an automated scanner) found on the desks before returning these items to the shelves. This method will underreport actual use because the library's customers will return items to the shelves, even when asked not to do so. Two reshelving studies using the sweep method found that it yielded results that underreported actual use from 20 to 40 percent.[107] In addition, this method will not identify use that is relatively short because the customer did not carry the item to a desk.

An alternative approach is to use direct observation to gain an estimate of total in-library use of the book or serial collection. During randomly assigned blocks of time, users are observed to see how many items are used and returned to the shelf and how many are left on the tables. Adding reshelved items to the items left on the tables provides a more accurate indication of in-library use.[108] Another study calculated the browsing ratio: volumes used in the library plus volumes checked out.[109]

An alternative method places stickers on each item; the library asks the customer to place a check mark on the sticker each time it is used. However, one study found such an approach underreported actual use by one-third.[110] Naylor found fewer reported uses from a user survey than were recorded by reshelving counts.[111] Sylvia and Lesher found that reshelving counts did not correspond to the number of citations in student papers.[112]

Another study examined the nonuse of current journal issues and no use of bound journals and microfilms of back journal issues and found that over half of the titles with unused current issues also had unused back issues.[113] One college used journal use, subscription prices, and academic department enrollment to calculate cost per use and use per department in an effort to determine low usage journals that could be moved to storage.[114]

Studies have suggested that there tends to be a stable *ratio* of total circulation to total in-library use of a library's collection, although the ratios noted in some studies have varied significantly (from less than 1:1 to more than 10 in-library uses to 1 borrowed item). Anthony Hindle and Michael Buckland found that books that circulate little get relatively little in-library use, and the more heavily borrowed books also have a higher in-library use.[115] They also noted that 40 percent of the collection had no recorded circulation yet accounted for nearly 20 percent of the in-library use.

Determining the ratio in a particular library is important to get a better understanding of the total use of a library's collection. This point was underscored in a study by Joan Stockard et al., who found a wide range of ratios when they examined in-library use in three libraries.[116]

To gather data for an in-library use analysis, most libraries will "sweep" up the materials sitting on tables and capture the data (manually or using a scanner) prior to reshelving the materials. This data collection method has several underlying problems:

- Despite the presence of signs asking customers not to reshelve materials, some items will be returned to the shelf.

- Some items left on a desk will be used more than once.

- Not all items that are used will be taken to a desk.

- The amount of use cannot be tracked (whether the user just scanned the table of contents or photocopied three articles).

- The data capture process is time-consuming and expensive, especially for journal collections.[117]

Harris[118] found that in-library collection use was as much as 20 times the use reflected in materials left on tables, while Lawrence and Oja suggested that in-library use of books was six times greater than circulation data in two University of California libraries.[119]

Formula Approach

Assuming there is a correlation between a library collection's adequacy and its size, Verner Clapp and Robert Jordan devised a formula for determining the minimal adequacy of an academic library's collection to support student and faculty needs. Developing a formula requires assigning quantities to various programmatic factors such as the number of faculty and students in various categories, the number of undergraduate and graduate subjects, or degree programs. The use of a formula is particularly appropriate for libraries in new colleges and universities.

Clapp and Jordan used a table to present their results for determining the minimum number of monographs and serial titles for a college library.[120] McInnis[121] converted this information into a formula with weighted variables:

$$V = 50,750 + 100F + 12E + 12H + 335U + 3,035M + 24,500D$$

Where   V = number of volumes
F = number of faculty
E = total number of students enrolled
H = number of undergraduate honors students
U = number of major undergraduate subjects
M = master degrees offered
D = doctoral degrees offered

and 50,750 is a constant. McInnis found that the Clapp and Jordan formula may report a low or conservative figure for the minimum levels of library size. The danger of the formula approach is that it may restrict growth of a library's collection and makes the assumption that all demand in the collection is uniform. Some have suggested that the formula approach should only be used when a library is being formed rather than in later, more mature stages.

Other formulas have been developed by the State of Washington[122] and Voigt.[123]

Curriculum Analysis

Another method involves assigning Library of Congress classification numbers to each course offering, sometimes called *course analysis*. The numbers of holdings for the corresponding classification numbers are counted in order to identify the resources available to support individual courses of instruction.[124] William McGrath used this approach at the University of Southwestern Louisiana and felt that it was a superior method to identify the scholarly interests in the campus departments.[125] McGrath's approach was replicated at the University of Nebraska at Omaha by Barbara Golden, who also added the number of enrolled students for each class to the analysis.[126] A similar analysis was prepared by Jenks[127] and Burr.[128]

Richard Dougherty and Laura Bloomquist used course analysis to compare collections at branch libraries on a large academic campus.[129] Others have used course analysis to improve acquisitions, prepare a collection development policy, and evaluate the collection.[130] In addition to using subject classification categories, Vernon Leighton suggested a library could use subject headings and keywords as queries in the online catalog to discover holdings.[131] Gwen Lochstet added faculty research activity to the course analysis approach and demonstrated its value for three departments at the University of South Carolina.[132]

Another variation of this approach is to compare faculty reserve lists and course bibliographies to the collection's content. Some bias may be present in any analysis since the library collection may have been used to create the lists.[133]

Course analysis allows the library to identify potential gaps in the collection. In addition, faculty will gain an understanding of the collection and how it supports the curriculum. And librarians will find their knowledge of the library's collection much improved. The disadvantage with this approach is that it is extremely time-consuming.

Interlibrary Loan Analysis

Another method of measuring collection adequacy against customer demand is to analyze a fairly large sample of interlibrary loan (ILL) requests. The requests are sorted by subject or program, publication date, language of publication, and format. Such an analysis can reveal whether there is unmet demand based on weaknesses in the library's collection.

Albert Henderson developed a library Collection Failure Quotient (CFQ), which is the ratio of interlibrary borrowing to collection size.[134] Using data from 36 academic libraries, Henderson noted that the average CFQ score had doubled between 1974 and 1992. Henderson also prepared a similar analysis for 80 university libraries and calculated their CFQ scores between 1974 and 1998; the results indicate that all scores doubled or tripled during the 25-year time frame of the analysis.[135]

A graph that shows the number and subject distributions of recent book acquisitions and of books borrowed using interlibrary loan can be an indication of current collection strength and balance, particularly for small to medium-sized libraries.[136] Jennifer Knievel and her colleagues suggest constructing a table of subject classifications and comparing the percent of holdings, the percent of circulation, and the ratio of holdings to interlibrary loan requests, to provide greater clarity when making collection management decisions.[137]

A longitudinal study prepared by Lynn Wiley and Tina Chrzastowski examined the number of ILL article requests among the 26 largest libraries in Illinois. Forty-four percent of the requests were filled in-state, and items from the sciences were requested by a two-to-one ratio over items from the social sciences and humanities. The results showed a showed a significant decline (26 percent reduction) as the result of these same libraries offering greater access to electronic journals; use of the full-text database increased about 10 percent per year.[138]

WEEDING THE COLLECTION

Another form of collection evaluation occurs when weeding items from the collection. Two popular weeding methods are

- Slote analysis, in which the time since last circulation is used to determine if an item should be discarded;[139] and

- Continuous Review, Evaluation, and Weeding, or CREW, in which the age of the item, last use date, and MUSTY (misleading, ugly, superseded, trivial, and no use in the library collections) are used to judge the suitability of weeding an item.

The need for weeding is based on the reality that most items now being borrowed were previously borrowed in the fairly recent past (thus the use of the last circulation date as a weeding criterion), and very few items that are now borrowed have sat on the shelves for a long period of time.

An analysis at a health sciences library found that recent print journals are accessed more frequently than older materials, with a significant drop in use of materials older than 15 years.[140] Colin Taylor developed his 15/5 rule as a way to identify items that are candidates for remote storage. He suggested that all volumes of a title that were published in the last 15 years and that had not been borrowed during the last 5 years should be moved to storage.[141]

PRESERVATION

An evaluation or assessment may be made from the perspective of the condition of the library's collection. The assessment is designed to identify that portion of the collection that may need to be repaired in order to preserve it. The evaluation collects data regarding the condition, age, paper pH, type of binding, date of last circulation, and so forth using a statistical sampling technique.[142]

VALUE

The vast majority of libraries assign a value to the library's collection for insurance purposes. But there is a much more important value that is difficult to conceptualize and quantify. That is, what are the consequences of use of the library's collection in the lives of its customers?

A few public libraries have attempted to compare the costs and the benefits of using the library using a cost-benefit analysis. Special libraries are in a fairly unique position in that they can ask their clients, usually employees of the organization, to identify and quantify the benefits that arise from use of the library—time savings, cost savings, generating new revenues, and so forth. Cost-benefit analysis is discussed in chapter 18.

Academic libraries have for a variety of reasons not put forth much effort in trying to understand the degree to which use of a library's collection improves the student learning process. The few studies that have been done are fairly old and reflect a library environment with only physical collections—the era prior to electronic databases.

Gorham Lane reported on several studies prepared at the University of Delaware in an attempt to discover the impact of library facilities and services on its undergraduates. One study investigated the long-term borrowing of books from the general collection. The majority of students did not borrow any materials from the library, although the percentage of students who did not borrow any materials declined somewhat from the freshman through the senior year. While students who did borrow materials were more likely to stay in school, the analysis revealed the correlation was not statistically significant. In summary, Lane found that the university's general collection was not widely used by undergraduates, and when it was used it did not have a significant relationship to academic achievement.[143]

Nichols found no statistically significant correlations between an institution's academic library resources and undergraduates' educational outcomes. The number of library books per student and library size and undergraduates' scores on the Graduate Record Examination (GRE) were analyzed.[144]

Another study examined the relationship between the number of books in the library and the number of books in the library per student with the scores on the GRE. After controlling for the students' background characteristics, Alexander Astin only found a weak positive correlation between library size and scores on the Graduate Record Examination (GRE).[145] An additional study also found a weak correlation between undergraduates' scores on both the GRE and the Scholastic Aptitude Test and the number of books in the library and the number of library books per student.[146] Implicit in these studies of the size of the library, sometimes called resource allocation analysis, was the assumption that "if you have it, they will use it."

Another study, prepared by Patrick Barkey at Eastern Illinois University, found that about two-thirds of students borrowed no materials from the library. Yet a direct correlation was noted between a student's grade point average and the number of items borrowed from the library, indicating that more of the better students used the library.[147] Jane Hiscock found very little connection between usage of libraries and academic performance in her study at the South Australian College of Advanced Education but did find a link between extensive use of library catalogs and high academic performance.[148]

Tony Mays examined circulation data and a survey completed by a sample of students in a university setting. He found that the library collection is deemed by many undergraduate students to be superfluous to their educational program and found no correlation between use of the library's collection and academic achievement. Furthermore, no predictions could be made about library use based on a student's discipline or field of study.[149]

James Self examined the use of reserve materials and the students' grades in a variety of courses at the University of Virginia. Almost half of the 8,454 students included in the analysis did not use any reserve materials. Also, while students with higher use of reserve materials tended to have higher grades, the statistical correlation was not significant, and thus use of reserve materials is not useful as a predictor of an individual's grade.[150]

A further study found only weak support for the use of materials found in the stacks of a library and better grades for students majoring in history and sociology.[151] Law students who were more active library book borrowers were more likely to receive honors upon graduation than students who were not active book borrowers.[152]

An examination of student characteristics and undergraduate library use was conducted and found that five variables influenced library use: hours spent on campus, credit hour enrollment, gender (male), grade point average, and academic major.[153] Jennifer Wells conducted a survey at the University of Western Sydney, Australia, and found a positive correlation between academic achievement and the use of different library resources and services.[154] She also found that the quantity of time spent in the library was not associated with academic success.

COLLECTION DEVELOPMENT

While the evaluation of collections might be viewed as an acceptable proxy for the evaluation of collection development, the reality is that over-selection and under-selection are not identified when the collection is evaluated. Under-selection results when materials that should have been acquired are not. Over-selection results when materials are acquired but never used. Under-selection can be mitigated through the use of interlibrary loan and document delivery services.

The consequences of over-selection are serious, even ignoring the costs to purchase, process, and shelve the item for many years to come. More important, the opportunity cost of the item—the value to the library's customers of what was *not* acquired due to the item that was selected—must be acknowledged. Moving little-used and never-used materials to a storage facility may lower the costs slightly, but ongoing costs to continue to store the materials and provide access are also significant.

Dennis Carrigan suggests using data from a library's automated circulation system to determine the proportional use by subject classification of a library's collection to reveal both under-selection and over-selection.[155] First introduced by George Bonn in 1974, the concept has been used at Virginia Tech libraries, among others.[156] A library would also need to prepare an analysis of interlibrary loan and document delivery data for a complete picture of the value of the collection development decisions that are being made on behalf of the library.

TOTAL COSTS

While purchase and processing costs of library materials are fairly easily identified, total life cycle costs of a library's collection are rarely considered. Using annual data reported by the Association of Research Libraries, costs are allocated to collections based on the size of the collection and its relative space. The analysis revealed that the life cycle costs of collections are many multiples of their purchase costs—seven times for monographs. And the life cycle costs of monograph collections overwhelm the costs of other collections—accounting for as much as 95 percent of all costs.[157]

SUMMARY

This chapter has presented a wide variety of methods that can be used to assess a library's physical collection. Among the more notable conclusions that can drawn from this discussion are the following:

- A small proportion of the collection receives the greatest proportion of use.

- Although the 80/20 rule is valid for many libraries, some libraries will have a slightly different ratio of circulation to holdings due to their age and size, which should be established through a local study.

- Circulation is not an accurate measure of total use, and the ratio of in-library use to circulation varies greatly and should be studied locally.

- Some research libraries have significant in-library use of low circulating items,

- Retention of print journals more than 15 years old may not be necessary in most academic libraries based on analysis of interlibrary loan data and citation analyses.

- Evaluating collection development is different than evaluating the collection, although similar tools are used for the analysis.

As resources available to libraries decline, it is critical that collections and services be continually and systematically reviewed, with the goal of keeping them aligned with the mission of the organization and the needs of the customers. To present a balanced view of any evaluation, it is suggested that two or more methods be used. Each evaluation methodology has strengths and weaknesses, which must be considered when making plans to assess a specific library's collection. The goals and objectives of the evaluation will usually determine what methodology should be used.

And for any type of library, consideration should be given to constructing and completing outcome studies that identify the benefits and impacts of the library's resources and its services on the lives of its customers.

NOTES

1. Elizabeth Futas and David L. Vidor. What Constitutes a "Good" Collection? *Library Journal*, 112, April 15, 1987, 45.

2. Diane Schmidt, Elizabeth B. Davis, amd Ruby Jahr. Biology Journal Use at an Academic Library: A Comparison of Use Studies. *Serials Review*, 20 (2), 1994, 45–64.

3. Robert N. Broadus. The Measurement of Periodical Use. *Serials Review*, 11 (2), 1985, 30–35.

4. Dennis R. Ridley and Joseph E. Weber. Toward Assessing In-house Use of Print Resources in an Undergraduate Academic Library: An Inter-Institutional Study. *Library Collections, Acquisitions & Technical Services*, 24, 2000, 89–103.

5. Harriet Lightman and Sabina Manilov. A Simple Method for Evaluating a Journal Collection: A Case Study of Northwestern University's Economics Collection. *The Journal of Academic Librarianship*, 26 (3), May 2000, 183–90.

6. Russell F. Dennison. Quality Assessment of Collection Development Through Tiered Checklists: Can You Prove You Are a Good Collection Developer? *Collection Building*, 19 (1), 2000, 24–26.

7. Nancy E. Gwinn and Paul H. Mosher. Coordinating Collection Development: The RLG Conspectus. *College & Research Libraries*, 44, March 1983, 128–40.

8. Howard D. White. *Brief Tests of Collection Strength: A Methodology for All Types of Libraries*. Westport, CT: Greenwood Press, 1995.

9. David Lesniaski. Evaluating Collections: A Discussion and Extension of Brief Tests of Collection Strength. *College & Undergraduate Libraries*, 11 (1), 2004, 11–24.

10. Allen D. Pratt and Ellen Altman. Live by the Numbers, Die by the Numbers. *Library Journal*, 122, April 15, 1997, 48–49.

11. Johann Van Reenen. Library Budgets and Academic Library Rankings in Times of Transition. *The Bottom Line*, 14 (4), 2001, 213–18.

12. A. K. Jain. Sampling and Data Collection Methods for a Book-Use Study. *Library Quarterly*, 39, July 1969, 245–52.

13. George S. Bonn. Evaluation of the Collection. *Library Trends*, 22, January 1974, 265–304.

14. Paul Metz. *The Landscape of Literatures: Use of Subject Collections in a University Library*. Chicago: American Library Association, 1983.

15. Terry R. Mills. *The University of Illinois Film Center Collection Use Study*. CAS Paper. Urbana: University of Illinois-Urbana, 1981.

16. Ken Dowlin and Lynn Magrath. Beyond the Numbers: A Decision Support System, in *Proceedings of the 1982 Clinic on Library Applications of Data Processing*. Urbana: University of Illinois, Graduate School of Library and Information Science, 1983, 27–58.

17. William Aguilar. The Application of Relative Use and Interlibrary Demand in Collection Development. *Collection Management*, 8 (1), Spring 1986, 15–24.

18. Joanne Ujiie and Stephen Krashen. Are Prize-Winning Books Popular Among Children? An Analysis of Public Library Circulation. *Knowledge Quest*, 34 (3), January/February 2006, 33–35.

19. Richard W. Trueswell. Some Behavioral Patterns of Library Users: The 80/20 Rule. *Wilson Library Bulletin*, 43, January 1969, 458–61.

20. William A. Britten. A Use Statistic for Collection Management: The 80/20 Rule Revisited. *Library Acquisitions: Practice & Theory*, 14, 1990, 183–89.

21. Seymour H. Sargent. The Uses and Limitations of Trueswell. *College & Research Libraries*, 40, September 1979, 416–23.

22. Michael K. Buckland. An Operations Research Study of a Variable Loan and Duplication Policy at the University of Lancaster. *Library Quarterly*, 42, 1972, 97–106.

23. D. Yvonne Jones. Oversized and Underused: Size Matters in Academic Libraries. *College & Research Libraries*, 67 (7), July 2006, 325–33.

24. Paul B. Kantor and Wonsik Shim. Library Circulation as Interaction Between Readers and Collections: The Square Root Law. *Proceedings of the American Society for Information Science*, 35, 1998, 260–66.

25. Allen Kent, Jacob Cohen, K. Leon Montgomery, James G. Williams, Stephen Bulick, Roger R. Flynn, William N. Sabor, and Una Mansfield. *Use of Library Materials: The University of Pittsburgh Study*. New York: Marcel Dekker, 1979.

26. Jasper G. Schad. Missing the Brass Ring in the Iron City. *Journal of Academic Librarianship*, 5, May 1979, 60–63; Melvin J. Voight. Circulation Studies Cannot Reflect Research Use. *Journal of Academic Librarianship*, 5, May 1979, 66; and Leslie Peat. The Use of Research Libraries: A Comment about the Pittsburgh Study & Its Critics. *Journal of Academic Librarianship*, 7, September 1981, 229–31.

27. Allen Kent. A Rebuttal. *Journal of Academic Librarianship*, 5, May 1979, 69–70; and Allen Kent et al. A Commentary on "Report on the Study of Library Use at Pitt by Professor Allen Kent et al." The Senate Library Committee, University of Pittsburgh, July 1969. *Library Acquisitions: Practice & Theory*, 4 (1), 1980, 87–99.

28. Larry Hardesty. Use of Library Materials at a Small Liberal Arts College. *Library Research*, 3, Fall 1981, 261–82.

29. Larry Hardesty. Use of Library Materials at a Small Liberal Arts College: A Replication. *Collection Management*, 10 (3/4), 1988, 61–80.

30. Debbi Dinkins. Circulation as Assessment: Collection Development Policies Evaluated in Terms of Circulation at a Small Academic Library. *College & Research Libraries*, 64 (1), January 2003, 46–53.

31. Robert M. Hayes. The Distribution of Use of Library Materials: Analysis of Data from the University of Pittsburgh. *Library Research*, 3, Fall 1981, 215–60.

32. Herbert H. Fussler and Julian L. Simon. *Patterns in the Use of Books in Large Research Libraries*. Chicago: University of Chicago Press, 1969.

33. Paul Metz and Charles A. Litchfield. Measuring Collections Use at Virginia Tech. *College & Research Libraries*, 49, 1988, 501–13.

34. Jonathan D. Eldridge. The Vital Few Meet the Trivial Many: Unexpected Use Patterns in a Monographs Collection. *Bulletin of the Medical Library Association*, 86 (4), October 1998,, 496–503.

35. Deborah D. Blecic. Monograph Use at an Academic Health Science Library: The First Three Years of Shelf Life. *Bulletin of the Medical Library Association*, 88 (2), 2000, 145–51.

36. Lucy E. Lyons. A Critical Examination of the Assessment Analysis Capabilities of OCLC ACAS. *The Journal of Academic Librarianship*, 31 (6), November 2005, 506–16.

37. W. S. Cooper, D. D. Thompson, and K. R. Weeks. The Duplication of Monograph Holdings in the University of California System. *Library Quarterly*, 45, 1975, 253–74.

38. B. Moore, I. J. Miller, and D. L. Tolliver. Title Overlap: A Study of Duplication in the University of Wisconsin System Libraries. *College & Research Libraries*, 43, 1982, 14–22.

39. Ruth H. Miller and Martha W. Niemeier. A Study of Collection Overlap in the Southwest Indiana Cluster of SULAN. *Indiana Libraries*, 9 (2), 1990, 45–54.

40. Thomas Nisonger. Editing the RLG Conspectus to Analyze the OCLC Archival Tapes for Seventeen Texas Libraries. *Library Resources & Technical Services*, 29, October/December 1985, 309–27.

41. William Gray Potter. Collection Overlap in the LCS Network in Illinois. *Library Quarterly*, 56 (2), 1986, 119–41.

42. Rob Kairis. Consortium Level Collection Development: A Duplication Study of the OhioLINK Central Catalog. *Library Collections, Acquisitions, & Technical Services*, 27, 2003, 317–26.

43. Sue Stroyan. Collection Overlap in Hospital Health Sciences Libraries: A Case Study. *Bulletin of the Medical Library Association*, 73 (4), October 1985, 358–64.

44. William G. Potter. Studies of Collection Overlap: A Literature Review. *Library Research*, 4, Spring 1982, 309–21.

45. William E. McGrath. Multidimensional Map of Library Similarities. *Proceedings of the American Society for Information Science*, 18, 1980, 298–300.

46. Alan Pritchard. Statistical Bibliography or Bibliometrics? *Journal of Documentation*, 25, December 1969, 48–49.

47. Schmidt et al., Biology Journal Use at an Academic Library.

48. Francis Narin. *Evaluative Bibliometrics: The Use of Publication and Citation Analysis in the Evaluation of Scientific Activity*. Cherry Hill, NJ: Computer Horizons, 1976.

49. Robert H. Austin, as quoted in Richard Monastersky. The Number That's Devouring Science. *The Chronicle of Higher Education*, October 14, 2005, 12.

50. P. Scales. Citation Analysis as Indicators of the Use of Serials: A Comparison of Ranked Title Lists Produced by Citation Counting and from Use Data. *Journal of Documentation*, 32, 1976, 17–25; and E. Pan. Journal Citation as a Predictor of Journal Usage in Libraries. *Collection Management*, 2, 1978, 29–38.

51. T. Stankus and B. Rice. Handle with Care: Use and Citation Data for Science Journal Management. *Collection Management*, 4, 1982, 95–110; and M. Tsay. The Relationship Between Journal Use in a Medical Library and Citation Use. *Bulletin of the Medical Library Association*, 86, 1998, 31–39.

52. Danny P. Wallace and Bert R. Boyce. Holdings as a Measure of Journal Value. *Library and Information Science Research*, 11, 1989, 59–71.

53. Thomas E. Nisonger. Use of the *Journal Citation Reports* for Serials Management in Research Libraries: An Investigation of the Effect of Self-Citation on Journal Rankings in Library and Information Science and Genetics. *College & Research Libraries*, 61 (3), May 2000, 263–75.

54. B. Rice. Selection and Evaluation of Chemistry Periodicals. *Science and Technology Libraries*, 4, 1983, 43–59; Schmidt et al., Biology Journal Use at an Academic Library, 45–64; and J. Wulff and N. Nixon. Quality Makers and Use of Electronic Journals in an Academic Health Sciences Library. *Journal of the Medical Library Association*, 92, 2004, 315–22.

55. D. Belecic. Measurements of Journal Use: An Analysis of the Correlations Between Three Methods. *Bulletin of the Medical Library Association*, 87, 1999, 20–25.

56. Joanna Duy and Liwen Vaughn. Can Electronic Journal Usage Data Replace Citation Data as a Measure of Journal Use? An Empirical Examination. *The Journal of Academic Librarianship*, 32 (5), September 2006, 512–17.

57. Robin B. Devin and Martha Kellogg. The Serial/Monograph Ratio in Research Libraries: Budgeting in Light of Citation Studies. *College & Research Libraries*, 51, January 1990, 46–54.

58. Richard Monastersky. Impact Factors Run into Competition. *The Chronicle of Higher Education,* October 14, 2005, 17.

59. Blaise Cronin and Lokman Meho. Using the h-index to Rank Influential Information Scientists. *Journal of the American Society for Information Science and Technology*, 57 (9), 2006, 1275–78.

60. Charles Oppenheim. Using the h-index to Rank Influential British Researchers in Information Science and Librarianship. *Journal of the American Society for Information Science and Technology*, 58 (2), 2007, 297–301.

61. Ben Toth. The Number Needed to Read—A New Measure of Journal Value. *Health Information and Libraries Journal*, 22, 2005, 81–82.

62. Note that Bradford multipliers may vary from zone to zone based on an analysis by I. K. R. Rao. An Analysis of Bradford Multipliers and a Model to Explain the Law of Scattering. *Scientometrics*, 41 (1/2), 1998, 93-100.

63. O. V. Groos. Bradford's Law and the Keenan-Atherton Data. *American Documentation*, 18, 1967, 46.

64. Liwen Qiu and Jean Tague. Complete or Incomplete Data Sets. The Groos Droop Investigated. Scientometrics, 19 (3/4), September 1990, 223–37.

65. R. E. Burton and R. W. Kebler. The "Half-life" of Some Scientific and Technical Literature. *American Documentation*, 11 (1), January 1960, 18–22.

66. Charles P. Bourne. Some User Requirements Stated Quantitatively in Terms of the 90 Percent Library, in Allen Kent and Orrin E. Taulbee (Eds.). *Electronic Information Handling*. Washington, DC: Spartan Books, 1965, 93–110.

67. B. C. Brookes. The Growth, Vitality and Obsolescence of Scientific Periodical Literature. *Journal of Documentation*, 26 (4), 1970, 283–94; and B. C. Brookes. Obsolescence of Special Library Periodicals: Sampling Errors and Utility Curves. *Journal of the American Society for Information Science,* 21 (5), 1970, 320–29.

68. D. J. De Solla Price. Networks of Scientific Papers. *Science*, 149, 1965, 510–15.

69. M. Stern. Characteristics of the Literature of Literary Scholarship. *College & Research Libraries*, 44, 1983, 199–209.

70. Jennifer E. Knievel and Charlene Kellsey. Citation Analysis for Collection Development: A Comparative Study of Eight Humanities Fields. *Library Quarterly*, 75 (2), 2005, 142–68.

71. Jan A. Pechenik, J. Michael Reed, and Melissa Russ. Should Auld Acquaintance Be Forgot: Possible Influence of Computer Databases on Citation Patterns in the Biological Literature. *BioScience*, 51 (7), July 2001, 583–88.

72. Rose Mary Magrill and Gloriana St. Clair. Undergraduate Term Paper Citation Patterns by Disciplines and Level of Course. *Collection Management*, 12 (3/4), 1990, 25–56.

73. T. J. Allen and P. G. Gerstberger. Criteria for Selection of an Information Source. *Journal of Applied Psychology*, 52, 1968, 272–79; Victor Rosenberg. The Application of Psychometric Techniques to Determine the Attitudes of Individuals Toward Information Seeking. *Information Storage and Retrieval*, 3, 1967, 119–27.

74. Erin T. Smith. Assessing Collection Usefulness: An Investigation of Library Ownership of the Resources Graduate Students Use. *College & Research Libraries*, 64, September 2003, 344–55.

75. M. E. Soper. The Relationship Between Personal Collections and the Selection of Cited Reference. *Library Quarterly*, 46, 1976, 397–415.

76. M. Liu. Progress in Documentation—The Complexities of Citation Practice: A Review of Citation Studies. *Journal of Documentation*, 49, 1993, 17–25.

77. H. D. White and K. W. McCain. Bibliometrics. *Annual Review of Information Science and Technology*, 24, 1989, 119–86.

78. Lois Kuyper-Rushing. Identifying Uniform Core Journal Titles for Music Libraries: A Dissertation Citation Study. *College & Research Libraries*, 60, 1999, 153–63.

79. Penny M. Beile, David N. Boote, and Elizabeth K. Killingsworth. A Microscope or a Mirror?: A Question of Study Validity Regarding the Use of Dissertation Citation Analysis for Evaluating Research Collections. *The Journal of Academic Librarianship*, 30 (5), September 2004, 347–53.

80. Johanna Tuñón and Bruce Brydges. Improving the Quality of University Libraries Through Citation Mining and Analysis Using Two New Dissertation Bibliometric Assessment Tools. *Presentation made at the 71st IFLA General Conference, 14–18 August 2005, Oslo, Norway.* Available at http://www.ifla.org/IV/ifla71/papers/078e-Tunon_Brydges.pdf.

81. Silas Marques De Oliveira. *Collection Evaluation Through Citation Checking: A Comparison of Three Sources.* Ph.D. dissertation, University of Illinois at Urbana-Champaign, 1991.

82. Beile et al., Microscope or a Mirror?, 347–53.

83. Shelley Mosley, Anna Caggiano, and John Charles. The "Self-Weeding" Collection. *Library Journal*, 119, October 15, 1996, 38.

84. Michelle Twait. Undergraduate Students' Source Selection Criteria: A Qualitative Study. *The Journal of Academic Librarianship,* 31 (6), 1995, 567–73; and Yunjie (Calvin) Xu and Zhiwei Chen.

Relevance Judgment: What Do Users Consider Beyond Topicality? *Journal of the American Society for Information Science and Technology*, 67 (7), 2006, 961–73.

85. Carol L. Barry. User-Defined Relevance Criteria: An Exploratory Study. *Journal of the American Society for Information Science,* 45 (3), 1994, 149–59; and Vicki Tolar Burton and Scott A. Chadwick. Investigating the Practices of Student Researchers: Patterns of Use and Criteria for Use of Internet and Library Sources. *Computers and Composition*, 17 (3), 2000, 309–28.

86. Thomas Stieve and David Schoen. Undergraduate Students' Book Selection: A Study of Factors in the Decision-Making Process. *The Journal of Academic Librarianship*, 32 (6), November 2006, 599–608.

87. Joan Bartram. Learning from the Big Guys: Small College Libraries Take Advantage of Big Brother's Hard Work. *Against the Grain*, 12 (2), April 2000, 31–32.

88. Daniel Gore. The Mischief in Measurement. *Library Journal*, May 1, 1978, 933–37.

89. Anne C. Ciliberti, Mary F. Casserly, Judith L. Hegg, and Eugene S. Mitchell. Material Availability: A Study of Academic Library Performance. *College & Research Libraries*, 48, November 1987, 513–27; Terry Ellen Ferl and Margaret G. Robinson. Book Availability at the University of California, Santa Cruz. *College & Research Libraries*, 47, September 1986, 501–8; Katherine A. Frohmberg, Paul B. Kantor, and William A. Moffett. Increases in Book Availability in a Large College Library. *Proceedings of the 43rd ASIS Annual Meeting*. Washington, DC: ASIS, 1980, 292–94; Paul B. Kantor. The Library as an Information Utility in the University Context: Evaluation and Measurement of Services. *Journal of the American Society of Information Science*, 27, 1976, 100–112; Paul B. Kantor. Availability Analysis. *Journal of the American Society of Information Science,* 27, 1976, 311–19; Stuart J. Kolner and Eric C. Welch. The Book Availability Study as an Objective Measure of Performance in a Health Sciences Library. *Bulletin of the Medical Library Association*, 73 (2), April 1985, 121–31; John Mansbridge. Evaluating Resource Sharing Library Networks. Ph.D. dissertation, Case Western University, Cleveland, Ohio, 1984; Elliot S. Palais. Availability Analysis Report, Arizona State. *User Surveys and Evaluation of Library Services*. Bethesda, MD: ERIC, 1981, 73–82. ED 214 541; Neil A. Radford. Failure in the Library—A Case Study. *Library Quarterly*, 53 (3), 1983, 328–39; Tefko Saracevic, William M. Shaw, and Paul B. Kantor. Causes and Dynamics of User Frustration in an Academic Library. *College & Research Libraries*, 38, 1977, 7–18; James L. Schofield and D. H. Waters. Evaluation of an Academic Library's Stock Effectiveness. *Journal of Librarianship*, 7, 1975, 207–27; William M. Shaw. Longitudinal Studies of Book Availability, in Neal Kaske and William Jones (Eds.). *Library Effectiveness: A State of the Art*. Chicago: American Library Association/LAMA, 1980, 337–49; Rita Smith and Warner Grande. AL Report, Undergraduate Library Availability Study 1975–1977, University of Tennessee. *User Surveys and Evaluation of Library Services*. Bethesda, MD: ERIC, 1981, 83–90. ED 214 541; Jo Bell Whitlatch and Karen Kieffer. Service at San Jose State University: Survey of Document Availability. *Journal of Academic Librarianship*, 4, 1978, 197–99; Yvonne Wulff. Book Availability in the University of Minnesota Bio-Medical Library. *Bulletin of the Medical Library Association*, 66, 1978, 349–50.

90. Paul B. Kantor. Demand-Adjusted Shelf Availability Parameters. *The Journal of Academic Librarianship*, 7 (2), 1981, 78–82.

91. Julia Shaw-Kokot and Claire de la Varre. Using a Journal Availability Study to Improve Access. *Bulletin of the Medical Library Association*, 89 (1), January 2001, 21–28.

92. Paul B. Kantor. The Library as an Information Utility in the University Context: Evaluation and Measurement of Services. *Journal of the American Society of Information Science*, 27, 1976, 100–112; Kantor, Availability Analysis, 311–19. See also Paul B. Kantor. *Objective Performance Measures for Academic and Research Libraries*. Washington, DC: Association of Research Libraries, 1984.

93. K. A. Frohmberg and W. A. Moffett. *Research on the Impact of a Computerized Circulation System on the Performance of a Large College Library: Part One—The Main Library*. Oberlin, OH: Oberlin College Library, 1981; Thomas R. Kochtanek. *User Satisfaction in the Hugh Stevens College Library*. Columbia, MO: University of Missouri, September 1979. ED 190 164; E. S. Palais. *Availability*

Analysis Report. SPEC Kit 71. Washington, DC: Association of Research Libraries, 1981; and G. K. Rinkel and P. McCandless. Application of a Methodology Analyzing User Frustration. *College & Research Libraries*, 44, 1983, 29–37.

94. Wulff. Book , 349–50; and Haseeb F. Rashid. Book Availability as a Performance Measure of a Library: An Analysis of the Effectiveness of a Health Sciences Library. *Journal of the American Society for Information Science*, 41 (7), 1990, 501–7.

95. J. B. Wood, J. J. Bremer, and S. A. Saraidaridis. Measurement of Service at a Public Library. *Public Library Quarterly*, 2, 1980, 49–57.

96. M. E. Murfin. The Myth of Accessibility: Frustration and Failure in Retrieving Periodicals. *Journal of Academic Librarianship*, 6, 1980, 16–19.

97. Rashid, Book Availability, 501–7.

98. Anne C. Ciliberti, Mary Casserly, Judy Hegg, and Eugene Mitchell. Material Availability: A Study of Academic Library Performance. *College & Research Libraries*, 48, November 1987, 513–27.

99. Anner Ciliberti, Marie L. Radford, Gary P. Radford, and Terry Ballard. Empty Handed? A Material Availability Study and Transaction Log Analysis Verification. *The Journal of Academic Librarianship*, 59, July 1998, 282–89.

100. Eugene S. Mitchell, Marie L. Radford, and Judith L. Hegg. Book Availability: Academic Library Assessment. *College & Research Libraries*, 55, January 1994, 47–55.

101. Michael K. Buckland. *Book Availability and the Library User*. New York: Pergamon, 1975.

102. Topsy N. Smalley. Assessing Collection Availability: A Snapshot Inventory. *Community & Junior College Libraries*, 5 (2), 1988, 69–75.

103. Thomas E. Nisonger. A Review and Analysis of Library Availability Studies. *LRTS*, 51 (1), January 2007, 30–49.

104. Neal K. Kaske. Materials Availability Model and the Internet. *Journal of Academic Librarianship*, 20, November 1994, 317–18.

105. Richard H. Orr, Vern M. Pings, Irwin H. Pizer, and Edwin E. Olsen. Development of Methodologic Tools for Planning and Managing Library Services: I. Project Goals and Approach. *Bulletin of the Medical Library Association*, 56 (3), July 1968, 235–40; Richard H. Orr, Vern M. Pings, Irwin H. Pizer, Edwin E. Olsen and Carol C. Spencer. Development of Methodologic Tools for Planning and Managing Library Services: II. Measuring a Library's Capability for Providing Documents. *Bulletin of the Medical Library Association*, 56 (3), July 1968, 241–67; Richard H. Orr, Vern M. Pings, Edwin E. Olsen, and Irwin H. Pizer. Development of Methodologic Tools for Planning and Managing Library Services: III. Standardized Inventories of Library Services. *Bulletin of the Medical Library Association*, 56 (3), July 1968, 380–403; and Richard H. Orr. Development of Methodologic Tools for Planning and Managing Library Services: IV. Bibliography of Studies Selected for Methods and Data Useful to Biomedical Libraries. *Bulletin of the Medical Library Association*, 58 (3), July 1970, 350–70.

106. Ernest R. DeProspo, Ellen Altman, and Kenneth E. Beasley. *Performance Measures for Public Libraries*. Chicago: American Library Association, 1979.

107. Colin R. Taylor. A Practical Solution to Weeding University Library Periodicals Collections. *Collection Management*, 1 (3/4), 1977, 27–45.

108. C. Wenger and J. Childress. Journal Evaluation in a Large Research Library. *Journal of the American Society for Information Science*, 28 (5), September 1977, 293–99.

109. Joseph E. Weber and Dennis R. Ridley. Assessment and Decision Making: Two User-Oriented Studies. *Library Review*, 46 (3), 1997, 202–9.

110. Dorothy Milne and Bill Tiffany. A Cost-per-use Method for Evaluating the Cost-effectiveness of Serials: A Detail Discussion of Methodology. *Serials Review*, 17 (2), 1991, 7–19; and Dorothy Milne and Bill Tiffany. A Survey of Cost-effectiveness of Serials: A Cost-per-use Method and Its Results. *Serials Librarian*, 19 (3/4), 1991, 137–49.

111. Maiken Naylor. Comparative Results of Two Current Periodical Use Studies. *Library Resources & Technical Services*, 38, 1994, 373–88.

112. Margaret Sylvia and Marcella Lesher. What Journals Do Psychology Graduate Students Need? A Citation Analysis of Their References. *College & Research Libraries*, 56, 1995, 313–18.

113. Jean S. Sauer. Unused Current Issues: A Predictor of Unused Bound Volumes? *Serials Librarian*, 18 (1/2), 97–107.

114. Steve Black. Journal Collection Analysis at a Liberal Arts College. *Library Resources & Technical Services*, 41 (4), 1997, 283–94.

115. Anthony Hindle and Michael K. Buckland. In-Library Book Usage in Relation to Circulation. *Collection Management*, 2 (4), Winter 1978, 265–77.

116. Joan Stockard, Mary Ann Griffin, and Clementine Coblyn. Document Exposure Counts in Three Academic Libraries: Circulation and In-Library Use, in *Quantitative Measurement and Dynamic Library Service*. Phoenix: Oryx Press, 1978, 136–47.

117. R. Broadus. A Proposed Method for Eliminating Titles from Periodicals Subscription Lists. *College & Research Libraries*, 46, 1985, 30–35.

118. C. A. Harris. A Comparison of Issues and In-library Use of Books. *ASLIB Proceedings*, 29, 1977, 118–26.

119. Gary S. Lawrence and A. R. Oja. *The Use of General Collections at the University of California*. Sacramento: California State Department of Education, 1980. ERIC ED 191 490.

120. Verner W. Clapp and Robert T. Jordan. Quantitative Criteria for Adequacy of Academic Library Collections. *College & Research Libraries*, 26, September 1965, 371–80.

121. R. M. McInnis. The Formula Approach to Library Size: An Empirical Study of Its Efficiency in Evaluating Research Libraries. *College & Research Libraries*, 33, 1972, 190–98.

122. Inter-institutional Committee of Business Officers. *A Model Analysis for Program 05 Libraries*. Olympia, WA: Evergreen State College, March 1970.

123. Melvin J. Voigt. Acquisitions Rates in University Libraries. *College & Research Libraries*, 36, July 1975, 263–71.

124. William E. McGrath. Significance of Book Use According to a Classified Profile of Academic Departments. *College & Research Libraries*, 33, 1972, 212–19; and William E. McGrath. Measuring Classified Circulation According to Curriculum. *College & Research Libraries*, 29, 1968, 347–50.

125. William McGrath and Norma Durand. Classifying Courses in the University Catalog. *College and Research Libraries*, 30, November 1969, 553–59.

126. Barbara Golden. A Method for Quantitatively Evaluating a University Library Collection. *Library Resources and Technical Services*, 18, Summer 1974, 268–75.

127. G. M. Jenks. Circulation and Its Relationship to the Book Collection and Academic Departments. *College and Research Libraries*, 37, 1976, 145–52.

128. Robert L. Burr. Evaluating Library Collections: A Case Study. *Journal of Academic Librarianship*, 5, 1979, 256–61.

129. Richard M. Dougherty and Laura L. Bloomquist. *Improving Access to Library Resources: The Influence of Organization of Library Collection and of User Attitudes Toward Innovative Services*. Metuchen, NJ: Scarecrow Press, 1974.

130. John H. Whaley Jr. An Approach to Collection Analysis. *Library Resources & Technical Services*, 25, July/September 1981, 330–38; Elliot Palais. Use of Course Analysis in Compiling a Collection Development Policy Statement for a University Library. *Journal of Academic Librarianship*, 13, March 1987, 8–13; and Michael R. Gabriel. Online Collection Evaluation, Course by Course. *Collection Building*, 8 (2), 1989, 20–24.

131. Vernon Leighton. Course Analysis: Techniques and Guidelines. *Journal of Academic Librarianship*, 21, May 1995, 175–79.

132. Gwen S. Lochstet. Course and Research Analysis Using a Coded Classification System. *Journal of Academic Librarianship*, 23, September 1997, 380–89.

133. M. B. Cassata and G. L. Dewey. Evaluation of a University Library Collection: Some Guidelines. *Library Resources & Technical Services*, 13, 1969, 450–57.

134. Albert Henderson. The Library Collection Failure Quotient: The Ratio of Interlibrary Borrowing to Collection Size. *The Journal of Academic Librarianship*, 26 (3), May 2000, 159–70.

135. Henderson, Library Collection Failure Quotient, 159–70.

136. Gary D. Byrd, D. A. Thomas, and Katherine E. Hughes. Collection Development Using Interlibrary Loan Borrowing and Acquisitions Statistics. *Bulletin of the Medical Library Association*, 70 (1), January 1982, 1–9.

137. Jennifer Knievel, Heather Wicht, and Lynn Silipigni Connaway. Use of Circulation Statistics and Interlibrary Loan Data in Collection Management. *College & Research Libraries*, 67 (1), January 2006, 35–49.

138. Lynn Wiley and Tina E. Chrzastowski. The Impact of Electronic Journals on Interlibrary Lending: A Longitudinal Study of Statewide Interlibrary Loan Article Sharing in Illinois. *Library Collections, Acquisitions, & Technical Services*, 29, 2005, 364–81.

139. Stanley J. Slote. *Weeding Library Collections: Library Weeding Methods*. Westport, CT: Libraries Unlimited, 1997.

140. Richard Kaplan, Marilyn Steinberg, and Joanne Doucette. Retention of Retrospective Print Journals in the Digital Age: Trends and Analysis. *Journal of the Medical Library Association,* 94 (4), October 2006, 387–93.

141. Taylor, Practical Solution to Weeding, 38.

142. Brain J. Baird. *Library Collection Assessment Through Statistical Sampling*. Toronto: Scarecrow Press, 2004.

143. Gorham Lane. Assessing the Undergraduates' Use of the University Library. *College & Research Libraries*, 27 (4), 1966, 277–82.

144. R. Nichols. Effects of Various College Characteristics on Student Aptitude Test Scores. *Journal of Educational Psychology*, 55 (1), 1964, 45–54.

145. A. Astin. Undergraduates' Achievement and Institutional "Excellence." *Science*, 161, 1968, 661–68.

146. D. A. Rock, J. A. Centra, and R.L. Linn. Relationship Between College C4aracteristics and Student Achievement. *American Educational Research Journal*, 7, 1970, 109–21.

147. Patrick Barkey. Patterns of Student Use of a College Library. *College & Research Libraries*, 26 (3), 1965, 115–18.

148. Jane Hiscock. Does Library Usage Affect Academic Performance? *Australian Academic & Research Libraries*, 17 (4), December 1986, 207–13.

149. Tony Mays. Do Undergraduates Need Their Libraries? *Australian Academic & Research Libraries*, 17 (2), June 1986, 56–62.

150. James Self. Reserve Readings and Student Grades: Analysis of a Case Study. *Library & Information Science Research*, 9 (1), January-March 1987, 29–40.

151. K. de Jager. Library Use and Academic Achievement. *South African Journal of Library & Information Science*, 65 (1), March 1997, 26–30.

152. J. M. Donovan. Do Librarians Deserve Tenure? Casting an Anthropological Eye on Role Definition within the Law School. *Law Library Journal*, 88 (3), 1996, 382–401.

153. Charles B. Harrell. The Use of an Academic Library by University Undergraduates. Ph.D. dissertation, University of North Texas, 1988.

154. Jennifer Wells. The Influence of Library Usage on Undergraduate Academic Success. *Australian Academic & Research Libraries*, June 1995, 121–28.

155. Dennis P. Carrigan. Collection Development—Evaluation. *The Journal of Academic Librarianship*, 22 (4), July 1996, 273–78.

156. George S. Bonn. Evaluation of the Collection. *Library Trends*, 29, January 1974, 272–73.

157. Stephen R. Lawrence, Lynn Silipigni Connaway, and Keith H. Brigham. Life Cycle Costs of Library Collections: Creation of Effective Performance and Cost Metrics for Library Resources. *College & Research Libraries*, 62 (6), November 2001, 541–53.

9

Evaluation of Electronic Resources

SERVICE DEFINITION

Libraries of all types and sizes are facing unrelenting pressure to provide access to an increasing number of electronic journals and other digital collections. The appeal for users is that they have desktop access to the electronic resources 24 hours a day without requiring a trip to the library itself. Libraries can link electronic journal contents from and to indexing and abstracting databases. Clearly digital collections save the library space, and given the relative ease with which they can be maintained, the library may experience some cost savings.

EVALUATION QUESTIONS

Libraries are in a period of transition as they move from traditional physical collections to a largely digital library. Some have called this a "hybrid" library. Having a clear understanding of who uses electronic resources and why they are being used can be helpful to libraries as they adjust their service delivery strategies to better meet the needs of their customers. Among the important questions that have been evaluated are the following:

- How do users of electronic resources differ from users of the library's physical collection?

- Do users use electronic resources exclusively, or do they also use the library's physical collection?

- What proportion of use of electronic resources occurs from within the library itself compared to access that is occurring from offices, dorm rooms, homes, and so forth?

- Why do people use electronic resources?

- Do users of electronic resources focus their use on a limited number of resources, or do they use a larger set of resources?

- What problems do people encounter when using a variety of electronic resources, each with its own unique user interface?

- What problems do libraries face when attempting to interpret access and download statistics?

Among the types of measures used to assess electronic resources are the following:

- **Transaction-based measures** include counts of search sessions, types of searches performed, number of records retrieved, and so forth.

- The transaction log file can also be examined to calculate **time-based measures** such as length of search sessions, system peak periods, time spent browsing versus downloading files, and so forth.

- **Cost-based measures** analyze the cost of providing the resources; determine the cost of providing the required hardware, software, networking, training, and site licensing; and so forth.

- **Use-based measures** examine the number of unique users, the number of times uses return each month, number of items viewed online, number of articles downloaded, user satisfaction, and so forth.

EVALUATION METHODS

Libraries can learn more about users and the uses of electronic resources through a variety of means, as shown in Table 9.1.

Table 9.1. Electronic Resources Evaluation Methods

Qualitative	Quantitative
Interviews	Surveys
Focus groups	Transaction log analysis
Observation	Download statistical analysis
Keeping a journal	Cost analysis
Paper prototypes and scenarios	Cost-benefit analysis
Card-sorting tests	

These methods, as well as their comparative strengths and limitations, were discussed in chapter 5. User surveys are often done, but the results vary depending on the type of questions asked. Assuming an adequate sample size, surveys allow for more accurate generalizations, but they are expensive and time-consuming to prepare, to conduct, and to interpret the results.

DISCUSSION OF PRIOR EVALUATIONS AND RESEARCH

Carol Tenopir prepared an excellent summary of user studies that have focused on electronic resources for the Council on Library and Information Resources.[1] Tenopir divided these studies into two groups. Tier 1 included major studies involving hundreds or thousands of subjects that employed a variety of evaluation methods and resulted in many publications. The Tier 2 category summarized the smaller, individual research studies.

Users

Obviously no single "user" is going to represent all users of electronic resources. In the academic environment, users of electronic resources are typically categorized into four primary groups—undergraduate students, graduate students, faculty, and researchers—and their use of electronic resources varies considerably. Public libraries will usually sort users into four groups as well: students, families, businesspeople, and senior citizens. Special libraries may separate users into two or three groups, but often users are analyzed in a single group.

The user of electronic journals will vary with subject discipline and the status of the individual:

- Faculty who use e-journals for research vary from a low of 61 percent (law) to a high of 83 percent (biological sciences).

- Faculty who use electronic journals for teaching range from a low of 28 percent (law) to a high of 56 percent (biological sciences).

- Student use also varies, from a low of 35 percent (law) to a high of 62 percent (biological sciences).[2] Of all survey respondents, 75 percent prefer online access to journal articles. And most respondents use online sources to find information about e-journals.

- Visits to the physical library by faculty and graduate students have declined, while visits to the virtual library have been increasing.[3]

- Disproportionately more use is made by graduate and postdoctoral students and faculty, while undergraduates' use is low compared to their population size.[4]

Susan Grajek found that about three-fourths of all users at Yale University Medical Center used their computers to access electronic journals. Grajek, who conducts an annual user's survey, has noted that use of electronic journals has been steadily increasing—from 50 percent in 1997 to 79 percent in 2004.[5] During a six-month period at the University of Southern California Medical Library, 28,000 full-text articles were viewed online, while only 1,800 uses were made of the corresponding print volumes.[6] A study at the Vanderbilt University Medical Center biomedical library found that students, residents, and fellows preferred electronic journals, while faculty preferred print journals. Although electronic journals are easier to access and search, print journals have higher quality text and figures.[7]

The importance of library gateways to electronic journals cannot be overemphasized. The biggest generators of ScienceDirect traffic are library gateways, followed by PubMed. In August 2005 ScienceDirect received over four million referrals from PubMed. Forty-three percent of full-text usage of ScienceDirect was for articles less than a year old, nearly 20 percent from articles one to two years old, and 27 percent for articles more than three years old.[8]

Faculty and students vary in their preferences for using print or online formats of journals. Most students preferred the convenience of online journal articles, while faculty members were more inclined to seek the best articles for their topic regardless of format.[9] In a comparison of the use of journals by faculty and students, Kathleen Joswick and Jeanne Stierman found that students preferred to use more generalized journals, while faculty often used highly specialized journals.[10] At the University of Maryland, faculty members were more likely to use electronic journals than print journals on a weekly or daily basis.[11] Faculty members who publish more frequently are more aware of and are more likely to submit articles to electronic journals.[12] Junior faculty tend to use electronic resources more than senior faculty.[13]

The finding that high school students and undergraduates prefer to search the Internet for school-related tasks has clearly and consistently been shown in a number of studies—see, for example, OCLC,[14] the Pew studies,[15] and Leah Graham.[16] The OCLC study found that 45 percent of U.S. respondents have never used an electronic database, and 57 percent were not sure the library offered access to online databases.

One recent project used a Web-based survey that measured both in-library and remote usage of networked electronic resources. The project, called MINES for Libraries—Measuring the Impact of Networked Electronic Services—asked survey respondents to indicate the purpose of their searching. The possible categories for using online resources included sponsored (funded) research, instruction/education/departmental research, patient care, and all other activities. The survey discovered that remote users of electronic resources exceed in-library use by a four to one or larger margin. Not surprisingly, those conducting sponsored research use the electronic resources from their offices rather than visiting the library. In addition, in-library and on-campus use of the electronic resources greatly exceeds off-campus usage. Most of the usage for sponsored research was done by faculty, staff, and researchers.[17] Grant-funded research accounted for almost one-third of networked electronic services activity, and this searching was done from on campus but not from within the library.[18]

Use

Scientists spend a considerable portion of their time reading journal articles. During the 1990s, scientists averaged 120 readings of scholarly journal articles per year; surveys in the 2000s indicate that the average has risen to 130. University scientists read more—they average 188 readings per year—and three-fourths of the readings are for research purposes. Forty percent of the readings are for teaching purposes. It is interesting to note that, on average, scientists whose work is recognized through achievement awards read more than non-award winners.[19] Medical scientists read much more than others, and engineers read the least. While medical faculty read more articles than others, they prefer to have the information digested in a way that saves them time.[20]

Typically scientists spend well over 100 hours per year reading scholarly articles, an indirect measure of the value these individuals attach to this activity. Not surprisingly, medical scientists spend more time reading—118 hours per year—than their peers in other disciplines.

All of this reading is done to improve the quality of teaching and research and to save time and money. The information is sought for a number of reasons, including

- primary research,
- current awareness or continuing education,
- communications-related purposes (making presentations, writing, consulting), and
- background research.

University medical scientists also read for the purposes of clinical practice and teaching.

Among the factors affecting choice of print or online journal articles, the time spent to acquire articles may have the strongest correlation to preference of format. Described by Barry Schwartz as a "satisficing" behavior, people may take what is available rather than seeking the best available due to time pressures, efficiency, ease of access, and around-the-clock availability of electronic resources from anywhere.[21] Several studies have shown that accessibility is associated with the amount of database use.[22]

Different motivations or information needs will affect information seeking and use. A study of students and faculty at the University of West England found that the greatest predictor of use of electronic resources was whether or not the individual was engaged in research.[23] Another study found that level of instruction is not correlated to amount of database use.[24] Yet another study determined there was no relationship between instruction in the use of electronic resources and increased use of those resources.[25]

For faculty, about half of the articles they read are identified by browsing recently published issues of journals as a by-product of keeping up with the literature and conducting background research. About a fourth of all readings are selected as the result of online searching of abstracting and indexing databases, Web search engines, and online journal collections and receiving a current awareness message. Other articles are identified as the result of a citation in another publication or from another colleague.[26] One analysis suggests that use of electronic resources are likely to be used most heavily in fields in which directed searching is the dominant search method and less in fields in which browsing and chaining are the preferred search methods.[27]

The majority of readings came from articles published in the previous year. Typically, for articles older than two years the scientists reading the articles reported that they were rereading them.[28] An analysis of the impact of online journals on the citation patterns of medical faculty over a 10-year period found that the number of journals cited per year increased and that the researchers were not more likely to cite online journals or less likely to cite journals only available in print.[29]

At Ohio State University, 69 percent of survey respondents use electronic resources weekly, yet half of all undergraduates never use any electronic resources or are not aware of the availability of such resources.[30]

OhioLINK is a consortium of 84 college and university libraries in Ohio that mounts electronic journals on its own automated library system, thus allowing it to track actual usage of this resource, which provides access to more than 5,200 journals from 22 publishers. The number of journal articles that have been downloaded has increased dramatically, to 16,500,000 in July 2007, as shown in Figure 9.1 (p. 154). The licensing of the electronic journals by the OhioLINK consortium has meant that each library saves money and still is able to provide its students and faculty access to a much larger array of journals than they would have on their own.[31] Forty percent of the journal titles account for 85 percent of the article downloads, and 1 percent of the journal titles account for about 10 percent of the downloads. Slightly more than half (58 percent) of the articles downloaded were from journals not held in print at the downloading user's library.[32] No institution will use every available title, and some journal titles will be used infrequently by all institutions.

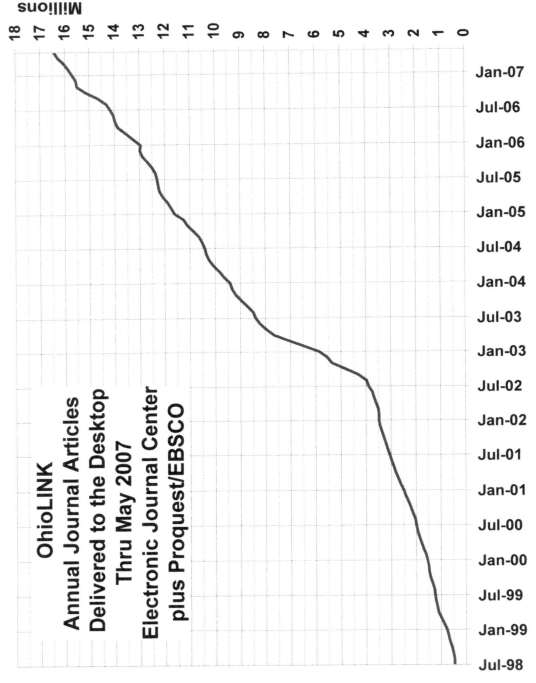

Figure 9.1. OhioLINK Annual Journal Articles Delivered to the Desktop Thru May 2007

A further analysis of the OhioLINK transaction logs showed that nearly two-thirds preferred the search engine and were more likely to look at a wider range of available journals. Another 23 percent of user sessions selected the alphabetical list option and were more likely to view only a single article.[33]

However, a large geographic consortium may not always be the best model. Philip Davis analyzed the use of 200 titles in the sciences and social sciences among the libraries that are members of the NorthEast Research Libraries Consortium and found that larger institutions used a wider range of journal titles, while smaller institutions only used about 30 percent of the electronic resources.[34] Davis suggested that consortiums based on size and type of library may be more cost effective.

A large percentage of use is concentrated in a small proportion of the journal titles, another manifestation of the 80/20 Rule, which seems to hold true for electronic journals, as noted by several studies that examined transaction logs.[35] James Stemper and Janice Jaguszewski suggest that the rule is closer to 70/30 in the online environment in a project that compared vendor and local data.[36]

John Crawford et al. noted that from 2001 to 2003, expenditures for electronic journals at the Glasgow Caledonian University increased more than six times (the percent of the acquisitions budget devoted to electronic resources rose from 4 percent to 22 percent in that time period).[37]

Most individuals report that they print selected articles from online sources for later reading and for their own archives, and they do not like the HTML format for printing.[38] Slightly more than three-fourths of the scholars begin their searching at a multi-journal Web site with links to full text, such as PubMed, ScienceDirect, Medline, or EbscoHost, rather than at a specific journal Web site.

Users of electronic journals typically search journal tables of contents, briefly scan the full text of the article, then request a PDF version of the article for printing or archiving. Younger scholars report that they are frequent e-journal users, while older scholars are troubled by the user interface at multi-journal Web sites and thus use e-journals less frequently.[40] Focus groups at the University of Washington noted that many of the databases licensed by the library are too complex to use, and there is not enough time or frequency of use to learn how to use them well.[41]

> One thing is clear. Users use what's available. And increasingly available means immediately.
> —Carol Diedrichs[39]

Since 1977 Donald King and his colleagues have asked faculty, researchers, scientists, and students about the time they spend reading and use of the print and electronic journal collections—including personal subscriptions and collections maintained by the library. A recent study at the University of Pittsburgh found that *if* the library's journal collection—physical and electronic—were not available, faculty would spend an additional 250,000 hours and some $2.1 million to use alternative sources to locate the desired articles.[42] Don King and his colleagues used a contingent valuation methodology, which asks survey respondents how much time and money they would spend to obtain the information they currently receive from the library's journal collection if the library collection were unavailable. Further analysis suggested that the total value of the library's journal collection to the university is $13.48 million less the costs for creating and maintaining the collection of $3.43 million, for a net value of $11.61 million. In other words, if there were no university library journal collection—print and electronic—it would cost the university 4.38 times the cost of the current library collection in faculty time and other expenditures for the same amount of research and information gathering to be carried out.

A survey of faculty members at the University of Idaho Library found that faculty wanted the library to assist in finding time by providing better electronic resources and services.[43] However, faculty were unaware of the range of electronic resources and lack the time to learn more about how to make effective use of electronic resources.

Ziming Liu surveyed graduate students and found that 84 percent use electronic resources all or most of the time.[44] College and university students report that they are frustrated with their campus libraries and would like the library to

- become more customer focused;

- make it easier to use and access library information;

- offer interactive maps, study guides, and resource guides;

- provide links to quality Web sites and other library catalogs; and

- make it easier to access electronic resources remotely.[45]

The Urban Libraries Council sponsored a large-scale telephone survey in early 2000 and found a difference in service ratings for the library and the Internet:[46]

Greater service ratings for the library	*Greater service ratings for the Internet*
Ease of use	Ease of getting there
Low cost	Time to get there
Availability of paper copy	Hours of access
Accuracy of information	Range of resources
Helpfulness of librarians	Expect to find what is sought
Privacy	Able to act immediately
	Currency of information
	Enjoyment of browsing
	Able to work alone
	Fun

E-Books

A comparison of 7,490 book titles and the same titles available as electronic books (e-books) at Duke University found that e-books received 11 percent more use than their print counterparts.[47] E-books are liked by students for several reasons:

- **Convenience:** Content is available immediately in digital format.

- **Cost savings:** They reduce the number of books purchased for classes.

- **Currency:** Recent content is valued.

- **Efficiency:** Users can browse or search and then print just those portions of interest. Students find reading online too disjointed.

- **An alternative copy:** They are available when the print version is checked out or no print version is available.[48]

A study of NetLibrary e-book use found that titles in economics, business, and computer science were most heavily used.[49] An analysis of Questia, a commercial online library service that provides access to e-books, found that literature was the most popular subject for research, followed by sociology and history, at the University of Rochester.[50]

From the perspective of the user, electronic resources are so attractive and heavily used because

- they provide access to information quickly;
- they provide access to a wide range of information;
- desktop access to information is easy—it saves time and energy—and can be done anytime and anywhere; and
- downloading and printing articles is now fairly routine.

Accuracy

Online journal articles in full-text databases are not always fully equivalent to print. Nancy Sprague and Mary Beth Chambers found that 45 percent of full-text articles were not as current as the print journal, 17 percent of major articles were missing, and many graphics were omitted in the databases.[51]

It is unclear why more research is not directed at the issue of accuracy and comprehensiveness of the available electronic resources.

Impact on Print Journals

The availability and use of electronic journals can have a significant impact on the use of the library's print journal collection. Sandra De Groote and Josephine Dorsch noted a sizeable decrease in print journal use, regardless of whether journals were available only in print or both online and in print.[52] A comparison of a matched set of biomedical journals available in print and online demonstrated that users overwhelmingly selected journals in the online format.[53] Others noting a reduction in the use of print journals include Vaughan[54] (a 47 percent drop from 1999 to 2002) and Pongracz Sennyey et al.[55] (a 41 percent decrease from 1998 to 2000). Chandra Prabha analyzed ARL data from 2002 to 2006 and noted a sevenfold increase in subscriptions to electronic-only journals and a reduction in subscriptions to print-only journals of over 50 percent, while subscriptions to both print and electronic journals remained about the same.[56]

A study in an academic medical sciences library compared print and online usage for 270 journals, both versions of which were available, over a two-year period. Print journal usage fell 22 and 30 percent over the two-year period, and frequently accessed print titles were also frequently accessed in their online versions. Also, usage of online journals outstripped that of print titles by a factor of 10 or more.[57] In a liberal arts college library, Steve Black noted that a decrease in print use is greater for those titles available online in full text, while use of print journals not available in full text dropped 34 percent from 1996 to 2003.[58]

Providing a contrary view, Tammy Siebenberg and her colleagues at Washington State University found that online availability definitely increased the total use of journals, and that users' migration from print to electronic resources depends on the subject area. From the user's perspective, quality and pertinence are still the dominant factors in journal selection.[59]

Impact on the Library

As demand for electronic resources has grown, there has been unrelenting pressure to spend more money on such resources, as evidenced by the increased percentage of the acquisitions budget spent on them.

Carol Montgomery prepared a comprehensive analysis of the impact that electronic journals are having on the various departments and activities within an academic library.[60] Montgomery noted, for example, that staff time to reshelve print journals decreased, while photocopying, use of reserve materials, and interlibrary loan requests for articles all also declined:

> Health science libraries have also noted a decline in the number of photocopies made, interlibrary loan requests, and physical attendance in the library as the result of providing access to a broad set of electronic resources.[61]

Providing access to electronic resources requires that a library reorganize its workflows and procedures. It will also have to hire or train staff with a new set of skills to negotiate the licenses for the electronic resources. David Lewis, director of the Indiana University Purdue University at Indianapolis library, noted during a presentation at the 2006 Living the Future Conference that unless current collection practices are changed, libraries cannot change except on the margins. He suggests that academic libraries need to "follow the user" and revise their collection development strategies by significantly reducing the number of books and print journal subscriptions and supporting open access by claiming responsibility for the institutional repository.[62]

Determining what print subscriptions to cancel will require the library to analyze use of both the print and electronic collections. Yet one of the challenges is the fact that libraries can provide access to electronic runs of journal that are relatively short. Thus, how should download statistics that are provided by vendors be used? Parker Ladwig and Andrew Sommese suggest adjusting use statistics using a journal's ISI *Journal Citation Reports* half-life. The authors contend that total use will be undercounted, but that the undercounting will be proportional across disciplines. Their approach allows a library to calculate an adjusted cost per use that can be used to assist in making cancellation decisions.[63]

SUMMARY

Caution must be exercised when attempting to draw conclusions about the availability of electronic resources because it is a fairly recent occurrence. It is important to know when a study has been conducted and how long electronic resources have been used by respondents in a specific study. A review of the available research about the availability and use of electronic resources suggests the following:

- Customers prefer online access to electronic resources that are licensed by the library.
- Libraries are spending an increasing percent of their acquisitions budget on electronic resources.
- A library should calculate a cost per use of a journal or a package of journals as part of an ongoing assessment process.
- Use of some electronic resources is quite high.
- Vendors need to improve the statistics that they provide to their library customers.
- The purchase of back files should be considered, as their cost is typically fairly moderate.
- Including costs for space, staff, and an automated system, the costs for electronic resources are lower than their print counterparts.

- Libraries will need to be more creative in communicating the value of and the availability of electronic resources to their current and prospective customers.

- The increasing use of electronic resources means that a library must adjust its expenditures on print journals and will likely need to restructure staff positions to cope with licensing and access issues.

FUTURE RESEARCH

A number of libraries, especially larger academic libraries, are involved in digitizing special collections and other unique materials. In a parallel vein, Google is involved in a mass digitization project that will convert more than five million books into machine-readable form. A similar project is underway involving several libraries, with funding provided by Microsoft, Yahoo, and others. Clearly having such a massive amount of content available online is going to have serious implications and consequences for all types of libraries, which will need to be studied. Among the issues that will likely be investigated and evaluated in the near-term future are the following:

- Should an increasing amount of materials now housed in a library be moved to storage facilities?

- Will a multiplicity of user interfaces provide so many obstacles that users will abandon all attempts at gaining access?

- How many users need to access the digital materials created by a library to make the investment cost effective?

- How does the availability of electronic resources affect a faculty member's ability to teach?

- Do the increasing amounts of electronic resources that are downloaded (saved or printed) increase the research productivity of users?

- Do graduate students who use electronic resources have better academic success?

- How can a library communicate the value of high-quality electronic resources to users in a way that will affect their searching behaviors?

- In short, what are the impacts of the ready availability of electronic resources?

NOTES

1. Carol Tenopir. *Use and Users of Electronic Library Resources: An Overview and Analysis of Recent Research Studies*. Washington, DC: Council on Library and Information Resources, August 2003. Available at http://www.clir.org/pubs/reports/pub120/pub120.pdf.

2. Amy Friedlander. Dimensions and Use of the Scholarly Information Environment: Introduction to a Data Set. Washington, DC: Council on Library and Information Resources, 2002. Available at http://www.clir.org/pubs/reports/pub110/contents.html. See also Leigh Watson Healy, Lynn Dagar, and Katherine Medaglia Wilkie. *Customer Report for the Digital Library Federation/Council on Library and Information Resources*. Burlingame, CA: Outsell, 2002.

3. Steve Hiller. How Different Are They? A Comparison by Academic Area of Library Use, Priorities and Information Needs at the University of Washington. *Issues in Science and Technology Librarianship*, 33, Winter 2002. Available at http://istl.org/istl/02–winter/article1.html.

4. Tschera Harkness Connell, Sally A. Rogers, and Carol Pitts Diedrichs. OhioLINK Electronic Journal Use at Ohio State University. *portal: Libraries and the Academy*, 5 (3), 2005, 371–90.

5. Susan Grajek. *Annual Medical Center Questionnaire of Library and Computer Use.* Available at http://its.med.yale.edu/about_itsmed/research/index.html.

6. David H. Morse and William A. Clintworth. Comparing Patterns of Print and Electronic Journal Use in an Academic Health Science Library. *Issues in Science and Technology Librarianship,* 28, Fall 2000. Available at http://istl.org/00–fall/refereed.html.

7. Nila A. Sathe, Jenifer L. Grady, and Nunzia B. Guise. Print Versus Electronic Journals: A Preliminary Investigation into the Effect of Journal Format on Research Processes. *Journal of the Medical Library Association,* 90 (2), April 2002, 235–43.

8. Alex Lankester. What We Know About ScienceDirect User Behavior. *Library Connect*, 4 (1), 2006, 10–11.

9. Juris Dilevko and Lisa Gottlieb. Print Sources in an Electronic Age: A Vital Part of the Research Process for Undergraduate Students. *Journal of Academic Librarianship*, 28 (6), November 2002, 381–92.

10. Kathleen E. Joswick and Jeanne Koekkock Stierman. Perceptions vs. Use: Comparing Faculty Evaluations of Journal Titles with Student Usage. *Journal of Academic Librarianship*, 21 (6), November 1995, 454–58.

11. Irma F. Dillon and Karla L. Hahn. Are Researchers Ready for the Electronic-Only Journal Collection? Results of a Survey at the University of Maryland. *portal: Libraries and the Academy*, 2 (3), 2002, 375–90.

12. Susan E. Hahn, Cheri Speier, Jonathan Palmer, and Daniel Wren. Advantages and Disadvantages of Electronic Journals: Business School Faculty Views. *Journal of Business and Finance Librarianship*, 5 (1), 1999, 19–31.

13. Erin T. Smith. Changes in Faculty Reading Behaviors: The Impact of Electronic Journals on the University of Georgia. *Journal of Academic Librarianship*, 29 (3), 2003, 162–68.

14. Cathy De Rosa, Joanne Cantrell, Janet Hawk, and Alane Wilson. *College Students' Perceptions of Libraries and Information Resources.* Dublin, OH: OCLC, 2006.

15. Steve Jones. *The Internet Goes to College.* Pew Internet & American Life Project. 2002. Available at http://www.pewinternet.org/reports/toc.asp?Report=71; Douglas Levin and Sousan Arafeh. *The Digital Disconnect: The Widening Gap Between Internet-Savvy Students and Their Schools.* Pew Internet & American Life Project. 2002. Available at http://www.pewinternet.org/reports/toc.asp?Report=67.

16. Leah Graham. Of Course It's True; I Saw It on the Internet!: Critical Thinking in the Internet Era. *Communications of the ACM*, 46 (5), 2003, 71–75.

17. Brinley Franklin and Terry Plum. Networked Electronic Services Usage Patterns at Four Academic Health Sciences Libraries. *Performance Measurement & Metrics*, 3 (3), 2002, 123–33.Available at www.arl.org/stats/newmeas/emetrics/Franklin_081102.pdf; see also Brinley Franklin and Terry Plum. Successful Web Survey Methodologies for Measuring the Impact of Networked Electronic Services (MINES for libraries). *IFLA Journal*, 32 (1), 2006, 28–40..

18. Brinley Franklin and Terry Plum. Library Usage Patterns in the Electronic Information Environment. *Information Research,* 9 (4), July 2004.

19. Carol Tenopir and Donald W. King. The Use and Value of Scientific Journals: Past, Present and Future. *Serials*, 14 (2), July 2001, 113–20.

20. Carol Tenopir, Donald W. King, and Amy Bush. Medical Faculty's Use of Print and Electronic Journals: Changes Over Time and in Comparison with Scientists. *Journal of the Medical Library Association*, 92 (2), April 2004, 233–41.

21. Barry Schwartz. The Tyranny of Choice. *Scientific American*, 290, April 2004, 70–75.

22. Yumin Jiang, Jeanne A. Baker, and Lynda S. Kresge. Toward Better Access to Full-Text Aggregator Collections. *Serials Librarian*, 39, 2000, 291–97; and Jie Tian, Sharon Wiles-Young, and Elizabeth Parang. The Convergence of User Needs, Collection Building and the Electronic Publishing Marketplace. *Serials Librarian*, 38, 2000, 333–39.

23. Dianne Nelson. The Uptake of Electronic Journals by Academics in the UK, Their Attitudes Towards Them and Their Potential Impact on Scholarly Communication. *Information Services & Use*, 21 (3/4), 2001, 205–14.

24. Carol Tenopir and Eleanor J. Read. Patterns of Database Use in Academic Libraries. *College & Research Libraries*, 61, 2000, 234–46.

25. Debbie Malone and Carol Videon. Assessing Undergraduate Use of Electronic Resources: A Quantitative Analysis of Works Cited. *Research Strategies*, 15 (3), 1997, 151–58.

26. Donald W. King, Carol Tenopir, Carol Hansen Montgomery, and Sarah E. Aerni. Patterns of Journal Use by Faculty at Three Diverse Universities. *D-Lib Magazine*, 9 (10), October 2003. Available at http://www.dlib.org/dlib/october03/king/10king.html.

27. Sanna Talja and Hanni Maula. Reasons for the Use and Non-use of Electronic Journals and Databases: A Domain Analytic Study in Four Scholarly Disciplines. *Journal of Documentation*, 59 (6), 2003, 673–91.

28. Carol Tenopir, Donald W. King, P. Boyce, M. Grayson, and K. L. Paulson, Relying on Electronic Journals: Reading Patterns of Astronomers. *Journal of the American Society for Information Science and Technology*, 56 (8), April 2005, 786–802.

29. Sandra L. De Groote, Mary Schultz, and Marceline Doranski. Online Journals' Impact on the Citation Patterns of Medical Faculty. *Journal of the Medical Library Association*, 93 (2), April 2005, 223–28.

30. Tschera Harkness Connell, Sally A. Rogers, and Carol Pitts Diedrichs. OhioLINK Electronic Journal Use at Ohio State University. *portal: Libraries and the Academy*, 5 (3), 2005, 371–90.

31. Carol Pitts Diedrichs. E-Journals: The OhioLINK Experience. *Library Collections, Acquisitions and Technical Services*. 25 (2), 2001, 191–210.

32. Thomas J. Sanville. A Method Out of the Madness: OhioLINK's Collaborative Response to the Serials Crisis Three Years Later: A Progress Report. *The Serials Librarian*, 40 (1/2), 2001, 129–55; and Anita Cook and Thomas Dowling. Linking from Index to Primary Source: The OhioLINK Model. *The Journal of Academic Librarianship*, 29 (5), September 2003, 320–26.

33. David Nicholas, Paul Huntington, Hamid R. Jamali, and Carol Tenopir. Finding Information in (Very Large) Digital Libraries: A Deep Log Approach to Determining Differences in Use According to Method of Access. *The Journal of Academic Librarianship*, 32 (2), March 2006, 119–26.

34. Philip M. Davis. Patterns in Electronic Journal Usage: Challenging the Composition of Geographic Consortia. *College & Research Libraries*, 63 (6), 2002, 484–97.

35. M. P. Day. Electronic Journal Usage and Policy at UMIST. *Information Services & Usage*, 21 (3/4), 2001, 135–37; Philip M. Davis. Patterns in Electronic Journal Usage: Challenging the Composition of Geographic Consortia. *College & Research Libraries*, 63 (6), 2002, 484–97; and Hans Roes. Promotion of Electronic Journals to Users by Libraries—A Case Study of Tilburg University Library. Presented at the UK Serials Group Promotion and Management of Electronic Journals in London, 28 October 1999. Available at http://drcwww.kub.nl/~roes/articles/london99.htm.

36. James A. Stemper and Janice M. Jaguszewski. Usage Statistics for Electronic Journals: An Analysis of Local and Vendor Counts. *Collection Management*, 28 (4), 2003, 3–22.

37. John Crawford, Angel De Vincente, and Stuart Clink. Use and Awareness of Electronic Information Services by Students at Glasgow Caledonia University: A Longitudinal Study. *Journal of Librarianship & Information Science*, 36 (3), September 2004, 101–17.

38. Institute for the Future. *E-Journal Usage and Scholarly Practice*. 2002. Available at http://ejust.stanford.edu/findings/full_0801.pdf. See also Institute for the Future. *Final Synthesis Report of the E-Journal User Study*. 2002. Available at http://ejust.stanford.edu/SR-786.ejustfinal.html.

39. Diedrichs, E-Journals, 208.

40. Institute for the Future, *E-Journal Usage and Scholarly Practice*.

41. Steve Hiller. Evaluating Bibliographic Database Use: Beyond the Numbers. *Against the Grain*, 15 (6), December 2003–January 2004, 26–30.

42. Donald W. King, Sarah Aerni, Fern Brody, Matt Hebison, and Amy Knapp. *The Use and Outcomes of University Library Print and Electronic Collections*. Pittsburgh: University of Pittsburgh, Sara Fine Institute for Interpersonal Behavior and Technology, April 2004; and Donald W. King, Sarah Aerni, Fern Brody, Matt Hebison, and Paul Kohberger. *Comparative Cost of the University of Pittsburgh Electronic and Print Library Collections*. Pittsburgh: University of Pittsburgh, Sara Fine Institute for Interpersonal Behavior and Technology, May 2004. See also Roger C. Schonfeld, Donald W. King, Ann Okerson, and Eileen Gifford Fenton. Library Periodicals Expenses: Comparison of Non-Subscription Costs of Print and Electronic Formats on a Life-Cycle Basis. *D-Lib Magazine*, 10 (1), January 2004. Available at http://www.dlib.org/dlib/january04/schonfeld/01schonfeld.html; Donald W. King, Carol Tenopir, Carol Hansen Montgomery, and Sarah E. Aerni. Patterns of Journal Use by Faculty at Three Diverse Universities. *D-Lib Magazine*, 9 (10), October 2003. Available at http://www.dlib.org/dlib/october03/king/10king.html.

43. Maria Anna Jankowska. Identifying University Professors' Information Needs in the Challenging Environment of Information and Communication Technologies. *The Journal of Academic Librarianship*, 30 (1), January 2004, 51–66.

44. Ziming Liu. Print vs. Electronic Resources: A Study of User Perceptions, Preferences, and Use. *Information Processing & Management*, 42, 2006, 583–92.

45. Steve Jones. *The Internet Goes to College*. Pew Internet & American Life Project. 2002. Available at http://www.pewinternet.org/reports/toc.asp?Report=71; Douglas Levin and Sousan Arafeh. *The Digital Disconnect: The Widening Gap Between Internet-Savvy Students and Their Schools*. Pew Internet & American Life Project. 2002. Available at http://www.pewinternet.org/reports/toc.asp?Report=67. See also OCLC. *How Academic Librarians Can Influence Students' Web-Based Information Choices*. OCLC White Paper on the Information Habits of College Students. Available at http://www2.oclc.org/oclc/pdf/printondemand/informationhabits.pdf.

46. George D'Elia, Corinne Jorgensen, Joseph Woelfel, and Eleanor Jo Rodger. The Impact of the Internet on Public Library Use: An Analysis of the Current Consumer Market for Library and Internet Services. *Journal of the American Society for Information Science and Technology*, 53 (10), 2002, 802–20.

47. Justin Littman and Lynn Silipigni Connaway. A Circulation Analysis of Print Books and E-Books in an Academic Research Library. *LRTS*, 48 (4), October 2004, 256–62.

48. Peter Hernon, Rosita Hopper, Michael R. Leach, Laura L. Saunders, and Jane Zhang. E-book Use by Students: Undergraduates in Economics, Literature and Nursing. *The Journal of Academic Librarianship,* 33 (1), January 2007, 3–13.

49. Carol Ann Hughes and Nancy L. Buckman. Use of Electronic Monographs in the Humanities and Social Sciences. *Library Hi Tech*, 19 (4), 2001, 368–75.

50. *netLibrary eBook Usage at the University of Rochester Libraries*. Available at http://www.library.rochester.edu/main/ebooks/studies/analysis.pdf.

51. Nancy Sprague and Mary Beth Chambers. Full Text Databases and the Journal Cancellation Process: A Case Study. *Serials Review*, 26 (3), October 2000, 19–31.

52. Sandra L. De Groote and Josephine L. Dorsch. Online Journals: Impact on Print Usage. *Journal of the Medical Library Association*, 89 (4), October 2001, 372–78; and Sandra L. De Groote and Josephine L. Dorsch. Measuring Use Patterns of Online Journals and Databases. *Journal of the Medical Library Association*, 91 (2), April 2003, 231–40.

53. David H. Morse and William A. Clintworth. Comparing Patterns of Print and Electronic Journal Use in an Academic Health Science Library. *Issues in Science and Technology Librarianship*, 28, Fall 2000. Available at http://www.istl.org/00-fall/refereed.html.

54. K. T. L. Vaughan. Changing Patterns of Print Journals in the Digital Age: Impacts of Electronic Equivalents on Print Chemistry Journal Use. *Journal of the American Society for Information Science and Technology*, 54 (12), October 2003, 1149–52.

55. Pongracz Sennyey, Gillian D. Ellern, and Nancy Newsome. Collection Development and a Long-Term Periodical Use Study: Methodology and Implications. *Serials Review*, 28 (1), Spring 2002, 38–44.

56. Chandra Prabha. Shifting from Print to Electronic Journals in ARL University Libraries. *Serials Review,* 12 (1), 2006, 4–13.

57. Oliver Obst. Patterns and Costs of Printed and Online Journal Usage. *Health Information and Libraries Journal,* 20, 2003, 22–32.

58. Steve Black. Impact of Full Text on Print Journal Use at a Liberal Arts College. *LRTS*, 49 (1), 2005, 19–26.

59. Tammy Siebenberg, Betty Galbraith, and Eileen E. Brady. Print versus Electronic Journal Use in Three Sci/Tech Disciplines: What's Going On Here? *College & Research Libraries*, 65 (5), September 2004, 427–38.

60. Carol Hansen Montgomery. Measuring the Impact of an Electronic Journal Collection on Library Costs. *D-Lib Magazine*, 6 (10), October 2000. Available at http://www.dlib.org/dlib/october00/montgomery/10montgomery.html.

61. Suzetta Burrows. A Review of Electronic Journal Acquisitions, Management, and Use in Health Science Libraries. *Journal of the Medical Library Association*, 94 (1), January 2006, 67–74.

62. David W. Lewis. Reflections on the Future of Library Collections. Presentation made at the Living the Future 6 Conference on 6 April 2006 in Tucson, Arizona. Available at http://www.library.arizona.edu/conferences/ltf/2006/proceedings.html#future.

63. J. Parker Ladwig and Andrew J. Sommese. Using Cited Half-Life to Adjust Download Statistics. *College & Research Libraries*, 66, November 2005, 527–42.

10

Evaluation of Reference Services

SERVICE DEFINITION

A library customer may approach a staff member at a number of service locations, which may be called by a variety of names—circulation desk, information counter, reference desk, or customer service—as well as via the Internet (e-mail or a virtual "Ask a librarian" service). Ignoring the quickly dispatched directional queries and the need to provide technical assistance with computers, printers, and so forth, the focus of this chapter is the evaluation of reference services. As shown in Figure 10.1, the provision of reference service involves a customer, a librarian, the interaction between the two, and access to a set of resources that can be used to answer the question.

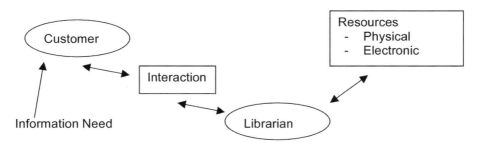

Figure 10.1. Components of Reference Service

The customer interacts with the librarian to resolve an information need using a variety of methods: face-to-face in the library, over a telephone, via e-mail, in a 24/7 chat-based electronic tool, via instant messaging, and so forth. The customer's knowledge about his or her information need may be complete and accurate or quite limited and ill-defined. But more important is the customer's ability to accurately communicate and interact with the reference librarian to fulfill the information need.

The librarian's ability to provide an accurate answer and a total experience that the customer will consider professional and satisfactory depends on a number of factors:

- The experience and training of the librarian
- The librarian's knowledge of and familiarity with the library's collection
- The librarian's knowledge of and familiarity with electronic resources
- The number of people waiting for service
- The "reference interview" communication skills
- The attitude of the librarian and his or her commitment to providing quality and friendly service
- The communication skills of the user to describe the information need
- Implementation of reference policies, reflected in management policies and reward and recognition practices

EVALUATION QUESTIONS

Libraries have examined a variety of issues surrounding reference service, including the following questions:

- Is use of reference services declining or increasing?
- Is an answer to a question provided?
- Is the answer provided accurate?
- How long does a customer wait for reference service?
- Is the customer satisfied with the answer provided?
- Is the customer satisfied with the complete reference experience?
- What interpersonal and other skills are important?
- What categories are used to record each reference transaction?
- What proportion of the physical reference collection is being used?
- What reference electronic resources are being used? Are other electronic resources needed?
- What is the cost to the library to answer each question?
- How does the cost to the library vary if service is provided in person, over the telephone, via e-mail, via fax, or using an electronic system?
- What is the value of providing reference to a library's customers?

EVALUATION METHODS

In general, there are a number of means for evaluating reference services. The more frequently used methods include surveys, focus groups, interviews, and observation. A broader classification of these methods includes

- descriptive analysis,
- obtrusive methods,
- unobtrusive methods,
- observation,
- conjoint analysis, and
- cost-benefit analysis.

DISCUSSION OF PRIOR EVALUATIONS AND RESEARCH

Libraries as a Source of Information

Some would suggest that libraries are either losing or have lost their quest to be the primary information provider for their service populations. Others would suggest that "losing" is a myth and that libraries were never frequently considered or used as a source for information even prior to the Internet. The recent evidence is fairly compelling. The use of reference services in large academic and public libraries has been declining in recent years. A recent OCLC survey found that people turn first to the Internet to get answers to their questions. Libraries are rarely, if ever, thought of as a potential source of information. Some 65 percent of survey respondents do not seek assistance, either while online or visiting the library.[1] However, of those who do seek assistance, more than three-fourths prefer to interact directly with a librarian. The survey respondents also indicated that search engines deliver better quality and quantity of information than librarian-assisted searching—and at greater speed. In addition, a recent study found that answers to ready reference questions on the Internet are very likely to be accurate, especially if the site is in the top five retrieved by Google. Many of the commonly proposed indicators of accuracy, for example, no advertising being present, were not related to accuracy.[2]

A survey of ARL libraries found that the number of reference transactions had declined 34 percent from 1991 to 2004. In addition, library customers now use a variety of methods to communicate with reference librarians—telephone, e-mail, chat reference, and reference question Web forms.[3]

Yet this is not a recent phenomenon, as Ching-chih Chen and Peter Hernon discovered more than 25 years ago when they surveyed 2,400 New England residents to learn about their information needs. The library ranked ninth, behind such sources as own experience; friends and acquaintances; newspapers or books; someone in a store or business; co-workers; professors, doctors, or lawyers; government officials; and television.[4]

Historically libraries have gathered counts of reference transactions to demonstrate the value of the service to funding decision makers (use equals value) and to better align staffing and service hours. Traditionally libraries have recorded each reference transaction as "directional," "ready reference," or "search/instructional." More recently Debra Warner suggested using the categories of non-resource-based, skill-based, strategy-based, or consultation.[5] However, reference staff are inconsistent about how they class and record data, regardless of the categories used. One study found as much as 45 percent variation in how staff recorded service transactions.[6]

Librarian Skills

A study by George Hawley suggested that libraries need to view reference as a service that incorporates a broader perspective and admit that it does a poor job of referring customers to other libraries or sources to satisfy the information need of the customer. In addition, the librarian is likely to be affected during the reference process by the user's status.[7]

The library profession has developed two guidelines for recommended behavior of reference service providers: *Facets of Quality for Digital References Services* and the RUSA *Guidelines for Behavioral Performance of Reference and Information Service Providers*. Reference staff members will adopt such behaviors through training and feedback about their actual performance. Actual behaviors have a strong impact on the perceived performance of service providers.[8] Nonverbal communication also plays an important role in the user's perception of the librarian's approachability. One study found that eye contact signaled to the user that the reference librarian was approachable.[9]

Several studies have shown that a library customer does not know who is a professional librarian and who is a paraprofessional. For example, Patricia Dewdney and Catherine Ross found that only 15 of their 72 proxies who were involved in their unobtrusive study of reference knew whether they had been helped by a librarian or a clerk.[10]

Interpersonal skills so necessary in a face-to-face reference transaction are also necessary, although modified, in a virtual reference situation.[11] One of the by-products of a virtual reference session is that the computer can save a transcript of all the interactions between the customer and the librarian. Periodically reviewing the transcripts offers an opportunity for improvement and feedback. The transcripts can be useful in a training setting.[12]

Historically the evaluation of reference has had a system-centric view of the world. However, thanks to the efforts of Brenda Dervin's sense-making communication theory,[13] Carol Kuhthau's diagnosis-intervention orientation model,[14] and Diane Nahl-Jakobovits's self-witnessing behavior model,[15] the user-centered perspective has been gaining strength. User-centered is a way of defining, measuring, and explaining the behavior of library users. Diane Nahl has prepared a thorough review of the research in this area.[16]

Descriptive Analysis

Most studies examining the quality of reference services are, by design, internally focused and consider such topics as the reference interval, service times, queuing times, librarian–customer interactions, and so forth. A majority of libraries collect output measures, which are gathered at the reference desk: number of customers served (often divided into blocks of time), time spent with each customer, and so forth. These statistics can be helpful in scheduling staff at the service desk, and the reporting of these measures in some manner is usually mandated. However, collecting these statistics is *not* a form of evaluation, because they cannot be used to assess quality or understand why people use reference services.

One academic library found a high correlation between gate count and use of reference services, so rather than capturing usage data each day, the library samples usage over three weekly periods and calculates annual reference statistics.[17]

Other studies of reference have categorized those that use the service (age, occupation, academic class standing, and so forth), degree of satisfaction with the service, visibility of the service, willingness of people to approach the service desk, types of questions asked (and answered), sources used, and so forth. The majority of the early studies focused on actual reference transactions as the unit of study. It is interesting to note that approximately 25 percent of reference transactions in public libraries are reported to be for someone else.[18] And those who came to the library on behalf of someone else rated library services higher than those who came seeking answers for their own questions.[19]

Assessing the customer's satisfaction with the reference interaction can provide valuable information, but it is only an indirect measure of reference service. Satisfaction has been defined as "the emotional reaction to a specific transaction or service encounter."[20] Customer satisfaction is basically a comparison between the expectations of the customer and his or her experience receiving the service. One study found evidence that customers appear to distinguish between their satisfaction with the service provided and satisfaction with the information that they obtain.[21]

Given the easy availability of options, it is not surprising that customers have high expectations for the skills of library staff and the overall quality of service they will receive. A study by Vicki Coleman et al. examined the quality of library services at three libraries and found that customers rated the libraries below or just barely above their minimum expectations.[22] In an earlier study, people sitting in an open area of an academic library were asked if they would approach a librarian for help if they had an information need. Of those with an information need, 42 percent indicated they would not ask for assistance because they were dissatisfied with service they had previously received.[23]

Jo Bell Whitlatch has suggested that since customers separately evaluate different aspects of service, a variety of performance measures, such as success in locating the desired information, should be analyzed.[24] She found that while customer and librarian ratings for service outcomes were almost always identical, substantial differences arose concerning the sufficiency of information provided and the usefulness of the information provided.

Unless a specific evaluation project is underway, in almost all cases the counting of transactions can be handled much more efficiently during sampling periods rather than collecting data on a daily basis. Assuming that the sampling periods occur several times per year and last from one to two weeks per occurrence, the resulting numbers can be extrapolated to identify the total volume of activity that occurs over a one-year time period. Staff will obviously spend less time making "tick" marks on a form, which should be appealing.

Obtrusive Methods

An obtrusive method is a technique to evaluate the use of a particular service during which the observer and user of the service directly interact. In the case of evaluating reference services, the observer, customer, and librarian would talk with one another about what they are doing and thinking. The observer could ask clarifying questions. In addition, a survey can be distributed to the customer or the librarian, or both.

A Library Survey

Some libraries have developed local surveys to determine the quality of reference services. In a study that involved five academic libraries in northern California, Jo Bell Whitlatch asked both users and librarians to complete a questionnaire regarding the reference transaction. The study found that requests for specific factual information are a small proportion of reference service: 12 percent.[25] Yet the librarians judged factual questions to be more difficult since responding to these queries involves the use of less familiar, less frequently used sources. Carolyn Jardine found that the reference librarian's attitude, behavior, interest, and enthusiasm influence customers' perceptions of the librarian and the service they receive.[26]

The WOREP Survey

One well-grounded tool is the Wisconsin-Ohio Reference Evaluation Program (WOREP), which asks the library customer to complete a short checklist about his or her query; the librarian fills out a corresponding form. The WOREP instrument—called the Reference Transaction Assessment Instrument—was developed by Charles Bunge and Marjorie Murfin and has been subjected to a rigorous set of reliability measures and validity tests.[27] A transaction is scored as successful only when the customer reports finding exactly what was wanted, marks being fully satisfied, and does not check any of the nine listed reasons for dissatisfaction. A library using WOREP can compare itself with similar types of libraries (for example, public libraries) as well as libraries of similar size. The survey is easy to administer and inexpensive to use, and the return rate is typically quite high.[28]

Wichita State University library used the WOREP survey, and staff were surprised to learn that the two highest user groups were freshmen and graduate students, contrary to the staff's impression that upper-level undergraduates were the biggest users.[29] An analysis of 7,013 reference transactions in 74 general reference departments in academic libraries around the United States found a mean success rate of 57 percent. Further analysis revealed that 46 percent of medium-sized libraries give quality reference service, compared to 30 percent of small libraries and 28 percent of large libraries.[30] Quality reference service was defined as providing an accurate answer (in the opinion of the customer) and having the customer rate the experience as satisfactory. Not surprisingly, having insufficient time for most customers and their questions usually had a negative effect on success in all sizes of libraries. Similar results were reported by June Parker in a study in the Government Documents Department at East Carolina University.[31]

The use of WOREP allows a library to discover its strengths and weaknesses and to compare itself to a set of peer libraries that have also completed the WOREP survey. The strength of the WOREP methodology is that it uses actual queries brought to the library by the customer or asked via the telephone, rather than using "test questions." One of the advantages of WOREP is its ability to highlight factors that are associated with less-than-successful reference transactions. The WOREP survey can be used repeatedly to track improvements resulting from staff training.[32]

Although large libraries, with their larger funding, collections, electronic resources, and trained staff, are able to provide a breadth and depth of reference services that simply cannot be duplicated in a smaller library, the large libraries may have too many resources and may provide a lower quality service than their medium-sized peers.

Unobtrusive Testing

In the unobtrusive testing method, library staff members are unaware that they are being tested as they attempt to respond to a query. Questions with predetermined answers are posed by "proxies" playing the role of customers. The questions may be specifically created for the study or derived from actual reference interactions. After the interaction the proxy completes a checklist to report answers, sources used, attitudes, and so forth.

Herbert Goldhor defined the quality of reference service as the accuracy of the information being provided in response to fact-type questions.[33] In 1971 Thomas Childers and Terence Crowley initiated a tradition of unobtrusive observation testing of reference services when they published the results of their dissertations.[34] An important distinction about these two studies was that Crowley administered the same 10 questions at 12 public libraries, while Childers dispensed 26 questions to all 25 libraries that were involved in his study. This type of study uses the correct answer rate—the proportion of correct answers to the total number of answers received (expressed as a percentage)—as a measure of reference performance.

This unobtrusive methodology was documented, and the results of a number of studies were discussed, in a book by Peter Hernon and Charles McClure.[35] Those who conducted these numerous studies found a consistent and low reference success rate. This led Hernon and McClure to suggest the "55 percent rule": Anyone asking an information question in a library has about a 55 percent chance of receiving the correct answer![36]

Their work led to a host of similar studies, some published and some not, and the results were often used to compare the quality of reference in one library to another.[37] It is important to note, however, that almost all studies after Childers and Crowley created a "pool of questions" from which only a few were administered to an individual library. Among the more notable was a study by McClure and Hernon in which they examined the quality of reference service in U.S. government depository libraries and found that correct responses ranged from 6 to 82 percent.[38] A similar study was performed by Juris Dilevko and Elizabeth Dolan in Canadian government depository libraries; they found that accuracy ranged from 15 to 79 percent.[39] This latter study used four categories to code or score each question: complete answer, partially complete answer, referral, and no or incorrect answer.

In general, despite the many reference accuracy studies done, there are inconsistent operational definitions of "accuracy" and outcome variables included in the analysis. Other problems with most of these studies include simplistic statistical analysis, a lack of random sampling, informational queries being only a part of the services offered at the reference desk, limited reliability of the study design, and so forth.[40] Studies that link reference performance to library size and budget have little utility in that the library is not likely to significantly change either variable. Crowley, using proxy customers to ask questions in 40 New Jersey public libraries, found that accuracy was *not* a function of the library's budget—defined by expenditures per capita.[41]

Thomas Childers, reflecting on his participation in launching a series of research projects that have evaluated reference service, has noted:

> The bad news about investigating queries with short, factual, unambiguous answers is that, in the minds of many—especially those interested in evaluating performance—it has assumed unrealistic proportions and come to stand for the whole of the reference function, yet there is no empirical foundation for it, no literature that links performance of one kind of reference service with performance on another kind of service.[42]

The inaccuracy of information provided by reference services has the potential for serious negative consequences, depending on how the information will be used. Paul Burton provided a summary of the numerous studies in this area and suggests that other professionals do not get it wrong 45 percent of the time. Burton recommends that librarians do more research into the contribution of information to work that users do and the environment in which their information needs arise.[43]

Kenneth Crews provides a valuable overview of most of the accuracy studies and suggests the need for further research.[44] In a comprehensive assessment and critique of the various reference accuracy studies, Matthew Saxton and John Richardson assert that there are a number of methodological difficulties, including the following:

- "Fact type" queries account for many and perhaps a majority of all queries received at the reference desk. "Open-ended" questions typically require more interaction and negotiation to arrive at a satisfactory answer from the customer's perspective.

- There are difficulties in determining categories for types of questions and what to count and what to exclude from a study.

- Definitions of independent and outcome variables are inconsistent from one study to another.

- Bias arises from self-selected samples and low sample sizes.

- Simplistic statistical techniques are used.

- Reporting of findings is inconsistent, and there is a general lack of attention to theory.[45]

An analysis by Saxton and Richardson of over 9,000 reference queries found that more than 90 percent of the answers were judged to be completely accurate or partially accurate, or the user was referred to another agency. The problem with this rosy assessment is that the authors are grouping together accurate and partially accurate categories, when in reality the answer is either accurate or it is not accurate.

More recently, Andrew Hubbertz has expressed three fundamental concerns about unobtrusive testing that raise serious questions about this type of research:[46]

- All libraries in such tests must be administered the same test—in other words, be asked the same questions. This will allow the identification of varying results to a single variable—library performance. Wondering about the wide variation in accuracy results, Hubbertz states that the difficulty of the questions or the skill, experience, training, and tenacity of the librarian could account for the differences, since the same questions were not administered at all locations.

- Such tests are principally useful for measuring relative performance rather than assessing the overall quality of service. The test questions do not represent the universe of questions that an individual library receives. That is, different libraries receive different mixes of reference queries, and the questions actually need to be representative of the entire mix the library receives in order to assess the overall quality of service of that library.

  Typically, possible questions are pretested, and those that score higher than 75 percent or lower than 25 percent are rejected. In reality, the range of accuracy scores varies from about 35 percent to 80 percent—about what one should expect given the design of the tests.[47] Hubbertz reanalyzed the two government depository studies and sorted the questions into "easy" and "hard" categories based on accuracy success. Overall, McClure and Hernon reported a 37 percent accuracy rate; the "easy" questions had a corresponding rate of 52 percent and the "hard" questions a 23 percent rate. Similarly, the Dilevko and Dolan study reported that full depository libraries had an accuracy rate of 37 percent; the "easy" questions had a 46 percent rate and the "hard" questions a 29 percent accuracy rate.

- This type of test should be used for the evaluation of reference collections and assessing the various modes of delivering service—in-person, 24/7 virtual reference, telephone, e-mail, chat, and so forth. Accuracy information about the comparative performance of each mode would be helpful to almost every library.

Joan Durrance examined the setting of the reference interview and found that customers were willing to return to a staff member who had made them feel more comfortable, was friendly, and appeared interested in their information need.[48] In an earlier study, Helen Gothberg found that customers of reference service were more satisfied when they encountered librarians who expressed warmth, empathy, and genuineness.[49] Roma Harris and Gillian Mitchell concluded from their study that the demeanor of the librarian during the reference interview may be as important as retrieving the correct information.[50] Continuing education and reference training seem to have little or no effect on accuracy.[51]

Patricia Dewdney and Catherine Ross asked students to visit a reference department in a library of their choice and ask a question of interest to them. The students were asked to rate, on a seven-point scale, the extent to which the staff member understood their questions and how friendly or pleasant they were. The students were asked to indicate their overall satisfaction level and their willingness to return to the same staff member. Dewdney and Ross found a positive correlation between the helpfulness of the answer and the friendliness of the staff member and overall satisfaction.[52] Another study, by Lynda Baker and Judith Field, found that overall satisfaction with a library's reference service depended primarily on the librarian's visible or verbal interest in the question or knowledge of appropriate sources. Dissatisfaction resulted from the absence of good listening skills and poor interpersonal skills.[53] A focus group study conducted by Virginia Massey-Burzio also noted the importance of friendliness and approachability.[54] Similar results were noted in studies conducted by Janine Schmidt[55] and Danny Wallace.[56] JoAnn Jacoby and Nancy O'Brien found that demonstrating service behavior that is friendly and helpful contributes to the students' "willingness to return" but may also help students to become more self-confident in their ability to find information on their own.[57]

One of the challenges facing a researcher when conducting a satisfaction survey is the tendency for respondents to answer with a middle or slightly positive category rather than choosing one extreme or the other. The overall responses are normally distributed as graphically shown in the bell-shaped curve.

Ross and Dewdney identified a list of negative actions that some librarians perform that prevent a successful reference transaction. Among these actions are

- immediately referring the user elsewhere,
- implying that the user should have looked elsewhere first,
- providing an unmonitored referral,
- convincing the user to accept other information more easily found,
- setting low expectations (i.e., indicating that defeat is likely),
- encouraging the user to give up,

- using nonverbal or verbal signals to suggest that the search is over when it actually isn't, and

- claiming that the information is not in the library or doesn't exist.[58]

One study found that only 12 percent of reference librarians concluded a reference transaction with the question, "Does this answer your question?" When the question was asked, correct answers were provided 76 percent of the time, while if it was not asked, the accuracy rate dropped to 52 percent.[59]

Providing reference services via chat, instant messaging, or using an electronic reference product affords the opportunity for testing but does raise different methodological issues. Marilyn White et al. performed a pilot study to understand and address the methodological concerns.[60] One of the by-products is a transcript of the session, which can later be analyzed or used for teaching or mentoring. One useful tool is Hirko and Ross's *Virtual Reference Training*.[61]

Most libraries that have offered a chat-based reference service have relied on using proprietary software that the library must license, and the user must also download some software. Alternatively, a library might provide a chat-based service using one of the more popular instant messaging programs available from several Internet services (e.g., AOL, Yahoo). Effective marketing efforts have used e-mails, listserv advertisements, and professional networking.[62] Despite the efforts of some libraries to promote chat-based reference services and high levels of user satisfaction with the service, use of chat services has declined or never gained much momentum.[63] For example, the Washington State University library provided a chat-based service from the fall of 2003 to July 2004 and only 101 transactions occurred—and another 35 attempts to use the service failed due to connection problems.[64] Students are typically heavy users of chat but are unaware that their own library offers a chat-based reference service.[65]

Another survey found that two-thirds of the respondents preferred face-to-face reference service, another 20 percent preferred e-mail service, and only 4 percent favored chat.[66] An analysis of why nine virtual reference (chat) services were discontinued revealed funding problems combined with low demand. Other problems included technical problems, staff problems, and institutional culture issues.[67] Another study has found that the virtual reference desk suffers from the same problems as the physical reference desk: inadequate reference interviewing, referral to alternative sources with a subsequent check on their suitability, and a lack of follow-up to determine satisfaction in general.[68] In short, chat reference does not do well compared to other available reference services.

Observation

A librarian can observe peers as they interact with customers at the reference desk. Acting as a coach or mentor, the librarian can offer specific suggestions for improving the way they interact with customers. In addition, the mentor might provide some coaching in the use of electronic sources or sources in the library that might be consulted. Users are aided to the extent that the answers to their questions help them accomplish something. Librarians who answer questions without knowing anything about the context may provide a correct answer but may otherwise be unhelpful in assisting the user.[69]

In the virtual environment, analysis of chat reference transcripts is another form of observation. NCknows is a collaborative, statewide, chat-based reference service in North Carolina. An analysis of the chat reference transcripts found that

- the quality of the chat-based reference service is high;

- compared to the 24/7 reference service, NCknows librarians are more engaged with users but are no more skilled in research or use of information sources; and

- while public librarians provide superior service, academic librarians provide superior referrals.[70]

Two other methods that have been used to better understand reference service but have not been used widely nevertheless provide an interesting perspective: conjoint analysis and cost-benefit analysis.

Conjoint Analysis

A few studies used a technique developed by market researchers to develop a model of users' preferences for a particular product or service when all the attributes are considered together. This technique, called conjoint analysis, allows all levels of each attribute to be compared to all levels of the other attributes. Attributes might be the speed of service, friendliness of the staff member, quality of the answer, and so forth. Applied within the context of academic reference services, several studies found that college students prefer a definite (rather than an uncertain) answer for which they only had to wait a brief period of time, and the answer was provided in a timely manner—no real surprise here.[71]

Cost-Benefit Analysis

One survey used the contingent valuation method to estimate the economic value that patrons attach to reference desk service at the Virginia Commonwealth University. David Harless and Frank Allen found that students were willing to pay $5.59 per semester to maintain current hours of the reference desk, while instructional faculty were willing to pay $45.76 per year to maintain current hours.[72] The students and faculty placed a value on the current hours of reference desk service that exceeded the cost by a ratio of 3.5 to 1.

The quality and costs of providing reference services are becoming much more visible. A recent study at Cornell University indicated that Google Answers,[73] an e-Bay-like marketplace for people with questions and others who are prepared to answer these questions, was significantly less expensive than comparable reference services at Cornell. Cornell was twice as expensive, and the Google Answers responses were nearly as good as the responses of the reference librarians.[74] In addition, 94 percent of the students who used Google Answers indicated that they would use the service again. (Google Answers is no longer available.)

Reference Resources

As noted in the large OCLC survey, 84 percent of the respondents use Internet search engines to begin their information searches, and only 2 percent begin searching using a library Web site or a library-provided online database.[75]

A recent report on a study noted that reference librarians use electronic resources six times more than print sources to respond to customer queries.[76] The top five sources used to respond to reference questions were electronic databases (24 percent), librarians (24 percent), the library catalog (15 percent), an internal Web page (12 percent), and reference books (9 percent). It is interesting to note that during the two semesters that the data were gathered, only 173 of the library's 9,587 reference collection titles were used—that is, less than 2 percent of the library's print reference collection. And for 75 percent of the questions, the librarians only referred to a single source for an answer. The switch by students to the direct use of

Internet-based resources (search engines) and avoiding the need to visit—in some way—the library has even been noticed by the popular press.[77]

For a significant number of years, libraries have been building and maintaining print reference collections. As reference librarians increasingly turn to electronic resources to respond to customer queries, an important question should be addressed: Is the print reference collection too large? This is particularly germane for libraries in which use of reference services has been declining for some years. Starting in 2000, libraries have been shifting a significant portion of their reference collection budget to electronic resources—27 percent or more in some libraries.[78] Librarians at the University of Georgia library report that they cancelled all their print indexes in favor of Web-based versions and now meet most of their undergraduates' needs without a print collection.[79]

A number of options exist for measuring the use of a print reference collection. Among them are the following:

- **Touch techniques:** A substance is placed on the print item that is affected in some way if the item is moved. The substance can be infrared dust, beads on the top of the book, or unexposed photographic paper. This method does not rely on the user for assistance in any way.

- **Tally slip:** A slip of paper is placed in each volume or on the spine of the item, and the user is asked to mark the slip of paper each time he or she opens a volume. Since this method depends on the cooperation of the user, results are problematic.

- **Interviews:** Interviewers approach each user of the reference collection during a sampling period and ask him or her to respond to a few questions. Not all individuals will be willing to participate, and the user's memory of what resources he or she has used will vary considerably.

- **Questionnaires:** Fussler and Simon placed a short questionnaire in a sample of volumes. When a volume was opened, the individual was asked to answer four questions: why the item was removed from the shelf; where and for what purpose the item would be used; and how valuable the item was to the user.[80]

- **Reshelving techniques:** The specific volume is recorded in some manner as it is reshelved. Some libraries have scanned the bar code and stored the information in a spreadsheet. Others have placed dots on the item for later counting. Different colored dots can be used to identify use by librarians. This method is problematic because patrons can use an item at the shelf and then reshelve it—even if there are signs requesting that items not be reshelved.[81] Others have printed a shelf list of reference materials and then manually recorded usage.

Eugene Engeldinger examined the use of the print reference collection at the University of Wisconsin—Eau Claire over a five-year period (using the dot method) and found that 35 percent of the collection was unused and 16 percent of the reference items had only been used once. Engeldinger noted that the reference staff members were surprised that so much material was used so infrequently, especially since staff were involved in an ongoing weeding program.[82] Mary Biggs and Victor Biggs reported that their survey of 471 libraries found that very few libraries (less than 10 percent) actually conducted use studies of their reference collections. As a result, the authors called in question the need for a library to maintain such large print reference collections.[83] A more recent survey of 550 college and university libraries found that few libraries weed their reference collections on a regular basis. The dominant reason was lack of staff time.[84]

In a study conducted at Stetson University, library staff collected reference materials from desks, tables, and shelves and recorded bibliographic information into a database over a four-month period. During the study period there were 9,755 titles and 25,626 volumes in the reference collection. The study found that only 8.5 percent of the total volumes in the print reference collection were used even once. Use of the collection mirrored the size of the reference collection by call number range.[85]

The Towson branch of the Baltimore County Public Library tracked usage from February to May 2005 and withdrew 15 percent of its reference collection, leaving 4,658 volumes.[86]

In 1997 Chuck Koutnik compared the process of answering questions using the Internet versus using print resources located in the library. He used 104 questions obtained from a reference textbook and found that the Web-based resources could answer over 30 percent of the questions correctly.[87] If such a study were to be repeated today, the percentage of correctly answered questions would be much higher, as the Web has increased exponentially in the intervening 10 years.

SUMMARY

Despite the relatively consistent research findings suggesting that reference librarians are correct only about 55 percent of the time, the methodological problems inherent in the studies of the unobtrusive testing of reference accuracy call into question a very large body of research. In sum, this research is murky, contradictory, and generally leads to misinformation—for both practicing reference librarians and their customers.

Obtrusive testing using the WOREP survey provides a foundation that is built on solid ground and includes the perspectives of both customer and librarian on a "real" reference transaction.

Other conclusions that can be drawn from the research include the following:

- The print reference collection should be evaluated for use and then weeded.

- The budget should be adjusted to provide more funding for electronic resources and less for the print reference collection.

- Training for reference staff may be needed so that they are more knowledgeable about electronic resources.

- Using several methods to evaluate reference services will provide a more complete picture of the range of services offered and their value.

NOTES

1. Cathy De Rose, Joanne Cantrell, Diane Cellentani, Janet Hawk, Lillie Jenkins, and Alane Wilson. *Perceptions of Libraries and Information Resources*. Dublin, OH: OCLC, 2005, 2–14.

2. Martin Fricke and Don Fallis. Indicators of Accuracy for Answers to Ready Reference Questions on the Internet. *Journal of the American Society for Information Science and Technology*, 55 (3), 2004, 238–45.

3. Eric Novotny. *Reference Service Statistics & Assessment*: SPEC Kit 268. Washington, DC: Association of Research Libraries, September 2002.

4. Ching-chih Chen and Peter Hernon. Library Effectiveness in Meeting Consumer's Information Needs, in *Library Effectiveness: A State of the Art: Preconference on Library Effectiveness*. Chicago: American Library Association, 1980, 50–62.

5. Debra G. Warner. A New Classification for Reference Statistics. *Reference & User Services Quarterly*, 41 (1), Fall 2001, 51–55.

6. Martin Kesselman and Sarah Barbara Watstein. The Measurement of Reference and Information Services. *Journal of Academic Librarianship*, 13, March 1987, 24–30.

7. George S. Hawley. *The Referral Process in Libraries: A Characterization and an Exhortation of Related Factors*. Metuchen, NJ: Scarecrow Press, 1987.

8. *Facets of Quality for Digital References Services*. June 2003. Available at http://www.vrd.org/facets-06–03.shtml; and MOUSS Management of Reference Committee. *Guidelines for Behavioral Performance of Reference and Information Service Providers*. June 2004. Available at http://www.ala.org/ala/rusa/rusaprotools/referenceguide/guidelinesbehavioral.htm.

9. Marie L. Radford. Approach or Avoidance? The Role of Nonverbal Communication in the Academic Library User's Role to Initiate a Reference Encounter. *Library Trends*, 46 (4), March 1998, 699–713.

10. Patricia Dewdney and Catherine S. Ross. Flying a Light Aircraft: Reference Service Evaluation from a User's Perspective. *RQ*, 34, 1994, 217–30.

11. Marie L. Radford. Encountering Virtual Users: A Qualitative Investigation of Interpersonal Communication in Chat Reference. *Journal of the American Society for Information Science and Technology*, 57 (8), 2006, 1046–59.

12. Buff Hirko and Mary Bucher Ross. *Virtual Reference Training: The Complete Guide to Providing Anytime, Anywhere Answers*. Chicago: American Library Association, 2004.

13. Brenda Dervin. Useful Theory for Librarianship: Communication, Not Information. *Drexel Library Quarterly*, 13, 1977, 16–32.

14. Carol Collier Kuhlthau. *Seeking Meaning: A Process Approach to Library and Information Services*. 2nd ed. Westport, CT: Libraries Unlimited, 2004.

15. Diane Nahl-Jakobovits. Problem Solving, Creative Librarianship, and Search Behavior. *College & Research Libraries*, 49 (5), 1988, 400–408.

16. Diane Nahl. The User-Centered Revolution: 1970–1995, in Allen Kent and James G. Williams (Eds.). *Encyclopedia of Microcomputers, Volume 19*. New York: Marcel Dekker, 1988, 143–99.

17. Gwen Lochstet and Donna H. Lehman. A Correlation Method for Collecting Reference Statistics. *College & Research Libraries*, 60 (1), January 1999, 45–53.

18. Melissa Gross and Matthew L. Saxton. Who Wants to Know? Imposed Queries in the Public Library. *Public Libraries*, 40 (3), May/June 2001, 170–76.

19. Melissa Gross and Matthew L. Saxton. Integrating the Imposed Query into the Evaluation of Reference Service: A Dichotomous Analysis of User Ratings. *Library & Information Science Research*, 24, 2002, 251–63.

20. K. Elliott. A Comparison of Alternative Measures of Service Quality. *Journal of Customer Service in Marketing and Management*, 1 (1), 1995, 35.

21. Marjorie E. Murfin and Gary Gugelchuk. Development and Testing of a Reference Transaction Assessment Instrument. *College & Research Libraries*, 48, July 1987, 321–22.

22. Vicki Coleman, Yi (Daniel) Xiao, Linda Blair, and Bill Chollett. Toward a TQM Paradigm: Using SERVQUAL to Measure Library Service Quality. *College & Research Libraries*, 58, 1997, 237–51.

23. Mary Jane Swope and Jeffrey Katzer. Silent Majority: Why Don't They Ask Questions. *RQ*, 12, 1972, 161–66.

24. Jo Bell Whitlatch. *The Role of the Academic Reference Librarian.* Westport, CT: Greenwood, 1990.

25. Jo Bell Whitlatch. Unobtrusive Studies and the Quality of Academic Library Reference Services. *College & Research Libraries,* 50 (2), March 1989, 181–94.

26. Carolyn W. Jardine. Maybe the 55 Percent Rule Doesn't Tell the Whole Story: A User-Satisfaction Survey. *College & Research Libraries,* 56, November 1995, 477–85.

27. Marjorie E. Murfin and Gary Gugelchuk. Development and Testing of a Reference Transaction Assessment Instrument. *College & Research Libraries,* 48, July 1987, 321–22.

28. Amy Paster, Kathy Fescemyer, Nancy Henry, Janet Hughes, and Helen Smith. Assessing Reference: Using the Wisconsin-Ohio Evaluation Program in an Academic Science Library. *Issues in Science and Technology Librarianship,* Spring 2006. Available at http://www.istl.org/ 06–spring/article2.html.

29. Janet Dagenais Brown. Using Quality Concepts to Improve Reference Services. *College & Research Libraries,* 55 (3), May 1994, 211–19.

30. John C. Stalker and Marjorie E. Murfin. Quality Reference Service: A Preliminary Case Study. *The Journal of Academic Librarianship,* 22 (6), November 1996, 423–29.

31. June D. Parker. Evaluating Documents Reference Service and the Implications for Improvement. *Journal of Government Information,* 23 (1), January/February 1995, 49–70.

32. Carolyn J. Radcliff and Barbara F. Schloman. Using the Wisconsin-Ohio Reference Evaluation Program, in Danny P. Wallace and Connie Van Fleet (Eds.). *Library Evaluation: A Casebook and Can-Do Guide.* Englewood, CO: Libraries Unlimited, 2001; see also Eric Novotny and Emily Rimland. Using the Wisconsin-Ohio Reference Evaluation Program (WOREP) to Improve Training and Reference Services. *The Journal of Academic Librarianship,* 31 (3), May 2007, 382–92.

33. Herbert Goldhor. *A Plan for the Development of Public Library Service in the Minneapolis—Saint Paul Metropolitan Area.* Minneapolis, MN: Department of Education, Library Division, 1967, 29.

34. Terence Crowley and Thomas Childers. *Information Service in Public Libraries: Two Studies.* Metuchen, NJ: Scarecrow Press, 1971.

35. Peter Hernon and Charles R. McClure. *Unobtrusive Testing and Library Reference Services.* Norwood, NJ: Ablex, 1984.

36. Peter Hernon and Charles R. McClure. Unobtrusive Reference Testing: The 55% Rule. *Library Journal,* 111, April 15 1986, 37–41.

37. Among the many studies, reported results include Marjorie E. Murfin and Gary M. Gugelchuk. Development and Testing of a Reference Transaction Assessment Instrument. *College & Research Libraries,* 48, July 1987, 314–38; Ian Douglas. Reducing Failures in Reference Service. *RQ,* 28, Fall 1988, 95–101; Joan C. Durrance. Reference Success: Does the 55 Percent Rule Tell the Whole Story? *Library Journal,* 49/50, 1995, 229–41; Loriene Roy. Reference Accuracy. *The Reference Librarian,* 49/50, 1995, 217–27; and Marjorie E. Murfin. Evaluation of Reference Service by User Report of Success. *The Reference Librarian,* 49/50, 1995, 229–41.

38. Charles R. McClure and Peter Hernon. *Improving the Quality of Reference Service for Government Publications.* Chicago: American Library Association, 1983.

39. Juris Dilevko and Elizabeth Dolan. *Government Documents Reference Service in Canada: Implications for Electronic Access.* Ottawa: Public Works and Government services Canada, 1999. Available at http://dsp-psd.pwgsc.gc.ca/Rapports/Dilevko_Dolan/dilevko-e.html. See also Juris Dilevko. *Unobtrusive Evaluation of Reference Service and Individual Responsibility: The Canadian Experience.* Westport, CT: Ablex, 2000.

40. Matthew L. Saxton. Reference Service Evaluation and Meta-Analysis: Findings and Methodological Issues. *Library Quarterly,* 67 (3), July 1997, 267–89.

41. Terence Crowley. The Effectiveness of Information Service in Medium Size Public Libraries, in *Information Service in Public Libraries: Two Studies*. Metuchen, NJ: Scarecrow Press, 1971, 16–21.

42. Thomas Childers. The Quality of Reference: Still Moot After 20 Years. *The Journal of Academic Librarianship*, May 1987, 73–74.

43. Paul F. Burton. Accuracy of Information Provision: The Need for Client-Centered Service. *Journal of Librarianship*, 22 (4), October 1990, 210–15.

44. Kenneth D. Crews. The Accuracy of Reference Service: Variables for Research and Implementation. *Library and Information Science Research*, 10, 1988, 331–55.

45. Matthew L. Saxton and John V. Richardson Jr. *Understanding Reference Transactions: Transforming an Art into a Science*. San Diego: Academic Press, 2002.

46. Andrew Hubbertz. The Design and Interpretation of Unobtrusive Evaluations. *Reference & User Services Quarterly*, 44 (4), Summer 2005, 327–35.

47. Terence Crowley. Half-Right Reference: Is It True? *RQ*, 25 (1), Fall 1985, 59–68.

48. Joan C. Durrance. Reference Success: Does the 55 Percent Rule Tell the Whole Story? *Library Journal*, 114 (7), April 15, 1989, 31–36.

49. Helen M. Gothberg. Immediacy: A Study of Communication Effect on the Reference Process. *Journal of Academic Librarianship*, 2, July 1976, 126–29.

50. Roma M. Harris and B. Gillian Michell. The Social Context of Reference Work: Assessing the Effects of Gender and Communication Skills on Observers' Judgment of Competence. *Library and Information Science Research*, 8, January–March 1986, 94–99.

51. Ronald R. Powell. An Investigation of the Relationship Between Quantifiable Reference Service Variables and Reference Performance in Public Libraries. *Library Quarterly*, 48, 1978, 1–19.

52. Patricia Dewdney and Catherine Sheldrick Ross. Flying a Light Aircraft: Reference Service Evaluation from a User's Perspective. *RQ*, 34, Winter 1994, 217–30.

53. Lynda M. Baker and Judith J. Field. Reference Success: What Has Changed Over the Past Ten Years? *Public Libraries*, 39, January/February 2000, 23–30.

54. Virginia Massey-Burzio. From the Other Side of the Reference Desk: A Focus Group Study. *Journal of Academic Librarianship*, 24, 1998, 217–30.

55. Janine Schmidt. Evaluation of Reference Services in College Libraries in New South Wales, Australia, in Neal K. Kaske and William Jones (Eds.). *Library Effectiveness: A State of the Art*. Chicago: American Library Association, 1980.

56. Danny Wallace. *An Index of Quality of Illinois Public Library Service, 1983*. Illinois Library Statistical Report, Number 14. Springfield: Illinois State Library, 1984.

57. JoAnn Jacoby and Nancy O'Brien. Assessing the Impact of Reference Services Provided to Undergraduate Students. *College & Research Libraries*, 66, July 2005, 324–40.

58. Catherine Sheldrick Ross and Patricia Dewdney. Negative Closure: Strategies and Counter-Strategies in the Reference Transaction. *Reference and User Services Quarterly*, 38, Winter 1998, 154–57.

59. Ralph Gers and Lillie J. Seward. Improving Reference Performance: Results of a Statewide Survey. *Library Journal*, 110, 1985, 32–35.

60. Marilyn Domas White, Eileen G. Abels, and Neal Kaske. Evaluation of Chat Reference Service Quality. *D-Lib Magazine*, 9 (2), February 2003. Available at http://www.dlib.org/dlib/february03/white/02white.html.

61. Hirko and Ross, *Virtual Reference Training*.

62. Deborah Lynn Harrington and Xiaodong Li. Spinning an Academic Web Community: Measuring Marketing Effectiveness. *The Journal of Academic Librarianship*, 27 (3), May 2001, 199–207.

63. Steve Coffman and Linda Arret. To Chat or Not to Chat: Taking Another Look at Digital Reference, Part 1. *Searcher*, 12 (7), July/August 2004, 38–46; and Steve Coffman and Linda Arret. To Chat or Not to Chat: Taking Another Look at Digital Reference, Part 2. *Searcher*, 12 (8), September 2004, 49–56.

64. Joel Cummings, Lara Cummings, and Linda Frederiksen. User Preferences in Reference Services: Virtual Reference and Academic Libraries. *portal: Libraries and the Academy*, 7 (1), 2007, 81–96.

65. Linda Frederiksen, Joel Cummings, and Lara Ursin. User Perceptions and Virtual Reference Services, in R. David Lankes et al. (Eds.). *The Virtual Reference Experience Theory Into Practice*. New York: Neal-Schuman, 2004, 43–61.

66. Cory M. Johnson. Online Chat Reference: Survey Results from Affiliates of Two Universities. *Reference and User Services Quarterly*, 43 (3), Spring 2004, 237–47.

67. Marie L. Radford and M. Kathleen Kern. A Multiple-Case Study Investigation of the Discontinuation of Nine Chat Reference Services. *Library & Information Science Research*, 28, 2006, 521–47.

68. Kristi Nilsen. The Library Visit Study: User Experience at the Virtual Reference Desk. *Information Research*, 9 (2), January 2004. Available at http://informationr.net/it/9-2/paper171.html.

69. Catherine Sheldrick Ross. How to Find Out What People Really Want to Know. *The Reference Librarian*, 16, 1986, 19–30.

70. Jeffrey Pomerantz, Lili Luo, and Charles McClure. Peer Review of Chat Reference Transcripts: Approaches and Strategies. *Library & Information Science Research*, 28, 2006, 24–48.

71. Gregory A. Crawford. A Conjoint Analysis of Reference Services in Academic Libraries. *College & Research Libraries*, 55, May 1994, 257–67; Michael Halperin and Maureen Stardon. Measuring Students' Preferences for Reference Service: A Conjoint Analysis. *Library Quarterly*, 50, 1980, 208–24; Kenneth D. Ramsing and John R. Wish. What Do Library Users Want? A Conjoint Measurement Technique May Yield the Answer. *Information Processing and Management*, 18, 1982, 237–42.

72. David W. Harless and Frank R. Allen. Using the Contingent Valuation Method to Measure Patron Benefits of Reference Desk Service in an Academic Library. *College & Research Libraries*, 60 (1), January 1999, 56–69.

73. Google recently announced that Google Answers was going to be discontinued. However, the popular Yahoo Answers continues to be available.

74. Anne R. Kennedy, Nancy Y. McGovern, Ida T. Martinez, and Lance J. Heidig. Google Meet eBay: What Academic Librarians Can Learn from Alternative Information Providers. *D-Lib Magazine*, 9 (6), June 2003. Available at http://www.dlib.org/ dlib/june03/kenney/06kenney.html.

75. Cathy De Rose, Joanne Cantrell, Diane Cellentani, Janet Hawk, Lillie Jenkins, and Alane Wilson. *Perceptions of Libraries and Information Resources*. Dublin, OH: OCLC, 2005, 1–17.

76. Jane T. Bradford, Barbara Costello, and Robert Lenholt. Reference Service in the Digital Age: An Analysis of Sources Used to Answer Reference Questions. *The Journal of Academic Librarianship*, 31 (3), May 2005, 263–72.

77. Patrick Boyle. What? Use a Book for Doing Research? College Students Forsake Library Shelves for Computers. *The Washington Post*, August 24, 2000, M07.

78. Brian Kenney and Eric Bryant. Reference Budgets: A Slow Revolution. *Library Journal*, 128 (19), November 15, 2003, 8–9, 12; and Mirela Roncevic. The E-Ref Invasion—Reference 2006. *Library Journal*, 130 (19), November 15, 2005, 8–13.

79. Roncevic, E-Ref Invasion, 8–13.

80. Herman H. Fussler and Julian L. Simon. *Patterns in the Use of Books in Large Research Libraries*. Chicago: University of Chicago Press, 1969.

81. Mary Biggs. Discovering How Information Seekers Seek: Methods of Measuring Reference Collection Use, in S. J. Pierce (Ed.). *Weeding and Maintenance of Reference Collections*. New York: Haworth Press, 1990, 103–14.

82. Eugene A. Engeldinger. "Use" as a Criterion for the Weeding of Reference Collections: A Review and Case Study, in Sydney J. Pierce (Ed.). *Weeding and Maintenance of Reference Collections*. New York: Haworth, 1990, 119–28.

83. Mary Biggs and Victor Biggs. Reference Collection Development in Academic Libraries: Report of a Survey. *RQ*, 27, Fall 1987, 66–79.

84. Eugene A. Engeldinger. Weeding of Academic Library Reference Collections: A Survey of Current Practice. *RQ*, 25 (3), Spring 1986, 366–71.

85. Jane T. Bradford. What's Coming off the Shelves? A Reference Use Study Analyzing Print Reference Sources Used in a University Library. *The Journal of Academic Librarianship*, 31 (6), November 2005, 546–58.

86. Rose M. Frase and Barbara Salit-Mischel. Right-Sizing the Reference Collection. *Public Libraries*, January/February 2007, 40–44.

87. Chuck Koutnik. The World Wide Web Is Here: Is the End of Printed Reference Sources Near? *RQ*, 36, 1997, 422–28.

11

Evaluation of Technical Services

To achieve the results they need, technical service departments need breakthrough, double-digit improvements in cost, time and effectiveness.

—Karen Calhoun[1]

SERVICE DEFINITION

The activities that encompass technical services are important because they support the services that the library's customers interact with. Selecting, cataloging, and processing the physical materials that are added to the library's collection, plus licensing the electronic databases, are all activities that add value. However, since technical services are providing service to other areas within the library and not directly to the customer, the focus of performance measurement and evaluation activities is necessarily internal.

EVALUATION QUESTIONS

Among the questions technical services evaluations have addressed are the following:

- How much time does it take to complete a variety of tasks?

- What are the costs to perform this variety of tasks?

- How does workflow analysis improve the productivity of a technical services department?

- What is the efficiency of operations in a library compared to a set of peer libraries?

- How do the quality and costs of in-library processing compare to using an outsourced vendor?

- How accurate is the work, especially cataloging, that is completed in technical services?

- Will enhancing bibliographic records improve the utility of records retrieved as a result of a user's search?

EVALUATION METHODS

Among the methods that have been used to evaluate technical services are

- activity surveys to gather information about time spent on a specific set of tasks;

- workflow analysis; and

- desk work analysis to determine costs, productivity, and accuracy of records.

DISCUSSION OF PRIOR EVALUATIONS AND RESEARCH

Time

We all are given a certain allotment of time to perform our work on a daily basis. We can attempt to prioritize and allocate a specific amount of time to various activities, or we can squander the time we spend at work each day. One of the components of efficiency is the time it takes to order, receive, catalog, and process an item until it finally reaches the shelf. And time can be broken into two components: the time to accomplish a particular task or activity and the time spent waiting between process activities.

One simple method for determining the time it takes to accomplish various technical services activities is for each staff member to record the task or activity being performed and the start and end times of the task. The slips or forms might be divided into two columns: tasks and time. In some cases, the slips are preprinted with a broad range of activities. These slips are used for a period of time sufficient so that a minimum of at least 500 slips can be collected. Assigning a unique ID number to each slip or form will ensure that all forms are returned and analyzed. The information is then tallied. Dividing the total time by the number of items handled for each task will reveal the time required to complete an activity or task for a single item. Other libraries have used a spreadsheet and a scanner to record the time spent on each activity.

Another approach is to use a random alarm unit that is carried by each staff member. When the alarm goes off, the staff member records the activity he or she is engaged in. If the alarm is used for a two- to three-week period, the resulting data will allow the library to prepare a chart of the time spent on each activity, by each staff member.

Some libraries have used the results as the basis for establishing performance or production standards. The standard is a specific, measurable statement of what is required for a job to be performed or how fast and how many. Tasks that are repetitive in nature are ideal candidates for establishing performance standards.

A study done in the technical services area of the East Carolina University library found that the time it took a firm order to move from being received to being placed on the shelf averaged 45 days—the range was from 1 to 170 days. The firm orders required cataloging to be accomplished by the library. PromptCat orders come with cataloging records, and the elapsed time averaged 38 days—with a range of 10 to 58 days.[2] A time-activity study conducted at the Carnegie Mellon University found that 83 percent of monographs were cataloged in less than 15 minutes. Further, the study found that the time from date cataloged to the date processing was completed was 1 to 5 days for 56 percent of the monographs, and 22 percent took longer than 30 days to complete.[3]

Costs

Those managing technical services are obviously concerned about total costs as well as the unit costs of performing each activity. A cost analysis can be done for a variety of reasons:

- It is useful as a management tool for controlling technical service activities.
- It is helpful in taking a progressive and proactive approach to management.
- It is useful for comparing costs with a set of peer libraries.
- It can be used to demonstrate transparent cost efficiency to funding decision makers.

As shown in chapter 3, it is not too difficult to calculate the costs for a specific activity or group of activities. However, caution must be used when attempting to compare the costs of one library with another because the cost figures were most likely not calculated in the same manner.

One interesting measure is the TSCORE—Technical Services Cost Ratio—which relates the costs of technical services to the cost of purchasing library materials. The total salaries for technical services are divided by the amount spent on purchasing materials in the same period.[4] For example, if a library spends $450,000 annually to purchase materials and pays $220,000 in salaries to those who work in technical services, then the library's TSCORE would be 220/450 or $.49. In this case, the library is spending 49 cents of every dollar it spends to acquire materials for its collection on technical services.

TSCOREs ranged from a low of 45 cents to a high of $1.00 in a survey of 10 university libraries and the TSCORE varied directly with the size of the library—larger libraries have higher TSCOREs. And a group of 12 large public libraries had an inverse relationship between the TSCORE and the size of the book budget—the larger the book budget, the smaller the technical services costs.[5]

Clearly the costs of technical services are going to be related to the tasks that are performed and the time it takes to perform each task.

The Iowa State University library conducted a series of time and cost studies from 1994 to 2001. During the period of the studies, cataloging costs per title declined consistently due to the collaborative efforts of catalogers and improved workflow procedures.[6] One interesting finding was that while automation had reduced costs and improved productivity, the library had for the most part only automated processes and activities that existed in the manual environment. The library had not been taking advantage of technology to transform the processes within technical services. Staff tracked how they spent their time for one-week intervals during sampling periods that ranged from four to six times a year. Although the library has made some changes to improve productivity, it has recognized that further change will require staff members to leave their present "comfort zones."[7] The bottom line for all of the analysis demonstrated that acquiring a monograph is now comparatively expensive relative to the costs of cataloging.[8] In addition to tracking costs for monographs, the Iowa State team also identified the time and costs to perform a number of tasks associated with the processing of serials.[9]

A thorough time and cost analysis was prepared at the University of Oregon library, which found that upgrading an OCLC record cost $9.23 per title and that original cataloging cost $24.92 per title.[10]

Taking a much broader perspective, Lawrence et al. used the Association of Research Libraries annual statistical data to aggregate costs in order to estimate the life cycle costs of collections. The annual costs included in the analysis were wages and salaries, operating expenses, building maintenance, and fixtures and equipment. The total annual operating costs were divided by the number of items by material types. The annual cost per material type was then multiplied by the expected life of the material. The analysis demonstrated that the purchase price of library materials is a small fraction of the life cycle ownership costs of maintaining library collections. For example, the researchers found that the expected cost of owning a monograph was more than seven times the original purchase price—consuming 95 percent of library life cycle expenditures.[11]

Historically libraries have used an analysis to identify the costs of doing business with one vendor compared to one or more other vendors. Recently, Paul Orkiszewski compared the costs of using Amazon.com with the library's existing vendor and found that the existing vendor offered better discounts to the library. However, Amazon.com compared favorably in terms of selection, availability, and fulfillment and considerably better in terms of speed.[12]

Workflow Analysis

One of the by-products of a time-activity study, previously discussed in this chapter, is that the library can also create a diagram of how materials flow in the technical services area. To do such a study, create a diagram of the technical services area that is to scale and then use the information from the forms to track the flow of materials. A good workflow will minimize the number of individuals who have to touch the materials as they move from receiving, to cataloging, to processing, and out the door.

One of the simplest tools to use to gain an understanding of the existing processes is a flow chart of activities and decisions made as part of each process. Redundant and unnecessary operations will be identified by carefully studying the flow chart. Myung Sung details the use of flow charts and other techniques to significantly improve the productivity of technical services and, as a result, eliminate a substantial backlog of materials.[13]

The Kent State University library developed an interdependent partnership with its book vendor that resulted in significantly reengineering its workflow by asking computers to perform the easy and dull work. The results were a significant decrease in the cost of cataloging and a reduction in the time it takes to get materials on the shelf.[14]

Efficiency

Efficiency measures divide the time or cost information for an activity by the volume of activity to create a time/activity or cost/activity ratio. Efficiency measures help the library determine whether it is doing things right. For example, if the library is spending $95,000 for original cataloging of a total of 1,460 titles over the course of the year, then the cost per title is $65.07. Similarly, if the library spends a total of 6,570 hours to complete all of the cataloging, then the time per title to complete original cataloging is 4.5 hours.

The vast majority of libraries have automated systems and use OCLC to obtain their cataloging records, yet a survey found the size of professional staff had remained the same at 47 percent, and had increased at 14 percent, of libraries.[15]

Time and cost efficiency measures for all of technical services, as well as the various components of the department, can be calculated. Due to the increasing pressures on the budgets of most libraries, there is an almost unrelenting need to ensure that the library is operating in a cost efficient manner. Yet if a knowledgeable librarian from another library or a consultant were to observe the operation of most technical service departments, he or she would find a host of nonessential and time-honored wasteful practices. Based on the evidence, the idea that intelligent and hard-working people will eliminate wasteful effort is a wonderful and hopeful, but ultimately unrealistic, expectation.

Starting in the early 1990s, Michael Hammer and James Champy introduced the notion of reengineering the organization, suggesting that three forces were driving organizations into unfamiliar territory: customers, competition, and change. Customers were becoming empowered because they had access to more information via the Internet about alternative product and service providers. In addition, competition was increasing, and change is a constant. Hammer and Champy defined reengineering as the fundamental rethinking and radical redesign of processes to achieve dramatic improvements in critical, contemporary measures of performance, such as cost, quality, service, and speed.[16] In the government sector, David Osborne and Ted Gaebler had a similar message.[17] These authors suggested creating teams to accomplish a broad range of activities, empowering the team members to make decisions and to eliminate all activities that were wasteful or did not add value for the customer. Eliminating tasks that duplicate one another or are unnecessary from the customer's perspective can significantly speed the throughput times of a process.

Penn State University Libraries used reengineering principles to reorganize the cataloging processes for monographs, with good results.[18] The University of Southern Mississippi libraries merged their acquisitions and cataloging units in 2001. After the merger and revising the workflows within the new unit, the ordering lag time was decreased by 30 to 60 days.[19]

The functionality of most automated library systems offers the opportunity to streamline workflows by combining processes performed at one workstation and reducing the number of staff who handle materials.

One of the unfortunate effects of the reengineering movement was that efforts to achieve cost reductions led to wholesale layoffs and retrenchment. As a result a new effort, called lean manufacturing, aims to improve the quality of product and services for customers while also reducing costs and improving productivity. "Lean" is aimed at the elimination of waste by organizing processes that add value for the customer. The four basic lean principles follow:

- Add nothing but value while eliminating waste.
- Do it right the first time. The key to rapid delivery is small batch sizes.
- People doing the work are adding value. They should be the center of the resources, information, process design, and decision-making authority.
- Deliver on demand means that work isn't done until a downstream process requires it—make only what the next process needs, when it needs it.[20]

Waste comes from a variety of sources, including the following:

- **Overproduction:** Producing more, sooner or faster than needed by the next process.
- **Inventory:** Any form of batch processing, whether it is electronic or physical.
- **Extra processing steps:** Reentering data, requiring extra copies, producing unused reports, expediting, travel expense reporting.
- **Motion:** Walking to perform an activity, such as picking up reports from a printer, fax machine, or other offices; moving book trucks; picking up supplies to complete a task.
- **Defects:** Data entry errors, errors in invoices, receiving of materials, staff turnover.

- **Waiting:** System downtime, system response times, approval for others, information from vendors, information from others within the department/library, scheduled times to complete activities.
- **Transportation:** Movement of materials and paperwork, including multiple hands-offs, multiple approvals, excessive e-mail attachments.

One indisputable sign that cataloging is a challenge for many libraries is the fact that

> [v]ast cataloging backlogs in many libraries provide even more convincing evidence that the cost of cataloging is too high. In many cases, though not all, backlogs exist because cataloging departments still seek to provide a level of service that is not supported by the institution. Backlogs can be eliminated by changing either the process or the product.[21]

Unfortunately, there is very little literature dealing with the topic of cataloging productivity. This means that the management of a library has a difficult time determining how many staff members it takes to handle a defined workload and to compare productivity with peer libraries. Although some libraries have established their own production standards, these vary significantly. Claire-Lise Benaud, Sever Bordeianu, and Mary Ellen Hanson suggested in 1999 that the profession should develop production expectations, yet such standards are still undefined, as shown in Table 11.1.[22] Smith suggested that a cataloger should be expected to catalog 250 to 400 titles a month and that original cataloging should take between 30 and 60 minutes per item depending on its complexity.[23]

Table 11.1. Examples of Cataloging Productivity

	Simple Monograph Copy	Complex Monograph Copy	Original Monograph
Professional catalogers	2 per hour	1 per hour	1 per hour
	3–4 per hour	2 per hour	.5 per hour
	5 per hour	3–5 per hour	2 per hour
	225 per month	100 per month	3 per hour
		120 per month	6 per day
		200 per month	90 per month
Paraprofessionals	2–5 per hour	1–5 per hour	1 per 1.3 hours
	3–10 per hour	5 per hour	7 per hour
	300–350 per month	100 per month	6 per day
	225–1,000 per month	200 per month	100 per month

Clearly the creation of cataloging production standards must encompass both quantity and quality measures. Mechael Charbonneau discusses the issues surrounding the development of such standards, particularly in the context of personnel appraisals.[24]

Ruth Fischer, Rick Lugg, and Kent Boese suggest that 10 business and productivity principles should affect technical services:

- **Know the current cost structures of technical services.** Including the cost for salaries, benefits, supplies, and overhead and dividing by the volume of activity will identify the cost to perform each activity.

- **Control the "expert mentality"** so that the discussion focuses on identifying alternatives for completing the required work.

- **Adhere to national standards rather than local practices.** For example, accepting duplicate call numbers will have little impact on the library's customers.

- **Maximize the use of available resources** by minimizing the review and editing of bibliographic records.

- **Design and produce an economically viable product.** Do existing cataloging practices produce records that clearly exceed the customer's needs?

- **Adjust capacity to match demand.**

- **Automate and/or outsource**, especially those activities that are repetitive and routine.

- **Establish production goals and measure performance** whether the work is done in the library or by an outside vendor.

- **Control quality via sampling;** it is not necessary to review each record added to the system. However, the library should establish an acceptable error rate—whether the work is done in the library or by an outside vendor.

- **Be strategic.** Determining how resources—financial, human, and technological—are allocated is what strategy is all about.[25]

Outsourcing

Outsourcing involves the purchasing, from an outside source, of goods and services that a library previously provided for itself. Some libraries have contracted out some technical services functions to vendors in the private sector, including collection development (approval plans and blanket orders), cataloging and authority control, materials processing, bindery services, and serials subscription service. Typically outsourcing is done to reduce costs or improve the speed of the service. A survey of academic libraries showed that outsourcing was not a strong trend, but that libraries that had outsourced were generally pleased with the results.[26]

Prior to signing a contract for an outsourced service, the library should prepare a cost analysis for that particular activity. A number of cost studies have compared in-library versus outsourced cataloging services. A Michigan State University library analysis concluded that its in-house work cost $6.22 per record, while the OCLC PromptCat service cost $3.99.[27] City University of New York determined that its in-house cost was $7.50 per title, versus $3.25 for outsourcing of cataloging.[28] At the University of Alabama a contrary view emerged; it calculated its in-house cataloging costs at $3.44 per title, compared to outsourcing costs of $9.80.[29] Wright State University outsourced all of its technical services, including cataloging activities, and saved the library about $253,000 per year.[30]

The acquisition of shelf-ready material—cataloging, bar codes, spine labels, covers, and the like—is another popular form of outsourcing. The University of Vermont found in-house processing costs of $6 to $7 per volume, while shelf-ready outsourcing cost $3 to $4 per volume.[31] Other libraries, including Adelphi University,[32] the University of Arizona,[33] and the Fort Worth Public Library,[34] found similar cost savings. In addition to cost savings, use of an outsourcing vendor can reduce the time to get materials on the shelf.

Outsourcing the selection and processing for shelf-ready, opening-day collections for branch libraries has been employed by a number of libraries.

Another variation of outsourcing is having a consortium of libraries centralize all technical services activities. Stumpf analyzed the feasibility of centralized cataloging and processing for a group of public libraries and determined that the concept would save the individual libraries money while improving throughput times.[35] Original cataloging was outsourced at the central Oregon Community College library, with turnaround time, error rates, and costs all declining.[36]

The topic of outsourcing is well summarized by James Sweetland,[37] and useful annotated bibliographies have been prepared by Marylou Colver[38] and Benaud and Bordeianu.[39] Clare Dunkle compares the pros and cons of outsourcing in libraries with the experiences of businesses outsourcing information technology services.[40] David Ball has suggested using a matrix to determine which services might be outsourced.[41] Some libraries have outsourced the cataloging of materials that are difficult to complete—for example, cataloging foreign language, legal, and medical materials. In some cases, outsourcing is used because it may be difficult to fill a cataloging position with a required set of skills. Among the questions that might be considered are the following:

- Does the service "define" the library?
- Are the costs for providing the service high?
- Is the turnaround time to provide a service greater than customer expectations?
- Has performance been declining of late?

While an outsourcing agreement is being negotiated, make sure that standards are clearly specified and that the consequences for failing to maintain the standards are articulated.

Regardless of the scope or specific service being outsourced, it is important to create an agreement that clearly identifies what is to be delivered (and for what price), as well as what performance measures will be used to verify the quality and timeliness of services.

Not surprisingly, outsourcing can engender considerable opposition. Ellen Duranceau suggested that

> [t]he question of whether and when to pay a vendor to do the work of professional in-house catalogers strikes to the very heart of our identity as librarians, calling into question our assumptions about our ultimate purpose, our place in the scholarly information chain, and how we can best serve our institutions.[42]

There is nothing more wasteful than doing efficiently that which is not necessary.

—Sir Royce[44]

A contrary point of view is expressed by James Rush: "I have long been fascinated by the fact that libraries spend so much of their scare resources on cataloging with so little resultant benefit."43

To improve the efficiency of technical services, the department should adopt a mantra:

- Simplify it!

- Eliminate it!

- Automate it!

QUALITY

The presence of a typographical error in a bibliographic record can negatively affect the ability of an individual to find needed information. This reality leads to my favorite definition of a library catalog: a place where bibliographic records get lost alphabetically. Typographical errors can occur in almost any part of the record itself. Errors in the primary fields—author, title, subject headings— are going to present more problems when searching, especially if the error occurs in the first word or two, than errors occurring in other parts of the record.

Your database is either getting worse every day, or through systematic intervention, it is getting better.

—Terry Ballard[45]

Jeffery Beall brought the importance of errors to the attention of librarians when he suggested the use of the "Dirty Database Test," which entailed performing keyword searches for 10 misspelled words and counting the number of records that were retrieved.[46] Terry Ballard systematically examined the database of Adelphi University and corrected more than 800 errors in a database that contained some 117,000 words. Most of the errors were found in the title proper, and in 40 percent of the cases, the error occurred in the first three words.[47] Terry Ballard and Arthur Lifshin analyzed the typographical errors found in a library's catalog and noted that the frequently misspelled words tend to have eight or more letters and at least three syllables. In addition, they noted that common words are more likely to have typos than esoteric technical terms.[48] Karen Markey and Marjorie Weller found that valid subject headings entered as a search request by users of the online catalog contained a spelling error in 6 percent of the cases. The 6 percent does not include spelling errors that failed to match the controlled vocabulary and keyword terms in the catalog.[49]

Another study examined the filing problems with initial articles in bibliographic records for European-language works and found that the number of errors was quite high.[50] Joseph Pollock and Antonio Zamora found a misspelling rate of 0.2 percent (2,000 misspelled words per million) and found that for words containing a spelling error, 90 to 95 percent contained a single error.[51] While the quality of the OCLC bibliographic database is quite good, the organization has an ongoing program to improve quality and reduce the number of misspellings.[52]

Sylvia Gardner classified spelling and typographical errors into four groups: errors of letter omission, errors of letter insertion, errors of letter substitution, and errors of letter transposition.[53] A more precise definition of errors was developed by Gentner et al. (see Table 11.2, p. 192).[54]

Table 11.2. Terminology of Errors

Error Category	Definition
Mis-strokes	Errors traced to inaccurate motion of the finger.
Transposition errors	Two consecutive letters in a word are interchanged.
Interchange errors	Two nonconsecutive letters are interchanged.
Migration errors	One letter moves to a new position.
Omissions	A letter in a word is left out.
Insertions	An extra letter is inserted into a word.
Substitutions	Occurs when the wrong letter is typed in place of the correct letter.
Doubling errors	A word containing a repeated letter is typed so that the wrong letter is doubled.
Alternate errors	A letter alternates with another, but the wrong alternation sequence is used.

A recent study examined the presence of typographical errors in library online catalogs. The errors were selected from the *Typographical Errors in Library Databases* Web site, which was created and maintained by Terry Ballard.[55] Jeffrey Beall and Karen Kafadar selected 20 typos in each of five categories (very high, high, medium, low, and very low) for a total of 100 words. These misspelled words were then searched on OCLC to identify library catalogs that contained the misspelled word in the bibliographic record. Five libraries were selected for each misspelled word, and then each library's online catalog was checked to see if the misspelled word had been corrected. The results indicate that very high, high, and medium frequency misspelled words had been corrected about 40 percent of the time, while low and very low frequency words were corrected only about 30 percent of the time.[56]

Typographical errors are not restricted to library online catalogs but are also to be found in electronic databases and journals.

A library can also perform an audit to determine the quality of its catalog. A sample of cataloging records is compared to the physical items and all errors are noted. Similarly, a sample of physical items is selected and then compared to their bibliographic records. For a margin of error of 4.9 percent, 3.5 percent, or 2.5 percent, choose a sample of 400, 800, or 1,500 items respectively. Using this method, one library found that about one-third of its catalog records contained at least one error.[57]

ENHANCED RECORDS

Adding additional content to a bibliographic record will improve the end user's chances for success while searching because the number of words that can be used to retrieve a record has been increased. Pauline Atherton first articulated the concept of enhanced records in 1978. The additional content might come from the table of contents, an abstract, a book jacket summary, entries from an index, or the preface.[58] Although the library can create its own enhanced records, by manually adding the content or adding the content from an online source, the library also has the option of contracting with a vendor to add the content. Aside from serving as a source of additional subject-rich indexing terms, the enhanced records will be of value to the user in determining the item's relevance.[59]

Gunnar Knutson's 1991 study showed an increase in circulation for titles to which additional or more specific subject headings were assigned in the bibliographic record. No increase was noted for titles with only contents notes added. A contrary view is provided by Ruth Morris, who found that titles with tables of contents increased the likelihood of usage by 45 percent. Titles with tables of contents added were more likely to be used in the library (by 43 percent) and to be circulated (by 33 percent).[60]

Peis and Fernandez-Molina found that precision and recall will improve simultaneously when the user is searching enhanced records compared to nonenhanced bibliographic records, as shown in Figure 11.1.[61]

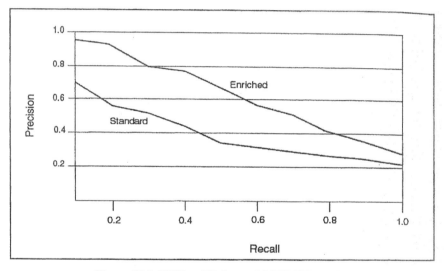

Figure 11.1. Utility of Enhanced MARC Records

A study at Stetson University library tracked 2,614 titles with enhanced bibliographic records. About 90 percent of the records had table of contents information added using a cut and paste approach, while the remaining 10 percent of the records had the contents added manually. The average cost for adding the contents was 94 cents per title. It was found that the titles with enhanced records increased circulation 5 percent.[62]

SUMMARY

A review of the research pertaining to technical services suggests that:

- Time and cost of technical services activities are quite variable. A library should periodically identify its performance and compare itself with a set of peer libraries.

- Workflow analysis and work simplification can assist a library in reducing the activities it performs that do not add value from the customer's perspective.

- Cataloging productivity is quite variable and seems to reflect management's expectations and the local culture of the library.

- Outsourcing, although controversial, can be selectively used to improve the time to get new materials on the shelf and may reduce costs.

- A library should periodically examine its online catalog database to determine the level of typos.

- The use of enhanced bibliographic records should be considered, given their value in improved searching from the user's perspective.

NOTES

1. Karen Calhoun. Technology, Productivity and Change in Library Technical Services. *Library Collections, Acquisitions & Technical Services*, 27 (3), Autumn 2003, 283.

2. Patricia Dragon and Lisa Sheets Barricella. Assessment of Technical Services Workflow in an Academic Library: A Time-and-Path Study. *Technical Services Quarterly*, 23 (4), 2006, 1–16.

3. Terry Hurlbert and Linda L. Dujmic. Factors Affecting Cataloging Time: An In-House Survey. *Technical Services Quarterly*, 22 (2), 2004, 1–14.

4. H. W. Tuttle. TSCORE: The Technical Service Cost Ratio. *Southeastern Librarian*, 19, 1969, 15–25.

5. H. M. Welch. Technical Service Costs, Statistics, and Standards. *Library Resources and Technical Services*, 11, 1967, 436–42.

6. Dilys E. Morris, Collin B. Hobert, Lori Osmus, and Gregory Wool. Cataloging Staff Costs Revisited. *Library Resources & Technical Services*, 44 (2), April 2000, 70–83.

7. David C. Fowler and Janet Arcand. Monographs Acquisitions Time and Cost Studies: The Next Generation. *Library Resources & Technical Services*, 47 (3), July 2003, 109–24.

8. Dilys E. Morris, Pamela Rebarcak, and Gordon Rowley. Monograph Acquisitions: Staffing Costs and the Impact of Automation. *LRTS*, 40 (4), 1996, 301–18.

9. David C. Fowler and Janet Arcand. A Serials Acquisitions Cost Study: Presenting a Case for Standard Serials Acquisitions Data Elements. *Library Resources & Technical Services*, 49 (2), April 2005, 107–22.

10. Nancy Slight-Gibney. How Far Have We Come? Benchmarking Time and Costs for Monograph Purchasing. *Library Collections, Acquisitions & Technical Services*, 23 (1), 1999, 47–59; and Nancy Slight-Gibney. Defining Priorities and Energizing Technical Services: The University of Oregon Self-Study. *Library Acquisitions: Practice and Theory*, 22 (1), 1998, 91–95.

11. Stephen R. Lawrence, Lynn Silipigni Connaway, and Keith H. Brigham. Life Cycle Costs of Library Collections: Creation of Effective Performance and Cost Metrics for Library Resources. *College & Research Libraries*, 62, November 2001, 541–53. Note: The Library Interactive Costing Spreadsheet is available online at http://bus.colorado.edu/faculty/lawrence/LICS.

12. Paul Orkiszewski. Notes on Operations: A Comparative Study of Amazon.com as a Library Book and Media Vendor. *Library Resources & Technical Services*, 49 (3), July 2005, 204–9.

13. Myung Gi Sung. Increasing Technical Services Efficiency to Eliminate Cataloging Backlogs. *Public Libraries*, 43 (6), November/December 2004, 52–43.

14. Margaret Beecher Maurer and Michele L. Hurst. Library-Vendor Collaboration for Re-Engineering Workflow: The Kent State Experience. *Library Collections, Acquisitions & Technical Services*, 27, 2003, 155–64.

15. L. Buttlar and R. Garcia. Catalogers in Academic Libraries: Their Evolving and Expanding Roles. *College & Research Libraries*, 59 (4), 1998, 311–21.

16. Michael Hammer and James Champy. *Reengineering the Corporation: A Manifesto for Business Revolution*. New York: HarperBusiness, 1993.

17. David Osborne and Ted Gaebler. *Reinventing Government: How the Entrepreneurial Spirit Is Transforming the Public Sector*. New York: Addison-Wesley, 1992.

18. Robert B. Freeborn and Rebecca L. Mugridge. The Reorganization of Monographic Cataloging Processes at Penn State University Libraries. *Library Collections, Acquisitions, & Technical Services*, 26, 2002, 35–45.

19. Ann Branton and Tracy Englert. Mandate for Change: Merging Acquisitions and Cataloging Functions into a Single Workflow. *Library Collections, Acquisitions, & Technical Services*, 26, 2002, 345–54.

20. Mary Poppendieck. *Principles of Lean Thinking*. Available at http://www.poppendieck.com/papers/LeanThinking.pdf.

21. Ruth Fischer, Rick Lugg, and Kent C. Boese. Cataloging: How to Take a Business Approach. *The Bottom Line*, 17 (2), 2004, 50.

22. Claire-Lise Benaud, Sever Bordeianu, and Mary Ellen Hanson. Cataloging Production Standards in Academic Libraries. *Technical Services Quarterly*, 16 (3), 1999, 43–67.

23. P. M. Smith. Cataloging Production Standards in Academic Libraries. *Technical Services Quarterly*, 6 (1), 1988, 3–14.

24. Mechael D. Charbonneau. Production Benchmarks for Catalogers in Academic Libraries: Are We There Yet? *Library Resources & Technical Services*, 49 (1), January 2005, 40–48.

25. Fischer, Lugg, and Boese, Cataloging, 50–54.

26. Katherine A. Libby and Dana M. Caudle. A Survey on the Outsourcing of Cataloging in Academic Libraries. *College & Research Libraries*, 58 (6), November 1997, 550–60.

27. Mary M. Rider and Marsha Hamilton. PromptCat Issues for Acquisitions: Quality Review, Cost Analysis and Workflow Implications. *Library Acquisitions: Practice and Theory*, 20 (1), 1996, 9–21.

28. Douglas Duchin. Outsourcing: Newman Library, Baruch College CCNY. *The Bottom Line*, 11 (3), 1998, 111–15.

29. Debra W. Hill. To Outsource or Not: University of Alabama Libraries Engage in Pilot Project with OCLC's TechPro. *Cataloging and Classification Quarterly*, 26 (1), 63–73.

30. Arnold Hirshon. Letter to the Editor. *Journal of Academic Librarianship*, 22 (5), 1996, 392.

31. A. J. Joy and R. Lugg. The Books Are Shelf-Ready, Are You? *Library Acquisitions: Practice and Theory*, 22 (1), 1998, 71–89.

32. B. Horenstein. Outsourcing Copy Cataloging at Adelphi University Libraries. *Cataloging and Classification Quarterly*, 28 (4), 1999, 105–16.

33. T. H. Marshall and J. W. Tellman. Processing Foreign Language Books Without Catalog Librarians at the University of Arizona Library. *Against the Grain*, 12 (3), 2000, 28–29.

34. C. A. Dixon and F. G. Bordonaro. From Selection to Shelf: Outsourcing Book Selection, Copy Cataloging, and Physical Processing at Forth Worth Public Library, in K. A. Wilson and Marylou Colver (Eds.). *Outsourcing Library Technical Services Operations: Practices in Academic, Public, and Special Libraries*. Chicago: American Library association, 1997.

35. Frances F. Stumpf. Centralized Cataloging and Processing for Public Library Consortia. *The Bottom Line*, 16 (3), 2003, 93–99.

36. Carol G. Henderson. Freelance Cataloging: Outsourcing Original Cataloging at Central Oregon Community College Library, in K. A. Wilson and Marylou Colver (Eds.). *Outsourcing Library Technical Services Operations: Practices in Academic, Public and Special Libraries*. Chicago: American Library Association, 1997, 38–45.

37. James H. Sweetland. Outsourcing Library Technical Services—What We Think We Know, and Don't Know. *The Bottom Line*, 14 (3), 2001, 164–75.

38. Marylou Colver. Selected Annotated Bibliography, in K. A. Wilson and Marylou Colver (Eds.). *Outsourcing Library Technical Services Operations: Practices in Academic, Public and Special Libraries*. Chicago: American Library Association, 1997, 193–220.

39. Claire L. Benaud and Sever M. Bordeianu. Outsourcing in Academic Libraries: A Selective Bibliography. *Reference Services Review*, 27 (1), 1999, 78–89.

40. Clare E. Dunkle. Outsourcing the Catalog Department: A Meditation Inspired by the Business and Library Literature. *The Journal of Academic Librarianship*, 146, January 1996, 33–43.

41. David Ball. A Weighted Decision Matrix for Outsourcing Library Services. *The Bottom Line*, 16 (1), 2003, 25–30.

42. Ellen Duranceau. Vendors and Librarians Speak on Outsourcing, Cataloging and Acquisitions. *Serials Review*, 20, Fall 1994, 69.

43. James E. Rush. A Case for Eliminating Cataloging in the Individual Library, in *The Changing Face of Technical Services*. Dublin, OH: OCLC, 1994, 1.

44. Quoted in Dorsey J. Talley. *Total Quality Management: Performance and Cost Measurement—the Strategy for Economic Survival*. Milwaukee, WI: ASQC Quality Press, 1991, 31.

45. Terry Ballard. Spelling and Typographical Errors in Library Databases. *Computers in Libraries*, 12 (6), June 1992, 14–19.

46. Jeffery Beall. The Dirty Database Test. *American Libraries*, 22, March 1991, 97.

47. Terry Ballard. Spelling and Typographical Errors in Library Databases. *Computers in Libraries*, 12 (6), June 1992, 15.

48. Terry Ballard and Arthur Lifshin. Prediction of OPAC Spelling Errors Through a Keyword Inventory. *Information Technology and Libraries*, 11, June 1992, 139–45.

49. Karen M. Drabenstott and Marjorie S. Weller. Handling Spelling Errors in Online Catalog Searches. *LRTS*, 40 (2), April 1996, 113–32.

50. Ralph Nielsen and Jan M. Pyle. Lost Articles: Filing Problems with Initial Articles in Databases. *Library Resources & Technical Services*, 39 (3), 1995, 291–92.

51. Joseph J. Pollock and Antonio Zamora. Collection and Characterization of Spelling Errors in Scientific and Scholarly Text. *Journal of the American Society for Information Science*, 34 (1), 1983, 51–58.

52. Edward T. O'Neill and Diane Vizine-Goetz. The Impact of Spelling Errors on Databases and Indexes, in *Proceedings of the 1989 National Online Meeting, 9–11 May 1989, New York*. Medford, NJ: Learned Information, 1990, 313–20; and Edward T. O'Neill and Diane Vizine-Goetz. Quality Control in Online Databases. *Annual Review of Information Science and Technology*, 23, 1988, 125–56.

53. Sylvia A. Gardner. Spelling Errors in Online Databases: What the Technical Communicator Should Know. *Technical Communications*, 39, 1992, 50–53.

54. D. R. Gentner, J. T. Grudin, S. Larochelle, D. A. Norman, and D. E. Rumelhart. A Glossary of Terms Including a Classification of Typing Errors, in William E. Cooper (Ed.). *Cognitive Aspects of Skilled Typewriting*. New York: Springer-Verlag, 1983, 39–43.

55. *Typographical Errors in Library Databases*. Available at http://faculty.quinnipiac.edu/libraries/tballard/typoscomplete.html.

56. Jeffrey Beall and Karen Kafadar. The Effectiveness of Copy Cataloging at Eliminating Typographical Errors in Shared Bibliographic Records. *Library Resources & Technical Services*, 48 (2), April 2004, 92–101.

57. Ann Chapman and Owen Massey. A Catalogue Quality Audit Tool. *Library and Information Research News*, 26 (82), Spring 2002, 26–37.

58. Pauline Atherton. *Books Are for Use: Final Report of the Subject Access Project to the Council on Library Resources*. Washington, DC: Council on Library Resources, 1978.

59. Stefanie A. Wittenbach. Building a Better Mousetrap: Enhanced Cataloging and Access for the Online Catalog, in Marsha Ra (Ed.). *Advances in Online Public Access Catalogs: Volume I*. Westport, CT: Meckler, 1992, 67–91.

60. Ruth C. Morris. Online Table of Contents for Books: Effect on Usage. *Bulletin of the Medical Library Association*, 89, 2001, 29–36.

61. E. Peis and J. C. Fernandez-Molina. Enrichment of Bibliographic Records of Online Catalogs Through OCR and SGML Technology. *Information Technology and Libraries*, 17 (3), March 1998, 161–72.

62. Debbi Dinkins and Laura N. Kirkland. It's What's Inside That Counts: Adding Contents Notes to Bibliographic Records and Its Impact on Circulation. *College & Undergraduate Libraries*, 13 (1), 2006, 59–71.

12

Evaluation of Interlibrary Loan

SERVICE DEFINITION

No library is going to be able to build a collection that will meet 100 percent of the needs of its customers. Therefore the sharing of resources, called interlibrary loan, has existed for a considerable period of time to assist libraries in bridging the gap of unmet needs. In most cases, journal articles are obtained from other libraries or a document delivery supplier, while books are normally borrowed from another library. The library customer may receive a paper copy of the journal article but may also download (or print) an electronic copy of the article. Many academic libraries have seen a significant growth in interlibrary loan borrowing over the last 10 years.

EVALUATION QUESTIONS

The evaluation of interlibrary loan and document delivery can be done for a variety of reasons:

- to assist requesting libraries in deciding among alternative supply sources;
- to enable suppliers to assess their own performance;
- to identify areas of weakness in order to make improvements; or
- to track performance over time to demonstrate improved levels of service, reduced costs, and so forth.[1]

EVALUATION METHODS

Document delivery and interlibrary loan (ILL) can be evaluated using a variety of measures, as shown in Table 12.1 (p. 200). The use of focus groups, a qualitative method, is discussed in chapter 4.

Table 12.1. Methods for Evaluating Interlibrary Loan

Qualitative	Quantitative
Focus groups	Speed (turnaround time)
	Fill rate
	Costs
	Access vs. ownership
	User surveys
	Requested items owned by library
	Concentration and scatter in requested materials

Other factors that have been evaluated include tracking the number of requests received, growth over time of the ILL service, document quality, safety of materials, and partner satisfaction. Peter Lor has suggested that a number of variables can be analyzed using a communication framework:[2]

- Who—requesting customers and libraries
- Requests what—requested materials
- Through which channel—procedures, channels, and transmission media
- From whom—supplying library or vendor
- With what effect—outcomes of requests.

DISCUSSION OF PRIOR EVALUATIONS AND RESEARCH

Two articles provide a thorough discussion of the interlibrary loan literature: Thomas Waldhart's 1985 article[3] and Joan Stein's 2001 article, which reviews the literature published from 1986 through 1998.[4] Waldhart noted a number of problems associated with the ILL research, including inadequate definitions of terms, an emphasis on local circumstances, limited use of statistical techniques, a superficial analysis of the collected data, and failure to build on prior research. These two articles are complemented by Lee Hilyar's article, which identifies the best practices for operating and managing interlibrary loan services in libraries.[5]

Rather than organizing the prior research around methods that have been used, this material is presented by examining the variables that have been studied.

Speed (Turnaround Time)

Just as this measure is known by many names—delivery time, turnaround time, turnaround, and delivery speed—so also has it been defined in a multiplicity of ways. Typically turnaround is the elapsed time between submission of the request and the item's being received by the library. However, some libraries and studies use the elapsed time until the document is received by the customer.

The *ISO 11620 Information and Documentation: Library Performance Indicators* standard includes measurement of speed of interlibrary lending.[6] This standard requires the library to construct a log and collect the dates of

- receiving the request from the user,
- initiating the search for materials,
- deciding on and initiating the interlibrary borrowing procedure,
- ordering the document from an external source,
- receiving the document from an external source, and
- notifying the user.

The speed of interlibrary lending can then be calculated for the proportion of documents received within the stated time periods.

Thomas Nisonger examined 75 studies published between 1992 and 2000 and found that the mean turnaround time ranged from 7 days to 38 days for ILL materials borrowed from other libraries, while commercial document delivery services ranged from 1 day to 23 days. The average turnaround time exceeded 10 days.[7] The average turnaround time for 97 ARL libraries was 16 days.[8]

In general, commercial document delivery firms provide faster but more expensive service. It should be noted that reported average turnaround times can often mask a great deal of variability. From the customer's perspective, consistency of speed may be more important than a "fast" service for some materials.

Among the variables that affect the results of the various studies are

- the definition used for *turnaround time*;
- how time is measured—calendar days or work days;
- how the request is transmitted—electronically, via fax, or via U.S. mail;
- whether the library is participating in a small group of libraries that provide "fast" service to one another; and
- whether the requests are verified.

Figure 12.1 (p. 202) illustrates the various points at which the clock can start and stop to determine turnaround time. The majority of interlibrary loan studies start the clock when the request is transmitted to the first of what may be several libraries and stop the clock when the material is received by the library (not in the hands of the customer). Starting the clock when the patron submits the request and stopping it when the item is received by the patron has been called the "satisfaction time."

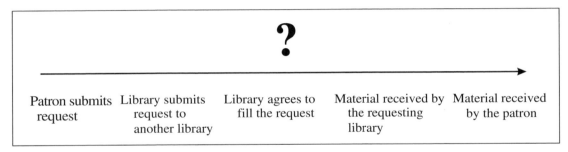

Figure 12.1. When Does the Turnaround "Clock" Start and Stop?

A survey of science faculty at Washington State University and Arizona State University found that 75 percent of the faculty did not want to wait longer than one to two weeks for document delivery.[9] The Oregon Document Delivery Service, a statewide courier network, achieves 24- to 48-hour turnaround for 95 percent of document requests.[10]

A service at the Texas A&M University Libraries called deliverEdocs provides desktop delivery of any article, even those on the Texas A&M library shelves. A customer survey revealed that 43 percent felt they should receive the article within two days and 32 percent within three days for materials owned locally. Further, 41 percent felt that interlibrary loan materials should be available within four to seven days, and 32 percent felt that two weeks was acceptable.[11]

The University of Nevada Las Vegas used a process improvement review team to modify existing workflow procedures, eliminated a backlog of requests, and was processing requests with 24 to 48 hours. The team used flow charts to document the existing workflow and to envision a new process.[12]

Clearly the use of electronic mail and online ordering systems has assisted libraries in reducing turnaround times. A study by the Research Libraries Group[13] and Sonja Landes[14] found that Ariel was the least expensive option for transmitting a 10-page journal article. A comparison of Ariel and Odyssey, the electronic delivery component of ILLiad, which allows articles to be sent directly to the customer without borrowing staff intervention, found—not surprisingly—that Odyssey was faster.[15]

More recently, the Colorado State University Libraries have developed RAPID, a system that includes the holdings for each participating library. The resource sharing database allows a library to exclude items that are oversized or rare, thus routing requests to libraries for materials they are willing to loan. RAPID interfaces with CLIO, ILLiad, and RLG's ILLManager, all of which are ILL management packages. Requests are handled electronically with no staff intervention save one keystroke. Libraries using RAPID have lower costs and improved turnaround times.[16]

Clearly the ready availability of electronic journals and other online materials is having an impact on interlibrary loan. An interlibrary loan article sharing data from the 26 largest libraries in Illinois shows a 26 percent drop in overall article requests from 1999/2000 to 2002/2003.[17]

Fill Rate

The fill rate, success rate, or satisfaction rate is the proportion of requested items that were received by the library, normally within a defined period of time. The majority of studies report a fill rate that exceeds 80 percent for both lending from other libraries and commercial services.

Factors that influence the results of a fill rate analysis include

- whether the analysis includes all designated suppliers or only the first designated supplier (the customer is only concerned with getting the material and not the number of suppliers approached);
- the type of item requested;
- whether potential or actual fill rates are being calculated;
- the point in the process at which the fill rate is being measured;
- the location of the measurement activity—requesting or supplying library; and
- whether the calculation is based on the number of requests or the number of attempts.

Lor conducted a study using four different methods to calculate the fill rate and found that it is important to carefully define the manner in which data are collected:[18]

- **Monthly statistical returns.** Suppliers had an overall fill rate of 74 percent for all requests. Requesters had a final fill rate of 80 percent, counting the final successful attempt.
- **Transaction tracking—longitudinal.** This approach yielded a 92 percent final fill rate, taking all attempts into account.
- **Transaction recording—cross-section.** This method only provides a snapshot view of the request status at one point in time and thus yielded a lower fill rate of 78 percent.
- **A questionnaire to determine customer perceptions of fill rates.** This method produced results that varied depending on the time interval between the request and when the material was received by the customer.

An analysis of interlibrary loan data over a three-year period for a consortium of large academic libraries (Committee on Institutional Cooperation) found that 19 percent of borrowing requests were unfilled.[19] Table 12.2 identifies the reasons why libraries are unable to fill requests. Reasons for the "owned but not available" category include items in circulation, not found on the shelf, and so forth.

Table 12.2. Reasons for Unfilled ILL Requests

Study*	Year	Volume Not Owned	Loan Prohibited	Owned But Not Available
Seaman	1992	60%	44%	38%
Guyonneau	1993		29% b	41% b
		53% j		27% j
Medina & Thorton	1996	39%		38%

b = books
j = journal articles

*Scott Seaman. An Examination of Unfilled OCLC Lending and Photocopy Requests. *Information Technology and Libraries*, 11 (3), 1992, 229–35; Christine H. Guyonneau. Performance Measurements for ILL: An Examination. *Journal of Interlibrary Loan, Document Delivery & Information Supply*, 3 (3), 1993, 101–26; and Sue Medina and Linda Thornton. Cannot Supply: An Examination of ILL Requests Which Could Not Be Filled by Members of the Network of Alabama Libraries. *Journal of Interlibrary Loan, Document Delivery & Information Supply*, 6 (4), 1996, 11–33.

Costs

Cost studies have been prepared at the state level and at the network or consortium level, although the majority of studies examine costs at the individual library level. Most libraries will track the cost per filled request, and the mean costs can be quite variable—from about $1 to slightly more than $18 per filled request.[20] The costs for materials filled by a commercial supplier are also variable—from a little more than $8 to slightly more than $33 per request.

Mary Jackson examined ILL costs in a study involving academic libraries and found that transaction costs had declined during the 1990s.[21] A summary of the costs and delivery speed for a number of studies is shown in Table 12.3.

Table 12.3. Summary of Interlibrary Loan Findings

Study*	Year	Cost of Borrow Request ($)	Cost of Lending Request ($)	Borrow/ Lending Cost ($)	Average Turnaround Time (Days)	Borrowing Fill Rate
Roche	1993	18.62	10.93	29.55		
Slolt	1995	14.72			10.5	82%
Levene —U of AR —IA State U	1996	2.11 1.46			15.4 8.4	
Naylor	1997	8.51	4.68			86%
Jackson —research —college	1998			27.83 19.33	15.6 10.8	85% 91%
Jackson —mediated ILL —RAPID	2004	17.50 5.41			7.6 3.4	

*Marilyn M. Roche. *ALG/RLG Interlibrary Loan Cost Study: A Joint Effort by the Association of Research Libraries and the Research Libraries Group.* Washington, DC: Association of Research Libraries, 1993; Wilbur A. Slolt, Pat L. Weaver-Meyers, and Molly Murphy. Interlibrary Loan and Customer Satisfaction: How Important Is Delivery Speed? In Richard AmRhein (Ed.). *Continuity and Transformation; The Promise of Confluence: Proceedings of the Seventh National Conference of the Association of College and Research Libraries, Pittsburgh, Pennsylvania, March 29–April 1 1995.* Chicago: Association of College and Research Libraries, 1995; Lee-Allison Levene and Wayne A. Pedersen. Patron Satisfaction at Any Cost? A Case Study of Interlibrary Loan in Two U.S. Research Libraries. *Journal of Library Administration,* 23 (1–2), 1996, 55–71; Jackson, *Measuring the Performance of Interlibrary Loan Operations*; Mary E. Jackson. *Assessing ILL/DD Services: New Cost-Effective Alternatives.* Washington, DC: Association of Research Libraries, 2004.

However, a great deal of caution should be exercised when attempting to compare costs from one library to another. Unless a group of libraries are participating in a cost analysis that carefully defines all cost components and provides a consistent process for reporting and analyzing the results, the comparisons are problematic because the cost components will vary and inflation will be a factor for studies conducted in prior years.

Among the variables that will influence the calculations of cost figures are the following:

- What components are included in the cost calculation[22]

  - Staff—can account for 75 percent or more of interlibrary loan operations in a library

  - Networking/communications

  - Delivery

  - Photocopying/scanning

  - Supplies

  - Software and computer equipment

  - Rental and maintenance

  - Direct borrowing costs

  - Indirect borrowing costs.

- The pay rates for different personnel classifications
- Whether indirect costs (benefits) and copyright cost are included
- The year the study was conducted

Reflecting the labor-intensive nature of the service, interlibrary resource sharing costs some $30 per transaction, one-third of which is borne by the lending institution.[23]

Access versus Ownership

One of the fundamental questions confronting any library is whether it is less expensive to own material or to provide access to it. Although most studies examine the tradeoffs associated with serials, some studies have looked at monographs. The literature suggests that there are two approaches in preparing an analysis:

- comparing actual expenses for purchasing material to the hypothetical cost of providing access; and

- comparing the costs of providing access (interlibrary loan/document delivery) to the hypothetical costs of purchase.

As shown in Table 12.4 (p. 206), the majority of studies suggest that access is considerably less expensive than ownership. However, ownership is clearly more cost effective for frequently used journal titles. Eleanor Gossen and Suzanne Irving found that the cost of providing access to all periodical subscriptions at SUNY Albany (based on observed usage) would have been $2,900,456, while the actual subscription costs were $1,273,531.[24] An analysis of interlibrary loan requests over one year (1992) found that only 4 percent of the journal articles were to be found in the electronic resources licensed by the library.[25] Surely that percentage would be much higher more than a decade later, with many more journal titles accessible online.

Table 12.4. Cost of Ownership vs. Access

Focus of Study	Cost of Ownership ($)	Cost of Access ($)	Author*	Location of Study
Journals accessed 5 times or more	220,000	4,034	Anthes	Wichita State University library
Journals requested 10 times or more	28,229	5,629	Kleiner & Hamaker	Louisiana State University library
Electrical engineering journal articles requested	89,544	6,264	Ferguson & Kehoe	Columbia University
Physics journal articles requested	33,628	1,872	Ferguson & Kehoe	Columbia University
aspalphaBiology periodical articles requested	343,926	28,674	Ferguson & Kehoe	Columbia University
Journal articles requested	62,800	8,700	Fusler	Colorado State University Libraries
Providing access to 1,060 articles from 480 canceled journals	207,000	12,278	Currie	Louisiana State University library
Access to articles from canceled journals	53,344	7,123	Wilson & Alexander	Texas A&M University library

*Mary Anthes. An Experiment in Unmediated Document Delivery: EbscoDOC at Wichita State University. *Library Collections, Acquisitions & Technical Services*, 23, Spring 1999, 1–13; Jane P. Kleiner and Charles A. Hamaker. Libraries 2000: Transforming Libraries Using Document Delivery, Needs Assessment and Networked Resources. *College & Research Libraries,* 58, July 1997, 355–74; Anthony W. Ferguson and Kathleen Kehoe. Access vs. Ownership: What Is Most Cost Effective in the Sciences. *Journal of Library Administration*, 19 (2), 1993, 89–99; Elizabeth A. Fuseler. Providing Access to Journals—Just in Time or Just in Case? *College & Research Libraries News*, 55, March 1994, 130–32, 148; Debra L. Currie. Serials Redesign: Using Electronic Document Delivery to Reshape Access to Agricultural Journal Literature. *Journal of Agricultural & Food Information*, 3 (2), 1995, 13–22; Mary Dabney Wilson and Whitney Alexander. Automated Interlibrary Loan/Document Delivery Data Applications for Serials Collection Development. *Serials Review*, 25 (4), 1999, 11–19.

Gossen and Irving suggest that access is cost effective for any serial title used five times or fewer during the year. Rather than using a rule of thumb, Bruce Kingma has suggested using graphs or a mathematical model to determine the access "break-even point": when access is more cost effective than ownership.[26]

User Surveys

A number of libraries have conducted one-time or periodic surveys of interlibrary loan users using a Likert scale to determine levels of satisfaction. Typically the results are reported as the percent of satisfied customers. Interestingly, a number of studies have found that delivery speed (turnaround time) is not correlated with customer satisfaction, and that interactions with service staff have a greater impact.[27]

Anna Perrault and Marjo Arseneau examined ILL customer satisfaction and found that about 60 percent of the faculty and graduate students felt that the highest priority should be on obtaining material regardless of speed and cost, and only about 15 percent of the respondents needed the material in less than a week.[28] An analysis of comments from a customer satisfaction survey of ILL services found that users value the service when staff interactions are experienced positively, and most respondents were unwilling to pay for expedited service.[29]

The ARL ILL/DD Performance Measures Study surveyed a random sample of users from each participating library and found high levels of satisfaction for timeliness, quality and completeness of materials, and staff helpfulness.[30]

Mark Kinnucan used the conjoint analysis approach in a series of interviews with faculty and graduate students and found that the price of the document was the most important consideration ($3 or less) and that turnaround time only had a modest effect.[31] A survey of ILL customers at the University of Arizona found that 64 percent of the respondents rated the overall service at better than average or better.[32]

Françoise Hébert used a SERVQUAL type of survey instrument and found that public library users of ILL ranked reliability as the most important dimension, followed by responsiveness. Again, staff interactions had a greater impact on overall customer satisfaction ratings than did turnaround times.[33] For more about SERVQUAL and customer satisfaction, see chapter 15.

In addition to doing a survey, some libraries have used a focus group to learn more about the perceptions of interlibrary loan users and their needs. Focus groups of ILL customers have been used at Emory University[34] and Carnegie Mellon University.[35]

Requested Items Owned by the Library

Requests made directly by users of an interlibrary loan system, often called an unmediated service, are frequently for materials already owned by the library. The percent of requests owned by the library varies greatly—from 15 percent to as much as 76 percent, according to several studies. There may be a number of reasons for this:

- The library's online catalog is not consulted prior to making an interlibrary loan request.

- The library's online catalog may not clearly reveal what holdings are owned by the library.

- The customer may prefer document delivery rather than retrieving the article from the library.

- The desired item may not be on the shelf—that is, it may be missing or checked out.

Any library using a patron unmediated interlibrary loan service will need to modify its workflow procedures to check whether the requested item is owned by the library, in order to keep costs down. Examining 325 requests that were not found on the shelves at the Texas A&M University libraries, it was found that better turnaround time would result if journal articles were ordered from a supplier rather than conducting a second and third search two or three days later.[36]

A consortium of large academic libraries found that an average of 25 percent of ILL borrowing requests were canceled due to local availability—the range was from 8 to 33 percent.[37]

A study conducted at Iowa State University library compared the time to recall an item in circulation to the time to retrieve the same item using interlibrary loan from anther library and found that recalled items were returned to the library in an average of 6.3 days, while interlibrary loan took an average of 7.3 days. The materials then sat on the hold shelf for the patron for another 3.2 days for recalled items and 4.5 days for ILL materials. The Iowa State University library continues to recall items that it owns but will use interlibrary loan if a second request is received for the same title.[38]

An analysis at the University of Colorado at Boulder compared interlibrary loan requests to the number of titles owned in 25 subject areas and found that for every request, the library owned from 9 to 144 titles.[39]

Concentration and Scatter in Requested Materials

A majority of items needed by a library's customers are going to be supplied through the use of the library's physical and electronic collections. Thus, it stands to reason that the majority of interlibrary loan requests will be for materials that are widely "scattered"—infrequently used. In many ways, libraries sharing their resources are similar to what Chris Anderson describes as the "long tail."[40] Also, Bradford's Law demonstrates that a subject area's journals can be divided into zones—a small number of highly used titles and a large number of infrequently used titles.

Yet analysis of interlibrary lending reveals a surprisingly different picture. Donald Urquhart was director of the British Science Museum Library, the forerunner of the British Library Lending Division, located in Bath. Analysis of lending data from 1956 led to Urquhart's Law, which states that interlibrary loan demand for a periodical is as a rule a measure of its total use within a local library. The analysis of the data showed that the distribution of interlibrary loans was highly skewed, with less than 10 percent of the journal collection accounting for about 80 percent of the loans, and the number of loans of given journals was highly correlated with the number of UK libraries holding these journals. Urquhart further suggested that the use of a single serial can be modeled by a Poisson distribution.[41]

One study found that 16 percent of 120 titles were requested more than five times, while 48 percent of the titles were selected only once.[42] Another study at SUNY Albany found that 80 percent of 291 journal titles were requested just once, while only 6 titles were requested more than five times.[43] A thorough analysis of NLM's DOCLINE interlibrary article requests found that 76 percent of the articles were requested once and less than 1 percent were requested 10 times or more.[44]

Other Topics

Clearly it is possible to conduct any number of studies pertaining to interlibrary loan and document delivery. Among the topics might be characteristics of the users of this service, characteristics of the requested materials, and reasons for not being able to fulfill a request.

An evaluation of unfilled interlibrary lending requests at the University of Indianapolis identified a number of reasons for the unavailability of the requested items. Problems within the library included poor working habits of the staff, cataloging errors, and loss of materials.[45]

SUMMARY

After reviewing the research pertaining to interlibrary loan and document delivery, it is possible to reach the following conclusions:

- The fill rates for interlibrary loan/document delivery are about the same for libraries and commercial firms.

- Commercial document delivery is more expensive but faster than interlibrary loan.

- Access is more cost effective for little-used materials, while ownership is best for more heavily used materials.

- A significant proportion of requests are for materials owned by the library.

- Libraries can make improvements in workflow procedures to improve turnaround times.

- User satisfaction is not related to speed of delivery.

NOTES

1. Maurice Line. Performance Measurement Within Interlending and Document Supply Systems, in *Interlending and Document Supply: Proceedings of the Second International Conference*. Boston Spa: IFLA Office for International Lending, 1992, 5–13.

2. Peter Lor. The Analysis of ILL Systems: A Taxonomy of Variables. *Journal of Interlibrary Loan, Document Delivery & Information Supply*, 1 (1), 1990, 43–66.

3. Thomas J. Waldhart. Performance Evaluation of ILL in the United States: A Review of the Research. *Library and Information Science Research*, 7 (4), 1985, 313–31.

4. Joan Stein. Measuring the Performance of ILL and Document Delivery Supply: 1986 to 1998. *Performance Measurement and Metrics*, 2 (1), April 2001, 11–72.

5. Lee Andre Hilyer. Interlibrary Loan and Document Delivery: Best Practices for Operating and Managing Interlibrary Loan Services in All Libraries. *Journal of Interlibrary Loan, Document Delivery & Electronic Reserve*, 16 (1/2), 2006, 1–147.

6. ISO. *ISO 11620 Information and Documentation: Library Performance Indicators*. Geneva: International Organization for Standardization, 1998.

7. Thomas E. Nisonger. Accessing Information: The Evaluation Research. *Collection Management*, 26 (1), 2001, 1–23.

8. Mary E. Jackson. Loan Stars. ILL Comes of Age. *Library Journal*, 123 (2), February 1, 1998, 44–47.

9. Elizabeth P. Roberts. ILL/Document Delivery as an Alternative to Local Ownership of Seldom-Used Scientific Journals. *Journal of Academic Librarianship*, 18, March 1992, 32, 34.

10. Sue A. Burkholder. By Our Own Bootstraps: Making Document Delivery Work in Oregon. *Computers in Libraries*, 12, December 1992, 19–24.

11. Zheng Ye (Lan) Yang. Customer Satisfaction with Interlibrary Loan Service—deliverEdocs: A Case Study. *Journal of Interlibrary Loan, Document Delivery & Information Supply*, 14 (4), 2004, 79–94.

12. Victoria A. Nozero and Jason Vaughan. Utilization of Process Improvement to Manage Change in an Academic Library. *The Journal of Academic Librarianship*, 26 (6), November 2000, 416–21.

13. Research Libraries Group. *Cost-Effectiveness of Ariel for Interlibrary Loan Copy Requests: Summary of a Report to RLG SHARES Participants.* 1996. Available at http://www.rlg.org/ariel/arifax.html.

14. Sonja Landes. Ariel Document Delivery: A Cost-Effective Alternative to Fax. *Interlending and Document Supply,* 25 (3), 1997, 113–17.

15. Ruth S. Connell and Karen L. Janke. Turnaround Time Between ILLiad's Odyssey and Ariel Delivery Methods: A Comparison. *Journal of Interlibrary Loan, Document Delivery & Electronic Reserve,* 16 (3), 2006, 41–55.

16. Jane Smith. The RAPIDly Changing World of Interlibrary Loan. *Technical Services Quarterly,* 23 (4), 2006, 17–25.

17. Lynn Wiley and Tina E. Chrzastowski. The Impact of Electronic Journals on Interlibrary Lending: A Longitudinal Study of Statewide Interlibrary Loan Article Sharing in Illinois. *Library Collections, Acquisitions, and Technical Services*, 29, 2005, 364–81.

18. Peter Lor. Measuring the Outcomes of Southern African Interlending Requests: A Comparison of Measurement Approaches. *South African Journal of Library and Information Science*, 57 (4), 1989, 362–71.

19. Anne K. Beaubien, Jennifer Kuehn, Barbara Smolow, and Suzanne M. Ward. Challenges Facing High-Volume Interlibrary Loan Operations: Baseline Data and Trends in the CIC Consortium. *College & Research Libraries*, 67 (1), January 2006, 64–84.

20. Thomas E. Nisonger. Accessing Information: The Evaluation Research. *Collection Management*, 26 (1), 2001, 1–23.

21. Mary E. Jackson. *Measuring the Performance of Interlibrary Loan Operations in North America Research and College Libraries: Results of a Study Funded by the Andrew W. Mellon Foundation.* Washington, DC: Association of Research Libraries, 1998. See also Mary E. Jackson. Measuring the Performance of Interlibrary Loan and Document Delivery Services. *ARL: A Bimonthly Newsletter*, 195, December 1997. Available at http://www.arl.org/newsltr/1997.html.

22. Anthony W. Ferguson and Kathleen Kehoe. Access vs. Ownership: What Is Most Cost Effective in the Sciences. *Journal of Library Administration*, 19 (2), 1993, 89–99.

23. Marilyn M. Roche. *ARL/RLG Interlibrary Loan Cost Study.* Washington, DC: Association of Research Libraries, 1993.

24. Eleanor A. Gossen and Suzanne Irving. Ownership Versus Access and Low-Use Periodical Titles. *Library Resources & Technical Services,* 39, January 1995, 43–52.

25. David Everett. Full-Text Online Databases and Document Delivery in an Academic Library: Too Little, Too Late? *Online,* 17, March 1993, 22–25.

26. Bruce R. Kingma. Economic Issues in Document Delivery: Access versus Ownership and Library Consortia. *Serials Librarian*, 34 (1–2), 1998, 203–11; Bruce R. Kingma. Interlibrary Loan and Resource Sharing: The Economics of the SUNY Express Consortium. *Library Trends*, 45, Winter 1997, 518–30; and Bruce R. Kingma and Suzanne Irving. The Economics of Access Versus Ownership: The Costs and Benefits of Access to Scholarly Articles via Interlibrary Loan and Journal Subscriptions. *Journal of Interlibrary Loan, Document Delivery & Information Supply,* 6 (3), 1996, 1–79.

27. Wilbur Stolt, Pat Weaver-Meyers, and Molly Murphy. Interlibrary Loan and Customer Satisfaction: How Important Is Delivery Speed, in *Continuity and Transformation: The Promise of Confluence: Proceedings of the Seventh National Conference of the Association of College and Research Libraries.* Chicago: Association of College and Research Libraries, 1995, 365–71; Lee-Allison Levene and Wayne Pedersen. Patron Satisfaction at Any Cost? A Case Study of Interlibrary Loan in Two U.S. Research Libraries. *Journal of Library Administration*, 23 (1–2), 1996, 55–71; Pat L. Weaver-Meyers and Wilbur A. Stolt. Delivery Speed, Timeliness and Satisfaction: Patrons' Perceptions About ILL Service. *Journal of Library Administration*, 23 (1–2), 1996, 23–42; and Sheila Walters. User Behavior in a

Non-Mediated Document Delivery Environment: The Direct Doc Pilot Project at Arizona State. *Computers in Libraries*, 15, October 1995, 22–24, 26.

28. Anna H. Perrault and Marjo Arseneau. User Satisfaction and Interlibrary Loan Service: A Study at Louisiana State University. *RQ*, 35, Fall 1995, 90–100.

29. Yem S. Fong. The Value of Interlibrary Loan: An Analysis of Customer Satisfaction Survey Comments. *Journal of Library Administration*, 23 (1/2), 1996, 43–54.

30. Jackson, *Measuring the Performance of Interlibrary Loan Operations*.

31. Mark Kinnucan. Demand for Document Delivery and ILL in Academic Settings. *Library and Information Science Research*, 15, 1993, 355–74; and Mark Kinnucan. Modeling User's Preferences for Document Delivery. *OCLC Systems and Services*, 10, 1994, 93–98.

32. L. Dols, K. Newsome and J. Veldof. A Process Improvement Approach to ILL, in *Arizona Libraries: Books to Bytes. Contributed Papers Presented at the AZLA Annual Conference, Phoenix Civic Plaza, 17–18 November 1995*. Phoenix: Arizona Library Association, 1996, 10–28.

33. Francoise Hébert. An Unobtrusive Investigation of ILL in Large Public Libraries in Canada. *Library & Information Science Research*, 16, 1994, 3–21; and Francoise Hébert. Service Quality: ILL in the Public Library, in J. Watkins (Ed.). *Interlending and Document Supply: Proceedings of the Fourth International Conference. Papers from the conference Held in Calgary, June 1995*. Boston Spa: IFLA, 1996, 111–17.

34. Molidori Group, Inc. *Emory University General Libraries ILL User Survey. Executive Summary*. Atlanta: Emory University General Libraries, 1997.

35. Joan Stein. ILL User Focus Groups: Final Report, Carnegie Mellon University Libraries. Unpublished report. Contact Joan at joan@andrew.cmu.edu.

36. Zheng Ye (Lan) Yang. Improving Turnaround Time for Document Delivery of Materials Owned But Not Found on the Shelf: A Case Study from an Academic Library. *The Journal of Academic Librarianship*, 32 (2), 2006, 200–204.

37. Anne K. Beaubien, Jennifer Kuehn, Barbara Smolow, and Suzanne M. Ward. Challenges Facing High-Volume Interlibrary Loan Operations: Baseline Data and Trends in the CIC Consortium. *College & Research Libraries*, 67 (1), January 2006, 64–84.

38. David J. Gregory and Wayne A. Pedersen. Book Availability Revisited: Turnaround Time for Recalls versus Interlibrary Loans. *College & Research Libraries*, 64, July 2003, 283–99.

39. Jennifer E. Knievel, Heather Wicht, and Lynn Silipigni Connaway. Use of Circulation Statistics and Interlibrary Loan Data in Collection Management. *College & Research Libraries*, 67 (1), January 2006, 35–49.

40. Chris Anderson. The Long Tail. *Wired*, 12 (10), October 2004; and Chris Anderson. *The Long Tail: Why the Future of Business Is Selling Less of More*. New York: Hyperion, 2006.

41. Stephen J. Bensman. Urquhart's Law: Probability and the Management of Scientific and Technical Journal Collection. Part 1. The Law's Initial Formulation and Statistical Bases. *Science & Technology Libraries*, 26 (1), 2005, 11–68; Part 2. Probability in the Development of a Central Document Delivery Collection. *Science & Technology Libraries*, 26 (2), 2005, 5–31; Part 3.The Law's Final Formulation and Implications for Library Systems. *Science & Technology Libraries*, 26 (2), 2005, 33–69.

42. Chandra Prabha and Elizabeth C. Marsh. Commercial Document Suppliers: How Many of the ILL/DD Periodical Article Requests Can They Fulfill? *Library Trends*, 45, Winter 1997, 551–68.

43. Eleanor A. Gossen and Sue Kaczor. Variation in Interlibrary Loan Use by University of Albany Science Departments. *Library Resources & Technical Services*, 41, January 1997, 17–28.

44. Eve-Marie Lacroix. Interlibrary Loan in U.S. Health Sciences Libraries: Journal Article Use. *Bulletin of the Medical Library Association*, 82, October 1994, 363–68.

45. Christine H. Guyonneau. Performance Measurements for ILL: An Evaluation. *Journal of Interlibrary Loan & Information Supply*, 3 (3), 1993, 101–26.

13

Evaluation of Online Systems

Numerous studies have shown users are often willing to sacrifice information quality for accessibility. This fast food approach to information consumption drives librarians crazy. "Our information is healthier and tastes better too" they shout. But nobody listens. We're too busy Googling.

—Peter Morville[1]

SERVICE DEFINITION

The more services and functionality are added to a library's Web site, the more important usability becomes. Similarly, the library's online catalog—as the primary finding tool for library resources—continues to play a vital role in the lives of both library staff and library customers. The interaction between an individual and an automated system is called an interface. A useful definition of *usability* states:

> The usability of an interface is a measure of the effectiveness, efficiency and satisfaction with which specified users can achieve specified goals in a particular environment with that interface.[2]

Jacob Nielsen suggests that there are five attributes of a usable interface:

- It is easy to learn—Can users accomplish basic tasks the first time they use the site?

- It is efficient to use—How quickly can users perform basic tasks?

- It is easy to remember—When users return to a Web site, how quickly can they reestablish proficiency?

- It causes few errors—How many and how severe are the errors users make that are caused by the user interface? The user may make errors independent of the user interface.

- It is pleasant to use—Is the total experience pleasant or one the user leaves quickly?[3]

The user's success with a particular user interface is predicated upon three primary factors:

- the amount of and accuracy of information,
- the choice of indexes and the vocabulary selected for a specific search request, and
- the difficulty/friendliness in learning to use the user interface itself.

EVALUATION QUESTIONS

An evaluation of the library's online systems is important for a number of reasons:

- The library's online catalog and Web site is often the first point of contact for a library customer.
- Improving usability will make the user more successful and thus more likely to return on a regular basis.
- If the library places resources on its Web site and they are used infrequently because it is hard to find them, resources are being wasted.

EVALUATION METHODS

As shown in Table 13.1, both qualitative and quantitative methods can be used to evaluate online systems.

Table 13.1. Methods for the Evaluation of Online Systems

Perspective	Qualitative	Quantitative
Internal Focus	Expert opinion Heuristic evaluation Checklists	Visualization tools Transaction log analysis Information retrieval analysis
External Focus	Interviews Focus groups Card sorting Ideal page design Observation—treasure hunt Think aloud/think after Tracking eye movement Diary Complaints Failure analysis	Surveys Experiments

When evaluating a library's online systems, it is important to use several methods so as to obtain a more balanced perspective of how well the library's online catalog and the library's Web site are meeting the needs of its customers.

DISCUSSION OF PRIOR EVALUATIONS AND RESEARCH

The whole experience of using a Web site is tied to a variety of factors, including how the site is organized and what navigation features, such as buttons, tabs, menus, links, graphics, site maps, and a site search engine, are provided. When they are visiting a Web site, users have a set of expectations; in order to be successful, the Web site must either meet or exceed those expectations. High-quality Web sites provide information and content of value to the customers!

A library's Web site will offer access to the online catalog as well as other electronic resources accessible through the library. It will provide information about the library, including it locations, hours, upcoming events, and so forth. A library's Web site may be in transition from one to another of three stages:

- **We are here.** The Web site provides basic library information and allows the user to perform a few rudimentary tasks.

- **User-centered Web site.** In addition to gaining access to the library's online catalog and other electronic resources, the user is able to accomplish a variety of other tasks—place a hold, change a mailing address, submit a request for purchase, place an interlibrary loan request, interact directly with a reference librarian, and so forth.

- **Personalization.** The user is able to customize the "look and feel" of the Web site and place a standing request to be placed in the hold queue for new books by a particular author, genre, and so forth.

The majority of libraries have an online catalog that is supplied by a vendor. Although a library can submit suggestions for enhancements, working collectively with other customers through a user's group to have the desired enhancements to a library's online catalog made by a vendor is likely to be a more effective method—the enhancements are likely to be included in a near-term software release.

Site level usability includes information architecture, navigation and search, linking strategy, overall writing style, page templates, layout and site design standards, use of common icons, clarity of headlines, and avoidance of jargon. The density of information on most Web sites is quite high, which essentially decreases the "findability" of information. Peter Morville suggests that "findability" is

- the quality of being locatable or navigable,

- the degree to which a particular object is easy to discover or locate, and

- the degree to which a system or environment supports navigation and retrieval.[4]

Qualitative Methods

A variety of qualitative methods are available for assessing the usability of a library's online systems. These will be addressed in some detail.

Expert Opinion

A knowledgeable individual can be approached to render an opinion about the usability of a library's online system. Typically this individual will have participated in a number of projects to improve the usability of Web sites and may have published an article or book about the topic of usability.

The use of an expert can result in very specific suggestions in a short period of time. The downside of this approach is that the recommendations only reflect the judgment and opinion of one individual.

Heuristic Evaluation

Heuristic evaluation is a usability engineering method for finding usability problems in a user interface design. Heuristic evaluation, originally developed by Jacob Nielsen, involves having a small set of evaluators examine the interface and judge its compliance with recognized usability principles—the "heuristics."[5] Nielsen suggests that the best results come from testing with no more than five evaluators, which will reveal about 85 percent of a site's usability problems.[6]

Each individual evaluator inspects the interface alone, and after all have finished they will then confer and discuss their findings. Each evaluator typically prepares a written report, which is used to assist the team in preparing a joint report. In some cases the evaluators are given a prescribed set of tasks to complete, and they can record their observations directly on the form. The output from the heuristic evaluation is a list of usability problems.

Checklists

A checklist is a relatively quick way to judge whether various elements have been included in a library Web site. A number of checklists have been developed over the last few years.[7] Several excellent books also provide checklists and other usability testing advice.[8] Roslyn Raward developed one such checklist that has been applied in several settings (see appendix A).[9] Raward used her checklist to evaluate the Web sites of 20 academic libraries and found no relationship with the type or age of the institution, but rather, good Web sites reflected the individual staff involved as well as the level of training and resources provided by each individual library.

Among the advantages of using a checklist for assessing the usability of a Web site are that it

- can be used to help design a new Web site or improve an existing one,
- uses a structured method of applying usability research to improve a Web site,
- is inexpensive and easy to implement,
- can be updated to reflect the latest advances in usability and technical communication techniques, and
- can be used multiple times during the development or improvement project.

Interviews

An interview is a guided conversation in which one person seeks information from another. Preparing the interview questions and knowing when and how to follow up with clarifying questions is critical to maximizing value for the process. One-on-one interviews can take significant time to conduct and then to prepare a transcript of the interview (if recorded) to formalize the notes that were taken. The written record of the interviews forms the basis for the analysis. The strength of an interview is that you will obtain detailed information not available from a survey. A more detailed discussion of the interview method may be found in chapter 4.

Focus Groups

Several focus groups composed of representatives of different types of users could be utilized to solicit information about what they like and don't like in an online system. As noted in chapter 4, this method requires a skilled moderator, and the library should have a clear idea of the topics to be covered.

Karen Markey has used focus groups to evaluate online catalogs.[10]

Card Sorting

Card sorting is an excellent method for learning more about users' mental models for a given situation. The tasks that can be performed, planned, or actual are each written on a separate card. Users are then asked to sort the cards into "related" stacks. This will help the Web site designer organize the Web pages so that information that "clumps" or is logically associated from the user's perspective will be found in the same place on the Web site. The mental models of Web site developers are often significantly different than those of the intended users.

Typically a group of participants are given the same set of cards to sort at one time. The card sorting technique can help the library understand

- the overall organization of the content of the Web site from the users' perspective,
- terminology preferred by users,
- labels users apply to different categories of information,
- unnecessary objects, and
- missing objects.

The card sort method was effectively used by the Cornell University Library to help determine how users would organize a set of concepts to be included in an online digital library help system.[11]

Ideal Page Design

In this method, a small group of users are asked to design their ideal page (a library home page, among several others). The resulting drawings are analyzed to identify what elements are used and their placement. The resulting report and original drawings are then shared with the Web page designer to produce mock-ups of the various pages. Typically these mock-ups are then shared with a different group of users, using a focus group or another method, to obtain their reactions.

Observation

Another method is to observe a series of users. In some cases, the user is asked to perform a general task, and at other times a user is given a series of very specific tasks to complete. In all cases, the path the user selects is recorded, using a video camera or by taking extensive notes. The challenge for the librarian is not to respond to questions, or, when the user encounters a problem, to make the observation a "teachable moment."

An analysis of a library Web site found that users had problems because too much expert knowledge was expected of them, and use of library terminology contributed to their difficulties.[12] Mark Spivey examined 60 academic library home pages and found the use of library jargon quite prevalent.[13] Table 13.2 presents a comparison of terminology that didn't work with the wording preferred by users.

John Kupersmith summarized 47 usability studies and found that

- the average user success rate for finding journal articles is only 53 percent;

- the terms most often misunderstood by users include acronyms and brand names, database, E-journals, index, periodical or serial, resource, reference and interlibrary loan; and

- terms most often understood by users include find books, find articles and terms accompanied by additional words or mouseovers that expand on their meaning.[14]

Table 13.2. Evaluation of Library Terminology*

What didn't work: Terms reported as being misunderstood, not understood, or not preferred	What did work: Terms reported as being understood or preferred
Databases—without referring to magazines, periodicals, or articles	The word *articles* prominently displayed as part of an icon representing periodicals and newspapers
Pathfinders	*Research by subject*
Web guides	*Tutorials*
Databases—described by one student as "the base that holds the data"	*Finding an article*
Browse vs. *Keyword*	*Title begins with . . .* *Subject begins with . . .*
Resources—No one used the term *resources* to describe anything	*Information by course* *Reference*
Database finder . . .	*Find articles*
Circulation	*Borrowing*
Online databases and indexes	*Find articles*
Database—Is it a spreadsheet?"	*Find articles*
Title words *Title browse*	*Title keywords* *Title begins with . . .*

*Adapted from a Web site maintained by John Kupersmith. He also provides a citation for each study included in his chart. Available at http://www.jkup.net/terms-studies.html.

A usability test at the Hunter College Libraries Web site used both qualitative and quantitative methods to analyze the data recorded on audiotapes and screen-capture software. The result was a list of features most in need of modification.[15]

Think Aloud/Think After

Scenario-based usability testing of the library's Web site can involve asking a group of real users (not library staff members) to perform certain specified tasks. The user is asked to think aloud as he or she attempts to complete the task (sometimes called the verbal protocol method). The participant is typically videotaped while completing the tasks (a videotape is simultaneously made of the screen to track the position of the pointer and where the user clicks). At a minimum, an audiorecording is made of the participant speaking as he or she works. Transcripts are normally made of the recording for analysis purposes, and this can be time-consuming.

Debbie Vaughn and Burton Callicott indicate that

- providing the evaluators with no hints will test *ease of use* of the Web site; and

- if hints or minimal instruction statements are provided, the evaluators will focus on *usefulness*.

In either case, the tasks assigned to the evaluators should focus on the usability of the site and not the information literacy skills of the participants.[16]

The goal is to analyze the data so that problems are recognized and possible solutions are identified. A usability study at the University of Buffalo library revealed that the structure and presentation of the existing Web site was surprisingly ineffective, without the study being terribly expensive or complicated.[17] Students at Roger Williams University were tape-recorded while performing personal research in the think aloud, observation/interview method.[18]

A study at Concordia University College of Alberta found that the think aloud method resulted in a greater quantity of data (and identified more problems) when compared to student interviews.[19] A study at the College of Charleston libraries using the talk aloud method revealed poor Web design and the participants' lack of research skills.[20]

Tracking Eye Movement

How text, images, and tools are displayed on the Web page is of great importance. Steve Krug has observed that many users spend little time reading a Web page but instead quickly scan sections to locate what they are looking for.

> What they actually do most of the time (if we are lucky) is glance at each page, scan some of the text, and click on the first link that catches their interest or vaguely resembles the thing they're looking for. There are actually large parts of the page that they don't even look at.[21]

Software has been developed that tracks eye movement when looking at an online system. This software will produce a "map" that traces the eye's movements and superimposes this "map" on top of an image of the Web site. A camera tracks the position of the subject's eyes on the screen using an infrared camera built into the monitor. The path the eye takes is divided into two categories—pauses (fixations) and movement. Clearly buying the necessary equipment and software and establishing a lab for testing is expensive, and most libraries will not be using this method.

When looking at the typical Web site, a majority of people will scan from left-to-right across the top of the Web page, move back to the left side of the page, scan down, scan across part way, return to the left-hand edge, and scan down some more. The resulting "map" resembles the letter "F" (see Figure 13.1). This suggests that most features of a Web site should be placed in the upper left-hand quadrant of the page. A video of eye tracking in action is also available.[22]

Figure 13.1. Eye Tracking Map. Provided courtesy of Sirsï Dynix.

Diary

The library asks a group of users to document their information-seeking activities for a period of time. The resulting information is then analyzed to look for common problems and challenges facing the users.

One library used a variation of a diary study, asking a group of graduate and undergraduate students to keep a diary and take photos and screen shots of their information-seeking activities for a week.

Complaints

The library may keep a log of all user complaints, however they are received, pertaining to the library's Web site or the online catalog. Often these complaints will reveal serious problems if the log is reviewed and the problems categorized. Tracking and analyzing complaints is a passive form of evaluation.

Failure Analysis

The computer system can keep a log of search requests that fail. Examining these failed searches allows an individual the opportunity to identify what went wrong and, by implication, what needs to be fixed. For example, some online catalogs require the author's last name to be entered prior to the first name. Searches with the author's first name will fail, so if the online catalog is modified to accept the author's name without regard to order, then the user will be more successful.

Karen Markey used a combination of methods, including failure analysis of subject searches, to better understand a new design for subject access in an online catalog.[23]

Quantitative Methods

Quantitative analysis provides very specific and detailed information about how an online system is actually used. This information can be used to complement the data gathered using qualitative methods.

Visualization Tools

Visualization tools will map a Web site so that the library can see how the site is structured and how many clicks it takes to get from one location to another.[24]

Transaction Log Analysis

The library can track the actual usage of its online systems both by using standard reports that are available from the automated library system as well as by analyzing the transaction logs that are kept by the system. The transaction log analysis will report the timing and actions of users, such as clicking on objects and links, mouse movements, typing, and so forth. The value of a transaction log analysis is that it clearly indicates what users actually do rather than what system designers expect users will do.[25] A transaction log analysis can focus on the individual commands or user's input, the search objective, or the complete session. However, the analysis needs to be viewed as a snapshot in time and cannot characterize user perceptions of the searches or activities that they perform.

Michael Berger made extensive use of transaction log analysis and found that problems in searching could be attributed to a combination of factors. The majority of searches could be placed in four categories: known item, personal author, periodical, and topical. When valid zero result searches are considered, zero result searches are much smaller than previously reported (50 percent was noted in a number of earlier studies). Success rates in all categories, except for topical, are fairly high.[26] The library at the University of Illinois at Chicago has found that the regular monitoring of OPAC transaction logs has allowed it to make improvements that lead to fewer problems for users.[27]

Transaction log analysis has been used to improve information retrieval systems,[28] determine what access points are actually used,[29] assess the success of point-of-use instructions,[30] determine what pages are viewed (and ignored) by the user, and verify users' perceptions of availability of materials.[31] See chapter 5 for further elaboration on the topic of transaction log analysis.

Information Retrieval Analysis

Precision and recall as measures of the efficiency of information retrieval have been used for a long time, although these measures do have their critics. *Precision* is the ratio of the number of relevant items found compared to the total number of items found (relevant and nonrelevant). In a perfect system, only relevant items are retrieved, and the value of precision would be 1.0. *Recall* is the ratio of the number of relevant items retrieved to the total number of relevant items in the system.

Retrieval studies have been conducted using bibliographic records (library online catalogs), full-text databases, Internet search engines, and Web sites. Since 1992, an annual Text Retrieval Conference (TREC) has been held to encourage research in information retrieval based on large text collections and to improve the evaluation techniques used to assess retrieval performance. Summarizing the precision and recall literature, it is possible to state the following:

- Precision and recall are traditional measures of retrieval performance.
- Precision and recall can be investigated using real systems and real users or be measured in a controlled situation (laboratory or experimental setting).
- Precision and recall are usually inversely proportional to one another.
- Nonrelevant items are sometimes called noise or misses.
- The size and composition of the sample used to assess the performance of a retrieval system will affect the outcome—precision and recall will vary.[32]

In many cases, it is impossible to know the total number of relevant items in a system, which makes any calculations of precision and recall suspect.

Anita Ondrusek prepared a comprehensive, systematic review of 163 studies that examined end-user behaviors and found that the studies producing the richest data sets were those projects that combined multiple methodologies and examined multiple variables. When combined with two or more other methods, transaction log analysis yields large data sets. The variables included in the various studies were grouped into six categories: end-user traits, system attributes, organizational setting, task and request characteristics, performance outcomes and obstacles, and results measures.[33]

Online Catalog

Examining the standard reports available from a library's online catalog will reveal information about how frequently an index is used, how often a search will fail, the point at which a search is abandoned, and so forth.

> *The user is not broken.*
> —Karen Schneider[34]

In 1996 Christine Borgman argued that the design of most online catalogs assumes that users formulate queries as a fixed goal and have complete knowledge about the author, title, or subject. Yet research has shown that users approach the catalog with incomplete information about any of the traditional access points, and thus online catalogs should be designed to answer questions instead of matching queries.[35] Although vendors have been adding functionality for years, the fact remains that the online catalog has remained essentially unchanged since their inception. In a recent article, Karen Markey reviewed the reasons why the online catalog has fallen from grace:

- Searching the library online catalog puts people on an emotional roller coaster.

- Translating information needs into words is difficult.

- Knowing what you want and where to look is important.

- Searching for something one does not know results in frenetic, aimless, and random activity.[36]

Users of a Web-based online catalog can often move from screen to screen quite easily, and yet their actions can lead to the wrong conclusions. A study at the Washington State University libraries found that users often conclude that when they do not find something, it is not owned by the library. The students also had a number of problems correctly using various features of the catalog, for example, the limiting feature.[37]

An observation study of four academic library online catalogs produced a total of 98 usability problems. These problems were sorted into six groups: layout (36 percent), ease of use (20 percent), functionality (17 percent), terminology (16 percent), feedback, and help.[38]

Not surprisingly, the Internet is clearly having an impact on users from all types of libraries. Eric Novotny found novice users were impatient in choosing their type of search and in evaluating their search results. They assumed search results were sorted by relevance and thus did not frequently browse past the initial screen of results. Interestingly, more experienced users used more specific keyword terms and were more persistent in reviewing their search results and considering their options.[39] No matter what type of search a task called for, participants tended to expect a simple keyword search to lead to optimal results presented in relevancy-ranked order.

Judith Kelly conducted a qualitative study, using the think aloud method complemented with an analysis of transaction logs, to gain a better understanding of the mental models constructed by users of the online catalog. She found that these individuals construct a broader mental model of information retrieval.[40]

Susan Augustine and Courtney Greene measured the amount of time and number of clicks to perform a given task and compared these measures with those of an "expert."[41] They found that users employ a trial-and-error method when searching online catalogs, are frequently unable to interpret the information they retrieve, and struggle to understand commonly used terminology. Similar results were noted in a Web usability study conducted at the University of Illinois at Chicago.[42]

Karen Markey and her colleagues examined end-user understanding of subject headings to determine the extent to which children and adults understood subdivided subject headings. A total of 48 children and 48 adults were recruited to participate in the study from three Michigan public libraries. The study found that about 36 percent of the meanings users gave to subject headings were correct. End-user understanding was not affected by context or subject heading order. The study team called on the library community to begin to grapple with the whole concept of subject access.[43]

Library Web Site

Clearly people experience the Web as a type of space through which they move. People construct cognitive maps and use a mix of trajectory and container metaphors to describe their experiences: "I went to . . . " and "I found it in . . .". People remember Web sites (bookmarks) and become confused. It is possible to move quite quickly from one Web site to another with just a simple click. The dominant form of communication on the Web is still text despite numerous sites that effectively use multimedia. Peter Morville suggests that "findability" is the bridge that spans the physical and digital worlds.[44]

Mooers' Law, first formulated by Calvin Mooers in 1959, states:

> An information retrieval system will tend *not* to be used whenever it is more painful and troublesome for a customer to have information than for him not to have it.[45]

The implications of Mooers' Law in the Web environment have led to usability studies and user-centered design. The mantra clearly is to make the library Web site simple and make it easy to use. And please, don't make me think!

A variety of tools are available that will track what portions of a Web site are visited and at what point users abandon the site. Portions of the Web site that are not used very frequently need to be repositioned or deleted.

Transaction log analysis is an unobtrusive method of tracking on the computer system the way users move around a Web site. Each "click" is logged and can be described in a variety of ways. However, it requires considerable time and computer programming talent to extract and analyze the transaction data. The real value of transaction log analysis is that the library will understand what users actually do compared to what they say they do.

Many studies of library Web sites have a developer or administrative focus rather than assessing the usability of the site from the user's perspective. For example, John D'Angelo and Sherry Little assessed 20 library Web sites to determine the extent to which they conformed to Web design guidelines.[46] Mark Stover and Steven Zink examined 40 academic library Web sites in a feature-counting comparison.[47] David King compared the layout and features found in 120 ARL Web sites.[48] Laura Cohen and Julie Still compared the structure and purpose of 100 academic library Web sites and developed four classifications: information, reference, research, and instruction.[49] A plethora of other how-we-did-it articles are available that describe how a usability test was conducted in a library.

Test questions in library Web site assessments typically follow a pattern similar to a bibliographic instruction session: Can the respondent find a journal article about a particular topic? Can the respondent find a specific book? Can the respondent change his or her patron profile? The answers to these questions comprise the "broccoli librarianship" cannon: information that librarians feel that users "should" know because it is "good for them."[50]

Caution should be exercised about usability testing because it creates an artificial situation, and the act of testing can affect the results. The conception of the test will determine the way in which the test is conducted and indirectly influence the results.[51] Testing is further complicated by the fact that many respondents will have difficulty since they lack fundamental library skills or are confused by the use of library terminology.

The manner in which information is organized on a Web site can adversely affect the way, or even whether, the site is used. A study of the University of Arizona library Web site, developed by a team of librarians, found that the developers mistakenly assumed that users understood how library information was organized.[52] The University of Washington libraries found that the layout and grouping of resources significantly affected the ability of users to distinguish between the catalog and online indexes.[53] A usability study at the Memorial University of Newfoundland libraries found that library Web sites fail to take into account how people approach the information-seeking problem and often reflect traditional library structures.[54]

Several studies have noted that library users do not understand the function or the content of the library's online catalog, online citation indexes, full-text databases, and lists of serial holdings. For example, surveys at Johns Hopkins University[55] and at the University of Northern Colorado[56] noted that students had difficulties with database searching and finding and using indexes to the periodical literature.

A study at Western Michigan University asked a group of students to find an article about a particular topic and found that 46 percent of the students were not successful starting from the library's Web site. The most common reason for failure was that the students searched the library's online catalog—of course the catalog lists books and not periodical literature.[57]

Several studies have noted that study participants often subjectively rate the user interface quite highly for its navigation and visual aesthetics, while a detailed analysis of their actual use of the Web site using transaction log analysis reveals that users are experiencing a good deal of difficulty.[58] Given the increasing use of library Web sites, especially by remotely located users, the Web interface should be clear, be easy to navigate, and have redundancy to accommodate different learning styles. Additional studies reveal that navigational assistance in the form of help and "how to find . . . " tools are hard to identify due to poor and inconsistent terminology.[59]

The University of Mississippi libraries used a number of methods in a usability assessment of the library Web site. Among the quantitative and qualitative measures collected were

- the number of clicks to reach a destination,
- the time required to complete a task,
- whether the task was completed successfully,
- the satisfaction level of the participant,
- signs of indecision,
- indications of frustration,
- user comments, and
- observer comments.[60]

Tip! For those really interested in usability testing, download the U.S. Department of Health and Human Services' *Research-Based Web Design & Usability Guidelines* (available at http://usability.gov/pdfs/guidelines_book.pdf). A total of 209 guidelines are provided. Each guideline shows a rating of its "Relative Importance" to the success of a Web site.

The vast majority of library Web usability testing focuses on "ease of use"—how quickly a user can complete a task. Very little effort is directed at testing "usefulness" and thus libraries are missing the big picture. Leslie Porter provides a good overview of various usability techniques used in the business world and illustrates how they can be applied to improve a library's Web site.[61] What is the value of the library Web site to their customers?

Surveys

It is also possible to prepare a survey and ask a group of respondents to indicate their level of satisfaction with various features and functions of a Web site. As noted above, a number of usability studies employed satisfaction surveys in conjunction with other evaluation methods. A further discussion of surveys and their development, use, and analysis of data may be found in chapter 5.

A survey at the University of the Pacific Library found that students were knowledgeable about searching for books in the online catalog but had greater difficulty identifying journal information.[62]

Experiments

Experiments allow the researcher to control a number of variables in order to better understand the relationship of one or more variables to another variable. A number of experiments have been used to examine the user interface and interaction of a human and the online catalog or Web site. Examples are Pauline Atherton's Books Project,[63] the British Okapi projects,[64] Nicholas Belkin's projects on relevance feedback,[65] and Karen Markey's online catalog projects.[66]

SUMMARY

Reflecting on these research findings, it is possible to reach the following conclusions about the evaluation of online systems:

- A qualitative method should be used to complement a quantitative method to provide a more balanced assessment of usability.

- Refining and improving an online system, particularly the library's Web site, should be done on a regular basis rather than letting one or more years elapse.

- Online systems should reflect a vocabulary that users will understand rather than using library terminology and jargon.

- The complexity that arises from the need to use multiple systems (to find books, journals, and articles about a topic) must be overcome so that the library will appeal to a broader audience.

- The time to develop the next generation online catalog is long overdue. The new online catalog must embrace a variety of features—ranked order retrieval, more like this, did you mean (correction of typos), and a simple user interface—commonly found on well-known Internet sites, such as Amazon and Google.

NOTES

1. Peter Morville. *Ambient Findability*. Sebastopol, CA: O'Reilly, 2005, 55.

2. *ISO 13407: Human-Centered Design Processes for Interactive Systems*. Geneva: International Organization for Standardization, 1999.

3. Jacob Nielsen. *Multimedia and Hypertext: The Internet and Beyond*. Boston: Academic Press, 1995, 281.

4. Morville, *Ambient Findability*.

5. Jacob Nielsen. Heuristic Evaluation, in Jacob Nielsen and R. Mack (Eds.). *Usability Inspection Methods*. New York: John Wiley, 1994.

6. Jacob Nielsen. Why You Only Need to Test with 5 Users. *Jacob Nielsen's Alertbox*. June 20, 2005. Available at http://www.useit.com/alertbox/20000319.html.

7. See, for example, Nancy Everhart. Web Page Evaluation. *Emergency Librarian*, 25 (5), May/June 1998, 22; John D'Angelo and Sherry K. Little. Successful Web Pages: What Are They and Do They Exist? *Information Technology and Libraries*, 17 (2), June 1998, 71–81. See also Steven Turner.

The HEP Test for Grading Web Site Usability. *Computers in Libraries,* 22 (10), November/December 2002, 37–39.

8. Jeffrey Rubin. *Handbook of Usability Testing: How to Plan, Design and Conduct Effective Tests.* New York: Wiley, 2002; and Elaina Norlin and C. M. Winters. *Usability Testing for Library Websites: A Hands-on Guide.* Chicago: American Library Association, 2002.

9. Roslyn A. Raward. A Report on the Development of a Usability Analysis Tool for the Evaluation of Library Websites, in *Information Online 2003: 11th Conference and Exhibition, 21–23 January 2003.* Available at http://conferences.alia.org.au/online2003/papers/raward.html.

10. Karen Markey Drabenstott. Focused Group Interviews, in Jack Glazier and Ronald R. Powell (Eds.). *Qualitative Research in Information Management.* Englewood, CO: Libraries Unlimited, 1992, 85–104.

11. Angi Faiks and Nancy Hyland. Gaining User Insight: A Case Study Illustrating the Card Sort Technique. *College & Research Libraries*, 61 (4), July 2000, 349–57.

12. Ruth Dickstein and Vicki Mills. Usability Testing at the University of Arizona Library: How to Let the Users in on the Design. *Information Technology and Libraries*, 19, 2000, 144–51.

13. Mark A. Spivey. The Vocabulary of Library Home Pages: An Influence on Diverse and Remote End-Users. *Information Technology and Libraries*, 19, September 2000, 152–56. See also Rachael Naismith and Joan Stein. Library Jargon: Student Comprehension of Technical Language Used by Librarians. *College & Research Libraries*, 50, September 1989, 543–52.

14. John Kupersmith maintains a Web site that summarizes usability studies: http://www.jkup.net/terms-studies.html.

15. Laura Cobus, Valeda Dent, and Anita Ondrusek. How Twenty-Eight Users Helped Redesign an Academic Library Web Site: A Usability Study. *Reference & User Services Quarterly*, 44 (3), Spring 2005, 232–46.

16. Debbie Vaughn and Burton Callicot. Broccoli Librarianship and Google-Bred Patrons, or What's Wrong with Usability Testing? *College & Research Libraries*, 64 (2), 2003, 1–18.

17. Brenda Battleson, Austin Booth, and Jane Weintrop. Usability Testing of an Academic Library Web Site: A Case Study. *The Journal of Academic Librarianship*, 27 (3), May 2001, 188–98.

18. Susan McMullen. Usability Testing in a Library Web Site. *Reference Service Review*, 29, February 2001, 7–22.

19. Heather G. Morrison. Online Catalogue Research and the Verbal Protocol Method. *Library HiTech*, 17 (2), 1999, 197–206.

20. Vaughn and Callicott, Broccoli Librarianship, 1–18.

21. Steve Krug. *Don't Make Me Think: A Common Sense Approach to Web Usability.* Berkeley, CA: New Rider, 2006, 21.

22. Available at http://sethgodin.typepad.com/seths_blog/2006/05/what_i_learned_.html.

23. Karen M. Drabenstott and Marjorie S. Weller. Failure Analysis of Subject Searches in a Test of a New Design for Subject Access to Online Catalogs. *Journal of the American Society for Information Science*, 47 (7), July 1996, 519–37.

24. For example, visualization tools include VISVIP and ScentViz, among others.

25. Bernard J. Jansen. Search Log Analysis: What It Is, What Has Been Done, How to Do It. *Library & Information Science Research*, 28, 2006, 407–32.

26. Michael G. Berger. Information-Seeking in the Online Bibliographic System: An Exploratory Study. Ph.D. dissertation, University of California, Berkeley, 1994.

27. Deborah D. Blecic, Nirmala S. Bangalore, Josephine L. Dorsch, Cynthia L. Henderson, Melissa H. Koenig, and Ann C. Weller. Using Transaction Log Analysis to Improve OPAC Retrieval Results. *College & Research Libraries*, 59 (1). January 1998, 39–50.

28. Thomas Peters. The History and Development of Transaction Log Analysis. *Library Hi Tech*, 11 (2), 1993, 41–66.

29. Brendan J. Wyly. From Access Points to Materials: A Transaction Log Analysis of Access Point Value for Online Catalog Users. *Library Resources & Technical Services*, 40, 1996, 211–36.

30. Michael C. Atlas, Karen R. Little, and Michael O. Purcell. Flip Charts at the OPAC: Using Transaction Log Analysis to Judge Their Effectiveness. *References and User Services Quarterly*, 37, 1997, 63–69.

31. Anne C. Ciliberti, Marie L. Radford, and Gary P. Radford. Empty Handed? A Material Availability Study and Transaction Log Verification. *Journal of Academic Librarianship*, 24, 1998, 282–88.

32. Carol Tenipor. Full-Text Databases, in Martha Williams (Ed.). *Annual Review of Information Science and Technology*. White Plains, NY: Knowledge Industries, 1984; Carol Tenopir and Jung Sung Ro. *Full-Text Databases*. New York: Greenwood, 1990; Gholamreza F. Araghi. Major Problems in Retrieval Systems. *Cataloging & Classification Quarterly*, 40 (1), 2005, 43–53; Marcia D. Kerchner. A Dynamic Methodology for Improving the Search Experience. *Information Technology & Libraries*, 25 (2), June 2005, 78–87; Charlotte Wien. Sample Sizes and Composition: Their Effect on Recall and Precision in IR Experiments with OPACs. *Cataloging & Classification Quarterly*, 29 (4), 2000, 73–85.

33. Anita L. Ondrusek. The Attributes of Research on End-User Online Searching Behavior: A Retrospective Review and Analysis. *Library & Information Science Research*, 26, 2004, 221–65.

34. Karen G. Schneider. *The User Is Not Broken: A Meme Masquerading as a Manifesto*. 2006. Available at www.freerangelibrarian.com.

35. Christine L. Borgman. Why Are Online Catalogs Still Hard to Use? *Journal of the American Society for Information Science*, 47 (7), July 1996, 493–503.

36. Karen Markey. The Online Catalog: Paradise Lost and Paradise Regained? *D-Lib Magazine*, 13 (1/2), January/February 2007. Available at http://dlib.org/dlib/january07/markey/01markey.html.

37. Janet Chisman, Karen Diller, and Sharon Walbridge. Usability Testing: A Case Study. *College & Research Libraries*, 60, November 1999, 552–69.

38. Hayley White, Tim Wright, and Brenda Chawner. Usability Evaluation of Library Online Catalogues. *Proceedings of the Seventh Australasian User Interface Conference, Hobart, Australia*, 2006, 50. Conferences in Research and Practice in Information Technology, Wayne Pickarski (Series Ed.). Available at crpit.com/confpapers/CRPITV50White.pdf.

39. Eric Novotny. I Don't Think I Click: A Protocol Analysis Study of Use of a Library Online Catalog in the Internet Age. *College & Research Libraries*, 65 (6), November 2004, 525–37.

40. Judith J. Kelly. What Do They Think They're Doing? Mental Models of Online Catalog Users in an Academic Library. Ph.D. dissertation, University of Georgia, Athens, 1995.

41. Susan Augustine and Courtney Greene. Discovering How Students Search a Library Web Site: A Usability Case Study. *College & Research Libraries*, 63 (4), July 2002, 354–65.

42. Steve Brantley, Annie Armstrong, and Krystal M. Lewis. Usability Testing of a Customizable Library Web Portal. *College & Research Libraries*, 67 (3), March 2006, 146–63.

43. Karen M. Drabenstott, Schelle Simcox, and Eileen G. Fenton. End-User Understanding of Subject Headings in Library Catalogs. *Library Resources & Technical Services*, 43 (3), July 1999, 140–60.

44. Morville, *Ambient Findability*.

45. Remarks by Calvin Mooers during a panel discussion at the annual meeting of the American Documentation Institute, October 24, 1959. See also Calvin N. Mooers. Mooers' Law: Or Why Some Retrieval Systems Are Used and Others Are Not. *American Documentation*, 11 (3), 1990, 1.

46. John D'Angelo and Sherry K. Little. Successful Web Pages: What Are They and Do They Exist? *Information Technology & Libraries*, 17, June 1998, 71–81.

47. Mark Stover and Steven D. Zink. World Wide Web Home Page Design: Patterns and Anomalies of Higher Education Library Home Pages. *Reference Services Review*, 24, 1996, 7–20.

48. David L. King. Library Home Page Design: A Comparison of Home Page Layout for Front-Ends to ARL Library Web Sites. *College & Research Libraries*, 59, September 1998, 458–65.

49. Laura B. Cohen and Julie M. Still. A Comparison of University Research and Two-Year College Library Web Sites. *College & Research Libraries*, 60, May 1999, 275–89.

50. Candice Benges and Janice J. Brown. Test, Review, and Retest: Usability Testing and Library Web sites. *Internet Reference Services Quarterly*, 5, 2001, 37–54.

51. Allison J. Head. Web Redemption and the Promise of Usability. *Online*, 23 (6), November/December 1999, 20–32.

52. Ruth Dickstein and Vicki Mills. Usability Testing at the University of Arizona Library: How to Let the Users in on the Design. *Information Technology and Libraries*, 19, 2000, 144–51.

53. Karen Eliasen, Jill McKinstry, and Beth Mabel Fraser. Navigating Online Menus: A Quantitative Experiment. *College & Research Libraries*, 58, November 1997, 509–16.

54. Louise McGillis and Elaine G. Toms. Usability of the Academic Library Web Site: Implications for Design. *College & Research Libraries*, 62, July 2001, 355–67.

55. Jill Coupe. Undergraduate Library Skills: Two Surveys at Johns Hopkins University. *Research Strategies*, 11, Fall 1993, 188–201.

56. Arlene Greer, Lee Weston, and Mary Alm. Assessment of Learning Outcomes: A Measure of Progress in Library Literacy. *College & Research Libraries*, 52, November 1991, 549–57.

57. Barbara J. Cockrell and Elaine Anderson Jayne. How Do I Find an Article? Insights from a Web Usability Study. *The Journal of Academic Librarianship*, 28 (3), May 2002, 122–32.

58. Maryellen Allen. A Case Study of the Usability Testing of the University of South Florida's Virtual Library Interface Design. *Online Information Review*, 26, 2002, 40–53; and Shelley Gullikson, Ruth Blades, Marc Bragdon, Shelley McKibbon, Marnie Sparling, and Elaine G. Toms. The Impact of Information Architecture on Academic Web Site Usability. *Electronic Library*, 17 (5), 1999, 293–304.

59. Susan McMullen. Usability Testing in a Library Web Site Redesign Project. *Reference Services Review*, 29, 2001, 7–22; Louise McGillis and Elaine G. Toms. Usability of the Academic Library Web Site: Implications for Design. *College & Research Libraries*, 62, 2001, 355–67; and Brenda Battleson, Austin Booth, and Jane Weintrop. Usability Testing of an Academic Library Web Site: A Case Study. *Journal of Academic Librarianship*, 27, 2001, 188–98.

60. Elizabeth Stephan, Daisy T. Cheng, and Lauren M. Young. A Usability Survey at the University of Mississippi Libraries for the Improvement of the Library Home Page. *The Journal of Academic Librarianship*, 32 (1), January 2006, 35–51.

61. Leslie Porter. Library Applications of Business Usability Testing Strategies. *Library Hi Tech*, 25 (1), 2007, 126–35.

62. Janice Krueger, Ron L. Ray, and Lorrie Knight. Applying Web Usability Techniques to Assess Student Awareness of Library Web Resources. *The Journal of Academic Librarianship*, 30 (4), July 2004, 285–93.

63. Pauline Atherton. *Books Are for Use: Final Report of the Subject Access Project to the Council on Library Resources*. Washington, DC: Council on Library Resources, 1978.

64. Stephen E. Robertson, Stephen Walker, and Micheline Hancock-Beaulieu. Experimentation as a Way of Life: Okapi at TREC. *Information Processing & Management*, 36 (1), January 2000, 95–108; Edward M Keen. The Okapi Projects. *Journal of Documentation*, 53, January 1997, 84–87.

65. Nicholas J. Belkin, Colleen Cool, and D. Kelly. Iterative Exploration, Design and Evaluation of Support for Query Reformulation in Interactive Information Retrieval. *Information Processing & Management*, 37 (3), May 2001, 403–34; Nicholas J. Belkin, Combining the Evidence of Multiple

Query Representations for Information Retrieval. *Information Processing & Management*, 31, May/June 1995, 431–48.

66. Karen Markey Drabenstott. *Testing a New Design for Subject Access to Online Catalogs*. Ann Arbor, MI: School of Information and Library Studies, 1995; and Karen Markey and Anh N. Demeyer. *Dewey Decimal Classification Online Project: Evaluation of a Library Schedule and Index Integrated into the Subject Searching Capabilities of an Online Catalog; Final Report to the Council on Library Resources*. Dublin, OH: OCLC, 1986.

14

Evaluation of Bibliographic/Library Instruction and Information Literacy

Carefully targeted, thoroughly prepared, well-presented, properly evaluated user education will be expensive indeed. We might remember S. R. Ranganathan's Fourth Law of Library Science: Save the Time of the Reader. This is more important than the Principle of Cost Effectiveness: Save the Time of the Librarian.

—Tom Eadie[1]

SERVICE DEFINITION

For a considerable period of time, libraries (generally academic libraries) have been offering and providing bibliographic instruction, sometimes called library research instruction, under one guise or another. It is interesting to note that little effort is expended by a library to reduce the complexity that leads to the need for bibliographic instruction.

Because most libraries are not equipped with the budget or staff to provide bibliographic instruction for all entering students, assuming such instruction were mandated, some libraries took the approach of integrating bibliographic instructional concepts into freshmen-level courses. In the best of all possible worlds, the content was cooperatively designed by a librarian and the course instructor.

EVALUATION QUESTIONS

Among the bibliographic instruction and information literacy questions that have been evaluated are the following:

- Do different types of instructional modes make a difference in acquiring skills?

- How improved are library skills as the result of instruction?

- Are students satisfied with the instruction?
- Do students who receive instruction use the library more often?
- Does academic performance improve as the result of instruction?

EVALUATION METHODS

The evaluation of bibliographic instruction and library instruction programs has produced a fair amount of literature, but the research done in this area is generally focused on methods to improve the instruction program rather than on an assessment of the impact of the program on the lives of the recipients.

The methods used to evaluate bibliographic instruction and library instruction programs include

- skill surveys,
- satisfaction surveys,
- identifying use of the library, and
- identifying improved academic performance.

DISCUSSION OF PRIOR EVALUATIONS
AND RESEARCH

Bibliographic instruction assessment efforts seem to fall into four categories: opinion surveys, knowledge testing, observing actual library use, and student persistence.[2] These categories are used to structure this overview.

Opinion Surveys

According to Richard Werking, what bibliographic instruction evaluation was done was not meaningful.[3] Typically the evaluations focused on user satisfaction rather than the development of learning competencies and other outcomes.[4] Aside from having difficulty identifying the benefits of instruction, the instruments that were used (surveys and skill tests) often lacked validity and reliability—it was not certain that the results were reliable because the responses might not be linked to the question being asked or the skill being assessed.[5] Despite their popularity, opinion surveys had the primary drawbacks that the questions often reflected the biases of the instrument's developers and that the data generated did not measure the effectiveness of the instruction within the institution's context. In addition, the self-reported data could lead to validity problems.

One study found that 85 percent of the respondents remained positive about the class and that they had retained their skills.[6] Another study, which tracked results over a six-year period, found little relationship between students' demographics, previous library instruction, or prior use of library resources and how they evaluated library instruction.[7]

Constance Mellon found that 75 to 85 percent of students described their initial response to the library in terms of fear or anxiety.[8] Studies that focus on measuring changes in student attitudes do not in any way measure any changes in student learning.

Knowledge Testing

One study used an advanced statistical methodology (multiple regression techniques) to evaluate the retention of long-term library skills and their impact on students who took a library skills course. While the students who actively used the learned skills after the course had the best skills retention (no surprise there), the study found no significant relationship between library skills retention and SAT scores or eventual grade point averages.[9] However, the use of a Library Orientation Test did appear to forecast academic success in terms of grade point average in a sample of 81 students.[10] Another study found no significant correlation between a library information competency class and the students' GPAs.[11]

Self-assessment imposes serious methodological problems because it is often not reliable or valid. For example, 90 percent of students rated their library skills as adequate, but in a test of competences, only 53 percent proved "minimally competent."[12]

Use of a pretest and post-test methodology has the potential for more accurately understanding knowledge transfer as a result of completing a class. One study using this approach with a sample of 404 students found no difference between pre- and post-test results.[13] Another study, with a larger sample of 1,197 students, found that the library class measurably improved the participants' library skills.[14] However, if the same instrument is used for the pre- and post-test, reported gains are suspect because students will likely remember questions and naturally improve their scores. Also, if students are tested immediately after receiving instruction, short-term gains are not likely to be sustained.

Focusing on a prescribed set of skills is not assessing the impact of instruction on actual use and behavior in a library.

Another study assessed the quality of term papers prepared by students and tracked the long-range course completion rates of students. The students who completed a library orientation course were found to have written better papers and had higher course completion rates when compared to students who did not take the orientation class.[15] Similar findings were also noted in earlier studies.[16] Providing a contrary point of view, another analysis found that a library instruction program made little difference in the types of materials students chose for their research papers.[17] In addition, focusing on the style of the citations, the total number of citations, and variety of citations is a library-centric view of the world. It is much more important to determine the degree to which the instruction helped the students write better papers and achieve better grades, among other possible outcomes.

A more recent study found that there were statistically significant differences in citation use (use of more scholarly resources and the number of incomplete citations) and the grade received in the course for students who took a library course than for those students who did not take the class.[18] A methodological problem associated with term paper analysis is that other variables, such as assistance from a reference librarian or friend, may interfere with the results.

Another study found significant differences between those who completed a bibliographic instruction class and a control group who did not attend the class. Bibliographic instruction class attendees had higher grade point averages and a higher persistence rate, yet there was no difference in graduation rates.[19] A three-year study determined that library use instruction is much more highly correlated with skill possession than either inherent intellectual ability or academic diligence.[20]

Donald Barclay suggested that the dearth of quality evaluations of library instructional classes was the result of limited institutional support, time constraints, and the difficulty of developing an effective evaluation process.[21] Barclay's solution was to "set [our] sights lower and do the best evaluation [we] can with what [we] have."[22] Rather than suggesting use of sloppy research, Barclay went on to recommend use of data, albeit less than perfect, which is better than either no data or the soft data based on anecdotal observations and student satisfaction surveys. Such an approach was followed at The Citadel library, which found that use of the library increased for students taking the bibliographic instruction class, as evidenced by pre- and post-test scores.[23]

A Johns Hopkins University study compared baseline measures of freshman library skills to upper-class students' skills and concluded that exposure to a library does not necessarily improve those skills, nor do students learn good library skills on their own.[24]

Carol Anne Germain et al. found that mediated online instruction resulted in greater pre- and post-test gain than traditional classroom instruction.[25] However, another study compared online and traditional and online instruction and found that while skills increased using both methods, there was no significant difference attributable to format.[26] At the University of the Pacific, Lorrie Knight found that classroom instruction resulted in improved pre- to post-test scores, while online instruction failed to provide enhanced scores.[27]

A quantitative analysis of student bibliographies submitted for courses in undergraduate institutions around Philadelphia found use of few electronic sources and no relationship between instruction in the use of electronic resources and increased usage of these sources.[28] A further study evaluated students taking a bibliographic instruction course and found that the students would obtain no greater bibliographical skills than those who did not take the course.[29]

One of the fundamental problems is that many instruments developed to measure the effectiveness of library research instruction lack important psychometric properties such as validity and reliability.[30]

Rather than traditional classroom instruction, interactive multimedia Web sites can provide instruction about specific library skills. An evaluation of the LUMENS Project found that users' topic knowledge increased after viewing the interactive materials—based on a pre- and post-test assessment of skills. However, planning the content and mastering the interactive technology requires librarians being able to work in a learning multimedia environment with few distractions.[31]

These studies are summarized in Table 14.1.

Table 14.1 Summary of Library Instruction Program Studies

Supportive	No Support
Opinion Surveys	
Wong et al. (2006). Positive feelings about instruction [395]	Werking (1980). What bibliographic instruction has been done is not meaningful
	Eadie (1982). Validity and reliability problems with locally developed instruments
	Landrum & Muench (1994). Surveys often reflect the biases of librarians who develop the instruments
	Moore-Jansen (1997). No link between instruction and library use and opinions [403]
	Stamatopols & Mackoy (1998). Student self-assessment of skills increased
Knowledge Testing	
Corlett (1974). Library orientation class was linked to improved GPA scores [81]	Hardesty et al. (1982). No correlation between library skills retention and SAT or GPA scores [162]
	Moore et al. (2002). Library skills class is not linked to GPA scores
	Ware et al. (1986). Self-assessment of skills not linked to reality
	Colborn & Cordell (1998). Pre- and post-test method reveals no improvement in library skills [404]
Breivik (1977). Library orientation course resulted in better term papers	Emmons & Martin (2002). Library use instruction made little difference in type of materials selected for a term paper [250]
King & Ory (1981); Dykeman & King (1983); Wilson (1986). Library skills class linked to better term papers	Malone & Videon (1997). Instruction does not lead to increased use of electronic sources in term papers [291]
Selegean et al. (1983). Bibliographic instruction resulted in higher GPA scores [512]	Eyman & Nunley (1977). Library skills course does lead to improved bibliographic skills
Carter (2002). Bibliographic instruction class resulted in increased use of the library	
Wang (2006). Library instruction course resulted in more scholarly citations and better grades [120 papers, 836 citations]	
Germain (2000). Online instruction resulted in better skills than classroom instruction [284]	Holman (2000). No difference between online and classroom instruction [56 & 27]

[#] = sample size

Actual Library Use

At Earlham College, bibliographic instruction was integrated into the course offerings of a majority of classes. It was found that the average graduate used the library in 54 percent of courses (bibliographic instruction was included in about 37 percent of courses). Unfortunately, no analysis was made to compare college graduates to drop-outs and their use (or nonuse) of the library.[32]

A fact that must be considered, then, is that to an extraordinary degree the primary literature indexes itself, and does so with greater comprehensiveness, better analytics, and greater precision than does the secondary literature. Footnotes are, after all, the traditional medium whereby scholars communicate with each other directly. That is their purpose.

—Stephen K. Stoan[33]

Student Retention Rates

Interestingly, several studies have noted a positive correlation between a freshman orientation course and student persistence and strengthened academic performance. One analysis examined data that covered a 15-year period and found that students who participated in the orientation class had higher sophomore return rates and graduation rates despite the fact that many were less prepared academically than their nonparticipant counterparts.[34]

A similar study found that freshman orientation course participant grades were higher, the students reported increased use of university resources such as the library and writing services, and their overall retention rate was higher than their counterparts'.[35] Freshman orientation courses are cost-effective given that they generate revenue due to increased student retention and thus offset the costs of the orientation class.[36]

Despite the studies noted here, the vast majority of libraries did little or no evaluation of bibliographic instruction because it was assumed to be a "good thing."

Bibliographic instruction seems to be perceived by many librarians simply as a self-evident social good, not needing an extensive rationale or empirical evidence to substantiate its effectiveness or even to support the need for it. Much of the literature of bibliographic instruction resembles a dialectic with the antithesis missing.[37]

In summarizing the plethora of articles reporting studies about library bibliographic instruction, a decidedly mixed picture emerges:

- The vast majority of new students who enter the college environment each year do not avail themselves of the opportunity to attend a library skills or bibliographic instruction class.

- A majority of collegiate courses do not have a bibliographic instruction component that is integrated into the course content.

- A fair amount of the research focuses on opinion surveys and pre- and post-test knowledge and library skill improvements, which do not evaluate student learning.

- The majority of instruments used to assess bibliographic instruction lack important properties such as validity and reliability.

- Improvement in basic library skills is the means and not the end, yet it is the latter that is the focus of most bibliographic instruction evaluation efforts.

- Few studies reported a link between bibliographic instruction and increased use of the library resources and services.

- Even fewer studies have focused on the link between bibliographic instruction and doing better academically (however this might be measured).

EVALUATION OF INFORMATION LITERACY PROGRAMS

Before the various studies of information literacy are reviewed, the topic of critical thinking is considered. Critical thinking is closely related to information literacy and can be defined as the ability to "interpret, evaluate, and make informed decisions about the adequacy of arguments, data, and conclusions."[38] One popular standardized test often used to assess critical thinking is the Watson-Glaser Critical Thinking Appraisal Test.[39]

One study was conducted to determine the relationship between an institution's academic library resources and services and undergraduates' library use and self-reported gains in critical thinking. Ethelene Whitmire found that the library's resources were related to self-reported gains in critical thinking for undergraduates attending research universities. Interestingly, she also found that academic library services were negatively related to undergraduates' use of the library. Undergraduates who were involved in more interactions with their faculty, engaged in more writing activities, and were active participants in the classroom reported more library use. In addition, full-time students report more library use than part-time students.[40]

In a related analysis, Whitmire noted that upperclassmen and students with better grades, students engaged in more focused library activities (compared to routine library use), and students actively participating in course learning and making conscientious revisions of their writings reported gains in their critical thinking.[41] Yet Whitmire also found that libraries with large numbers of bibliographic instruction participants, with more service hours, and with greater utilization of document delivery and interlibrary loan services reported that fewer undergraduates used the library. Confounding the picture even further, Patrick Terenzini and others found negative relationships between library experiences and critical thinking scores.[42]

Starting late in the 1980s, Patricia Breivik and others presented the idea of information literacy, suggesting that it was an essential skill in lifelong learning.[43] These individuals believed that integration of information literacy into the curriculum serves as a major goal for the future success of academic libraries. Shirley Behrens provided a conceptual analysis and historical overview of information literacy.[44]

While bibliographic instruction tended to focus on the organization of the library and its physical collections, the use of primary reference sources, and how to search the library catalog more effectively, information literacy focuses on the skills needed to handle and manipulate information in an online and Internet era.

Undergraduate students from high schools with library media teachers are more familiar with basic library use concepts, fundamental ideas of how information is organized and made accessible, and how to use online catalogs to advantage than are students from high schools without librarians. The students with good information literacy skills coming from high schools with librarians received better grades than students who attended schools without librarians.[45]

Academic librarians have turned to the concept of information literacy as a way to designate the importance of understanding how information is organized, how to find appropriate information resources, and how to assess information that is encountered during the search process. Unfortunately, "there is a temptation for students to settle for information that meets the 'three Fs' requirement: first, fastest, and full text."[46]

In general, information literacy involves recognizing a need for information, identifying what is needed, evaluating and organizing information, and learning to use it effectively. While it is obvious that developing information literacy skills will be important throughout the lives of undergraduate and graduate students, the issues of how to impart and assess those skills are very similar to those encountered by librarians when they were evaluating bibliographic instruction.

The *Information Literacy Competency Standards for Higher Education*, developed by the Association of College & Research Libraries (ACRL), state:

> Information literacy forms the basis for lifelong learning. It is common to all disciplines, to all learning environments, and to all levels of education. It enables learners to master content and extend their investigations, become more self-directed, and assume greater control over their own learning. An information literate individual is able to:
>
> - Determine the extent of information needed
> - Access the needed information effectively and efficiently
> - Evaluate information and its sources critically
> - Incorporate selected information into one's knowledge base
> - Use information effectively to accomplish a specific purpose
> - Understand the economic, legal, and social issues surrounding the use of information, and access and use information ethically and legally.[47]

Teaching information literacy skills is generally viewed as affecting student outcomes, because these skills support such educational outcomes as critical thinking, problem solving, and lifelong learning. Unfortunately this view is an assumption that has yet to be proven in a series of studies that can be replicated.

A 1990 study done at Cornell University employed two surveys: one to employers of Cornell graduates to identify which skills were needed to retrieve and manage information, and the other to graduates of the library's instruction program to identify which skills were retained and were useful in their careers.[48]

Methods of information literacy instruction include

- instruction at the reference desk,
- course-integrated instruction,
- for-credit classes, and
- tutorials.

A systematic review to assess which library instruction methods are most effective for improving the information literacy skills of undergraduate students considered 257 articles and used 55 studies for critical appraisal. Studies measured outcomes that correlated with Benjamin Bloom's lower levels of learning—remember, understand, and apply. The review found that

- computer-assisted instruction is as effective as traditional instruction;

- traditional instruction is better than no instruction; and

- self-directed, independent learning is more effective than no instruction.[49]

Susan Taylor studied three colleges with well-regarded information literacy programs and noted the factors that were common to all:

- There was leadership by the librarians.

- There was faculty interest and support.

- The curriculum required library use.

- The library's collection development involved faculty.[50]

The majority of the information literacy literature focuses on three topics: opinion/satisfaction surveys, testing of skills by the participants of the information literacy courses, and actual information-seeking behavior. The Information Literacy Test developed by the Educational Testing Service was administered to 3,000 college students from 44 institutions and found that only 13 percent were deemed information literate.[51] Only 49 percent could identify faux Web sites using evaluation criteria of objectivity, authority, and timeliness, and no more than 35 percent knew how to narrow an overly broad search.

Opinion Surveys

Often this literature suggests that improvements should be made to teaching methods and modes of delivery of the information literacy content. For example, one study found that students of color, students satisfied with campus library facilities, and students engaged in interactions with faculty self-reported greatest satisfaction with their information literacy skills.[52]

Skills Testing

Another study that used testing to gauge gains in information literacy as well as obtaining the perspectives of librarians involved in instruction and of the students claimed "success" but did not use an independent means to verify improved student grades.[53]

We have years of study to indicate that isolated skills lessons are not effective, not even when they are related to a topic of study.

—Ken Haycock[54]

One evaluation of a curriculum-integrated information literacy program for undergraduate students showed that the participants experienced little or no long-term impact on their searching skills.[55] Another study found that the differences between those who had attended library information literacy education sessions and those who had not were not that great.[56] Another problem that arises is that "library jargon" is often used in the instruction program, and as one study noted, students could only correctly define an average of 9 out of 15 terms. Terms the least understood included *Boolean logic, controlled vocabulary, truncation,* and *precision.*[57]

A study assessing information literacy at the University of California, Berkeley, found that students think they know more about accessing information and conducting library research than they are able to demonstrate when put to the test.[58] A different study found that students had difficulties defining a problem, determining where to go for information (that is, which sources to use), developing an effective search strategy, finding material in the library, and developing insights.[59]

One recent study at Southeastern Louisiana University found that students who partici-pated in an information literacy class had improved confidence levels in using the library yet failed to improve their pre- to post-test performance on content questions.[60] Between 35 and 81 percent of the test participants received poor or failing scores. Similar disappointing findings were found in a study at Johns Hopkins University[61] and Indiana University, South Bend.[62]

Challenges arise when a library attempts to use a pre- and post-test method of assessment. Locally developed questions are often not subjected to rigorous analysis to screen out use of jargon or the answer being indicated in another item. If the pretest scores are high, there is very little room to differentiate the impact of the training from incidental changes, including test/re-test effects.[63]

The King's College (Pennsylvania) library has spent several years developing a 25-item Information Literacy Assessment instrument, with five questions for each of the five ACRL *In-formation Literacy Competency Standards*. The library decided to use a relatively brief but rig-orous instrument with a reliability of .67 as measured by Cronbach's alpha. Doubling the number of questions would increase the reliability to a projected .78 but could lead to "fatigue" among the students completing the assessment.[64] Rather than the traditional librarian-centered instructional class, students are asked to complete 10- to 15-minute preclass exercises, which are reviewed by the librarian prior to the class meeting. During the class students are asked to demonstrate the concepts so that they learn from each other to make the experience more learning centered.

Project SAILS (Standardized Assessment of Information Literacy Skills) is a Web-based, multiple-choice knowledge test targeting a variety of information literacy skills. A number of academic libraries have administered the test. Participants are presented with 45 randomly generated multiple-choice or multiple-response questions from a test bank of 130 questions. In general, the findings suggest that students' information literacy seems to improve throughout their academic careers due to their participation in an information literacy class.[65]

It is also possible to use an evaluation rubric to assess the information literacy skills of in-dividuals. Megan Oakleaf found that multiple raters can use rubrics to produce consistent scor-ing of information literacy artifacts of student learning. However, different groups of raters arrived at varying levels of agreement. And while students could give specific indicators of au-thority when evaluating a Web site, they had difficulty choosing an appropriate Web site for a specific assignment.[66]

Observed Behavior

One study found that while students' learning is influenced by their previous experiences, they will engage with information literacy programs only to the extent that they perceive pro-fessors and instructors require them to do so.[67] Other studies have raised serious questions about students' abilities to seek and use information.[68]

An analysis of college students found that they are not being exposed to library and infor-mation literacy environments, and those students greatly overestimated their skill levels. Few faculty members participate in information literacy skills modeling for students, and students are not familiar with basic library research skills.[69]

Nancy Seamans used a qualitative approach and found that students do not see libraries and library personnel as part of their information-support network. Further, students appear to be generally uncritical in using and evaluating resources.[70] Alison Brettle prepared a system-atic review of the literature and observed that there is limited evidence to show that training im-proves skills, insufficient evidence to determine the most effective methods of training, and limited evidence to show whether training leading to increased knowledge of health care improves patient health care.[71]

Clearly the readily availability of a wide range of Internet-based resources (some of dubious quality and value) is having an impact on academic libraries. The well-publicized decline in ARL reference statistics is one handy indicator. One study of student searching behavior shows that commercial Internet search engines dominate students' information-seeking strategies. Some 45 percent of students use Google as their primary access method when attempting to locate information, while only 10 percent rely on the university library online catalog.[72] A companion survey, sponsored by the Pew Trust, found that 55 percent of college students completely agree that Google provides worthwhile information, compared with only 31 percent for library databases. In addition, Internet-based search engines are the first choice for research for 80 percent of the respondents; the online library only 6 percent. Further, the respondents indicated that they see little difference between Internet resources and library-provided electronic databases.[73]

The OCLC survey indicates that search engines are used most often to begin information searches (89 percent), while a library Web site is selected by just 2 percent of college students.[74] The survey also found that college students favor libraries as a place to study, for free Internet access, and for materials, while they favor bookstores for coffee shops, current materials, and meeting their friends.

An analysis of over 300,000 student respondents to the College Student Experiences Questionnaire over a 19-year period found that library experiences do not seem to directly contribute to gains in information literacy, to what students gain overall from college, or to student satisfaction.[75]

A summary of the studies related to information literacy is in Table 14.2.

Table 14.2. Summary of Information Literacy Studies

Supportive	No Support
Smalley (2004). High school students with good information literacy skills received better grades than students who attended high schools without librarians [506]	Whitmire (1998). Libraries with large numbers of bibliographic instruction students report that few undergraduates used the library [18,157]
Skills Testing	
Julien & Boon (2004). Claimed gains in information literacy but no testing [28]	Brewer (1999). Information literacy program had no impact on students' searching skills
	Rabine & Cardwell (2000). Few differences between those who attended an information literacy class and those who did not [414]
	Maughan (2001). Students' perceptions of their skills is greater than reality [185]

Supportive	No Support
	Hepworth (1999). Students not retaining information literacy skills
	Dunnington & Strong (2006). Student confidence levels improved but actual skills did not [635]
	Coupe (1993). Student skill levels did not improve
	Schuck (1992). Instruction course produced no improvements
Observed Behavior	
	Hartmann (2001). Participation in information literacy is driven by professor requirements [focus groups]
	Turnbull et al. (2000). Students reluctant to seek and use information
	Kuh & Gonyea (2003). Library experiences do not lead to gains in information literacy [300,000]

[#] = sample size

James Marcum has asked whether "information" is the appropriate literacy. He suggested that other literacies deserved some consideration and were perhaps better suited for a student's long-term success in the job marketplace. Among the possible literacies vying for supremacy are visual literacy, technological literacy, computer-mediated communication literacy, computational literacy, and knowledge media literacy.[76] Perhaps literacy is not the appropriate focus, but rather academic libraries should be concentrating on competencies, fluency, or expertise.

Allan Martin has suggested the use of the term "e-literacy" to describe the combination of computer literacy and information literacy encompassing

- awareness of IT and the information environment,
- confidence in using generic IT and information tools,
- evaluation of information-handling operations and products,
- reflection of one's own e-literacy development, and
- adaptability and willingness to meet e-literacy challenges.[77]

FACULTY–LIBRARIAN RELATIONSHIPS

The perception of librarians by academic faculty members will clearly have a major impact on the success of information literacy efforts. Some librarians have observed that faculty members are either apathetic about or obstructive toward their efforts to initiate joint instructional activities. Several studies suggest that librarians are valued for the support services they provide but are not perceived to be academic equals, as evidenced by the lack of scholarly published literature.[78] And while librarians are concerned about their relationships with faculty, faculty members do not seem to be too concerned about theirs with librarians.[79]

The most thorough analysis to date remains Hardesty's 1991 study, which developed the *Library Educational Attitudes Scale* to measure faculty members' attitudes toward the role of the library in undergraduate education.[80] Other studies soon followed, including Cannon,[81] Thomas,[82] and Leckie and Fullerton.[83] The studies suggested that arts and humanities faculty were more likely to invite a librarian to instruct their classes than were their science counterparts. In addition, there is little support among faculty for instructional methods requiring a high degree of library–faculty cooperation, such as team teaching, credit courses, or jointly developed assignments.

Librarians at Oregon State University found that a surprising number of faculty and students did not know about the several one-credit, discipline-specific library research courses, and that a for-credit course was the least preferred method for receiving information literacy instruction.[84] More recently, Claire McGuinness found that faculty believe that students gradually become information literate through class assignments and individual initiative as part of a "law of exposure." The findings lead to the assumption made by faculty that students will develop information literacy skills although the faculty make no attempt to design assignments with this outcome in mind.[85]

All of this suggests that librarians need to reconsider their opinions about what students need to be taught and how librarians contribute to the student learning process. Implicit in this reconsideration is the need to focus library efforts on the outcomes of information literacy rather than on ways to improve the process of imparting skills or assessing the satisfaction levels of students who complete an information literacy course.

SUMMARY

In summarizing the information literacy literature, a fairly clear picture comes into focus:

- A majority of the literature has centered on the testing of discrete skills or competencies to improve the delivery of information literacy content. Such a perspective focuses on the instructor, instruction method, or instruction materials and is too narrowly focused.

- Little research has addressed the value of improved information literacy skills and success in the academic environment.

- Faculty members will of necessity have to be involved in the assessment of information literacy outcomes.

- No research has been done to determine the extent to which good information literacy skills assist in lifelong learning and greater success in student careers after graduation—a "big picture" perspective.

NOTES

1. Tom Eadie. Immodest Proposals: User Instruction for Students Does Not Work. *Library Journal*, 115 (17), October 15, 1990, 44.

2. John C. Selegean, Martha Lou Thomas, and Marie Louise Richman. Long-Range Effectiveness of Library Use Instruction. *College & Research Libraries*, 44 (6), November 1983, 476–80.

3. Richard Werking. Evaluating Bibliographic Instruction: A Review and Critique. *Library Trends*, 29, Summer 1980, 153–72.

4. Tom Eadie. Beyond Immodesty: Questioning the Benefits of BI. *RQ*, 21, 1982, 331–33.

5. Eric Landrum and Diana Muench. Assessing Student Library Skills and Knowledge: The Library Research Strategies Questionnaire. *Psychological Reports*, 75, 1994, 1617–24.

6. Gabrielle Wong, Diana Chan, and Sam Chu. Assessing the Enduring Impact of Library Instruction Programs. *The Journal of Academic Librarianship*, 32 (4), July 2006, 384–95.

7. Cathy Moore-Jansen. What Difference Does It Make? One Study of Student Background and the Evaluation of Library Instruction. *Research Strategies*, 15 (1), 1997, 26–38.

8. Constance A. Mellon. Library Anxiety: A Grounded Theory and Its Development. *College & Research Libraries*, 47, March 1986, 162–3.

9. Larry Hardesty, Nicholas P. Lovrich Jr., and James Mannon. Evaluating Library-Use Instruction. *College & Research Libraries*, 43, January 1982, 38–46.

10. Donna Corlett. Library Skills, Study Habits and Attitudes, and Sex as Related to Academic Achievement. *Educational and Psychological Measurement*, 34 (4), 1974, 967–69.

11. Deborah Moore, Steve Brewster, Cynthia Dorroh, and Michael Moreau. Information Competency Instruction in a Two-Year College: One Size Does Not Fit All. *Reference Services Review*, 30, November 2002, 300–306.

12. Susan A. Ware, J. Deena, and A. Morganti. Competency-Based Approach to Assessing Workbook Effectiveness. *Research Strategies*, 4 (9), Winter 1986, 4–10.

13. Nancy W. Colborn and Rossane M. Cordell. Moving from Subjective to Objective Assessments of Your Instruction Program. *Reference Services Review*, 26, Fall/Winter 1998, 125–37.

14. John S. Riddle and Karen A. Hartman. But Are They Learning Anything? Designing an Assessment of First Year Library Instruction. *College & Undergraduate Libraries*, 7, 2000, 66.

15. Patricia S. Breivik. Brooklyn College: A Test Case, in *Open Admissions and the Academic Library*. Chicago: American Library Association, 1977.

16. Amy Dykeman and Barbara King. Term Paper Analysis: A Proposal for Evaluating Bibliographic Instruction. *Research Strategies*, 1, December 1983, 14–21; David F. Kohl and Lizabeth A. Wilson. Effectiveness of Course Integrated Bibliographic Instruction in Improving Course Work. *RQ*, 26, December 1986, 203–211; and David N. King and John C. Ory. Effects of Library Instruction on Student Research: A Case Study. *College & Research Libraries*, 42 (1), January 1981, 31–41.

17. Mark Emmons and Wanda Martin. Engaging Conversation: Evaluating the Contribution of Library Instruction to the Quality of Student Research. *College & Research Libraries*, 63 (6), November 2002, 545–60.

18. Rui Wang. The Lasting Impact of a Library Credit Course. *portal: Libraries and the Academy*, 6 (1), January 2006, 79–92.

19. John C. Selegean, Martha Lou Thomas, and Marie Louise Richman. Long-Range Effectiveness of Library Use Instruction. *College & Research Libraries*, 44 (6), November 1983, 476–80.

20. Larry Hardesty, Nicholas P. Lovrich Jr., and James Mannon. Library-Use Instruction: Assessment of Long-Term Effects. *College & Research Libraries*, 43, 1982, 38–46.

21. Donald Barclay. Evaluating Library Instruction: Doing the Best You Can with What You Have. *RQ*, 33, Winter 1993, 194–99.

22. Barclay. Evaluating Library Instruction, , 196.

23. Elizabeth Carter. "Doing the Best You Can with What You Have": Lessons Learned from Outcomes Assessment. *The Journal of Academic Librarianship*, 28 (1), January–March 2002, 36–41.

24. Jill Coupe. Undergraduate Library Skills: Two Surveys at Johns Hopkins University. *Research Strategies*, 11 (4), Fall 1993, 187–201.

25. Carol Germain, Trudi E. Jacobson, and Sue A. Kaczor. A Comparison of the Effectiveness of Presentation Formats for Instruction: Teaching First-Year Students. *College & Research Libraries*, 61 (1), January 2000, 65–72.

26. Lucy Holman. A Comparison of Computer-Assisted Instruction and Classroom Bibliographic Instruction. *Reference and User Services Quarterly*, 40 (1), 2000, 53–60.

27. Lorrie A. Knight. The Role of Assessment in Library User Education. *Reference Services Review*, 30 (1), 2002, 15–24.

28. Debbie Malone and Carol Videon. Assessing Undergraduate Use of Electronic Resources: A Quantitative Analysis of Works Cited. *Research Strategies*, 15 (3), 1997, 151–58.

29. David Eyman and Alven Nunley. *Effectiveness of Library Science 101 in Teaching Bibliographic Skills.* May 1977. ERIC Document ED150 962.

30. E. Eric Landrum and Diana M. Muench. Assessing Students Library Skills and Knowledge: The Library Research Strategies Questionnaire. *Psychological Reports*, 75, 1994, 1619–28.

31. Karen Markey, Annie Armstrong, Sandy De Groote, Michael Fosmire, Laura Fuderer, Kelly Garrett, Helen Georgas, Linda Sharp, Cheri Smith, Michael Spaly, and Joni E. Warner. Testing the Effectiveness of Interactive Multimedia for Library-User Education. *portal: Libraries and the Academy,* 5 (4), 2005, 527–44.

32. Sara J. Penhale, Nancy Taylor, and Thomas G. Kirk. *A Method of Measuring the Reach of a Bibliographic Instruction Program.* Available at www.ala.org/ala/acrlbucket/nashville1997pap/penhaletaylor.htm.

33. Stephen K. Stoan. Research and Library Skills: An Analysis and Interpretation. *College & Research Libraries*, 45, March 1984, 103.

34. M. Shanley and C. Witten. University 101 Freshman Seminar Course: A Longitudinal Study of Persistence, Retention, and Graduation Rates. *NASPA Journal*, 27, 1990, 344–52.

35. C. Wilkie and S. Kuckuck. A Longitudinal Study of the Effects of a Freshman Seminar. *Journal of the Freshman Year Experience*, 1, 1989, 7–16.

36. K. Ketkar and S. D. Bennett. Strategies for Evaluating a Freshman Studies Program. *Journal of the Freshman Year Experience*, 1, 1989, 33–44.

37. J. Benton. Bibliographic Instruction: A Radical Assessment, in C. Oberman-Soroka (Ed.). *Proceedings from the Second Southeastern Conference on Approaches to Bibliographic Instruction, 22–23 March 1979.* Charleston, SC: College of Charleston, 1980, 53–68.

38. Earnest T. Pascarella and Patrick T. Terenzini. *How College Affects Students: Findings and Insights from Twenty Years of Research.* San Francisco: Jossey-Bass, 1991, 118.

39. Available at http://harcourtassessment.com.

40. Ethelene Whitmire. Academic Library Performance Measures and Undergraduates' Library Use and Educational Outcomes. *Library & Information Science Research*, 24, 2002, 107–28.

41. Ethelene Whitmire. Development of Critical Thinking Skills: An Analysis of Academic Library Experiences and Other Measures. *College & Research Libraries*, 59 (3), May 1998, 1–8.

42. Patrick T. Terenzini and Leonard Springer. Influences Affecting the Development of Students' Critical Thinking Skills. *Research in Higher Education*, 36 (1), 1995, 23–40; and Patrick T. Terenzini and Leonard Springer. First-Generation College Students: Characteristics, Experiences, and Cognitive Development. *Research in Higher Education*, 37 (1), 1996, 1–23.

43. Patricia S. Breivik and Gordon Gee. *Information Literacy: Revolution in the Library.* New Your: American Council on Education/Macmillan, 1989; and Patricia S. Breivik. *Student Learning in the Information Age.* Phoenix: American Council on Education/Oryx, 1998.

44. Shirley J. Behrens. A Conceptual Analysis and Historical Overview of Information Literacy. *College & Research Libraries,* July 1994, 309–22.

45. Topsy N. Smalley. College Success: High School Librarians Make the Difference. *The Journal of Academic Librarianship*, 30 (3), May 2004, 193–98.

46. Laurie A. MacWhinnie. The Information Commons: The Academic Library of the Future. *portal: Libraries and the Academy*, 3 (2), 2003, 241–57.

47. Available at www.ala.org/ala/acrl/acrlstandards/informationliteracycompetency.htm.

48. Mary Ochs, Bill Coons, Darla Van Ostrand, and Susan Barnes. *Assessing the Value of an Information Literacy Program*. Ithaca, NY: Cornell University, Albert R. Mann Library, October 1991. ERIC ED 340 385.

49. Denise Koufogiannakis and Natasha Wiebe. Effective Methods for Teaching Information Literacy Skills to Undergraduate Students: A Systematic Review and Meta-Analysis. *Evidence Based Library and Information Practice*, 1 (3), 2006, 3–22.

50. Susan D. K. Taylor. *An Examination of Course-Integrated Library Instruction Programs at Three Small Private Liberal Arts Colleges*. Manhattan: Kansas State University, 1991.

51. Andrea L. Foster. Students Fall Short on 'Information Literacy,' Educational Testing Service's Study Finds. *Chronicle of Higher Education,* 53 (10), October 2006, A36.

52. Ethelene Whitmire. Factors Influencing Undergraduates' Self-Reported Satisfaction with Their Information Literacy Skills. *portal: Libraries and the Academy*, 1 (4), 2001, 409–20.

53. Heidi Julien and Stuart Boon. Assessing Instructional Outcomes in Canadian Academic Libraries. *Library & Information Science Research*, 26, 2004, 121–39.

54. Ken Haycock. Information Literacy as a Key Connector for All Libraries: What All Librarians Can Learn from Teacher Librarians, in *Concept, Challenge, Conundrum: From Library Skills to Information Literacy; Proceedings of the Fourth National Information Literacy Conference Conducted by the University of South Australia Library and the Australian Library and Information Association Information Literacy and Special Interest Group, 3–5 December 1999*. Adelaide: University of South Australia, 2000, 15–24.

55. Chris Brewer. Integrating Information Literacy into the Health Sciences Curriculum: Longitudinal Study of an Information Literacy Program for the University of Wollongong. Paper presented at the 4th National information Literacy Conference, Adelaide, South Australia, December 1999.

56. Julie Rabine and Catherine Cardwell. Start Making Sense: Practical Approaches to Outcomes Assessment for Libraries. *Research Strategies*, 17 (4), 2000, 319–35.

57. Norman B. Hutcherson. Library Jargon: Student Recognition of Terms and Concepts Commonly Used by Librarians in the Classroom. *College & Research Libraries*, 65 (4), July 2004, 349–54.

58. Patricia Davitt Maughan. Assessing Information Literacy among Undergraduates: A Discussion of the Literature and the University of California-Berkeley Assessment Experience. *College & Research Libraries*, 62 (1), January 2001, 71–85.

59. Mark Hepworth. A Study of Undergraduate Information Literacy and Skills: The Inclusion of Information Literacy and Skills in the Undergraduate Curriculum. Paper presented at the 65th IFLA Council and General Conference, Bangkok, Thailand August 20–28, 1999. Available at http://www.ifla.org/IV/ifla65/papers/107–124e.htm.

60. Angela Dunnington and Mary Lou Strong. What's Assessment Got to Do with It?! Exploring Student Learning Outcomes. Presentation given at the ALA Annual Conference, New Orleans, Louisiana, June 24, 2006. Personal communication with the authors.

61. Jill Coupe. Undergraduate Library Skills: Two Surveys at Johns Hopkins University. *Research Strategies*, 11, Fall 1993, 188–201.

62. Brian R. Schuck. Assessing a Library Instruction Program. *Research Strategies*, 10, Fall 1992, 152–60.

63. Joan R. Kaplowitz and Janice Contini. Computer Assisted Instruction: Is It an Option for Bibliographic Instruction in Large Undergraduate Survey Classes? *College & Research Libraries*, 59 (1), 1998, 19–27.

64. Terrence Mech. Developing an Information Literacy Assessment Instrument, in Peter Hernon, Robert E. Dugan, and Candy Schwartz (Eds.). *Revisiting Outcomes Assessment in Higher Education.* Westport, CT: Libraries Unlimited, 2006.

65. See the Project SAILS Web site at www.projectsails.org.

66. Megan J. Oakleaf. Assessing Information Literacy Skills: A Rubric Approach. Ph.D. dissertation, University of North Carolina at Chapel Hill, 2006.

67. Elizabeth Hartmann. Understandings of Information Literacy: The Perceptions of First-Year Undergraduate Students at the University of Ballarat. *Australian Academic & Research Libraries*, 32 (2), 2001, 110–22.

68. Deborah Turnbull, Denise Frost, and Nicola Foxlee. Infoseek, InfoFind! Information Literacy and Integrated Service Delivery for Researchers and Postgraduates. Paper presented at the Information Online 2003 Conference, Sydney, New South Wales, January 2003; and Margaret C. Wallace, Allison Shorten, and Patrick Crookes. Teaching Information Literacy Skills: An Evaluation. *Nurse Education Today*, 20, 2000, 485–89.

69. Teresa Y. Neely. Aspects of Information Literacy: A Sociological and Psychological Study. Ph.D. dissertation, University of Pittsburgh, 2000.

70. Nancy H. Seamans. Student Perceptions of Information Literacy: Insights for Librarians. *Reference Services Review*, 30 (2), 2002, 112–23.

71. Alison Brettle. Information Skills Training: A Systematic Review of the Literature. *Health Information and Libraries Journal*, 20 (Supplement 1), June 2003, 3–9.

72. Jillian R. Griffiths and Peter Brophy. Student Searching Behavior and the Web: Use of Academic Resources and Google. *Library Trends*, 53 (4), Spring 2005, 539–54.

73. Steve Jones. The Internet Goes to College: How Students Are Living in the Future with Today's Technology. *Pew Internet and American Life Project.* Available at http://www.pewinternet. org/pdfs/PIP_College_Report.pdf.

74. Cathy De Rosa, Joanne Cantrell, Janet Hawk, and Alane Wilson. *College Students' Perceptions of Libraries and Information Resources.* Dublin, OH: OCLC, 2006.

75. George D. Kuh and Robert M. Gonyea. The Role of the Academic Library in Promoting Student Engagement in Learning. *College & Research Libraries*, 64 (7), July 2003, 256–82.

76. James W. Marcum. Rethinking Information Literacy. *The Library Quarterly*, 72 (1), January 2002, 1–26.

77. Allan Martin. Towards e-Literacy, in Allan Martin and Hannelore Rader (Eds.). *Information and IT Literacy: Enabling Learning in the 21st Century.* London: Facet, 2003, 18.

78. See, for example, Margaret K. Cook. Rank, Status and Contribution of Academic Librarians as Perceived by the Teaching Faculty at Southern Illinois University, Carbondale. *College & Research Libraries*, 42, May 1981, 214–22; Robert T. Ivey. Teaching Faculty Perceptions of Academic Librarians at Memphis State University. *College & Research Libraries*, 55, January 1994, 69–82; LeeAnn Withnell. Faculty Opinions of Academic Library Service Policies. *Journal of Interlibrary Loan, Document Delivery & Information Supply*, 4, 1994, 23–79; Gaby Divay, Ada M. Ducas, and Nicole Michaud-Oystryk. Faculty Perceptions of Librarians at the University of Manitoba. *College & Research Libraries*, 48, January 1987, 27–35; Larry R. Oberg, Mary Kay Schleiter, and Michael Van Houten. Faculty Perceptions of Librarians at Albion College: Status, Role, Contribution and Contacts. *College & Research Libraries*, 50, March 1989, 215–30.

79. Lars Christensen, Mindy Stombler, and Lyn Thaxton. A Report on Librarian-Faculty Relations from a Sociological Perspective. *Journal of Academic Librarianship*, 30, March 2004, 116–21.

80. Larry Hardesty. *Faculty and the Library: The Undergraduate Experience.* Norwood, NJ: Ablex, 1991.

81. Anita Cannon. Faculty Survey on Library Research Instruction. *Reference Quarterly*, 33, Summer 1994, 524–41.

82. Joy Thomas. Faculty Attitudes and Habits Concerning Library Instruction: How Much Has Changed Since 1982? *Research Strategies*, 12, Fall 1994, 209–23.

83. Gloria J. Leckie and Anne Fullerton. Information Literacy in Science and Engineering Undergraduate Education: Faculty Attitudes and Pedagogical Practices. *College & Research Libraries*, 60, January 1999, 9–29.

84. Jeanne R. Davidson. Faculty and Student Attitudes Toward Credit Courses for Library Skills. *College & Research Libraries*, 62 (2), March 2001, 155–63.

85. Claire McGuiness. What Faculty Think—Exploring the Barriers to Information Literacy Development in Undergraduate Education. *The Journal of Academic Librarianship*, 32 (6), November 2006, 573–82.

15

Evaluation of Customer Service

SERVICE DEFINITION

Historically, library customer satisfaction surveys have been known as user surveys. Only in the last 10 years or so have surveys been developed that focus on user satisfaction or customer satisfaction. And while it is possible to assess the degree of satisfaction for a specific library service, the focus of this chapter is on determining satisfaction with the library and all of its systems and services as a whole. It is important to remember that libraries—physical or virtual—are only used by people who *choose* them.

Phillip Kotler and Alan Andreasen suggest that nonprofit organizations that are focused on themselves rather than their customers will display specific characteristics, including seeing their services as inherently desirable, blaming customer ignorance or lack of motivation when their services are not being used, relegating research about customers to a minor role, tending to define marketing as promotion, and assuming that there is no competition.[1]

When it comes to customer satisfaction, the perception of the customer—right or wrong, informed or uninformed—is the only "reality" that counts. A tendency exists for any library to become defensive about its ratings by asserting that "we really do a better job than the numbers reflect" or "the users just aren't aware of," attitudes that simply mask the reality that the library has failed in some way. There may be many reasons for lower than expected ratings: not delivering the desired services, lack of quality in services, need for staff training, or not communicating the library's value to customers and decision stakeholders.

A recent survey found that over 50 percent of public and academic libraries had no way of quantifiably tracking organizational success and used informal customer feedback as their primary metric of success.[2]

Terry Vavra has suggested that an organization create a chart that identifies why people use a particular service and determine the associated customer requirements for each use motive. This, in turn, will lead to identifying corresponding performance measures that matter, as shown in Table 15.1 (p. 250).

Table 15.1 The Structure of Customer Requirements

Use Motives	Customer Requirement	Performance Measures
Currency of resources	Library has what I want	Purchase requests/ILL requests
		Turnover rate of collection
		Complaints
Availability of resources	Items available to borrow	Availability survey
		Complaints
Read best sellers	Wait time	Wait time (no. days)
		Complaints
Proximity of library to home/office	Convenience	Average travel time
		Average travel distance
Ease of navigation in library	Can find my own way	No. directional questions
		Complaints
Hours of operation	Convenience	Complaints
Cleanliness of library	Comfort and security	Cleanliness index
Courteous staff	Friendly	Customer satisfaction survey
Helpful staff	Help when I need it	Customer satisfaction survey

Many librarians maintain that only they, the professionals, have the expertise to assess the quality of library service . . . . Such opinions about service, in fact, are irrelevant. The only thing that matters is the customers' opinions, because without users there is no need for libraries except as warehouses.

—Ellen Altman and Peter Hernon[3]

EVALUATION QUESTIONS

A number of customer service–related questions have been the focus of evaluation efforts, including the following:

- How should a library define quality?
- Is customer satisfaction important to a library?
- Should increasing customer satisfaction be important to a library?
- Our library's customer survey indicates we are doing "good." What now?
- How can a library improve its customer satisfaction rating?
- What are the trade-offs when using LibQUAL+?
- Is it possible to distinguish between information product and information service satisfaction?

EVALUATION METHODS

The methods that have been used to evaluate customer service can be divided into qualitative and quantitative (see Table 15.2).

Table 15.2. Customer Service Evaluation Methods

Qualitative	Quantitative
Focus groups	Locally developed surveys
Mystery shoppers	Standardized surveys
Complaints	Defining service characteristics

DISCUSSION OF PRIOR EVALUATIONS AND RESEARCH

Service Quality

Service quality has garnered significant attention in the professional management and library literature in the last few years. It is is an antecedent of customer satisfaction (there is some debate about this), and higher quality service levels will result in increased customer satisfaction. Yet a client can visit the library and obtain a correct answer to a question and still be unsatisfied due to a variety of reasons. Some writers have confused service quality with or likened it to satisfaction. Danuta Nitecki suggests that quality is a long-run, overall evaluation, whereas satisfaction represents a short-term, transaction-specific measure.[4]

Richard Orr is often credited as an early proponent of identifying quality of libraries and suggests a distinction between quality and value. Orr indicates that *quality* should reflect how good the service is, in comparison to *value*, which should reflect how much good it does.[5]

Service quality has been defined from four primary perspectives:

- **Excellence** is usually externally defined and is used by many organizations. The brand of "excellence" is slowly created over time by many companies and not-for-profit organizations. However, attributes of excellence may change over time. Excellence is achieving or reaching for the highest standard and never being satisfied with second best. In some cases, excellence may be externally defined.

- **Value** stresses the benefits that will be received by the recipient, while quality is the perception of meeting or exceeding expectations. Quality and value are thus different concepts. The focus is on internal efficiency and external effectiveness. In this case, quality is judged relative to price.

- **Conformance to specifications** requires a detailed specification of requirements—some or most of which the customer may not be aware of. While this approach facilitates precise measurement, it is an internally focused view of the world. For example, Joseph Juran—one of the pioneers in quality control—separated quality into two components: quality of design and quality of conformance to design specifications. Most customers will not care about service specifications—only the results of the specifications.

- **Meeting and/or exceeding expectations** crosses the boundaries of most service industries, although it should be noted that expectations, although subjective, are customer-centric, and are neither static nor predictable.[6] After all, ultimately it is the customer who judges the quality of a service. Customer expectations will change as the result of experiences with other service providers. The majority of research pertaining to service quality and customer satisfaction focuses on this dimension. Service quality can be defined as reducing the gap between the services provided (real or perceived) and customer expectations.

Service quality actually has two components **what** is provided to the customer and **how** the service is delivered—or deliverables and interactions. Deliverables describe what is provided to the customer. Interactions describe the characteristics of staff and equipment that impact how customers experience the service process. A large amount of the library literature has focused on the "what" to the exclusion of the "how."

Customer satisfaction has been defined as "the emotional reaction to a specific transaction or service encounter."[7] Satisfaction has two components. The first is *service encounter satisfaction*, which is the degree of satisfaction or dissatisfaction experienced by the individual in a specific service transaction. Jan Carlson, former president of SAS Airlines, coined the phrase "moments of truth" to describe any point in time during which a customer comes into contact with an organization.[8] Examples of "moments of truth" in a library include contact at the information desk, reference desk, or circulation desk or asking for assistance from a page in the stacks as well as use of the library's Web site or receiving an overdue notice.

The second component is *overall service satisfaction*, or the level of client satisfaction or dissatisfaction based on multiple transactions or experiences.[9] Thus, the overall service satisfaction is built up over time and is the result of numerous transactions of varying quality. Others have suggested that *customer satisfaction* refers to a specific transaction, while *service quality* is the collective judgment based on all of the previous encounters.

It is possible to conceive of the relationship between satisfaction and performance from two perspectives:

- Library performance is equated with customer satisfaction.

- A series of variables other than performance alone contribute to user satisfaction.

Rachael Applegate suggested that it is possible to distinguish between material and emotional satisfaction, and there are three possible models to describe the satisfaction formation process:

- **Material Satisfaction Model.** In this model system performance determines material satisfaction. However, the results from several studies suggest mixed or weak support between performance measurement variables and user satisfaction.[10]

- **Emotional Satisfaction Model—Simple Path.** In this model emotional satisfaction is caused by material satisfaction. Yet several studies have found weak relationships between emotional satisfaction and performance—almost as if users were reluctant to criticize the library.[11] Applegate called this a "false positive."[12]

- **Emotional Satisfaction Model—Multiple Path.** In this model three variables are analyzed—product settings, product performance, and disconfirmation. Disconfirmation refers to the difference between an individual's expectations of performance and the actual perception of performance. Applegate found in her OPAC retrieval experiment that disconfirmation plays an important role in explaining the formation of satisfaction.[13]

These findings are complemented by Xi Shi's study, which separated the measurement of user satisfaction by both information product and information system/service, which were typically measured as one concept in prior studies.[14] Customer satisfaction can also be manifest at the micro level and macro level, as noted by Rowena Cullen.[15] Fei Yu found that the performance variable precedes only repeat users' satisfaction. Further analysis suggested that users' emotional and material satisfaction can determine user behavior—next time library use or library use loyalty. Thus, it is much easier to achieve service use loyalty for repeat users for specific services rather than achieving general library use loyalty for occasional users.[16]

A simplified model of the interactions among and between client expectations, perceptions, satisfaction, assessment of service quality, and the resulting overall customer satisfaction is shown in Figure 15.1. The various quality-related survey instruments are assessing the "perceived quality" rather than attempting to determine an "objective measure of quality."

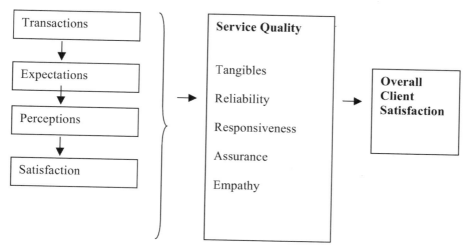

Figure 15.1. Client Satisfaction and Service Quality Model. Adapted from Rowena Cullen. Perspectives on User Satisfaction Surveys. *Library Trends*, 49 (4), Spring 2001, 662–86.

Some have objected to the focus on customer satisfaction and service quality in assessing the value of libraries. For example, John Budd suggests that such a strategy results in emphasizing the exchange value of libraries and their services to the detriment of relying on use as a value of libraries. In short, Budd argues that the focus on customer satisfaction is a way for libraries to increase their share of the budget.[17]

SATISFACTION

Satisfaction is a sense of contentment that results from an actual experience in relation to an expected experience. Satisfaction surveys ask the client to assess the quality and utility of library services. If applied in an appropriate manner, a customer satisfaction survey allows the library to learn what matters to customers and apply that information to improve service delivery. Most satisfaction surveys ask the client to evaluate the effectiveness of the service(s) provided and assess the degree to which his or her needs were met. Customer satisfaction, by its very nature, is inward and backward looking (a lagging indicator of performance).[18] In order to improve customer satisfaction, the gaps that exist between a customer's expectations and the service actually provided must be reduced over time.

Too often, customer satisfaction is approached as a report card rather than as a source of information about services where improvement and further analysis and thinking are required. George D'Elia and Sandra Walsh suggested that user satisfaction surveys are useful for evaluating the performance of a library but should not be used to compare presumed levels of performance for libraries serving different communities.[19] Illustrating the challenges that will arise from such an effort, Sebastian Mundt reports that a joint user satisfaction survey conducted by 15 German university libraries found the results lead to identifying "best practice" activities and revealed structural strengths and weakness among the libraries. The libraries decided to keep the results anonymous to avoid the public branding of "winners and losers."[20]

In some cases, user satisfaction surveys are used as an indirect assessment of outcomes.

Using customer satisfaction data is complicated by the lack of clarity about what customer satisfaction ratings actually measure. A customer's experience with a library service(s) is dictated by a simple formula:

Customer satisfaction = Performance minus Expectations.[21]

Customers are pleased when the perception of performance meets or exceeds their expectations (see Figure 15.2). Libraries must pay attention to both performance and customer expectations. Expectations range on a continuum or hierarchy from worst possible, to low, to minimally acceptable, to high, to ideal.[22] Should a library deliver a service that is below what is expected by the customer, the only result is dissatisfaction. Excitement or delight will only produce very satisfied customers since the level of service provided is totally unexpected.

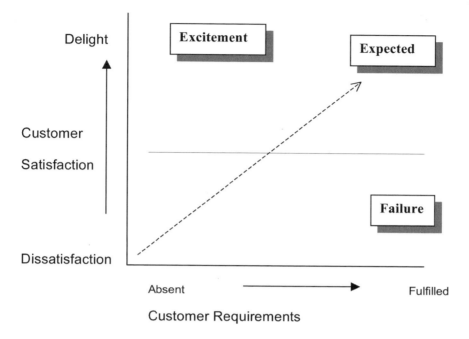

Figure 15.2. Levels of Customer Satisfaction

As noted by Peter Hernon and John Whitman, expectations can be divided into three groups:

- **Core expectations:** elements of service assumed to be common to all people (courtesy, respect, dignity, and so forth)

- **Learned expectations:** Developed from experience and a widening exposure to the world

- **Anticipated expectations:** An aspect or element of service that is not currently offered.[23]

Methods for Determining Satisfaction

It is possible to use either qualitative methods or quantitative technique to determine the levels of customer satisfaction (see Table 15.3).

Table 15.3. Customer Satisfaction Evaluation Methods

Qualitative	Quantitative
Focus groups	Surveys
Mystery shopper	Locally developed surveys
Complaints	Standardized surveys

Focus Groups

One popular qualitative method is to use several focus groups, each group representing a different customer segment, and ask them to discuss the library, its services, and the participants' use of the library and their levels of satisfaction.

The use and limitations of focus groups are discussed in chapter 4.

Mystery Shoppers

Another qualitative method, the use of a mystery shopper, offers the opportunity to discover a new dimension for the assessment of quality and perceived value of services provided by the library. The strength of the mystery shopper approach is to learn how staff attitudes, attributes, and behaviors influence overall customer satisfaction. The concept of mystery shoppers asks individuals to act as customers to evaluate and report on the total customer experience—from first impressions through to the use of specific resources and services. Of particular note, the consistency, reliability, and accuracy of promised services as well as the responsiveness of staff can be assessed.[24] The "shopper's" experience is documented by completing a survey after each service transaction.[25] A library can design the shopping experience questionnaire, and the cost to use a commercial shopping firm is usually modest. Some academic libraries have hired and trained students to act as "shoppers."

The University of Wollongong library used mystery shoppers to capture more detailed, qualitative information about its services outside the somewhat artificial focus group setting.[26]

More commonly, a library will use a survey that will generate numerical responses indicating the degree of satisfaction. These surveys can be developed locally or a library can use a standardized survey such as LibQUAL+.

Complaints

Customer complaints are simply a fact of life for any organization. Research conducted by a customer service consulting firm found that the average organization will not hear from 96 percent of unhappy customers (for every complaint, 26 people will not complain). And more important, 13 percent of those having a problem will relate their experience to 20 or more people.[27] This negative word-of-mouth advertising is what leads some people who have not visited a library to stay away.

The important point about complaints is what the library does about them. There seem to be two approaches to the "problem" of complaints:

- Complaints indicate a "failure" and are something to be avoided. The emphasis is on taking care of the problem and placating customers. Often the same problems and complaints recur since the library does nothing to correct the underlying root cause. This approach is reflective of an inward-looking, library-centric view of the world.

- Complaints are "welcomed" and the library uses the complaint as an opportunity to learn something from the customer's perspective and examines the policies and training that led to the problem. This approach is reflective of an outward-looking, customer-centric view of the world. The library will keep a log of all complaints, which are sorted into categories. While staff are trained to provide an immediate solution to resolve the customer complaint, complaints are periodically analyzed in an attempt to take corrective actions so that the same problem is not repeatedly encountered by customers.

Locally Developed Surveys

Satisfaction surveys can be created and conducted by library staff. A survey can focus on general satisfaction, which is an evaluation of the library as a whole, or on satisfaction with one or more specific library services. The focus of this chapter is on the former; satisfaction with specific library services is addressed in part III. A number of library user surveys are available via the Internet.[28]

There are difficulties associated with a satisfaction survey. They are usually technical, such as ensuring that an appropriate sample size is obtained, that the sample is random, and that the questions are appropriately worded. In addition, the numerical values assigned to customer satisfaction ratings are largely misunderstood, misused, and misapplied. The assumed, though incorrect, linear and interval properties of satisfaction ratings can cause serious misunderstandings. And numerical averages, or means, are not a reliable way to summarize or track periodic performance.[29]

However, the chief underlying difficulty connected with any survey is making sure that the right questions are being asked.

A false sense of security. In any survey, the distribution of satisfaction ratings is presumed to be a reflection of "true" satisfaction. Yet in most library customer satisfaction surveys the distribution of responses is abnormally skewed, that is, the majority of the survey respondents report high levels of satisfaction (see Figures 15.3 and 15.4, p. 258).[30] When reflecting on the results of a satisfaction survey, libraries must recognize that they are considered a "good thing"—much like apple pie and motherhood.[31] Companies have learned that only when customers rate their buying experience as either completely or extremely satisfied can they count on customers' repeat purchasing behavior.[32] Perhaps frequent library users are those who rate their library experience as "completely or extremely satisfied."

D'Elia and Walsh questioned the value of user satisfaction because the user's expectations of a service are conditioned by what he or she has been used to receiving.[33] In addition, one of the problems with satisfaction surveys is that an individual's expectations may change. An individual may be pleased with a particular product or service (and would rate such a product or service quite high in a satisfaction survey) until he or she discovers an alternative product or service that provides vastly improved levels of satisfaction. Suddenly that person's satisfaction with the old product or service is quite low.[34]

Disconfirmation theory is a popular model for predicting customer satisfaction or dissatisfaction. This model suggests that customers have some standard in their minds to guide their activities—purchase of a product or use of a service. One study found that it is the disconfirmation of user needs and expectations, not user needs or expectations alone, that determines library user satisfaction. This suggests that satisfaction with the information product may be more important for overall satisfaction than is satisfaction with the system or service.[35]

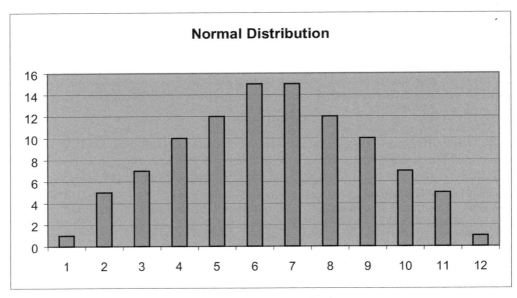

Figure 15.3. Normal Distribution

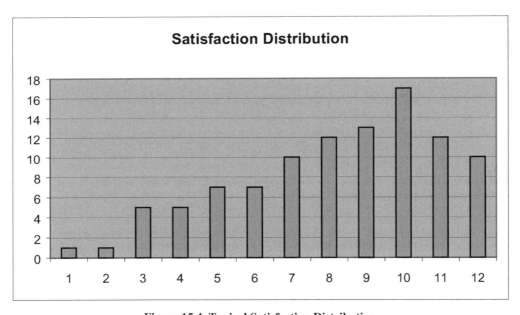

Figure 15.4. Typical Satisfaction Distribution

Avoiding self-absorption. The typical customer satisfaction survey asks, "How are we doing?" To the extent that this perspective fosters an attitude that the library is doing well, it may mean that the library is missing an opportunity to better understand the real needs of its users. As we have seen, the broad customer satisfaction survey responses will typically be very high for the library. But what about the user's satisfaction with particular services and products offered by the library? This requires a probing and inquisitive nature and the ability to move beyond the good feelings that arise when the library is rated highly.

Missed opportunities. Asking users how *they* are doing, perhaps in a series of focus groups, will reveal the motivations and frustrations that they experience in using the library. Perhaps there are real barriers to access and service that can be eliminated about which the library is unaware or that it never considered from the perspective of the user.

One survey of library users noted that satisfaction levels were quite high (96 percent) when people succeeded in finding what they wanted but dropped almost by half when they failed to find what they wanted.[36] George D'Elia, attempting to ascertain the determinants of user satisfaction in a library setting, found that there were none. He examined user demographics, the various uses of the library by the user, and the user's evaluation of the characteristics of the library used.[37] While satisfaction is important as a perceived value of library service, it does not demonstrate how the individual or the community has benefited from the services provided by the library.

Failing to understand expectations. Most often customer satisfaction surveys focus on customer *perceptions* of service delivery but rarely afford the customer a chance to articulate *expectations* of service delivery. Since customers compare their expectations with their experiences, having a good understanding of expectations is important to better serving the needs of library users.

Another problem with satisfaction surveys is that they often fail to probe beneath the surface of responses provided, and in fact respondents may be reluctant to criticize libraries generally. However, one study found that people were willing to suggest or agree with specific criticisms or complaints.[38]

Providing a level of service that users rate as satisfactory may not be enough. In fact, different satisfaction levels may reflect different issues and therefore require different corrective actions. Several research studies have demonstrated that only completely satisfied customers will be loyal.[39]

Perspective. In some cases it is possible to improve the quality, timeliness, and utility of an information service and see a corresponding increase in customer satisfaction surveys over time. Yet even in the face of objective measures that demonstrate improvements in service levels, satisfaction surveys (a subjective measure) might report the same or only slight increases in customer satisfaction levels. This may be the case since input, process, and output measures typically are collected and reported as administrative performance measures, while customers' evaluations are likely to be based on outcomes that are meaningful to them.[40]

Methodology problems. Satisfaction data collected using different means (in-person or telephone surveys versus self-administered survey forms) are not comparable. In some cases, oral data-gathering techniques may increase satisfaction ratings by 10 to 12 percent compared to data gathered using self-administered surveys.[41] Further, how a question is asked appears to affect the level of satisfaction. A positive form of the question ("How satisfied are you?") seems to lead to greater reported levels of satisfaction than a negative form (Did you experience a problem that led to your being dissatisfied?).

Survey scores don't link to actual performance. Links between the actual performance of a library, as measured by subjective or objective measures, to customer satisfaction survey results, have not been established.

Survey fatigue. A great many people are simply turned off by customer satisfaction surveys—too many questions and too many surveys. Their response? Trash them.

How to take corrective action. Once the results of a survey are in, the library management team and the employees of the library simply have no idea how to make improvements so that the library's customer satisfaction scores will go up.

An analysis of customer experiences in using public and academic libraries found that both overall satisfaction and willingness to return to the library were significantly related to the librarian's behavior (smiling and displaying welcoming body language) and the quality of the reference answer.[42] Further support for this finding was noted by Joan Durrance, who found a strong relationship between overall satisfaction and the friendliness of library staff.[43]

A survey at the University of Illinois at Urbana-Champaign library found that staff-provided services were rated negative (expectations exceeded service), while the physical and electronic collections were rated positive (service exceeds expectations).[44] A survey at Valdosta State University library found that students' comments were much more valuable than the objective questions and gave specific insight into each area of customer service.[45]

Single Survey Question

Can a single survey question serve as a predictor of actual customer behavior? In the business world, customer loyalty results in individuals who tend to buy more over time or devote a larger share of their wallets to a company they feel good about. And loyal customers talk up a company to their friends, family, and colleagues.

For example, Enterprise Rent-a-Car asks their customers a single question when they return a rented car :

How likely is it that you will recommend Enterprise to a friend or colleague?

The results are tallied for each branch, each day to develop an Enterprise Service Quality index (ESQi). Employees earn bonuses based on their ESQi ratings. The company found a strong relationship between branches with high ESQi ratings and sustained growth for the branch.[46]

Extending the concept of the single survey question to a number of other companies, Frederick Reichheld developed the Net Promoter Score (NPS) using a 10-point Likert scale. The Net Promoter Score is the percentage of those who will recommend to family and friends ("promoters") minus the percentage of detractors (those who rate the company poorly).[47] Some well-known companies have NPS scores above 50 percent, while others have quite low scores—5 to 10 percent. An important question to consider for your library is: What is your library's NPS score?

Priority Setting

Asking users about the relevance of existing and possible library services is another form of client satisfaction survey that can have direct and positive impact. The users will benefit because the library will better appreciate what services have the greatest clear-cut impact in their personal or professional lives. The library, in turn, can benefit from such a survey in that it will identify what services are most important but also understand how users rate the library's current performance for each specific service offering.

Using a priority and performance evaluation or PAPE survey, the user is asked to indicate the priority the library should give to each service, using a Likert scale.[48] Following this, the user is asked to rate the library's performance in providing the service (see a sample PAPE survey instrument in Figure 15.5). In addition to asking users to participate in a PAPE survey, asking the library's funding decision makers and library staff to complete the questionnaire also will allow the library to compare and contrast the responses from these three important groups. Any differences that emerge between the groups will require further attention and consideration. One PAPE study found that while there was general congruence between library staff and their customers, there was a tendency for library staff members to underestimate the importance of performing the promised service dependably and accurately.[49]

In your opinion, what priority should the library give each of the following?

Please circle the number that best gives an indication of your assessment.

	Low Priority					Very High Priority		Don't Know
	←--------------------------→							
Availability & accessibility of library staff	1	2	3	4	5	6	7	D
Availability of reference services	1	2	3	4	5	6	7	D
Checking out books	1	2	3	4	5	6	7	D
Able to browse magazines & newspapers	1	2	3	4	5	6	7	D
Interlibrary loan service	1	2	3	4	5	6	7	D
Access to online databases	1	2	3	4	5	6	7	D

And so forth . . .

In your opinion, how well does the library perform in each of the following areas? Please circle the number that best gives an indication of your assessment.

	Low Priority					Very High Priority		Don't Know
	←--------------------------→							
Availability of reference services	1	2	3	4	5	6	7	D
Checking out books	1	2	3	4	5	6	7	D
Availability & accessibility of library staff	1	2	3	4	5	6	7	D
Access to online databases	1	2	3	4	5	6	7	D
Interlibrary loan service	1	2	3	4	5	6	7	D
Able to browse magazines & newspapers	1	2	3	4	5	6	7	D

And so forth . . .

Figure 15.5. Sample PAPE Questionnaire

Note: The order of the library services in the second section should be different than the sequence of the first section of the survey. This forces the respondent to carefully read and rate each library service.

A sample of the results from a PAPE survey is shown in Figure 15.6 (p. 262). In all, 21 library services have been prioritized and evaluated (identified using the letters of the alphabet). Notice that for the first 14 services, the priority assigned by the library's clients exceeded the library's ability to deliver the expected level of service (with three exceptions). And for the services with lower priorities, actual performance exceeded expectations in only two cases. Yet some adjustment of the service levels for these two highly rated services might be advisable.

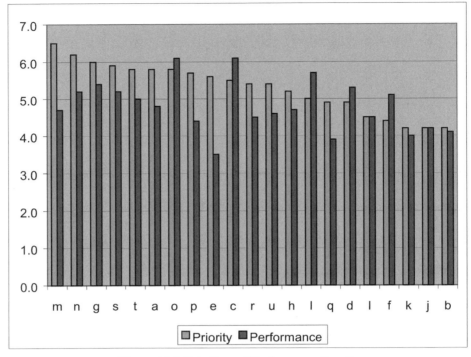

Figure 15.6. Priority and Performance Results

A somewhat similar presentation approach is called a quadrant analysis (see Figure 15.7). Plotting the scores of priority and performance will allow the library to see what services should be focused on in order to make improvements that will have the greatest impact on the library's customers.[50]

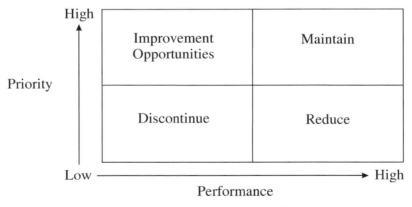

Figure 15.7. Quadrant Analysis Illustration

Libraries that have used PAPE have found it to be a useful tool that can be administered annually to capture any shifts of the priorities of their users as well as to track improvements in the services provided.

Budget Allocation

A method of studying user preferences that has been infrequently used in a library setting is to ask a sample of users to allocate hypothetical library budgets over a range of services. The user is given a supplemental budget of $200,000 over the existing budget, a supplemental budget of $100,000 over the existing budget, and no new funds—the user must make adjustments to the mix of services without increasing the budget. Note that a library will need to adjust the supplemental budget amounts to reflect its own situation. That is, if a library has a budget of $5 million, then the supplemental budget amounts would be higher.

In 1969 Jeffrey Raffel and Robert Shishko analyzed responses from 283 M.I.T. users (40 percent response rate to the survey) and found that the rank order of services selected varied little at each budget level. Users were principally interested in improving availability of materials and lowering the cost of making photocopies.[51] Slightly different results were obtained when the responses were sorted by type of user. Given increased funding, undergraduates wanted improved access to reserve materials; graduate students were interested in more new books and increased access to the materials in other libraries; while faculty expressed preferences for departmental libraries.

Standardized Survey

One popular service quality assessment tool developed in the retail industry, called SERVQUAL (Service Quality), has been adapted for libraries.[52] In the SERVQUAL model, quality is defined as "perceived quality" rather than "objective quality" and compares the expectations of customers and performance using five attributes:

- **Tangibles**. Physical appearance of the library, library staff members, equipment, and communication materials (signage, handouts, and so forth).

- **Reliability**. Is the service reliable and consistent? This is the *most* important factor among the five attributes being evaluated by the client.

- **Responsiveness**. How timely is the service? Are staff members willing to provide assistance?

- **Assurance**. Do staff convey competence and confidence? Are they knowledgeable, professional, and courteous?

- **Empathy**. Are staff members cheerful? Do they provide individualized attention to clients?

A shorter, competing survey instrument, called SERVPERF (Service Performance), was developed to better address the issue of predicting overall variance.[53]

The SERVQUAL instrument is based on the Gap Model of Services, developed by a team of marketing researchers.[54] Customer satisfaction constitutes the gap or difference between the service a customer expects to receive and the service received. It is possible to use the data gathered by SERVQUAL to identify five different gaps, as shown in Figure 15.8.[55] The *service quality gap* arises from the difference between the perceived service and the expected service. Other gaps will likely be contributing to the service quality gap.

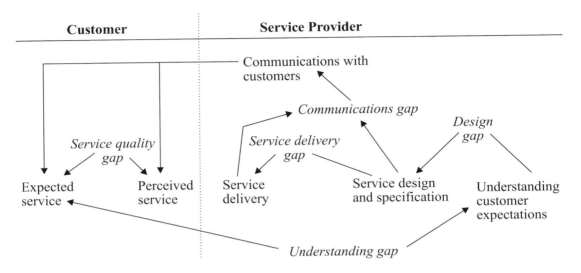

Figure 15.8. Service Quality Gaps. Adapted from Mik Wisniewski and Mike Donnelly. Measuring Service Quality in the Public Sector: The Potential for SERVQUAL. *Total Quality Management,* 7 (4), 1996, 357–65.

The *understanding gap* comes about due to the differences between customer service expectations and management's understanding of customer expectations. Such a gap may arise due to a less-than-clear understanding of customer needs or poor communication within the library.

The *design gap* is the gap between management's understanding of customer expectations and the design and specifications of service quality. The management team provides the training to the library's employees about what constitutes acceptable levels of service. The *delivery gap* will arise due to the gap between the specification of service quality and the actual quality of service delivered.

Finally, the *communications gap* is that between what is actually delivered and what has been promised in terms of external communications, comparison by the customer of experiences with other similar services, and so forth.

There have been several criticisms of the SERVQUAL approach, including fundamental measurement problems, the belief that use of perceptions is better than use of this particular scale, shortcomings in how the scale was developed, the presence of both positive and negative wording of questions, and problems using the scale across organizations.[56] Michael Roszkowski et al. provide a detailed summary of the criticisms leveled at SERVQUAL.[57] These problems arise, in part, because the data are collected after a service encounter, and questions about service expectations may be based on memory or be biased by the services actually received.

Hébert used a version of the SERVQUAL instrument to examine the quality of interlibrary loan services and suggested that there are two service dimensions: technical quality (an objective measure of *what* customers receive) and functional quality (a subjective measure of *how* customers receive a service). Hébert found a mismatch between library measures of interlibrary loan performance (fill rate and turnaround time) and customer perceptions of quality.[58]

Versions of SERVQUAL have been used successfully in a number of library settings.[59] A survey of three academic libraries in the Erie, Pennsylvania, area and an analysis of the data using regression models showed that three factors—assurance, resources, and tangibles (physical condition of the library)—explained about 64 percent of satisfaction. Also, staff responsiveness to customer requests had no effect on user satisfaction.

One adaptation of SERVQUAL, which has been named LibQUAL+, has been pilot tested by a large number of Association of Research Libraries since the spring of 2000. Initially five dimensions were identified as being useful for assessing library service: affect of service, reliability, library as place, provision of physical collections, and access to information.[60] Through the extensive testing of the instrument, the Web-based LibQUAL+ has been refined and now includes 22 survey questions providing information about three dimensions: affect of service, information control, and library as place.[61] (See appendix B for a copy of the 22 LibQUAL+ questions.) An additional eight questions deal with general satisfaction and information literacy, up to five local library questions, and some demographic questions, and there is an open-ended box for comments from the respondents. Some libraries have found that as many as one-third of all respondents will provide an open-ended comment.

> LibQUAL+ measures dimensions of perceived library quality; that is, each survey question is part of a broader category and scores within those categories are analyzed in order to derive more general information about library users' perceptions of service.[62]

Guidry noted that some LibQUAL+ respondents have difficulty discerning the differences among the three service levels—minimum, desired, and perceived—upon which the gap model is based. Further, Roszkowski et al. analyzed one library's LibQUAL+ data and found that the "perceived ratings" correlated more highly with global measures of library performance than did the "superiority gap" scores (desired minus perceived scores).[63]

When using LibQUAL+, data can be collected from different groups—undergraduates, postgraduates, academic staff, and library staff. The survey asks the respondent to identify *minimum* levels of service, the *desired* levels of service, and the *actual* level of service. An analysis of the differences and similarities in the ratings between the groups can be revealing and helpful in assessing the quality of library services. The LibQUAL+ instrument can be and has been used by other than academic libraries.

An analysis of LibQUAL+ survey responses from several UK university libraries found that undergraduates had lower response rates yet were more likely to use library resources —specifically to obtain texts and readings needed for course assignments. Postgraduates were more likely to use electronic resources, and they were interested in the library's book and journal collections.[64] Further, the analysis of the survey data revealed that samples of less than 400 were used (a sample of 400 would typically be considered the minimum acceptable to provide reasonably accurate results).

LibQUAL+ does have its critics. For example, Xi Shi and Sarah Levy have noted several problems:[65]

- **Conceptual problems.** The LibQUAL+ instrument is conceptually different from the frameworks suggested by the original service quality research of Parasuraman, Berry, and Zeitheml.[66] Also, the definitions of the tested constructs, expectations, and needs are confusing.

- **Sample problems.** For many campuses, the response rate has been less than 5 percent. Given this low rate, is it possible to use the resulting data with confidence? The LibQUAL+ staff suggest a 10 percent response rate as reasonable, assuming the sample represents the demographic pattern of the total population.

- **Data analysis problems.** Determinants of service quality perception cannot use descriptive statistics.

In another critique of LibQUAL+, William Edgar asks eight questions raising issues that should be seriously considered:[67]

1. How do libraries operate to serve their users?

2. What is the value provided to library users?

3. Are library users able to be self-reliant?

4. Are library users who are satisfied with library service delivery likely to be those who are well served by the service's underlying essence?

5. Are academic library users also its customers?

6. Are library users the only constituency with legitimate claims to library effectiveness?

7. On what basis should obligations of an academic library be distributed?

8. How do users' perceptions of service delivery relate to their perceptions of the service's underlying "essence," its reality?

An individual can also have valid reasons for dissatisfaction after a visit to the library. For example, the individual might receive a correct negative to an unanswerable question, might not get the answer at that time (although the library could have provided it if more time had been available), or might not be satisfied with the answer even though the answer was correct.[68]

A further analysis of customer satisfaction suggests that libraries should focus on their resources (the collection and providing access to electronic resources) and staff demeanor or attitude.[69] An analysis of the LibQUAL+ data and the information garnered from a series of focus groups noted user dissatisfaction with incomplete runs of titles, both serials and monographs.[70] A different analysis of LibQUAL+ data from 35 Association of Academic Health Sciences Libraries found no relationship between overall satisfaction and the library's reporting structure, size of library staff, and number of constituents.[71] However, the ratio of the number of constituents to library staff was correlated with user satisfaction ratings.

In Australia, a number of libraries have used a survey developed by the Rodski Research Group that is similar to LibQUAL+.[72]

In addition to conducting surveys of customer satisfaction and quality assessment, a library might perform a "walk-through audit" to assess the total customer experience.[73] The audit comprises a number of questions to be answered by a team of library managers that take the managers through the customer's experience stage by stage. The results of the audit can highlight areas in which the library can change or to improve the "experience" of going to the library.

Defining Service Characteristics

One of the challenges facing any service provider, such as a library, is gaining an understanding of what service characteristics are expected as a matter of course and what characteristics will delight the customer. Dr. Noriaki Kano, a Japanese quality expert, developed the "Kano model" to assist in this process. Kano's model predicts the degree of customer satisfaction, which is dependent on the degree of fulfillment of customer requirements, and that customers have different types of customer expectations.

The Kano model relates three factors to their degree of implementation (see Figure 15.9). The three factors are basic or expected (must be) factors, normal or fundamental (more is better) factors, and delighter or latent (excitement) factors. The degree of customer satisfaction ranges from disgust, through neutrality, to delighted.

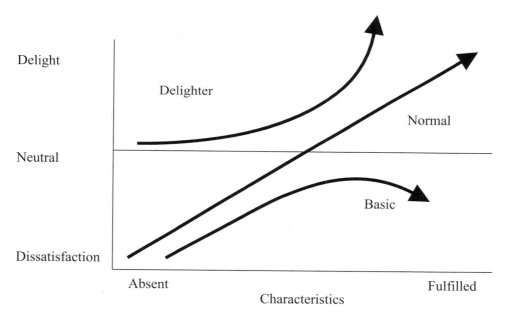

Figure 15.9. The Kano Model

Basic requirements are those that are so obvious to customers that they do not state them overtly. They are normally so obviously essential to the customer that stating these requirements seems a bit silly. For example, you would expect to hear a dial tone when you pick up a telephone. If you don't, then you are unhappy. Failing to provide basic requirements will result in customer complaints.

Normal requirements are those that a customer is cognizant of and can readily articulate. When these needs are met, customers are satisfied, and when they are not met, dissatisfaction arises. If more than "standard" customer requirements are delivered, then additional perceived benefits are generated.

Delighter requirements or exciting requirements are needs that some or all customers may not be aware of. Thus, these are often referred to as latent requirements. These are "out of the ordinary" service or product features or characteristics. If a provider understands such a need and fulfills it, the customer is delighted and will have a "wow" reaction. If these needs are not met, there is no customer response since customers are unaware of the need.

A library can analyze an existing or planned service by involving users to discover the types of customer requirements. This is done by using a two-sided question. The same question is asked of a number of users in positive and negative forms. For example:

- How do you feel if our service has feature X?
- How do you feel if our service does not have feature X?

The respondent is presented with four choices for these two questions:

- I like it.
- It is normally that way (feature is expected).
- I don't care.
- I don't like it.

The results are then tallied. Features or requirements that have high counts represent one of the three types of customer requirements (see Table 15.4). It should be remembered that over time, some service characteristics will move from delightful to normal and from normal to basic.

Table 15.4. Kano Model Response Table

Positive Question Answers	Negative Question Answers			
	Like	**Normal**	**Don't Care**	**Don't Like**
Like		Delightful	Delightful	Normal
Normal				Basic
Don't Care				Basic
Don't Like				

A library can use this methodology to systematically examine all of the characteristics and features of a service in order to discover what characteristics are particularly important to the user. These service characteristics can be identified by using a systems analysis approach to break a service down into its component steps and processes. This can be complemented by observing users as they interact with the service. Questions that should be addressed include the following:[74]

- What do customers find frustrating or confusing about the service?
- Does the user experience any anxiety using the service?
- Are there any time-consuming tasks or wasted time in using the service?
- What things does the user do that are "wrong"?
- What is causing a customer to use the service once and not return?
- Are any other irritants experienced by users when they use the service?

In addition, the library might also use a focus group to identify other characteristics or features for a particular library service, such as, circulation, reference, and so forth.

IMPLEMENTING QUALITY

If a library wants to make improvements in the quality of services that it offers to its customers, then staff will need training and encouragement to embrace change. Improving quality will, almost by definition if not necessity, require changing the way in which the library completes its activities and delivers service.

It should not be surprising that a library that is attempting to embrace service quality will meet resistance on some level. Peter Hernon et al. articulate 16 reasons why resistance will likely be encountered.[75] Frankie Wilson and Stephen Town suggest that a library will move through several evolutionary stages or levels as it seeks to embrace a culture of continuous improvement. They have developed a Quality Maturity Model with five levels:[76]

- **Level 1—Initial.** The quality management process is ad hoc, and success depends on individual effort and heroics.

- **Level 2—Repeatable.** Basic quality management processes are established since staff have received some training, and management ensures that the processes are followed.

- **Level 3—Defined.** The quality processes are standardized and documented. Staff receive training and understand how their activities and responsibilities fit into the organization's strategy.

- **Level 4—Managed.** Detailed performance measures of the quality process are routinely collected, analyzed, and acted upon.

- **Level 5—Optimizing.** Continuous quality improvement is enabled by the ongoing data collection processes, and new processes are pilot tested to identify best practices.

SUMMARY

This chapter has presented a number of methods that can be used to assess customer satisfaction. Among the more notable conclusions that can drawn from the above discussion are the following:

- Customer satisfaction surveys are the most popular and frequently used method of assessment.

- Use of two or more methods provides a more complete picture of customer satisfaction.

- Librarians try to make small adjustments in services to increase customer satisfaction.

- Adjusting a service may not lead to improved customer satisfaction ratings.

- Deciding on what expectation to meet has important service delivery implications.

- Focusing on customers requires staff to be trained and to accept that service quality is a worthy goal.

- How the library will assess progress toward the achievement of customer satisfaction goals is an important concern.

NOTES

1. Phillip Kotler and Alan Andreasen. *Strategic Marketing for Nonprofit Organizations.* Englewood Cliffs, NJ: Prentice-Hall, 1991.

2. Stratton Lloyd. Building Library Success Using the Balanced Scorecard. *Library Quarterly*, 76 (3), July 2006, 352–61.

3. Ellen Altman and Peter Hernon. Service Quality and Customer Satisfaction Do Matter. *American Libraries*, August 1998, 53–54.

4. Danuta Nitecki. Quality Assessment Measures in Libraries. *Advances in Librarianship*, 25, 2001, 133–62.

5. Richard Orr. Measuring the Goodness of Library Services. *Journal of Documentation*, 29 (3), 1973, 315–52.

6. Carol A. Reeves and David A. Bednar. Defining Quality: Alternatives and Implications. *Academy of Management Review*, 19 (3), 1994, 419–45; Peter Hernon and Danuta A. Nitecki. Service Quality: A Concept Not Fully Explored. *Library Trends*, 49 (4), Spring 2001, 687–708.

7. K. Elliott. A Comparison of Alternative Measures of Service Quality. *Journal of Customer Service in Marketing and Management*, I (1), 1995, 35.

8. Jan Carlson. *Moments of Truth.* Cambridge, MA: Balinger, 1987.

9. Peter Hernon and Ellen Altman. *Assessing Service Quality: Satisfying the Expectations of Library Customers.* Chicago: American Library Association, 1998. See also Peter Hernon and Ellen Altman. *Service Quality in Academic Libraries.* Norwood, NJ: Ablex, 1996.

10. Carol H. Fenichel. Intermediary Searchers' Satisfaction with the Results of Their Searches, in A. Benefeld and E. Kazlauskas (Eds.). *Proceedings of the 43rd ASIS Annual Meeting.* New York: Knowledge Industry for ASIS, 1980, 58–63. See also S. E. Hilchey and J. M. Hurych. User Satisfaction or User Acceptance? Statistical Evaluation of an Online Reference Service. *RQ*, *24*(4), 1985, 452–59; and R. Tagliacozzo. Estimating the Satisfaction of Information Users, *Bulletin of the Medical Library Association*, 65, 1977, 243–49.

11. Melvon Ankey. Evaluating End-User Services: Success or Satisfaction? *Journal of Academic Librarianship*, *16*, 1991, 352–56; H. J. Butler and G. M Kortman,. InfoTrac: Is It an Appropriate Reference Tool? *Reference Librarian,* 19, 1988, 225–37; and Prudence Dalrymple. Retrieval by Reformulation in Two Library Catalogs: Toward a Cognitive Model of Searching Behavior. *Journal of the American Society for Information Science*, 41, 1990, 272–81.

12. Rachel Applegate. Models of User Satisfaction: Understanding False Positive, *RQ*, *32*(4), 1993, 525–39.

13. Rachel Applegate. User Satisfaction with Information Services: A Test of the Disconfirmation-Satisfaction Model with a Library OPAC. Ph.D. dissertation, University of Wisconsin-Madison, 1995.

14. Xi Shi. An Examination of Information User Satisfaction Formation Process. Dissertation Abstracts International. 2000, (UMI No. 3010763); and Shi, X. Satisfaction Formation Processes in Library Users: Understanding Multisource Effects. *Journal of Academic Librarianship*, *30*(2), 2003, 121–31.

15. Rowena Cullen. Perspectives on User Satisfaction Surveys. *Library Trends*, 49 (4), 2001, 662–87.

16. Fei Yu. Users' Emotional and Material Satisfaction at the Micro/Macro Levels in an Academic Library. Ph.D. dissertation, University of Pittsburgh, 2006.

17. John M. Budd. A Critique of Customer and Commodity. *College & Research Libraries*, 58, July 1997, 309–20.

18. Jennifer Cram. Six Impossible Things Before Breakfast: A Multidimensional Approach to Measuring the Value of Libraries. Keynote address to the 3rd Northumbria International Conference on Performance Measurement in Libraries and Information Services, 27–31 August 1999. Available at http://www.alia.org.au/~jcram/six_things.html.

19. George D'Elia and Sandra Walsh. User Satisfaction with Library Service—A Measure of Public Library Performance? *The Library Quarterly*, 53 (2), April 1983, 109–33.

20. Sebastian Mundt. Benchmarking Users Satisfaction in Academic Libraries—A Case Study. *Library and Information Research*, 27 (87), Winter 2003, 29–37.

21. Richard L. Lynch and Kelvin F. Cross. *Measure Up! Yardsticks for Continuous Improvement.* London: Basil Blackwell, 1991.

22. Roland T. Rust, Anthony J. Zahorik, and Timothy L. Keiningham. *Return on Quality: Measuring the Financial Impact of Your Company's Quest for Quality.* New York: McGraw-Hill, 1994.

23. Peter Hernon and John R. Whitman. *Delivering Satisfaction and Service Quality.* Chicago: American Library Association, 2001.

24. G. Deane. Bridging the Value Gap: Getting Past Professional Values to Customer Value in the Public Library. *Public Libraries*, 42 (5), 2003, 315–19.

25. Philip Calvert. It's a Mystery: Mystery Shopping in New Zealand's Public Libraries. *Library Review*, 54 (1), 2005, 24–35.

26. Marjie Jantti. Assessing the Service Needs and Expectations of Customers—No Longer a Mystery. Paper presented at the Library Assessment Conference, Charlottesville, Virginia, September 25–27, 2006.

27. Robert G. Sines and Eric A. Duckworth. Customer Service in Higher Education. *Journal of Marketing for Higher Education*, 5, 1994, 1–15.

28. See, for example, the Colorado Library Research Service Web site at http://www.lrs.org/usersurveys.asp.

29. Timothy Keiningham and Terry Vavra. *The Customer Delight Principle: Exceeding Customers' Expectations for Bottom-Line Success.* New York: McGraw-Hill, 2001.

30. Douglas Badenoch, Christine Reid, Paul Burton, Forbes Gibb, and Charles Oppenheim. The Value of Information, in Mary Feeney and Maureen Grieves (Eds.). *The Value and Impact of Information.* London: Bowker Saur, 1994, 9–78.

31. Ruth Applegate. Models of User Satisfaction: Understanding False Positives. *RQ*, 32 (4), 1993, 525–39.

32. Thomas O. Jones and W. Earl Sasser Jr. Why Satisfied Customers Defect. *Harvard Business Review*, November–December 1995, 88–99.

33. George D'Elia and Sandra Walsh. User Satisfaction with Library Service—Measure of Public Library Performance? *Library Quarterly*, 53 (2), 1983, 109–33.

34. John Guaspari. The Hidden Costs of Customer Satisfaction. *Quality Digest*, February 1998, 45–49.

35. Xi Shi, Patricia J. Holahan, and M. Peter Jurkat. Satisfaction Formation Processes in Library Users: Understanding Multisource Effects. *The Journal of Academic Librarianship*, 30 (2), March 2004, 122–31.

36. Barry Totterdell and Jean Bird. The Effective Library: Report of the Hillingdon Project on Public Library Effectiveness. London: The Library Association, 1976.

37. George D'Elia. User Satisfaction as a Measure of Public Library Performance, in *Library Effectiveness: A State of the Art. Papers from a 1980 ALA Preconference, June 27 & 28, 1980, New York, NY.* Chicago: American Library Association, 1980, 64–69.

38. Totterdell and Bird, Effective Library.

39. Thomas O. Jones and W. Earl Sasser Jr. Why Satisfied Customers Defect. *Harvard Business Review*, 73, November/December 1995, 88–99.

40. Janet M. Kelly and David Swindell. A Multiple-Indicator Approach to Municipal Service Evaluation: Correlating Performance Measurement and Citizen Satisfaction Across Jurisdictions. *Public Administration Review*, 62 (5), September/October 2002, 610–21.

41. Robert A. Peterson and William R. Wilson. Measuring Customer Satisfaction: Fact and Artifact. *Journal of the Academy of Marketing Science*, 20 (1), Winter 1992, 61–71.

42. Patricia Dewdney and Catherine S. Ross. Flying a Light Aircraft: Reference Service Evaluation from a User's Viewpoint. *RQ*, 34, Winter 1994, 217–30.

43. Joan C. Durrance. Reference Success: Does the 55 Percent Rule Tell the Whole Story? *Library Journal*, 114, April 15, 1989, 31–36.

44. Karen Schmidt and Sue Searing. UIUC Library: User Survey and Needs Assessment Spring 1998. Summary. Unpublished report by the University of Illinois at Urbana-Champaign Library.

45. Deborah S. Davis and Alan M. Bernstein. From Survey to Service: Using Patron Input to Improve Customer Satisfaction. *Technical Services Quarterly*, 14 (3), 1997, 47–62.

46. Frederick F. Reichheld. The One Number You Need to Grow. *Harvard Business Review*, 81 (12), December 2003, 46–57.

47. Frederick F. Reichheld. *The Ultimate Question: Driving Good Profits and True Growth*. Boston: Harvard Business School Press, 2006.

48. Marianne Broadbent and Hans Lofgren. Information Delivery: Identifying Priorities, Performance and Value, in *OPAC and Beyond*. Hilton on the Park, Melbourne, Australia, Victorian Association for Library Automation 6th Biennial Conference and Exhibition, 11–13 November 1991, 185–215; Marianne Broadbent. Demonstrating Information Service Value to Your Organization. *Proceedings of the IOLIM Conference*, 16, 1992, 65–83; Marianne Broadbent and Hans Lofgren. *Priorities, Performance and Benefits: An Exploratory Study of Library and Information Units*. Melbourne, Australia: CIRCIT Ltd. and ACLIS, 1991.

49. Susan Edwards and Mairead Browne. Quality in Information Services: Do Users and Librarians Differ in Their Expectations? *Library & Information Science Review*, 17, 1995, 163–82.

50. Danuta A. Nitecki. Quality Assessment Measures in Libraries. *Advances in Librarianship*, 25, 2001, 133–62.

51. Jeffrey A. Raffel and Robert Shishko. *Systematic Analysis of University Libraries*. Cambridge, MA: MIT Press, 1969.

52. A. Parasuraman, Valarie A. Zeithaml, and Leonard L. Berry. SERVQUAL: A Multiple-Item Scale for Measuring Consumer Perceptions of Service Quality. *Journal of Retailing*, 64, 1988, 12–37; Valarie A. Zeithaml, A. Parasuraman, and Leonard L. Berry, *Delivering Quality Service: Balancing Customer Perceptions and Expectations*. New York: Free Press, 1990; Parasuraman, Valarie A. Zeithaml, and Leonard L. Berry. Reassessment of Expectations as a Comparison Standard in Measuring Service Quality: Implications for Further Research. *Journal of Marketing*, 58 (1), January 1994, 111–24.

53. Joseph J. Cronin and Steven A. Taylor. SERVPERF versus SERVQUAL: Reconciling Performance-Based and Perceptions Minus Expectations of Service Quality. *Journal of Marketing*, 58 (1), January 1994, 125–31.

54. A. Parasuraman, Leonard Berry, and Valarie A. Zeithaml. A Conceptual Model of Service Quality and Its Implications for Future Research. *Journal of Marketing*, 49 (4), 1985, 41–50.

55. Mik Wisniewski and Mike Donnelly. Measuring Service Quality in the Public Sector: The Potential for SERVQUAL. *Total Quality Management*, 7 (4), 1996, 357–65.

56. See, for example, Tom J. Brown, Gilbert A. Churchill Jr., and J. Paul Peter. Improving the Measurement of Service Quality. *Journal of Retailing*, 66 (1), Spring 1993, 127–39; J. Joseph Cronin Jr.

and Stephen A. Taylor. Measuring Service Quality: A Re-examination and Extension. *Journal of Marketing*, 56 (3), July 1992, 55–68; James M. Carman. Consumer Perceptions of Service Quality: An Assessment of SERVQUAL Dimensions. *Journal of Retailing*, 66 (1), Spring 1990, 33–55; Emin Babakus and Gregory W. Boller. An Empirical Assessment of the SERVQUAL Scale. *Journal of Business Research*, 24 (3), Winter 1994, 253–68; Syed Saad Andaleeb and Amiya K. Basu. Technical Complexity and Consumer Knowledge as Moderators of Service Quality Evaluation in the Automobile Industry. *Journal of Retailing*, 70 (4), Winter 1994, 367–81.

57. Michael J. Roszkowski, John S. Baky, and David B. Jones. So Which Score on the LibQUAL+ Tells Me if Library Users Are Satisfied? *Library & Information Science Research*, 27, 2005, 424–39.

58. Francoise Hébert. Service Quality: An Unobtrusive Investigation of Interlibrary Loan in Large Public Libraries in Canada. *Library & Information Science Research*, 16, 1994, 3–21.

59. Syed S. Andaleeb and Patience L. Simmonds. Explaining User Satisfaction with Academic Libraries. *College and Research Libraries,* 59, March 1998, 156–67; Yoshinori Satoh, Haruki Nagata, Paivi Kytomaki, and Sarah Gerrard. *Performance Measurement & Metrics*, 6 (3), 2005, 183–93; Vicki Coleman, Yi (Daniel) Xiao, Linda Bair, and Bill Chollett. Toward a TQM Paradigm: Using SERVQUAL to Measure Library Service Quality. *College & Research Libraries,* 58, May 1997, 237–51; Susan Edwards and Mairead Browne. Quality in Information Services: Do Users and Librarians Differ in Their Expectations? *Library & Information Science Research,* 17, Spring 1995, 163–82.

60. Colleen Cook, Fred Heath, and Bruce Thompson. *LibQUAL+: One Instrument in the New Measures Toolbox.* Available at http://www.arl.org/newsltr/212/libqual.html; Colleen Cook and Bruce Thompson. Higher-Order Factor Analytic Perspectives on Users' Perceptions of Library Service Quality. *Library Information Science Research*, 22, 2000, 393–404; Colleen Cook and Bruce Thompson. Users' Hierarchical Perspectives on Library Service Quality: A LibQUAL+ Study. *College and Research Libraries*, 62, 2001, 147–53.

61. Yvonna S. Lincoln. Insights into Library Services and Users from Qualitative Research. *Library & Information Science Research*, 24 (1), 2002, 3–16; A copy of the 2002 version of the LibQUAL+ survey instrument may be found in Colleen Cook, Fred Heath, Bruce Thompson, and Duane Webster. LibQUAL+: Preliminary Results from 2002. *Performance Measurement and Metrics*, 4 (1), 2003, 38–47.

62. Roszkowski et al., So Which Score.

63. A. Parasuraman. Foreword to the Special Issue of *Performance Measurement & Metrics*, 3 (2), 2002, 37–39.

64. Claire Creaser. One Size Does Not Fit All: User Surveys in Academic Libraries. *Performance Measurement and Metrics*, 7 (3), 2006, 153–62.

65. Xi Shi and Sarah Levy. A Theory-Guided Approach to Library Services Assessment. *College & Research Libraries*, 66 (3), May 2005, 266–77.

66. A. Parasuraman, Leonard L. Berry, and Valarie A. Zeitheml. A Conceptual Model of Service Quality and Its Implications for Future Research. *Journal of Marketing*, 49, 1985, 41–50; and Parasuraman et al. SERQUAL: A Multiple-Item Scale for Measuring Consumer Perceptions of Service Quality. *Journal of Retailing*, 64, 1988, 12–40.

67. William B. Edgar. Questioning LibQUAL+: Expanding Its Assessment of Academic Library Effectiveness. *portal: Libraries and the Academy*, 6 (4), 2006, 445–65.

68. Roy Knight. The Measurement of Reference Use, in *Output Measurement*. London: Public Libraries Research Group, 1974.

69. Andaleeb and Simmonds, Explaining User Satisfaction, 156–67.

70. Amy E. Knapp. We Asked Them What They Thought, Now What Do We Do? The Use of LibQUAL+ Data to Redesign Public Services at the University of Pittsburgh. *Journal of Library Administration*, 40 (3/4), 2004, 151–71.

71. Douglas J. Joubert and Tamera P. Lee. Empowering Your Institution Through Assessment. *Journal of the Medical Library Association*, 95 (1), January 2007, 46–53.

72. Nicole Clark and Grace Saw. Reading Rodski: User Surveys Revisited. Paper presented at The 25th IATUL Annual Conference, Krakow, Poland, 2004. Available at http://www.library.uq.edu.au/papers/reading_rodski.pdf.

73. Jennifer Rowley. Customer Experience of Libraries. *Library Review*, 43 (6), 1994, 7–17.

74. Kurt R. Hofmeister, Christi Walters, and John Gongos. Discovering Customer Wow's. *ASQC 50th Annual Quality Conference Proceedings*, May 13–15 1996. Milwaukee, WI: ASQC, 1996, 759–70.

75. Peter Hernon, Danuta A. Nitecki, and Ellen Altman. Service Quality and Customer Satisfaction: An Assessment and Future Directions. *The Journal of Academic Librarianship*, 25 (1), January 1999, 9–17.

76. Frankie Wilson and J. Stephen Town. Benchmarking and Library Quality Maturity. *Performance Measurement and Metrics*, 7 (2), 2006, 75–82.

Part IV

Evaluation of the Library

16

Evaluating the Broader Perspective

Libraries are often faced with providing, in some manner, an indication of the value of the library and all of its services to interested stakeholders. Thus, it is necessary to go beyond the evaluation of a specific library service and attempt to assess the total impact of the library on the lives of its customers. The obvious question then arises: How can a library determine its value to its parent organization, to the overall college or university environment, or to its community?

Attempting to answer the question, "How is the library doing?" is really trying to measure how effective the library is. Effectiveness is trying to answer the question, "Are we doing the *right* things?" During the planning process the library makes decisions about the mix of services that it will offer and who the library's primary customers are going to be. An evaluation of the total library is an attempt to demonstrate how effective the library is in its community (city or county, academic campus, government agency, or company). Such an evaluation may also be attempting to demonstrate the value of the library in the lives of its customers and the broader organization that it serves.

Funding any library is an expensive proposition: print and electronic collections, buildings and equipment, along with the ongoing costs of recruiting and retaining staff. The benefits gained from funding any library are increasingly being questioned by the funding stakeholders. Among the questions often raised are the following:

- Does the investment in libraries represent value for money?

- Are there demonstrable, tangible benefits that arise from library use?

- Does the library meet the needs of its service community?

The next three chapters explore ways in which libraries have attempted to determine their effectiveness and define the value of the library. The primary means of describing the value of the library have occurred in the areas of accomplishments, economic benefits, and, for public libraries, social impacts of the library on the lives of customers.

Due to the elusive nature of organizational effectiveness (sometimes called "goodness"),
Lawrence Mohr has called it the "Holy Grail of management research."[1] The pursuit of the Grail
of Library Goodness[2] has led to studies attempting to demonstrate the goodness of the library.

One of the principal differences between a service organization such as a library and a for-profit business, according to Peter Drucker, is that a business receives resources (it must "earn" its revenues) by satisfying the customer, whereas the service organization receives a budget allocation from a funding source.[4] The problem is that there is little direct relationship between how effective a library is and the satisfaction experienced by the customer or user. Ultimately, it is not unusual for a budget-based institution such as a library to judge its effectiveness by the amount of next year's budget allocation. Often "performance" is the ability to maintain or increase the library's budget. Drucker suggests that service organizations like libraries should

> *The financial crisis is looking even worse, but you will be pleased to know that the librarian reports that the library performance went up a half a point on the library goodness scale last week.*
>
> —Michael Buckland[3]

1. answer the question, "What is our business and what should it be?";
2. derive clear objectives and goals from their definition of function and mission;
3. identify priorities of concentration that enable them to select targets, set deadlines, and make someone accountable for results;
4. define measurements of performance;
5. build feedback from results into their systems; and
6. perform an audit of objectives and results to identify those objectives that no longer serve a useful purpose.

Thomas Childers and Nancy Van House[5] made a similar observation about the lack of a connection between services offered and the availability of revenues:

- Revenues and outputs are separated.
- A common metric (the bottom line in corporations) is lacking in nonprofit sector organizations.
- The decision-making process is bigger than the library.
- The library has neither champions nor foes.
- Library benefits are not widely self-evident.

Another challenge associated with assessing the goodness of the library is based on two different values. Librarians are primarily concerned about providing access to resources and information using professional and experienced service staff. As such, librarians have an internal focus, seeing themselves as "doing good," and are less concerned about assessing outputs and impacts. The library's funding decision makers have an external view and want to ensure that the library is operating efficiently and effectively—that is, meeting the needs of the community of users.

The three primary challenges that must be confronted when considering organizational effectiveness are the definition, measurement, and determinants of effectiveness. Quite clearly, the definition of effectiveness is going to be multidimensional, since a single perspective is not likely to do justice to any organization. And the definition of effectiveness is going to vary not only by type of organization but also by the services the library decides to offer and the strategies it employs to provide those services.

A number of problems in assessing organizational effectiveness have been identified, including the following:

- Different approaches to assessing effectiveness are products of varying, arbitrary models of organizations.

- Effectiveness is a product of individual values and preferences, and thus the best criteria for assessing effectiveness cannot be identified.

- The construct space of effectiveness has never been bounded.

- Not all relevant criteria of effectiveness have been identified.[6]

Given these problems, it has proven difficult to define organizational effectiveness. Kim Cameron identified four general models of ways organizations tend to define their effectiveness:[7]

- The *goal model, goal attainment model,* or *rational system model* views effectiveness in terms of achievement of specific goals and objectives. The focus is on productivity and outputs. Establishing goals maybe arbitrary or subjective. If a library does not have clearly defined goals, it will be impossible to articulate criteria of effectiveness, thus rendering this model useless. However, caution should be exercised since a library may only select already existing measures to the exclusion of new measures, e.g., outcome measures.

- The *internal process* or *natural systems model* sees an organization seeking to achieve goals as well as desiring to maintain itself as a social unit. Organizational health, stability, internal processes, and the attainment of goals measure effectiveness.

- The *open systems model* or *system resource model* focuses on the interdependence of the organization with its environment. The organizational survival and growth depend on acquiring resources, in particular budgetary resources, from external groups.

- The *multiple constituencies model* or *participant satisfaction model* sees effectiveness as the degree to which the needs of the various constituencies or stakeholders are met. Some of the stakeholders to be satisfied are not going to control needed fiscal resources (which is the system resource model). The challenge with this perspective is to reconcile the often conflicting needs and wishes of different stakeholders, each of which will have different criteria of effectiveness.

These models have been used by others to study the applicability of Cameron's models in a library setting:[8] One of the important implications of these models is that the choice of any one model will, of necessity, capture only a portion of the organization described by the model. Other segments of the organization will not be included in the measurement and thus it will not reflect the performance of the total organization.

PUBLIC LIBRARY STUDIES

Thomas Childers and Nancy Van House conducted a library effectiveness study with the goal of identifying the perceptions of seven groups (users, friends, trustees, local officials, community leaders, library managers, and library service staff) about what performance measures indicate the effectiveness of a library. An analysis of 2,500 survey respondents found that six items were in the top ten preferences for all of the groups: convenience of hours, range of materials, range of services, staff helpfulness, services suited to community, and materials quality (see Table 16.1, p. 280).[9] As the library transitions to a mix of physical and virtual services, it will be interesting to determine how the perceptions of different stakeholders change.

Table 16.1. Top 15 Effectiveness Indicators, Ranked by Each Group

Community Leaders	Local Officials	Trustees	Friends	Users	Library Managers	Service Librarians
1. Convenience of hours	Convenience of hours	Convenience of hours	Convenience of hours	Convenience of hours	Convenience of hours	Staff helpfulness
2. Range of materials	Range of materials	Staff helpfulness	Range of materials	Range of materials	Staff helpfulness	Range of services
3. Range of services	Services suited	Services suited	Staff helpfulness	Range of services	Range of materials	Range of materials
4. Staff helpfulness	Range of services	Range of materials	Range of services	Staff helpfulness	Services suited	Convenience of hours
5. Services suited	Staff helpfulness	Range of services	Services suited	Materials quality	Range of services	Services suited
6. Materials quality	Materials availability	Public opinion	Convenience of location	Convenience of location	Circulation	Circulation
7. Materials availability	Convenience of location	Managerial competence	Materials quality	Materials availability	Public opinion	Materials quality
8. Awareness of services	Materials quality	Staff morale	Community well-being	Service freeness	Materials quality	Staff morale
9. Convenience of location	Awareness of services	Materials quality	Awareness of services	Services suited	Number of visits	Awareness of services
10. Service freeness	Users' evaluation	Staff quality	Materials Availability	Newness of materials	Awareness of services	Staff quality
11. Community well-being	Community well-being	Users' evaluation	Service freeness	Parking	Convenience of location	Public opinion
12. Users' evaluation	Public opinion	Awareness of services	Staff quality	Speed of services	Staff quality	Number of visits
13. Speed of service	Number of visits	Community well-being	Building easy to identify	Interlibrary cooperation	Users' evaluation	Convenience of location
14. Staff quality	Managerial competence	Number of visits	Public opinion	Handicapped access	Users per capita	Users' evaluation
15. Public opinion	Speed of services	Convenience of location	Special group services	Awareness of services	Materials availability	Materials expended

Quite obviously there are more similarities than differences when looking at the indicators across all groups. It is interesting, however, to compare and contrast the responses of users to those of all the other groups. Users' preferences seem reasonable. A good library is one that is open at convenient times, has a good range of materials and services, and has helpful staff members. Notice particularly that library staff place greater importance on different criteria of goodness than do the other groups.

The other picture that emerges is that each group has a slightly different perspective that must, in part, be recognized as the library struggles to put together a set of performance measures to demonstrate the value of the library to all stakeholders.

Using the responses from the survey noted above, the statistical technique factor analysis was used by Childers and Van House to identify eight broad dimensions of effectiveness: outputs and inputs, internal processes, community fit, access to materials, physical facilities, management elements, service offerings, and service to special groups. It is then possible to sort these eight dimensions into one of the four organizational effectiveness models previously noted, as shown in Table 16.2.

Table 16.2. Models and Dimensions of Organizational Effectiveness

Goal Model	Process Model	System Resource Model	Multiple Constituencies Model
Outputs & Inputs	Internal Processes	Outputs & Inputs	Community Fit
Community Fit	Management Elements	Internal Processes	
Access to Materials		Physical Facilities	
Service Offerings		Management Elements	
Service to Special Groups			

Clearly the goal model and the system resource model have the preponderance of the performance measures that have been developed by librarians as a way to demonstrating the value or effectiveness of the library. However, librarians and interested stakeholders should recognize that other perspectives exist and might be more appropriate to use in some situations.

The library effectiveness study was replicated in New Zealand, and the results of the survey rankings and the factor analysis were similar to those identified in the United States.[10] People in most of the groups surveyed recognized that perceptions of effectiveness are multidimensional and that a number of measures will be needed when communicating the value of the library to stakeholders. And while there are no differences in the perceptions of library effectiveness between geographical areas, no one model of organizational effectiveness dominates among the perceptions of various stakeholders.[11] The good news is that librarians, users, and city council members have relatively congruent views about what constitutes an effective library. However, it should be recognized that since the library is a social creation, librarians need to involve multiple stakeholders in a process to identify possible measures of a library's "goodness."

In a 1996 survey conducted in 500 communities, library directors and officials differed significantly in their perception of the library and its value to the community when compared to other tax-supported services. Among the officials, the library provided a lower "return for tax dollars spent," even when the local library was judged as being close to ideal.[12]

Glen Holt has risen to the challenge and suggests that there are seven measurable criteria for defining a "great library":

- Great libraries provide measurably superior service
- Great libraries have great funding
- Great libraries train and retrain their staffs
- Great libraries integrate the marketing of virtual, place and outreach services
- Great libraries serve both the weakest and strongest among their constituents
- Great libraries provide constituents with education and entertainment
- Great libraries use virtual tools to offer a full range of timely information and services.[13]

ACADEMIC LIBRARY STUDIES

Kim Cameron, in a series of studies conducted in the later 1970s and 1980s, examined organizational effectiveness in higher education and suggested that there were nine possible dimensions of effectiveness:

- **Students' educational satisfaction** with their educational experiences at the institution
- **Student academic development,** indicating academic attainment, growth, and progress of students at the institution
- **Student career development** and the opportunities for career development provided by the institution
- **Student personal development**, focusing on non-career and nonacademic oriented aspects
- **Faculty and administrators' employment satisfaction** with their jobs at the institution
- **Professional development and quality of the faculty**, focusing on the amount of stimulation toward professional development provided by the institution
- **Systems openness and community interaction** with, adaptation to, and service in the external environment
- **Ability to acquire resources** from the external environment
- **Organizational health,** including benevolence, vitality, and viability in the internal operations and practices at the institution[14]

Cameron notes that effectiveness in one domain may not necessarily relate to effectiveness in another domain. Also, organizational effectiveness in external domains may militate against effectiveness in internal domains. Cameron suggests that effectiveness is a mental construct inferred from an organization's behavior and not something observed directly.[15]

Effective organizations generate valued and desired outcomes. Another study suggested that managerial strategies are more important than structure, demographics, finances, and other factors. Colleges and universities with proactive strategies and those with an external emphasis are more successful than those with internal and reactive strategies.[16] Also, higher education institutions with declining resources can be as effective as institutions with abundant resources, provided the process for coping with fewer resources is open and transparent.[17]

Building on the work of Childers and Van House, Rowena Cullen and Philip Calvert used the same four models in a survey of six New Zealand academic institution stakeholders: resource allocators, senior library staff, other library staff, academic staff, graduate students, and undergraduate students. The survey respondents were asked to rate 99 indicators of library service using a 5-point Likert scale. Factor analysis was used to derive 13 dimensions of performance. The results show some similarities and some differences in what each constituency expects from the library. Yet the library management team is confronted with the task of allocating resources to meet varying expectations.[18] One of the implications of these studies is that the library management team needs to clearly understand what the key stakeholders are expecting of the library.

Joseph McDonald and Lynda Micikas surveyed academic libraries in institutions without doctoral programs in seven states using an adaptation of Kim Cameron's work. Respondents were asked to rate 95 measures of library performance using a 7-point Likert scale. Analysis was performed on survey responses received from 131 institutions (a 50 percent response rate) and 384 surveys. Twenty-one factors emerged, and these were grouped into four main domains: major resources—staff size and diversity, college support for the library, and library collection adequacy; services—access/use of outside libraries, cooperative associations, and librarian professional service; library/stakeholder interaction—staff development, shared goals, shared organizational direction, faculty relations, and evaluation of the library; and access—collection physical organization and access/use of campus library.[19] It is important to note that given this type of analysis, no two groups in the same institution—let alone different organizations—will ever have the same ratings. Ellen Altman, in a review of the McDonald and Micikas book, suggested that the study had a number of problems, including faulty question design, possible sampling bias, and statistical analysis problems.[20]

John Crawford et al. conducted a large-scale study of 15 academic universities in England, and a total of 4,193 fully completed surveys were returned—about a 15 percent response rate. The goal was to identify the differing perceptions of various stakeholder groups: undergraduates, graduate students, research staff, academic staff, and library staff. Not surprisingly, the various stakeholder groups have different agendas.[21]

Library stakeholders, in particular funding decision makers, are concerned about understanding the performance of the library from several perspectives:

- What are the *goals and objectives* that the library is striving to reach? What proportion of the population is the library serving?

- A set of measures is needed that indicate what *progress* is being made to achieve the library's goals and objectives. In most cases, this will be a combination of output and outcome measures.

- *Efficiency measures* demonstrate that the library is operating efficiently and that the library is a good custodian of the funds provided by the taxpayers in the community.

- *Trends and comparisons* show how the library has done over time compared with other comparable libraries.

LIBRARY GOODNESS

Clearly no single measure of library goodness is going to fulfill the expectations of the multiple groups that need to be satisfied. Without a clear understanding of and agreement on the mission and vision of the library, there may be conflicts over how

A major aspect of library effectiveness is representing the library to key stakeholders.
—Thomas A. Childers and
Nancy A. Van House[22]

well the goals of the library are actually achieved. The reality is that the library is controlled to a large extent by the resources that are made available to it (and the library does not have direct control over the allocation of these resources). Providing the tools and resources allows a well-trained staff to provide services in an efficient manner.

In the past, little was required of a library beyond having the library director adhere to budget allocations. In such an environment there was little encouragement and few rewards for being ' "good" beyond personal satisfaction. While library stakeholders, including the funding decision makers, have historically accepted the conventional wisdom of the "community goodness" provided by the library, stakeholders are increasingly demanding tangible proof that the library is delivering quality library services that meet the needs of the customers using cost efficient means. The bottom line is a demand for increased accountability.

And this demand is not new. Back in 1973, Orr suggested that libraries needed to focus on providing answers to three "goodness" questions:

- How good is the library? The focus is on quality and capabilities.

- What good does the library do? The focus is on beneficial use.

- How well is the library managed?[23]

Yet librarians have difficulty knowing how to approach this issue of reporting performance, for several reasons:

- **Lack of consensus.** The library profession has not spoken with one clear voice about what performance measures should be used to report the library's accomplishments.

- **Lack of definitions.** The library profession has failed to adopt a consistent set of definitions for the plethora of performance measures that already exist. The result is that two libraries can be reporting the same statistic but actually be measuring two different perspectives of a service, be collecting the data differently, and so forth.

- **Lack of understanding.** Library directors and managers often have a poor understanding of the potential value and utility of performance measures, which when consistently applied can assist in improving the operation of the library. As such, these individuals are ambivalent toward evaluation in general and specifically toward the difficulty of attempting to assess the outputs of the library that affect the individual user and the local community.

- **Lack of structure.** There may be several reasons that prevent libraries from effectively using performance measures. Among these are the library's culture, a desire not to waste time and resources, the need for staff to become more knowledgeable, and the need for training.

- **Statistical overload.** Most libraries collect a great many performance measures. The state library and federal surveys often mandate the collection of some statistics, while the local library continues to gather other measures it has "always" collected. As a result, staff are more than likely to be overwhelmed by the prospect of collecting some "new" performance measures without considering the possibility of deciding to stop collecting others.

- **It is hard work.** As Orr noted, attempting to measure quality and beneficial use requires a great deal of thinking about the issues and how to measure the two concepts. Historically librarians have tended to fall back on measures that serve as surrogates— collection completeness and circulation, respectively.

As a result, the library profession has been unable to answer even such basic questions as:

- What is a good library?

- What is a bad library?

- How can we move from being "bad" to being "good"?

THE 90 PERCENT LIBRARY

An important strategic planning decision for a library board and library stakeholders is: What percent of all service needs can be met by the resources contained within our library? Any library is going to be faced with a group of users with a wide variety of interests and information needs, yet no library can anticipate and plan for meeting all users' needs. Thus the question arises: What level of resources and services will meet "X" percent of the needs of our population's needs? The library will handle the remainder of needs in some other way. The percent level selected by the library will determine, in large part, the budgetary needs of the library.

Charles Bourne asked: What does a library have to do to satisfy 90 percent of a library population's needs?"[24] User requirements could be stated in the following terms:

90 percent of the information needs of a given user population is satisfied by:

- Books that are less than _____ years old
- A book collection size of _____ volumes
- A media collection size of _____ items
- A print journal collection of _____ titles
- A print journal collection that are less than _____ years old
- An electronic journals collection of _____ titles
- Interlibrary loan journal articles delivered in _____ days
- Computer workstations to minimize wait times below _____ minutes
- And so forth.

Given the distributions of Bradford and Zipf and the rate of obsolescence of materials found in a library, it should be possible to estimate collection size and other service needs for a given service population at the desired service levels. A library should also consider policies that it might have in place to discourage use of one or more services. For example, does the library charge for interlibrary loan? Does a patron have to wait months to borrow a best seller? Does the library charge to borrow videos and DVDs?

SUMMARY

The problem of demonstrating the "goodness" of the library, which librarians historically have focused on through their use of input, process, and output measures, is much less important than being able to establish the effectiveness of the library from the perspective of the user. This challenge of demonstrating effectiveness is being exacerbated by the wide range of services offered by libraries as well as the transition from the traditional print-based library to providing access to a combination of print and electronic resources (the hybrid library).

In addition, the library must overcome the inertia of continuing to do what it has always done while resisting calls to provide relevant information about the utility of the library. Historically and today, the generally accepted folk wisdom has regarded the library as a good thing. Yet folk wisdom is no substitute for demonstrating the relevance of the library to its stakeholders, especially the mayors, city managers, county administrators, and boards who control the library's purse strings. Ultimately, the challenge of demonstrating effectiveness is based on the need to focus on the difference the library makes in the lives of individuals and in the community itself.

NOTES

1. Lawrence B. Mohr. *Explaining Organizational Behavior: The Limits and Possibilities of Theory and Research*. San Francisco: Jossey-Bass, 1982.

2. Michael Buckland. *Library Services in Theory and Context*. New York: Pergamon, 1988, 241–44.

3. Michael K. Buckland. Concepts of Library Goodness. *Canadian Library Journal*, 39 (2), April 1982, 63–66.

4. Peter F. Drucker. Managing the Service Institution. *The Interest*, 33, Fall 1973, 43–60.

5. Thomas Childers and Nancy A. Van House. *What's Good? Describing Your Library's Effectiveness*. Chicago: American Library Association, 1993.

6. Kim S. Cameron and David A. Whetten. *Organizational Effectiveness: A Comparison of Multiple Models*. New York: Academic Press, 1983.

7. Kim S. Cameron. Domains of Organizational Effectiveness in Colleges and Universities. *Academy of Management Journal*, 24, 1981, 254–47; and Kim S. Cameron. A Study of Organizational Effectiveness and Its Predictors. *Management Science*, 32, 1986, 87–112.

8. Thomas Childers and Nancy Van House. The Grail of Goodness: The Effective Library. *Library Journal*, 114, October 1, 1989, 44–49; Thomas Childers and Nancy Van House. Dimensions of Library Effectiveness. *Library and Information Science Review*, 11, 1989, 273–301; Nancy Van House and Thomas Childers. Dimensions of Library Effectiveness II: Library Performance. *Library and Information Science Review*, 12, 1990, 131–53.

9. Childers and Van House, *What's Good?*.

10. Rowena J. Cullen and Philip J. Calvert. Further Dimensions of Library Effectiveness: Report of a Parallel New Zealand Study. *Library and Information Science Review*, 15, 1993, 143–64; Philip J. Calvert and Rowena J. Cullen. Further Dimensions of Library Effectiveness II: The Second Stage of the New Zealand Study. *Library and Information Science Review*, 16, 1994, 87–104.

11. Philip J. Calvert and Rowena J. Cullen. Performance Measurement in New Zealand Libraries: A Research Project. *Australasian Library & Information Services*, 5 (1), March 1992, 3–12; Philip J. Calvert and Rowena J. Cullen. The New Zealand Libraries Effectiveness Study and the New Zealand University Libraries Effectiveness Study. *Australian Academic & Research Libraries*, 26 (2), June 1995, 97–106.

12. Leigh Estabrook and Edward Lakner. A Survey of Libraries and Local Government. *Illinois State Library: Special Report Series*, 4, 1997, 54–62.

13. Glen E. Holt. What Makes a Library Great? *Public Library Quarterly*, 24 (2), 2005, 83–89.

14. Kim Cameron. Measuring Organizational Effectiveness in Institutions of Higher Education. *Administrative Science Quarterly*, 23, December 1978, 604–29.

15. Kim Cameron. Domains of Organizational Effectiveness in College and Universities. *Academy of Management Journal*, 24 (1), 1981, 254–47.

16. Cameron, Study of Organizational Effectiveness, 87–112.

17. Kim Cameron and John Smart. Maintaining Effectiveness Amid Downsizing and Decline in Institutions of Higher Education. *Research in Higher Education*, 39 (1), 1998, 654–86.

18. Rowena J. Cullen and Philip J. Calvert. Stakeholder Perceptions of University Library Effectiveness. *The Journal of Academic Librarianship*, 21 (6), November 1995, 438–48; and Rowena J. Cullen and Philip J. Calvert. New Zealand University Libraries Effectiveness Project: Dimensions and Concepts of Organizational Effectiveness. *Library and Information Science Research*, 18, 1996, 99–119.

19. Joseph A. McDonald and Lynda Basney Micikas. *Academic Libraries: The Dimensions of Their Effectiveness*. Westport, CT: Greenwood Press, 1994.

20. Ellen Altman. A Review of Academic Libraries. *The Journal of Academic Librarianship*, 21 (2), March 1995, 128–29.

21. John Crawford, Helen Pickering, and Dorothy McLelland. The Stakeholder Approach to the Construction of Performance Measures. *Journal of Library & Information Science*, 30 (2), June 1998, 87–112.

22. Childers and Van House, *What's Good?*

23. Robert H. Orr. Measuring the Goodness of Library Services: A General Framework for Considering Quantitative Measures. *Journal of Documentation*, 29 (3), September 1973, 314–32.

24. Charles P. Bourne. Some User Requirements Stated Quantitatively in Terms of the 90 Percent Library, in Allen Kent and Orrin E. Taulbee (Eds.). *Electronic Information Handling*. Washington, DC: Spartan Books, 1965, 93–110.

17

Accomplishments:
The Key to Realizing Value

When an individual uses a library the immediate benefits will occur within the lifetime of that person. Robert's Orr's Input-Process-Output-Outcomes evaluation model was discussed in some detail in chapter 2. It is in the last category of Orr's model, outcomes, that an individual translates the immediate benefit from use of a library into an accomplishment—an outcome.

Tefko Saracevic and Paul Kantor developed a framework and taxonomy for establishing the value that may arise from using library and information services based on the vocabulary of users in responding to a questionnaire.[1] They suggest that an individual has three potential reasons to use a library or information service: (1) to work on a task or project, (2) for personal reasons, or (3) to get an object or information or to perform an activity.

They assert that when an individual interacts with a library service, there are three areas of interaction that should be considered:

- **Resources**. From the individual's viewpoint, three perspectives might be considered in this area.

  - *Availability*. This traditional evaluation measure attempts to assess whether the library has the given resource, item, or service desired by the client.

  - *Accessibility*. This measure focuses on the ease with which the service can be accessed. Is a visit to the library required, for example? Is the resource available online?

  - *Quality*. This measure assesses the degree to which a service or resource is accurate, current, timely, and complete.

- **Use of Resources, Services**. In examining this area, the library could ask its customers to assess five potential measures:

  - The degree of *convenience* in using the resource or service.

  - *Ease of use*. How difficult is it to use a resource or library service?

  - What *frustration*, if any, results from using the resource or library service?

289

- How *successful* is the client in using a library service or resource?

- How much *effort* is required to move from one service to another? For example, performing a search to identify citations and then to retrieve the desired journal articles or other resources.

- **Operations and Environment**. There are four categories in which an individual can be asked to rate the library and its services:

  - How reasonable and clear are the library's *policies and procedures*? Do they facilitate access to the library's services or act as impediments?

  - Are the *facilities* of adequate size? Does the physical layout and organization of the library resources facilitate access to the resources and services?

  - Are library *staff members* helpful, efficient, and knowledgeable? Is there a clear understanding of the goals and objectives of the organization and a desire by library staff to offer a quality service?

  - Is the *equipment* reliable and easy to use? Are user instructions or guides readily available? Is the library's Web site easy to use and kept current?

But most important, Saracevic and Kantor focused on the results, outcomes, or the impact that a library or information service has on the organization. An "organization" can be defined as a community, an academic institution, or a profit or not-for-profit concern. Given a reason to use the library, and having had an interaction with one or more library services, what is the effect? The six categories include the following:

- **Cognitive results**. Use of the library may have an impact on the mind of the individual. The intention of this category is to ask, "What was learned?" Thus, the individual may have

  - refreshed memory of detail or facts;

  - substantiated or reinforced knowledge or belief;

  - provided new knowledge,

  - changed in viewpoint, outlook, or perspective;

  - got ideas with a slightly different or tangential perspective (serendipity); or

  - got no ideas.

- **Affective results**. Use of the library or its services may influence or have an emotional impact on the individual. The individual may experience

  - a sense of accomplishment, success, or satisfaction;

  - a sense of confidence, reliability, and trust;

  - a sense of comfort, happiness, and good feelings;

  - a sense of failure; or

  - a sense of frustration.

- **Meeting expectations**. When using the library or an information service, the individual may
  - be getting what was needed, sought, or expected;
  - be getting too much;
  - be getting nothing;
  - have confidence in what was received;
  - receive more than expected; or
  - seek substitute sources or action if what was received did not meet expectations.
- **Accomplishments** in relation to tasks. As a result of using the library, the individual is
  - able to make better informed decisions;
  - achieving a higher quality performance;
  - able to point to a course of action;
  - proceeding to the next step;
  - discovering people and other sources of information; or
  - improving a policy, procedure, and plan.
- **Time aspects**. Some of the real value for the user of a library is the fact that the information provided might lead to a savings in time in several possible ways. The individual may
  - save time as a result of using the service,
  - waste time as a result of using the service,
  - need to wait for service,
  - experience a service that ranges from slow to fast, or
  - need time to understand how to use a service or resource.
- **Money aspects**. Using the library or information service may, in some cases, clearly result in saving money or generating new revenues. The individual may be able to provide an
  - estimate of the dollar value of results obtained from a service or information received,
  - estimate of the amount of money saved due to the use of the service,
  - estimate of the cost in using the service,
  - estimate of what may be spent on a substitute service, or
  - estimate of value (in dollars) lost where the service was not available or use was not successful.

Most libraries will find the survey instrument developed by Saracevic and Kantor too long and difficult to replicate. A more simplified process will produce roughly similar results. It should be noted that the first three results (cognitive, affective, and expectations) would normally translate in some way to having an impact on the latter three outcomes (accomplishments, time, and money).

The principal focus of this chapter is on accomplishments. Accomplishments for the special library translate into time and money impacts, as noted in the next chapter. Accomplishments for public libraries translate into economic and social benefits, which are discussed in more detail in the following two chapters.

Accomplishments for academic libraries, it is hoped, are beginning to command the attention of librarians as they seek to demonstrate the outcomes and benefits of the campus library. The library offers a variety of services and products, including access to the physical collection, access to electronic resources, reference services, instruction programs (bibliographic instruction or information literacy instruction), access to technology, and a physical space for meetings or studying. In broad terms, the impact of an academic library may occur in three possible areas:

- student learning,
- teaching, and
- research.

EVALUATION METHODS

As shown in Table 17.1, a number of approaches can be used to assess the outcomes or impact of a library service in student learning, teaching, and research.

Table 17.1. Assessing the Outcomes of the Academic Library

	Student Learning	Teaching	Research
Access to the physical collection	Evaluation of term papers, projects. Do library users get better grades? Graduate sooner?	Teachers' assessment of materials presented during a course, assigned readings	Citation analysis of materials in research reports, articles and books published, conference presentations Value of the collection for research
Access to the electronic collection	Evaluation of term papers, projects. Do library users get better grades? Graduate sooner?	Teachers' assessment of materials presented during a course, assigned readings	Citation analysis of materials in research reports, articles and books published, conference presentations Value of the collection for research
Reference services	Value of the service to students	Value of the service to professors	Value of the service to researchers

	Student Learning	**Teaching**	**Research**
Instruction programs	Evaluation of term papers, projects. Do students who receive instruction get better grades? Graduate sooner?	Assessment of faculty of the value of the instruction—better papers, projects?	Assessment of researchers of the value of the instruction—better research, save time, assist in keeping current?
Access to technology located in library	Indirect link to outcomes	Indirect link to outcomes	Indirect link to outcomes
Space for meetings in library	Indirect link to outcomes	Indirect link to outcomes	Indirect link to outcomes
Space for studying in library	Indirect link to outcomes	Indirect link to outcomes	Indirect link to outcomes

A few studies have attempted to identify the academic library's impact on the lives of students, professors, and researchers. The studies that have been done generally have had small sample sizes and did not use a control group to distinguish the role of the library. For a more detailed discussion of the issues of assessment in the academic environment, consult *Library Assessment in Higher Education*.[2]

LIBRARY'S ROLE IN STUDENT LEARNING

One study examined student characteristics and undergraduate library use and found that five variables influenced library use: hours spent on campus, credit hour enrollment, gender (male), grade point average, and academic major.[3] Similar results were noted in a study by Ethelene Whitmire, who observed that the more students studied, the more they used the library.[4] However, a contrary point of view resulted from an analysis that found the quantity of time spent in the library was not associated with academic success, and a weak positive correlation was observed between academic achievement and the use of different library resources and services.[5]

A longitudinal analysis of faculty who used library information-seeking assignments found that such assignments are volatile due to turnover, use of adjuncts versus full-time faculty, and individual faculty preferences changing from year to year.[6] A study at Penn State University found that only 8 percent of courses required much library use (students needed to gather information independently for a term paper), while nearly two-thirds of courses required no library use.[7]

A survey of students at the University of Maryland found that remote access to full-text materials as well as citation and abstract databases is the most important service offered by the library.[8] While moving to electronic subscriptions can save the library money,[9] none of the surveys or other assessment methods have yet to tell the library why users select certain resources, or what value results from the resources provided by the library—value to the user and to the institution.

Examining the relatively consistent findings of the studies, it is possible to come to the following conclusions:

- There is no clear evidence that library use is linked to learning or academic success.

- A considerable proportion of all undergraduate students borrow no materials from the library.

- A small proportion of students (10 to 15 percent) are responsible for a majority of borrowed materials.

- Assigned readings and course-related readings (reserves) account for the majority of circulation in most undergraduate libraries.

- The amount of borrowing varies by discipline or field of study.

- Borrowing by undergraduates increases by class rank—lowest among freshmen and highest among seniors.

- A few courses on a campus will generate the majority of library use.

- The studies do not control for student abilities and typically rely on a single measure of use and success.

- Studies that rely on self-evaluation of success may not be an accurate assessment of library skills.

- The correlation between library use and academic achievement is weak at best.

- Improvement in basic library skills is the means and not the end, and yet the latter is the focus of most bibliographic instruction evaluation efforts.

- Few studies reported a link between bibliographic instruction and increased use of the library resources and services.

- Little research has addressed the value of improved information literacy skills and success in the academic environment.

LIBRARY'S ROLE IN TEACHING

Almost no research has been done to evaluate the library's role in helping professors provide instructional materials and course content. Professors spend a fair amount of time reading in an attempt to keep current in their field of specialization. Some of what these professors read obviously comes from the library.

A study at the University of California, Berkeley, found that professors include images and visual materials in course content in order to improve their students' learning, to integrate primary sources into their teaching, to provide students with a context for a topic, and to include materials that would otherwise not be available.[10] Faculty members found the digital content by performing a Google search or by including materials from their own collection of digital resources.

LIBRARY'S ROLE IN RESEARCH

Learning how researchers use and obtain value from the library's physical and electronic resources will become increasing important as a library is asked to demonstrate the value of its resources and services.

One study examined the number of publication citations across 169 universities in Canada, the United Kingdom, and the United States. A strong relationship existed between the number of institutional associated publications and the number of academic staff, the number of research students, the number of library books and journals, and the level of university revenues.[11] Yet the value of these findings, especially those on library holdings, no longer hold, given the evidence of other studies.

For example, bigness seems to count at a basic level: Large universities produce a large number of publications, and their libraries spend large amounts of money on these and other materials and thus have large collections. One method to determine the actual productivity of an institution, especially when making comparisons to other universities, is to calculate the number of citations by faculty member or by full-time researchers. Examining the citations in the Institute for Scientific Information (ISI) and library measures derived from the Association of Research Libraries, John Budd found medium to high correlations between the number of publications and number of volumes, materials expenditures, total expenditures, and number of professional staff.[12] Similar results were noted by James Baughman and Martha Kieltyka.[13]

Gerstberger and Allen found a direct relationship between perceived accessibility of information and several measures of utilization. Researchers appeared to follow Zipf's Law of Least Effort: Individuals choose the option to obtain information that involves the least effort.[14] One of the implications of the Gerstberger and Allen study is that improving the quality or quantity of library resources will be wasted unless ways are found to bring information to the researchers. Victor Rosenberg studied a group of researchers and found that the primary attribute of any information-gathering method is its ease of use.[15]

Brinley Franklin found that remote usage significantly exceeds in-library usage of electronic resources, sometimes by as much as four to one. Researchers depend more on electronic resources than on traditional print journals, and patterns of use vary by academic discipline.[16]

Academic Analytics, a commercial company, has developed a Faculty Scholarly Productivity Index. Faculty members are judged using three factors: publications, which include the number of books and journal articles published; federal-grant dollars awarded; and honors and awards. The individual faculty member's score is aggregated into a departmental and university score. The scholarly productivity is expressed as a z-score, a statistical measure that reveals how far and in what direction a value is from the mean. The z-score allows the performance of programs to be compared across disciplines.[17]

SCHOOL LIBRARIES

Keith Curry Lance and his colleagues have been involved in a series of studies that have sought to assess the impact of school library media centers on student academic achievement. Studies have been completed in Colorado, Alaska, Pennsylvania, Oregon, Iowa, and New Mexico.[18]

These studies used a multivariate statistical analysis to control for competing predictors of achievement such as other school factors (teacher qualifications and experience, teacher-pupil ratio, per-pupil expenditures) and community conditions (adult educational attainment, racial and ethnic demographics, and poverty).[19]

The original Colorado study found that the size of the library in terms of staff and collection was a direct predictor of reading scores—the variation ranged from 5 to 15 percent. A majority of test score variation was explained by socioeconomic factors.

Principals have a strong impact on school library programs. They are willing to take risks, provide strong leadership, have problem-coping skills, and clearly communicate their expectations, which in turn lead to changed teacher behaviors.[20]

Examining these studies collectively, it is possible to identify three major sets of findings:

- **School library development:** Higher levels of professional and total staffing, larger collections of print and electronic resources, and more funding result in students doing better on standardized reading tests.

- **Leadership:** Meeting frequently with the principal, attending and participating in faculty meetings, serving on standards and curriculum committees, and meeting with library colleagues outside the local school.

- **Collaboration activities:** Identifying useful materials for teachers, planning instruction cooperatively with teachers, providing in-service training for teachers, and teaching students both with classroom teachers and independently were linked to higher reading scores.[21]

SUMMARY

Clearly there are significant opportunities for the library community to begin to better understand the relationship of the library's resources and services and the outcomes and impacts in the lives of customer, students, faculty, and researchers. Research and assessment activities will require some creative approaches to better understand the contributions of the library. Seeking to assess impact will require any library to move from a traditional, library-centric view of the world to looking at the deeper issues associated with the library's actual contribution to learning, teaching, and research.

NOTES

1. Tefko Saracevic and Paul B. Kantor. Studying the Value of Library and Information Services. Part I. Establishing a Theoretical Framework. *Journal of the American Society of Information Science*, 48 (6), 1997, 527–42; Tefko Saracevic and Paul B. Kantor. Studying the Value of Library and Information Services. Part II. Methodology and Taxonomy. *Journal of the American Society of Information Science*, 48 (6), 1997, 543–63.

2. Joseph R. Matthews. *Library Assessment in Higher Education.* Westport, CT: Libraries Unlimited, 2007.

3. Charles B. Harrell. The Use of an Academic Library by University Undergraduates. Ph.D. dissertation, University of North Texas, 1988.

4. Ethelene Whitmire. The Relationship Between Undergraduates' Background Characteristics and College Experiences and Their Academic Library Use. *College & Research Libraries*, 62 (6), November 2001, 528–40.

5. Jennifer Wells. The Influence of Library Usage on Undergraduate Academic Success. *Australian Academic & Research Libraries,* June 1995, 121–28.

6. Rachel Applegate. Faculty Information Assignments: A Longitudinal Examination of Variations in Survey Results. *The Journal of Academic Librarianship*, 32 (4), July 2006, 355–63.

7. Linda K. Rambler. Syllabus Study: Key to a Responsive Academic Library. *Journal of Academic Librarianship*, 8, July 1982, 155–59.

8. Kimberly B. Kelley and Gloria J. Orr. Trends in Distant Student Use of Electronic Resources: A Survey. *College & Research Libraries*, 64 (3), 2003, 176–91.

9. Carol H. Montgomery and Donald W. King. Comparing Library and User Related Cost of Print and Electronic Journal Collections: A First Step Towards a Comprehensive Analysis. *D-Lib Magazine*, 8 (10), October 2002. Available at http://dlib.org/dlib/october02/montgomery/10montgomery.html.

10. Diane Harley. Why Study Users? An Environmental Scan of Use and Users of Digital Resources in Humanities and Social Sciences Undergraduate Education. *First Monday*, 12 (1), January 2007.

11. J. P. Rushton, and S. Meltzer. Research Productivity, University Revenue, and Scholarly Impact (Citations) of 169 British, Canadian, and United States Universities. *Scientometrics*, 3, 1981, 275–303.

12. John M. Budd. Faculty Publishing Productivity: An Institutional Analysis and Comparison with Library and Other Measures. *College & Research Libraries*, 56 (6), November 1995, 547–54; and John M. Budd. Increases in Faculty Publishing Activity: An Analysis of ARL and ACRL Institutions. *College & Research Libraries*, 60, 1999, 308–15.

13. James C. Baughman and Martha E. Kieltyka. Farewell to Alexandria: Not Yet! *Library Journal*, 124 (5), 1999, 48–49.

14. G. K. Zipf. *Human Behavior and the Principle of Least Effort*. Cambridge, MA: Addison-Wesley, 1949.

15. Victor Resenberg. Factors Affecting the Preferences of Industrial Personnel for Information Gathering Methods. *Information Storage and Retrieval*, 3, 1967, 119–27.

16. Brinley Franklin and Terry Plum. Successful Web Survey Methodologies for Measuring the Impact of Networked Electronic Services (MINES for Libraries). *IFLA Journal*, 32 (1), 2006, 28–40; and Brinley Franklin, Martha Kyrillidou, and Toni Olshen. The Story Behind the Numbers: Measuring the Impact of Networked Electronic Services (MINES) and the Assessment of the Ontario Council of University Libraries' Scholars Portal. Presented at the 6th Northumbria International Conference on Performance Measurement in Libraries and Information Services, Durham, England, August 22–23, 2005.

17. More information about the 2004 and 2005 Faculty Scholarly Productivity Index is available at http://www.academicanalytics.com/.

18. For a list of the many state projects that have focused on the value of school libraries visit http://www.lrs.org/impact.asp.

19. Keith Curry Lance and Becky Russell. Scientifically Based Research on School Libraries and Academic Achievement: What Is It? How Much of It Do We Have? How Can We Do It Better? *Knowledge Quest*, 32 (5), May/June 2004, 13–17.

20. Ken Haycock. Research in Teacher-Librarianship and the Institutionalization of Change, in A. Clyde (Ed.). *Sustaining the Vision: A Collection of Articles and Papers on Research in School Librarianship*. San Jose, CA: Hi Willow Research and Publishing, 1996, 13–22.

21. Keith Curry Lance. What Research Tells Us About the Importance of School Libraries. *Knowledge Quest*, 31 (1), September/October 2002, supplement, 17–22.

18

Economic Impacts

Libraries must increasingly justify the amount of money they receive and provide evidence about the extent of the library's use. Attempting to determine the benefits of any library is a challenging proposition fraught with definitional problems about the type of benefits as well as trying to determine the magnitude of the economic impact. It is possible to consider three categories of benefits:

Use Benefits

- Direct benefits

    - Cost savings from avoiding the purchase of materials (books, CDs, videos, magazines, newspapers, reference materials, electronic resources, and so forth).

    - Free or low-cost access to computers, photocopiers, audio and video equipment, meeting rooms, programs, and so forth.

    - Access to trained professionals for assistance in finding information

    - Economic impact of library spending on jobs, supplies, and so forth in the local community

    - Economic spending by library users in nearby business establishments

- Indirect benefits

    - Improving skills—reading literacy, job skills, computer skills—for children and adults of all ages

    - Educational programs

    - Library as a community amenity

    - Community interactions

    - Support for a democratic society

    - Social welfare

Nonuse Benefits

- Option for an individual to use the library at some time in the future. The library is appreciated and valued as an institution that improves the quality of life in the community.

- Option for others to use now and in the future. Indicates the willingness of individuals to support the library so that others may benefit. Nonuse benefits are difficult to quantify and if measured open to considerable discussion and debate. Thus, nonuse benefits are typically ignored in order to produce a more conservative estimate of benefits.

The total value of a library is determined by adding use and nonuse values.

It is also important to think about value from the perspective of the library customer. Value should be considered as the worth of a product or service in terms of organizational, operational, social, and financial benefit to the customer. All library product offerings and services have both a value and a cost in the mind of the customer. The cost of the offering may be monetary but it more than likely also includes such factors as time, effort, or equipment needed to make use of a library service. And the customer will be comparing the value and the costs associated with using the library with the value and costs of using an alternative.

The principal method for evaluation of the economic benefits of a library involves the use of a survey, often several surveys to different types of actual and potential library customers. Any evaluation must address several important issues: who receives the value, when the value accrues, whether an immediate benefit also translates into a long-term value, and how to identify and quantify the tangible and intangible derived from library use. The end result is the preparation of a cost-benefit analysis, which attempts to compare the total costs and the value of the total benefits to make an evaluation of the utility of the library.

Several methods have been used in an attempt to determine the economic value of a library, including

the direct survey,

the client value model,

contingent valuation,

consumer surplus,

the formula approach,

return on capital investment,

an economic impact analysis, and

a data envelopment analysis.

Determining the value of a library and its services typically involves conducting a survey and asking the library's customers to provide feedback about the value of the library in their lives. The prospect for determining the value of a public library is more complicated, as will be seen in a later section of this chapter.

DIRECT SURVEY

The outcome or impact the special library and its information services have on the larger organization can be summarized here using three major outcome categories: accomplishments, time, and money.

Accomplishments can be viewed as the category of outcome or impact that is not related to time or money impacts. Further, accomplishments can be viewed both from a positive perspective and avoiding negative consequences, as articulated most clearly by Joanne Marshall in some of her studies. For example, Marshall[1] suggests that information services can assist the organization by avoiding

poor business decisions,

conflict within the institution, and

conflict with another institution.

A case in point illustrates the consequences of a poor decision-making process when incomplete information about a particular topic becomes one of the components of a decision. A medical researcher at Johns Hopkins University conducted an online search about the potential side effects of a particular chemical compound, which was being considered for testing on humans.[2] The researcher did not conduct a thorough search of the published paper-based literature, found in the library, which preceded the start of the online database. Based on the search results, the trial for human testing commenced and one of the volunteers subsequently died. For a period of time, all medical trials at Johns Hopkins University were stopped. Now researchers must collaborate with a librarian and a pharmacist to ensure that a search of medical literature is comprehensive and thorough.[3]

Time. One of the principal values of a special library and its information services is that it significantly improves the productivity of the clients of the library, and thus the efficiency of the larger organization is improved. The principal reason this is so is that the cost of an information professional's time continues to be less than that of other professionals (for example, doctors, engineers, lawyers, senior managers). Also, an information professional is trained and is thus much more efficient in finding information resources, conducting online searches, and so forth. Thus the combination of the cost differential plus more efficient searching assists in making the organization's professionals more productive and ultimately leads to a cost savings for the organization.

Helen Manning, the librarian at Texas Instruments, surveyed library users and asked them to identify the impact of library services on their job, the number of hours saved as a result of using library services, and the number of hours saved by the librarian.[4] Despite a low response rate to the survey, Manning calculated that the total savings to Texas Instruments from the library totaled $959,000. Given the operating budget of $186,000, the return on investment was 515 percent or a benefit/cost ratio of 5.15:1.

In a wide range of studies, José-Marie Griffiths and Don King have focused on the apparent value of information services. That is, they focused on the time and effort that would be required by a individual to identify, locate, order, receive, and use the needed information compared to the time (and thus, cost) if these tasks were performed by a library.[5] The typical special library spends a range of $525 to $1,325 per year per professional employee (2005 dollars). If the library were eliminated and other sources of information were used to provide the equivalent information, the organization would spend considerably more than it does for a library (Griffiths and King report a 3:1 return on investment).

The net result of the Griffiths and King studies is that libraries provide better information, faster and less expensively than is possible with other alternatives. By providing timely, quality information services that meet the needs of the professionals within an organization, the library helps to increase the quality, timeliness, and productivity of these individuals and ultimately enhances the performance of the larger organization.

Griffiths and King report that professionals spend a considerable amount of time reading journal articles, books, internal reports, and other documents (professionals average 198 readings per year). The professionals spend a considerable amount of time acquiring and reading documents, even those provided by the library (an average of 288 hours per year). This reading, in turn, leads these professionals to avoid having to do certain work at all, modify their existing work, or stop an unproductive line of work.

Professional employees spend an average of 9.5 hours a week obtaining, reviewing, and analyzing information.[6] This is roughly one-quarter of the time they spend working each week and represents a significant expenditure of their time at the workplace. These same professionals have also estimated the value of receiving information from the library as opposed to their acquiring the documents themselves. On average, the return on investment ranged from 7.8:1 to 14.2:1.

Gwen Harris and Joanne Marshall prepared a cost-benefit analysis that examined a library's current awareness bulletin using the approach of identifying the value of time (and hence money) saved by reading the bulletin as compared to needing to spend the time and energy to seek the information from other sources. They found a benefit to cost ratio of 9:1.[7] Readers of the current awareness bulletin felt that they saved time but also were introduced to new ways of doing things, avoided duplication of effort, and increased their individual productivity.

There is a flip side to the positive impact of improving a person's productivity, as noted by Marshall.[8] Without the appropriate information, a person can experience loss (waste) of his or her own time or loss of another person's time. This expenditure of time or attention is the currency of exchange for information. This scarcity of attention relative to the abundant amount of available information provides for an attention economy, according to Warren Thorngate.[9]

The constantly increasing volume of information means that any criteria developed to separate the informational wheat from the chaff are going to be problematic. As we seek information, we are likely to make two kinds of errors: of commission (reading something that has little or no value) and of omission (overlooking something we shouldn't). Sampling an ever-decreasing proportion of worthwhile articles, reports, and so forth means that we are ever more likely to overlook that which would provide insight, solve a problem, suggest a new direction for research, and so forth.

Money. Two approaches to identifying the cost aspects of the library and its information services can be used: ascertaining (1) the relative value and (2) the consequential value of an information service.

The *relative value* approach seeks to identify the cost to use alternative sources of information compared to the nominal cost of providing the library service. According to Griffiths and King, on average, an organization without a library will spend more than three times per year as much per professional to obtain information services as an organization with a library (2005 dollars):

Without library	$6,588
With library	$1,408

Using the information obtained from these various surveys, Griffiths and King were able to establish the value for a particular library service if the library performed the service on behalf of a client. This estimated value approach is based on the assumption that each service transaction results in true "savings" for an organization, but clearly this is not always the case. Yet this approach can be an effective starting point for the library director when discussing the value of the library with the management team of the organization.

The second approach is to identify the *consequential value* of using the library and its information services. The approach here is to ask the library client (user) what is the financial impact for each information service transaction (or for a sample of transactions). The decision of whether to use a sample would be based on the volume of activity within the library (a sample size of several hundred would be desirable). The trade-off involves asking the client at the end of each information transaction or only for the sample (the possible nuisance factor declines when using a sample).

Some libraries wait about a week and then contact by telephone the individual who responded to the survey. The survey questions are repeated. In some cases, the individual is able to think of some additional benefits that will accrue through the use of the information service that he or she has overlooked initially. Alternatively, the data about the utility of the library or information center could be obtained using an annual survey. The disadvantage of the annual survey is that it relies on customers to make estimates about the impact of the library during the past year, and these estimates are likely to be on the conservative side.

Once the data about the financial impact have been gathered, a cost-benefit analysis can be prepared. On the one hand the benefits from using the library have been identified by the clients (quantifying the benefits). On the other hand, the costs for providing library services are fairly well known (using the library's budget and preparing an activity based costing analysis to identify the indirect and overhead costs to the organization).[10] The cost-benefit analysis allows the library to prepare an estimate of the library's return on investment, or ROI.

Frank Portugal suggests that two variations can be followed when the cost-benefit analysis is prepared. The first approach tallies all the financial benefits in the form of savings and reports the result. The second approach tallies all the financial benefits in the form of savings and also includes estimates of losses that may have occurred as the result of using the information service.

Depending on which option is chosen, the cost-benefit ratio will range from 28:1 to 18.8:1. Clearly, either option demonstrates that the library is providing real dividends as the result of its services, and thus the library should not be considered an overhead expense.

Griffiths and King studied the savings that resulted from the application of the information obtained through reading. They conducted research across three industries and found that benefits ranged from 2.6:1 to 17:1.

Other studies report similar results. Leigh Estabrook, in her analysis of document delivery studies, found that there was a range of benefits that varied from $2 to $48 saved for every $1 spent.[11] In an earlier review of cost-benefit studies, Manning reported a ratio of savings to cost of about 5 to 1.[12] And Michael Koenig, in an article that reviewed the cost-benefit methodologies, identified a number of studies that resulted in a range of benefits to cost of 2.5:1 to 26:1. Koenig suggested a conservative approach that would summarize the value ratio as 2:1.[13]

Freeing up a professional's time to identify and obtain relevant information can have a considerable beneficial impact on an organization. One survey of nine corporations found that the professionals were able to quantify the value of information received—the value of which ranged from $2,500 to $15,000 per document used.[14]

In addition to saving money, the information provided by the library may spur additional revenues (revenues from existing products and services to existing customers and/or attracting and retaining new customers), lead to the development of new products and services, shorten the product/service development life cycle, and so forth.[15] The U.S. Department of Transportation produced a study that demonstrated that good information reduces costs, saves time, improves decision making, and improves customer satisfaction.[16]

Failing to conduct a thorough search for relevant information can lead to significant expenditures of funds that would not have been spent if the information had been known. A survey in England estimated that between 10 and 20 percent of research was unintentionally duplicated, costing British companies from £6 to £12 million in 1962.[17] The survey revealed instances in which the belated discovery of information

- if previously known, would have saved time, money, or research work (43 percent);
- did, in practice, cause an alteration in the plan of research (25 percent);
- revealed that their research unintentionally duplicated other work (18 percent): and
- if previously known, would have caused a different research plan to be pursued (15 percent).

A more recent study conducted by the UK Patent Office found few companies that investigated previous research and development results. Further, the Patent Office found that about one-third of the applications had already been patented and thus the efforts had been duplicated. This duplication of effort was estimated to cost the European Union £20 billion a year in 1998.[18]

CLIENT VALUE MODEL

Guillaume Van Moorsel has suggested creating a client value model, which establishes a common "value vocabulary" for libraries and their customers, thereby establishing a basis for making planning decisions about library product and service offerings.[19] A relative value index is created for alternative products or service offerings that can be used to assess each alternative.

CONTINGENT VALUATION

There are two methods for valuing public goods such as a public library: those based on revealed preferences and those based on stated preferences. The stated preferences method will capture both use and nonuse values. The *contingent valuation* (CV) method, developed by Nobel laureate economists Kenneth Arrow and Robert Solow, uses surveys to value nonmarket goods and services. The respondent is presented with a description of the service, its present quantity and quality, and an estimated change in quantity or quality. In order to be valid, contingent valuation must be able to integrate valuation motives that extend beyond the pursuit of self-interest, and must not violate the assumption of rationality. The respondent is then asked to state the value of the proposed change in terms of his or her maximum willingness to pay. In the willingness to accept approach, the respondents are asked how much they would accept to give up something they already have.

The strength of the contingent valuation method is its directness. Contingent valuation has been applied to more than 50 cultural studies, including assessing the value of cultural and national heritage, museums, theaters, art and paintings, and libraries.[20] Another study examined over 2,000 papers and studies from more than 40 countries that applied the technique in different contexts.[21]

Ideally the two contingent valuation methods—willingness to pay and willingness to accept—would provide similar estimates of benefits. However, the willingness to accept method will typically provide the highest benefits estimates, since respondents normally include not only direct benefits but also societal or collective benefits. The willingness to pay approach provides a more conservative estimate, since some respondents assume someone else in society will fund the service even if they choose not to support it—the "free rider problem." The contingent valuation studies completed in several libraries are reviewed below.

St. Louis Public Library

Two contingent valuation methods were used at the St. Louis Public Library in 1999 to determine a cost-benefit ratio as part of a project funded by the Institute of Museums and Library Services (IMLS). The first approach asked a random sample of library card holders what they would be willing to pay in taxes to enjoy the library services as they then existed. The respondents indicated that they would be willing to pay at the same rate as the library's budget—a 1:1 ratio.[22]

A second approach, the willingness to accept method, asked what the respondents would accept in terms of a reduced tax bill if the library system were to close. The respondents indicated that the average amount that they would accept would be a $7 reduction. However, 88 percent of the respondents refused to answer the question, indicating that the library was too valuable or too important to consider closing; that the community and their children needed the public library. The end result using the willingness to accept method was a 7:1 benefit to cost ratio; however, use of this ratio should be carefully considered given the low response rate of values provided by respondents.

Respondents' expectations, reasons for using a public library, and prior experiences in using the library will in large part determine their assessment of the value of library services.

Phoenix Public Library

In 2001 the Phoenix Public Library participated in a project to estimate the benefits of library services to its citizens. Telephone interviews were conducted with a random sample of library card holders, who were asked how much they would be willing to pay (in taxes) to enjoy the library privileges they already had. Respondents were also asked how much of a tax cut they would accept in exchange for closing all public libraries.[23]

In addition, a sample of teachers was asked how much their school educational budgets would have to increase to provide the same quality of education if the Phoenix Public Library did not exist. Similarly, businesses were asked how much their firms would have to be compensated to be "whole" again, if services of the library were no longer available. A total of 516 individuals were interviewed.

The willingness to pay approach estimated benefits of $248,044,585, while the willingness to accept approach produced a much larger estimated benefit of $1,255,099,086. Since over 80 percent of the households interviewed refused to answer the willingness to accept question, caution should be exercised in using this figure. Given the library's annual budget of $24,470,084, the benefit to cost ratio using the willingness to pay method is 10.1:1. The willingness to accept method produces a much higher ratio—51.2:1.

The study also used the consumer surplus method as well as calculating the return to capital assets; these methods are discussed later in this chapter. Overall, the study found that users of the Phoenix Public Library received from $250 to $400 million of benefits. For each dollar of the library's budget, its patrons received benefits of more than $10. And the library has physical assets worth approximately $150 million, which provide an annual rate of return of 150 percent.

The British Library

In 2004 the British Library commissioned a study to determine the library's contribution to the national economy. The study used the contingent valuation method to determine the direct and indirect benefits arising from the use of the library. More than 2,000 people were interviewed, and the study concluded that for every £1 pound of public finding the British Library receives annually, £4.40 is generated for the UK economy. And if the British Library did not exist, the UK would lose £280 million of economic value per annum.[24]

Norway

A contingent valuation study was conducted throughout all of Norway using a telephone survey of 999 individuals. The sample reflected the characteristics of the total population of Norway. This study was unique in that it asked the respondents to assign a value to the motivations for using a public library—direct, indirect, and nonuser values.

The results revealed that direct use had the highest value among the respondents—40 percent. The value of having the option to use the public library should the need arise, sometimes called the potential use value, was the second highest value—20 percent. The altruistic motivation value for others in the community, not the respondents or their family, and their use of the public library, was the third highest value—17 percent. Adding all the other options to the altruistic value provides a total of 40 percent for nonuse values.[25] The importance of nonuse values shows that a majority of the respondents appreciate and value social benefits of public libraries and will support libraries from a broader perspective than direct self-interest only. Interestingly, households with higher education and fewer children are more likely to give greater weight to altruistic or nonuse values. Further, some 94 percent of the Norwegian population perceive that they have property rights to their local library. Also, using a willingness to accept method, a cost-benefit ratio was reported as 1:4.[26]

Specific Library Services

The contingent valuation method has also been used to assess a specific library service. For example, David Harless and Frank Allen used this method to estimate the economic value that patrons attach to reference services in an academic library. This study, conducted at the Virginia Commonwealth University library, surveyed 382 students and faculty and found that students were willing to pay $5.59 per semester to maintain current hours at the reference desk. Faculty members indicated that they were willing to pay $45.76 per year to maintain current hours. After estimating the costs of providing reference services, the authors concluded that the benefit to cost ratio was 3.5 to 1.[27]

Don King and his colleagues used a contingent valuation methodology at the University of Pittsburgh and asked survey respondents how much time and money they would spend to obtain the information they currently received from the library's journal collection if the library collection were unavailable. The study found that *if* the library's journal collection—physical and electronic—were not available, faculty would spend an additional 250,000 hours and some $2.1 million to use alternative sources to locate the desired articles.[28] Further analysis suggested that the total value of the library's journal collection to the university is $13.48 million less the costs for creating and maintaining the collection of $3.43 million, for a net value of $11.61 million. Thus, the benefit to cost ratio is 4.38:1.

CONSUMER SURPLUS

Consumer surplus is used by economists to determine the value consumers place on the consumption of a good or service in excess of what they must pay to get it. While library services are free, customers do pay in the form of time and direct transportation costs to use the public library. This effort to use the library represents an implicit price or transaction cost to the customer. Since many alternatives to almost all library services are available in the marketplace, it is possible to determine the price of the market alternative plus its transaction cost.

In conducting a consumer surplus survey, the respondents are asked, for example, about the number of books that they borrow from the library, the number of books that they buy, and the number of additional books that they would buy if they could not borrow from the library. Comparing the number of borrowed books with the number of purchased books, it is possible to calculate the value that the library user places on borrowing privileges. Such estimates can also be made for each library service used by each user surveyed. All of these estimates are then totaled to provide an estimate of the total direct annual benefits for all library users measured in dollars.

A survey of general users, teachers, and businesspeople using the consumer surplus method, conducted on behalf of the Phoenix Public Library, found that the estimated total benefits were $400,724,998. This resulted in a benefit to cost ratio of 16:1.

State of Florida

In a study of public libraries in Florida, survey participants were asked to indicate in dollar terms the value to them of individual library programs and services. The study team calculated overall user benefits by deriving an average retail price for each service. The value for each service was then totaled to derive the total benefits received by library users. A return on investment of $6.27 was calculated for each tax dollar invested.[29]

A comprehensive study of the economic contribution and return on taxpayer investment in Florida's public libraries was conducted in 2004. The study used both the contingent valuation method and an economic impact analysis, using data gathered from a statewide telephone survey of adults, in-library user surveys of adults, a follow-up survey of libraries, and surveys of organizations—schools, businesses, and so forth.

The survey found that in addition to borrowing materials for recreational or entertainment reasons, adults used the public library for three reasons:

- **Personal or family needs:** job seeking, health issues, consumer purchasing, and so forth.

- **Educational needs:** as students, teachers, home schooling, and lifelong learning.

- **Work-related purposes:** contributions to businesses, schools, universities, nonprofit organizations, government agencies, and hospitals.

The study found that the investment in Florida's public libraries in 2004 was $449 million and the economic returns amounted to $2.9 billion, yielding an overall return on investment of 6.54 to 1.[30]

The benefit to the state—in terms of the availability of Florida public libraries—is $2.3 billion, measured as the total cost to use alternatives if the public libraries did not exist. Given that the annual budget for all Florida public libraries is $449 million, the result is a benefit to cost ratio of 5.2:1.

An earlier survey of 1,991 Florida public library customers, reported by Bruce Fraser et al., found that a significant number of respondents felt that the library had contributed to the patrons' financial well-being, provided benefits to local businesses, and contributed to the prosperity of the local/state community.[31] Note that this survey did not ask the respondents to identify the value of the perceived financial benefits.

State of South Carolina

A study was conducted in 2004 to determine the economic impact of the public libraries of South Carolina. The study found that the total direct economic impact for the state's public libraries (only the value of circulation and reference services were calculated) was estimated at $222 million, while the actual cost of providing services was $77.5 million. This results in a benefit to cost ratio of 2.86:1.

Rather than relying on a survey to establish the direct economic impact, the study team used the annual statistics reported to the State Library and a series of formulas. The formulas included the following:

- **Books:** 50 percent of the average price of hardbacks and trade paper books of $10 or $5 per item results in (total circulation of juvenile books + total circulation of adult books) X $5

- **Nonprint materials:** 25 percent of the average price for tape cassettes, compact discs, and VHS cassettes results in (total circulation of juvenile nonprint materials + total circulation of adult nonprint materials) X $8.76

- **Magazines and newspapers:** The average subscription cost of magazines and newspapers ($200) times the number of subscriptions held

- **Reference questions:** Assuming a user spent 30 minutes to find an answer, and a South Carolina median hourly wage of $12, a value of $6 per reference transaction was used. This resulted in the formula: Total of reference transactions X $6

- **In-library use of materials:** The Study Team used a conservative estimate of $2.43 for each visitor, assuming the visitor spent an average of 30 minutes in the library. This resulted in the formula: The total of in-library use of materials X $2.43

The indirect economic impact of public library expenditures—wages, supplies, new materials, construction, and so forth—was almost $126 million. The indirect benefits provide a benefit to cost ratio of 1.62 to 1. Thus, the total direct and indirect return on investment is $4.48 for every dollar spent by South Carolina public libraries—a benefit to cost ratio of 4.48:1.[32]

British Public Libraries

Analyzing the available statistical data, a study team concluded that British public libraries produce £98 million more value than they cost to provide—a return on investment of 13.6 percent. The borrowing of books and the dominant use of the public library, allows the user to obtain the benefit at a fraction of what it would cost to purchase the book or to read books that would be too expensive to buy. Thus, different types of people, according to their education, wealth, age, and personal interest, generate a mixture of educational, informative, cultural, and recreational benefits.[33]

A SHORTCUT METHOD

Conducting a telephone or paper survey using the consumer surplus method is obviously costly and time-consuming. A shortcut method is available that will produce very similar results without incurring the costs of the survey. For each library service a substitute price is determined by checking various sources in the local community or online. The results of such an analysis are shown in Table 18.1 (p. 310). The prices are then multiplied by the output measure for each category—annual circulation, attendance at programs, number of reference queries answered, and so forth.

As shown in Figure 18.1 (p. 311), the San Diego Public Library concluded that the benefits exceed costs by a factor of 6:1. Similar results were noted by the Miami-Dade Public Library System, which also found a benefit to cost ratio of 6:1 (see Table 18.2, p. 312). Using this shortcut method, a library can calculate its own benefit-cost ratio. Determining and communicating the benefit-cost ratio for your library is important for both interested funding stakeholders and the citizens of a community.

Table 18.1. Pricing of Substitute Market Services

Service	Substitute	Price ($)	Source
Children's books (paperback)	Bookstore	8.00	*Bowker Annual*
Books for adults (paperback)	Bookstore	14.00	*Bowker Annual*
Video/DVD films	Rental	4.00	Blockbuster Video
Audio/music	Purchase	13.00	Wal-Mart
Magazines	Newsstand	3.00	Local newsstand
Newspapers	Newsstand	1.00	Local newsstand
Toys	Educational store	15.00	Local educational store
Reference and research services	Information broker	50.00/hour	Information broker
Special Events	Cultural center	9.00	Local cultural center
Craft and activity programs	YMCA	1.00/hour	YMCA
Social skills/etiquette training	YMCA	1.00/hour	YMCA
Computer services	Local coffee shop	Free	Local coffee shop
Adult education	Public schools	Free	Public schools
Family or parenting programs	Public schools	Free	Public schools
Storytelling programs	Local bookstore	Free	Local bookstore
Meeting space	Local Public School	Free	Local public school
Encyclopedia	Purchase a CD	75.00	*Encarta*
Dictionaries and almanacs	Local bookstore	10.00	Local bookstore

The business of the public library is to gather books, information, and related material to make them available, **Free** to the residents of the City of San Diego, CA. If our patrons had had to buy these materials and services in Fiscal Year 2001 they would have paid at least . . . .
$160,207,881!

For example:

- 6,587,872 items (including books, audiovisual materials, etc.) were borrowed. At an average retail price of $20, these would have cost **$131,757,540.**

- 1,617,633 books, periodicals and newspapers were used in libraries but not checked out. Had the library user had to purchase these materials at an average retail price of $10 these would have cost **$16,176,330.**

- 1,835,706 questions were answered in person and by telephone by library staff. Had the library user had to pay $2 for each inquiry, the cost would have been **$3,671,412.**

- 308,362 persons used the electronic magazines and newspapers on the library's IAC database. If the user had to purchase these materials or pay for access at $5 each, these activities would be worth **$1,541,810.**

- 536,974 persons signed up and used the Internet on a Library workstation. If the user had to pay for access at $10 each, these activities would be worth **$5,369,740.**

- 154,017 persons attended 4,370 library programs (excluding the film and Chamber Music series). At a $2.50 admission these activities would be worth **$385,034.**

- 22,400 children and teens registered for the Summer Reading Program. If each had paid a $5 registration fee, this would have cost **$110,200.**

- 618 literacy and ESL tutors provided 43,554 hours of tutoring to 839 learners. At $25/hour, this service would have cost **$1,088,850.**

- 227 students spent 6,170 hours using computer resources at the Library's Literacy Computer Lab. At $10/hour, this would have cost **$61,700.**

- 4,853 persons attended Monday evening and Sunday afternoon film series. At a $5 admission, these activities would be worth **$24,285.**

- 2,100 persons attended the Chamber Music series at the Central Library. At $10 admission, these activities would be worth **$21,000.**

These are just some of the services the public library provided in FY 2001. The value was much more to many more users than the estimate of $160,207,881. However, all of the library's services in FY 2001 cost the taxpayer of the City of San Diego only $27,675,365.

Figure 18.1. How Much Is Library Service Really Worth?

Table 18.2. Miami-Dade Public Libraries Estimated Return on Investment, 1998–1999

Materials and Services	Estimated Benefits ($)
4,751,514 books and materials borrowed at an average retail price of $20 each.	95,030,280
4,614,903 books, periodicals and newspapers were used in libraries, if purchased the average retail price of each would be $10.	46,149,030
5,435,095 reference questions answered in person by library staff, if each charge were $2 per inquiry.	10,870,190
625,292 Internet sessions at a $2 per session access fee.	1,250,584
420,581 persons attended 8,546 programs and exhibitions, if there were a $2 admission.	841,162
19,000 children and teens participated in the Mayor's Summer Reading Program, if there were a $5 registration fee.	95,000
279 literacy tutors provided 10,015 hours of one-on-one tutoring to 239 Project LEAD participants, if each charge were $25/hour.	250,375
Total Benefits	154,486,621
Less Taxpayers Investment (Annual Library Budget)	–24,645,113
Total Return on Investment	**$129,841,508**
Benefit to Cost Ratio	**$6.3:$1**

One of the problems associated with the use of the benefit-cost ratio as calculated above is that each use of a particular item is treated as if it were a new purchase by the library on behalf of the user. In addition, the material in the library's collection will be there for several years and will be used with less frequency over time. Clearly material in a library's collection is going to have a value each time it is used, but from an economic viewpoint the value will be less than the original purchase price. A number of studies have attempted to calculate a more realistic value of an item being circulated (used by a library customer) as a percent of the purchase price of the item.

Joseph Newhouse and A. J. Alexander constructed an economic model based on data collected at the Beverly Hills (CA) Public Library that suggested that the value of an item being loaned was 10 percent of the purchase price of a book. Analyzing circulation data over a 46-week period, the authors calculated the circulation rate for each item, its price, and the percent of the community that would buy the book if they did not own it, as well as including a discount rate for the value of money. The analysis was based on the assumption that the individual derives a fractional benefit of "ownership" from borrowing the item from the library. They concluded that the maximum benefit was derived from books that were issued frequently over a long period of time.[34]

A "Value Added Library Methodology" (V+LM) was developed in New Zealand that was based on the assumption of a hypothetical commercial market with willing buyers and sellers that would price the outputs of the service. The results of the New Zealand approach were to use an average book loan value of NZ$7.96 or 25 percent of the average book purchase price.[35]

The V+LM approach was to identify and quantify what the library does that adds value, what activities add the greatest value, whether the budget allocation is appropriate, and any inconsistencies between principles and actions.[36] A library's service is valued with the V+LM methodology using three main measures:

- **Market price proxy,** which estimates the market price in an imagined situation where there is a willing seller and a willing buyer.

- **Replacement cost,** which estimates what it would cost to replace the service.

- **Opportunity cost**, which estimates the value from using a service assuming less time is spent on searching for information.

Public, academic, and special libraries have used the V+LM methodology. For example, the Manakau Public Libraries, which has a budget of NZD 12 million, calculated a return to the community of at least NZD 18 million (a 66 percent return on the library's annual budget).

Two studies were conducted to identify the benefits from cataloging records provided by national libraries. A study performed for the National Library of Canada (NLC) found that using NLC records as the basis for copy cataloging rather than doing original cataloging of items, a total of $1,725,000 was saved by Canadian university libraries and large urban public libraries.[37] A similar study performed on behalf of the National Library of New Zealand found a total economic benefit of NZD $160.6 million.[38]

FORMULA APPROACH

A project in England to determine the value of public library benefits estimated the value of the loaning of materials a and found that the value of benefits slightly exceeded the costs of providing the service. The project developed a simplified equation to estimate benefits:

$$V = 0.15IP$$

where V = value, I = circulation of books, and P = the average price of acquiring the book.[39] This formula has the following attributes:

- Books acquired but not loaned will depress the value.

- The higher the circulation, the higher the value.

- More expensive books have a greater impact on value (the user receives more benefit).

- The value of paperback books is accurately reflected.

- Hardback books have a longer lending life than paperbacks.

- The formula is simple to use.

The disadvantage of this method is that only circulation of materials is being valued, to the exclusion of all other services. Adding additional components to the formula for other library services would probably make the formula too complicated.

RETURN ON CAPITAL INVESTMENT

Comparing annual benefits of the library versus the annual tax-supported budget provides an estimate of the annual percent return on taxes paid. Tax support is the base that makes the existence of the library possible and hence its provision of services feasible. To determine the rate of return to the public library capital investment requires valuation of the physical assets of the library. These assets include land and buildings, furniture and equipment, and collections. Land is typically valued at estimated market value. Other assets are valued at their current replacement costs.

Glen Holt and his colleagues calculated the return on capital investment for several libraries,[40] which included the following:

- Baltimore County Public Library—72 percent
- Birmingham Public Library—5 percent
- King County Library System—94 percent
- Phoenix Public Library—150 percent
- St. Louis Public Library—22 percent

ECONOMIC IMPACT ANALYSIS

Economic impact studies compare local or regional economic conditions with an activity present versus the activity's absence. The economic benefit calculation estimates the change in economic indictors due to the activity.[41] An economic impact analysis uses a basic input-output model of economic activity to identify the specific stimulus, such as an investment in a new library building or the annual expenditures for the library's operations. The model identifies how transactions impact the production and consumption of goods and services in an economy. As the result of direct spending by the library for salaries and supplies, the model estimates the recycling of funds in the local or regional economy. This magnification of library spending is known as the "multiplier effect."

The library provides data on the location of vendors and suppliers for all library expenditures. A survey of library customers is then conducted to determine the value of their expenditures as a result of their visit to the library. Library customers might spend money on transportation, parking, food, shopping, movie, museum, motels, and so forth.

Seattle Public Library

The opening of a new downtown main library in Seattle, Washington, has resulted in a 250 percent increase in the number of visitors to the Central Library. Approximately 30 percent of the 2.5 million individuals who visited the library (725,000 people) are projected to be out-of-town visitors. An economic impact analysis demonstrated that these out-of-town visitors will spend $16 million in net new spending in downtown Seattle (hotels, restaurants, car rentals, ferries, and so forth).[42]

Carnegie Library of Pittsburgh

In 2006 an economic impact analysis was prepared for the Carnegie Library of Pittsburgh. The analysis concluded that the library provides an economic benefit of $3 for every dollar it spends. The Carnegie Library of Pittsburgh is the most visited regional asset. These visitors to the library spend a total of $9.8 to $15.6 million annually at nearby businesses. The library supported more than 900 jobs and $80 million in economic output in Allegheny County through its operations and renovations. The library provides more than $75 worth of benefits for every resident of Allegheny County.[43]

State of Florida

As part of a study conducted on behalf of the state of Florida, an econometric input-output model was used to estimate the economic effects of public libraries on the gross regional product (GRP), employment, and real disposable income (wages) from the public funding, investment, and earnings for 2004. The statewide GRP is estimated to have increased by $4.0 billion as a result of publicly funded public library expenditures in the state. A total of 68,700 jobs were created from the spending increases, and personal income increased by $5.6 million.[44]

DATA ENVELOPMENT ANALYSIS

Data envelopment analysis (DEA) is a statistical technique used to evaluate a number of producers, or in the jargon of the DEA literature, a "decision making unit." A library can be a decision-making unit for the purposes of analysis. The production process for each decision-making unit is to convert a set of inputs and produce a set of outputs. The DEA technique was developed by Charnes, Cooper, and Rhodes.[45]

A typical statistical approach is characterized as a central tendency approach and evaluates producers relative to an average producer. In contrast, DEA compares each producer with only the "best" producers. A data envelopment analysis might be prepared for a group of separate libraries or all branch libraries in a system. The inputs used in the analysis might be size of the facility, total number of materials in the collection, number of staff members, hours open per week, and so forth. The output measures might include circulation, reference queries answered, attendance at programs, gate count, and so forth.

The data envelopment analysis provides three types of evaluation information:

- A single summative score is assigned to each library. This series of efficiency scores can then be used to relate one decision-making unit to all others.

- Any perceived slack (or waste) in the input used and the output produced is identified.

- A set of weights is attached to each decision-making unit relative to all other units.

Obviously the choice of what inputs and outputs to include in the analysis is very important. In most cases, a statistical technique called correlation is used to test for a statistical relationship between the input variables and the output variables. After all, preparing a data envelopment analysis using variables that are not related to one another will not produce any helpful information. The strengths of a DEA analysis include the following:

- Multiple input and output models can be handled.

- It does not require an assumption of a functional form relating inputs to outputs.

- A producer is compared to a peer or a combination of peers.

- Inputs and outputs can have different units—dollars, counts, and so forth.

- Insights are gained into ways to increase outputs /or conserve inputs to make a library more efficient.

- The analysis can be run several times, changing the mix of input and output measures in order to better understand the operations of the libraries.

One DEA study compared different size university libraries. The study team developed a "service index" for 24 university libraries in Taiwan. The input variables included data concerning collections, personnel, expenditures, buildings, and services provided. The resulting analysis produced a service frontier curve (see Figure 18.3).[46]

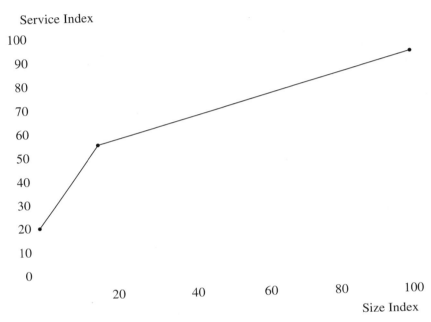

Figure 18.3. Service Frontier of the 24 University Libraries

Wonsik Shim and Paul Kantor prepared a DEA analysis of the Association of Research Libraries using data from 1994–1995. Their study examined 10 input measures and 5 output measures. The ARL libraries were divided into two groups: public and private. About 49 percent of the public institutions appear inefficient, while only 17 percent of the private institutions do.[47]

Another study compared 118 university libraries from German-speaking countries and English-speaking countries. Ten libraries were rated fully efficient; however, there were no significant differences between libraries from English-speaking and German-speaking countries or between small and large university libraries.[48]

Chen prepared a study that evaluated the 23 university libraries in Taipei—using four input and five output variables—and found that 11 libraries were relatively efficient.[49]

An application of the data envelopment analysis examined the 47 branch public libraries in Hawaii. Four input measures (collection size, number of library staff, days open, and nonpersonnel expenditures) and three output measures (circulation, patron visits, and reference transactions) from 1995 were used in the analysis. The estimated technical efficiency scores for the branch libraries ranged from 0.45 to 1.00. Among a number of additional library characteristics that were analyzed, only floor space and the size of the collection had positive effects on library performance—that is, larger libraries did better. The results of the analysis can be used to help improve the inefficient libraries.[50]

OTHER METHODS

Other measures that might be used to determine the economic value of the library that have not been discussed in this chapter are

- subsidies the public library provides to other organizations in the community such as schools, nonprofit organizations, and other government agencies;

- cost avoidance that results from the fact that the library provides a service and thus other government or nonprofit organizations need not expend monetary resources;[51]

- conjoint analysis using statistical techniques to compare one attribute of a service with all other attributes to ascertain people's preferences; and

- path analysis using a series of regressions with a different number of variables entered at different stages to examine the causal relationships. Lewis Liu used path analysis to examine the relationships among public libraries, literacy levels, and economic productivity measured by gross domestic product per capita. Liu concluded that public libraries contribute to long-term economic productivity primarily through literacy programs.[52]

A more recent report by the Urban Libraries Council summarizes the public library's contributions to local economic development. This readable report discusses the impact of library services in the areas of early literacy and school readiness, strategies for building workforce participation, small business support, and the power of place.[53]

SUMMARY

This chapter has presented a number of methods that can be used to determine the economic value of a library. As shown in Table 18.3 (p. 318), the various methods produce a range of benefits compared to cost. The good news is that regardless of the method selected, the results generally fall into the same range. That is, the typical benefit to cost ratio ranges from 4:1 to 6:1.

Table 18.3. Benefit to Cost Ratios

Author	Year	Willingness to Pay	Willingness to Accept	Consumer Surplus	Direct Survey Value of Time
Estabrook	1986				2:1 to 48:1
Manning	1987				5:1
Koenig	1992				2.5:1 to 26:1
Griffiths & King	1994				7.8:1 to 14.2:1
Harris & Marshall	1996				9:1
Holt & Elliott St. Louis Public	1999	1:1	7:1		
Elliott Phoenix Public	2001	10.1:1	51.2:1	10:1 to 16:1	
Holt et al. Baltimore County	2001			3:1 to 6:1	
Holt et al. Birmingham Public	2001			1.3:1 to 2.7:1	
Holt et al. King County Library	2001			5:1 to 10:1	
Griffiths et al. State of Florida	2004			6.54:1 to 5.2:1	
British Library	2004			4.4:1	
Barron et al. State of South Carolina	2005			4.48:1	

Other observations about determining the economic value of a library include the following:

- A direct survey of library customers can be used to determine the positive impact of the library in reducing costs, saving time, accomplishments, and so forth. The direct survey is most often used in the special library environment but has also been used in academic and public libraries.

- A contingent valuation study is time-consuming and expensive because it typically involves a telephone survey to gather the needed data. As such, this method is beyond the means of most libraries.

- The consumer surplus method can be readily adapted and has been used successfully by a number of libraries.

- The shortcut method can be easily used by a library to demonstrate its value to its community.

- The return on capital investment can be easily determined for most libraries, and the findings may resonate with local stakeholders.

- The economic impact method can be used to show both the direct and indirect economic benefits of a local library or a group of libraries.

- If two or more methods are used to estimate the economic benefits, there will likely be increased confidence in the results.

- Some studies have only reported the direct benefits in order to communicate a more conservative estimate of the economic benefits.

- Regardless of the method selected, the results should be clearly and consistently communicated to the library's funding decision makers and its customers.

NOTES

1. Joanne Gard Marshall. *The Impact of the Special Library on Corporate Decision-Making.* Washington, DC: Special Libraries Association, 1993.

2. Collaboration with Librarian Required in Hopkins' Report. *Corporate Library Update*, 10 (13), September 15, 2001, 1. All documents related to the report can be found at www.hopkins-medicine.org.

3. For more information about the revised research procedures, visit http://www.hopkinsmedicine.org/press/2001/august/actionplan.htm.

4. Helen Manning. The Corporate Librarian: Great Return on Investment, in James M. Matarazzo et al. (Eds.). *President's Task Force on the Value of the Information Professional.* Final Report. Preliminary Study. Washington, DC: Special Libraries Association, 1987, 23–34.

5. José-Marie Griffiths and Donald W. King. *Special Libraries: Increasing the Information Edge.* Washington, DC: Special Libraries Association, 1993.

6. Mary Corcoran and Anthea Stratigos. Knowledge Management: It's All About Behavior. Information About Information Briefing. Burlingame, CA: Outsell, January 2001.

7. Gwen Harris and Joanne G. Marshall. Building a Model Business Case: Current Awareness Service in a Special Library. *Special Libraries*, 87 (2), Summer 1996, 181–94.

8. Joanne Gard Marshall. *The Impact of the Special Library on Corporate Decision-Making.* Washington, DC: Special Libraries Association, 1993.

9. Warren Thorngate. On Paying Attention, in Wiliiam J. Baker, Leendert P. Mos, Hans V. Rappard, and Henderikus J. Stam (Eds.). *Recent Trends in Theoretical Psychology.* New York: Springer-Verlag, 1987, 247–63.

10. Alison M. Keyes. The Value of the Special Library: Review and Analysis. *Special Libraries*, 86 (3), Summer 1995, 172–87.

11. Leigh Estabrook. Valuing a Document Delivery System. *Research Quarterly*, 27 (1), Fall 1986, 59–62.

12. Helen Manning. The Corporate Librarian: Great Return on Investment, in *President's Task Force on the Value of the Information Professional.* Washington, DC: Special Libraries Association, 1987.

13. Michael Koening. The Importance of Information Services for Productivity "Under-Recognized" and Under-Invested. *Special Libraries*, 83 (3), Fall 1992, 199–210.

14. Margareta Nelke. Swedish Corporations Value Information. *Information Outlook*, 3 (2), February 1999, 10.

15. For a more detailed discussion of the economic value of special libraries, see Joseph R. Matthews. *The Bottom Line: Determining and Communicating the Value of Special Libraries.* Westport, CT: Libraries Unlimited, 2002.

16. Susan C. Dresley and Annalynn Lacombe. *Value of Information and Information Services.* Cambridge, MA: U.S. Department of Transportation, Volpe National Transportation Systems Center, October 1998.

17. John Martyn. Unintentional Duplication of Research. *New Scientist*, 377, 1968, 338.

18. Patent Omission Costs £20b. *Professional Engineering*, 11 (11), June 10, 1998, 12.

19. Guillaume Van Moorsel. Client Value Models Providing a Framework for Rational Library Planning (or, Phrasing the Answer in the Form of a Question). *Medical Reference Services Quarterly,* 24 (2), Summer 2005, 25–40.

20. D. Noonan. *Contingent Valuation Studies in the Arts and Culture: An Annotated Bibliography.* Chicago: The Cultural Policy Center at the University of Chicago, 2002. Available at http://culturalpolicy.uchicago.edu/publications.html.

21. Richard T. Carson, Jennifer L. Wright, N. J. Carson, A. Alberini, and Nicholas E. Flores. *A Bibliography of Contingent Value Papers and Studies.* La Jolla, CA: Natural Resource Damage Assessment, 1995.

22. Glen E. Holt and Donald Elliott. Proving Your Library's Worth: A Test Case. *Library Journal*, 123 (18), November 1998, 42–44; Glen E. Holt, Donald Elliott, and Christopher Dussold. A Framework for Evaluating Public Investment in Urban Libraries. *The Bottom Line*, 9 (4), Summer 1996, 4–13; Glen E. Holt, Donald Elliott, and Amonia Moore. Placing a Value on Public Library Services. A St. Louis Case Study. *Public Libraries*, 38 (2), March–April 1999, 98+.

23. Donald Elliott. *Cost-Benefit Analysis of Phoenix Public Library.* Phoenix: Phoenix Public Library, April 2001.

24. Spectrum Strategy Consultants and Independent. *Measuring Our Value.* London: The British Library, 2004. Available at http://www.bl.uk/about/valueconf/valuepresentations.html; Caroline Pung, Ann Clarke, and Laurie Patten. Measuring the Economic Impact of the British Library. *New Review of Academic Librarianship,* 10 (1), 2004, 79–102; and Gary Warnaby and Jill Fenney. Creating Customer Value in the Not-for-profit Sector: A Case Study of the British Library. *International Journal of Nonprofit Voluntary Sector Marketing,* 10, 2005, 183–95.

25. Svanhild Aabo and Jon Strand. Public Library Valuation, Nonuse Values, and Altruistic Motivations. *Library & Information Science Research*, 26, 2004, 351–72. See also Svanhild Aabo and Ragnar Audunson. Rational Choice and Valuation of Public Libraries: Can Economic Models for Evaluating Non-Market Goods Be Applied to Public Libraries? *Journal of Librarianship and Information Science*, 34 (1), March 2002, 5–15; Svanhild Aabo. Valuation of Public Libraries, in Carl Gustav Johannsen and Leif Kajberg (Eds.). *New Frontiers in Public library Research.* Lanham, MD: Scarecrow Press, 2005.

26. Svanhild Aabo. Are Public Libraries Worth Their Price? *New Library World*, 106 (11/12), 2005, 487–95.

27. David W. Harless and Frank R. Allen. Using the Contingent Valuation Method to Measure Patron Benefits of Reference Desk Service in an Academic Library. *College & Research Libraries,* January 1999, 56–69.

28. Donald W. King, Sarah Aerni, Fern Brody, Matt Hebison, and Amy Knapp. *The Use and Outcomes of University Library Print and Electronic Collections.* Pittsburgh: University of Pittsburgh, Sara Fine Institute for Interpersonal Behavior and Technology, April 2004; and Donald W. King, Sarah Aerni, Fern Brody, Matt Hebison, and Paul Kohberger. *Comparative Cost of the University of Pittsburgh Electronic and Print Library Collections.* Pittsburgh: University of Pittsburgh, Sara Fine Institute for Interpersonal Behavior and Technology, May 2004. See also Roger C. Schonfeld, Donald W. King, Ann Okerson, and Eileen Gifford

Fenton. Library Periodicals Expenses: Comparison of Non-Subscription Costs of Print and Electronic Formats on a Life-Cycle Basis. *D-Lib Magazine*, 10 (1), January 2004. Available at http://www.dlib.org/dlib/january04/schonfeld/01schonfeld.html; Donald W. King, Carol Tenopir, Carol Hansen Montgomery, and Sarah E. Aerni. Patterns of Journal Use by Faculty at Three Diverse Universities. *D-Lib Magazine*, 9 (10), October 2003. Available at http://www.dlib.org/dlib/october03/king/10king.html.

29. Charles McClure, Bruce Fraser, Timothy W. Nelson, and Jane B. Robbins. *Economic Benefits and Impacts from Public Libraries in the State of Florida*. Tallahassee: Florida State University, Information Use Management and Policy Institute, January 2001. Available at http://dlis.dos.state.fl.us/bld/finalreport/.

30. José-Marie Griffiths, Donald W. King, and Christinger Tomer. *Taxpayers Return-on-Investment (ROI) in Florida Public Libraries. Part I: The Use, Impact and Value of Florida's Public Libraries—Detailed Study Methods and Summary Results*. Tallahassee: Center for Economic Forecasting and Analysis, Florida State University, August 2004; Tim Lynch and Julie Harrington. *Taxpayers Return-on-Investment (ROI) in Florida Public Libraries. Part II: The Economic Impact and Value of Public Libraries in Florida—The REMI Analysis*. Tallahassee: Center for Economic Forecasting and Analysis, Florida State University, August 2004.

31. Bruce T. Fraser, Timothy W. Nelson, and Charles R. McClure. Describing the Economic Impacts and Benefits of Florida Public Libraries: Findings and Methodological Applications for Future Work. *Library & Information Science Research*, 24, 2002, 211–33.

32. David D. Barron, Robert V. Williams, Stephen Bajjaly, Jennifer Arns, and Steven Wilson. *The Economic Impact of Public Libraries on South Carolina*. Columbia: University of South Carolina, School of Library and Information Science, January 2005. Available at http://www.libsci.sc.edu/SCEIS/home.htm.

33. Anne Morris, Margaret Hawkins, and John Sumsion. *The Economic Value of Public Libraries*. London: Resource: The Council for Museums, Archives and Libraries, 2001. See also Anne Morris, John Sumsion, and Margaret Hawkins. The Economic Value of Public Libraries. *Libri*, 52, 2002, 78–87.

34. J. P. Newhouse and A. J. Alexander. *An Economic Analysis of Public Library Services*. Santa Monica, CA: Rand Corporation, 1972.

35. Library & Information Association of New Zealand. *Manukau Libraries: Trial of the V+LM Value Added Library Methodology*. Trial Report. New Zealand: LIANZA, October 12, 2000.

36. Ruth MacEachern. Measuring the Added Value of Library and Information Services: The New Zealand Approach. *IFLA Journal* 27, (4), 2001, 232–37.

37. Jamshid Beheshti. *The Use of NLC MARC Records in Canadian Libraries, Phase 1: University and Large Urban Public Libraries, Final Report, 31 March 2002*. Montreal: McGill University, Graduate School of Library and Information Studies, 2002.

38. McDermott Miller, Ltd. *National Bibliographic Database and National Union Catalogue: Economic Evaluation for the National Library of New Zealand*. 2002. Available at www.natlib.gov.nz/files/EconomicValuationReport.pdf.

39. John Sumsion, Margaret Hawkins, and Anne Morris. Estimating the Economic Value of Library Benefits. *Performance Measurement and Metrics*, 4 (1), 2003, 13–27.

40. Glen E. Holt, Donald S. Elliott, Leslie E. Holt, and Anne Watts. *Public Library Benefits Valuation Study: Final Report to the Institute of Museum and Library Services for National Leadership Grant*. St. Louis, MO: St. Louis Public Library, 2001. See also Donald S. Elliott, Glen E. Holt, Sterling W. Hayden, and Leslie Edmonds Holt. *Measuring Your Library's Value: How to Do a Cost-Benefit Analysis for Your Public Library*. Chicago: ALA Editions, 2006.

41. Glen E. Holt, Donald S. Elliott, and Christopher Dussold. A Framework for Evaluating Public Investment in Urban Libraries. *The Bottom Line*, 9 (4), 1996, 4–13.

42. Berk & Associates. The Seattle Public Library Central Library: Economic Benefits Assessment. The Transformative Power of a Library to Redefine Learning, Community, and Economic Development. Seattle: Berk & Associates, 2005. Available at http://www.spl.org/default.asp?pageID=branch_central_about&branchID=1.

43. Carnegie Mellon University. *Carnegie Library of Pittsburgh: Community Impact and Benefits.* Pittsburgh, PA: Carnegie Mellon University, Center for Economic Development, April 2006.

44. Griffiths, King, and Tomer, *Taxpayers' Return-on-Investment (ROI)*; Lynch and Harrington, *Taxpayers' Return-on-Investment.*

45. Abraham Charnes, William W. Cooper, and E. Rhodes. Measuring the Efficiency of Decision Making Units. *European Journal of Operations Research*, 2, 1978, 429–44. See also Abraham Charnes, William W. Cooper, Arie Y. Lewin, and Lawrence M. Seiford (Eds.). *Data Envelopment Analysis: Theory, Methodology and Applications.* Norwell, MA: Kluwer Academic Publishers, 1994.

46. Chiang Kao and Ya-Chi Lin. Comparing University Libraries of Different University Size. *Libri*, 49, 1999, 150–58.

47. Wonsik Shim and Paul B. Kantor. A Novel Economic Approach to the Evaluation of Academic Research Libraries. *Proceedings of the American Society for Information Science*, 35, 1998, 400–410.

48. Gerhard Reichmann. Measuring University Library Efficiency Using Data Envelopment Analysis. *Libri*, 54, 2004, 136–46.

49. Tser-yieth Chen. An Evaluation of the Relative Performance of University Libraries in Taipei. *Library Review*, 46 (3), 1997, 190–201.

50. Khem R. Sharma, PingSun Leung, and Lynn Zane. Performance Measurement of Hawaii State Public Libraries: An Application of Data Envelopment Analysis (DEA). *Agricultural and Resource Economics Review*, 28 (2), October 1999, 190–98.

51. Jennifer Abend and Charles R. McClure. Recent Views on Identifying Impacts from Public Libraries. *Public Library Quarterly*, 17 (3), 1999, 3–29.

52. Lewis G. Liu. The Contribution of Public Libraries to Countries' Economic Productivity: A Path Analysis. *Library Review*, 53 (9), 2004, 435–41.

53. The Urban Libraries Council. Making Cities Stronger: Public Library Contributions to Local Economic Development. Evanston, IL: The Urban Libraries Council, 2007. vailable at http://www.urbanlibraries.org/files/making_cities_stronger.pdf.

19

Evaluation of Social Impacts

The evaluation of the social impacts of a library will focus exclusively on public libraries. Most special libraries are designed to serve only a very narrowly defined clientele and not the public. School and academic libraries have the potential for impacting the larger community within which they serve, but here also most of the use and therefore the benefits are going to accrue to those who use the academic library.

The majority of the literature pertaining to the social benefits of public libraries involves the author asserting what the benefits are rather than reporting on a research project. One of the most visible examples of this is a Canadian project that produced a report called *Dividends: The Value of Public Libraries in Canada.*[1] This report drew upon a number of sources and suggested that the benefits of the public library can easily be divided into two categories: economic and social (see Table 19.1).

Table 19.1. The Benefits of Public Libraries

Economic	Social
Access to information is vital to the success of organizations and businesses	Libraries are used extensively
Libraries support the local economy	Support Canadian culture
Support the cultural industry sector—book and periodical trade	Support a democratic society
	Support children and students
	Support lifelong learning
	Provide access to information technology and the Internet

The notion that public libraries have a social impact is an old one. Historically, the purpose of public libraries was to safeguard democracy and divert behavior from socially destructive activities by exposing the population of a community to literature and acceptable recreation.[2] The terms "social impact," "social benefit," social cohesion," and "social inclusion" are often used interchangeably. However, these terms are all descriptors of the broader concept of "social capital."

Social capital accumulates as a by-product of interactions, which result in a sense that a service or institution enhances functioning within the wider society. In general, social capital refers to the networks and links within a community. It encompasses the level of cooperation, trust, mutual support, and participation of residents in community activities that strengthen their sense of social belonging and community well-being. Social capital consists of relationships among individuals, organizations, businesses, and government.

Social capital can be thought to exist in three ways:

- **Bonding social capital** refers to the ties between people and organizations.

- **Bridging social capital** refers to ties across groups who are not alike.

- **Linking social capital** promotes involvement and inclusion across social strata.[3]

Almost all of the research to identify the social benefits of a public library has involved qualitative methods. Surveys have been used occasionally, primarily to determine the level of support for public libraries in a community, in a state, or across the nation.

QUALITATIVE METHODS

Most of the studies exploring the social impacts or benefits of the public library in a community have relied on qualitative measures. Among these are interviews, focus groups, observations, asking users to keep diaries, and so forth.

Barbara Debono, in a review of the social impact of public libraries, suggests that two approaches can be taken in investigating the effects, experiences, or differences: an emphasis on a neutral outcome and an emphasis on positive impacts or benefits.[4]

An analysis in England suggested that libraries needed to move beyond the lending of materials and traditional library services to embrace new services and partnerships and work as a tool for active development with life enhancing consequences for the community.[5] Fran Matarasso suggests that there is a broader value of library services in alleviating social problems and laying the foundations of sustainable communities.[6]

One study investigated the impact of providing in-library access to information technology resources and found a positive impact on both the communities and the individuals supporting a range of activities—from study to job seeking to building and maintaining social networks using the Internet.[7]

A study in an Australian community examined the economic and social benefits of the public library. The study found that the library contributed to key social values in the community, especially equity and social justice; contributed to the quality of life; and was a symbol and institution of the community.[8]

A study of 10 public libraries in the Sydney, Australia, area involved making observations on a number of days as well as distributing surveys to users and nonusers. The study found that the library was accessed not only for its resources but for the opportunity to socialize. Parents generally regarded libraries as safe places and were happy to allow their children to frequently spend time at the library. The desire to socialize with staff was also noted for older, more frequent users of the library.[9]

Another Australian study involving all 43 public library systems in the state of Victoria analyzed more than 10,000 surveys designed to gather views about the contribution to and impact of their libraries on their local communities. The project used a combination of methods to gather the data—interviews, focus groups, and online and telephone surveys. This Libraries/Building/Communities project reported the contributions of public libraries to their communities under four main themes:[10]

- Developing social capital
    - Providing a welcoming environment
    - Creating pride of place
    - Attracting users from all walks of life
    - Reaching out to the community
    - Appreciation of cultural differences
    - Building bridges to the government
    - Encouraging collaboration across the community
- Overcoming the digital divide
    - Making technology accessible
    - Exploiting technology to benefit the community
- Creating informed communities
    - Community information
    - Government information
    - Providing a gateway to the world of information
- Convenient and comfortable places of learning
    - Developing information skills
    - Stimulating ideas and discussion
    - Supporting vulnerable learners
    - Supporting students.

Candy Hildenbrand suggests that public libraries create social capital in a number of ways, through

- encouraging civic engagement by delivering programs that bring citizens together—breaking down barriers;
- encouraging trust through social cohesion and inclusion by providing resources and a meeting place accessible to everyone—creating communities;
- facilitating local dialogue and dissemination of local information—building bonding social capital;
- upholding democratic ideals by making information freely available to all citizens—creating an informed citizenry;

- providing a public space where citizens can work together on personal and community problems—fostering community participation; and
- engaging in partnerships with other community organizations—building bridging social capital.[11]

The Social Audit

In England, the British Library financed several research projects to examine the utility of a social audit as a potential tool in assessing the social and economic impacts of public libraries.[12] A social audit is a means of assessing the social impact of an organization in relation to its aim and those of its stakeholders. The team conducting the social audit has to contact actual and potential library users and especially focus on the needs of library nonusers.[13]

Rebecca Linley and Bob Usherwood used a "social process audit,"[14] which collects information through the use of interviews and focus groups with stakeholders. When conducting a social audit, the main criterion for evaluation is the impact of policy on social need, which raises the obvious question of what constitutes social need and what the public library's responsibility is in meeting some portion of a social need.[15]

The results of the social audit suggested that the public library's established roles (culture, education, reading and literacy, and information) have an enduring relevance.

- The library is a center of cultural life.
- Library services support both adults' and children's educational needs.
- The library supports the development of children's reading skills.
- The library is a suitable "nonstigmatized" place for adult literacy classes.
- The library remains important as a source of *free* reading material, especially for people with limited economic means.
- The library provides equitable access to information and other resources.

The public library also has a social and caring role:

- Individuals gain new skills and confidence from using the library.
- The library is a place where people meet and share interests, sometimes described as "the cement in the social fabric."
- The library promotes greater understanding among different cultural groups.
- The library sustains local identity by developing and maintaining community self-esteem.
- The library has a beneficial effect on psychological health and well-being—especially for the isolated and vulnerable.

The findings of a social audit are derived from qualitative, often anecdotal, evidence and suggest that public libraries enrich the lives of many people. Proponents of the social audit process suggest that use of this technique is what makes the enriching process visible. Opponents of the technique point to the lack of any objective or quantitative performance measures to support the conclusions made as a result of the audit.

QUANTITATIVE METHODS

A telephone survey of 1,004 individuals across the United States was conducted by the Marist College Institute for Public Opinion in 2003. The results of this poll suggest that

- 67 percent of the respondents felt it was *very valuable* to have access to a public library in their community, and another 27 percent felt it was valuable;

- almost two-thirds of the respondents would support an increase in taxes to support public library services;

- the respondents would, on average, be willing to pay an additional $49 per year for public libraries; and

- the priorities for library services included: programs for children, open hours in evenings and on weekends, computers for public use, and homework help centers, among many more.[16]

The results of this survey suggest that people are willing to pay for improved library services even when they may not be active library users.

A Zogby poll sampled New York State residents in 2002. The results revealed that

- almost all respondents felt the public library was important to them (95 percent) and almost three-fourths indicated that the library was "very important" (71 percent);

- more than 75 percent of the respondents would be willing to increase their taxes to improve support for the library; and

- a sizable majority (89 percent) felt it was important for state government to do more for local public libraries.[17]

A New York State survey in 1999 by the Regents Commission of 1,004 adults found that

- use of public libraries in New York is higher than average (73 percent),

- local public libraries are very important to the quality of life, and

- slightly more than two-thirds of the respondents would double the financial support for libraries.[18]

The Counting on Results project analyzed survey responses from more than 5,500 respondents from 45 libraries in 20 states. The purpose of the project was to learn more about the outcomes of public library use. The results indicated the following:

- **General information outcomes:** Reading for pleasure was the most popular response (74 percent), followed by learning more about a skill, hobby, or other personal interest (56 percent) and finding information for school, work, or a community group (46 percent).

- **Local history and genealogy outcomes:** Respondents made progress researching family history (53 percent), identified a new source to search (50 percent), and obtained a document or record (42 percent).

- **Library as place (Commons) outcomes:** Respondents learned about new books, videos, or music (67 percent); found a quiet place to think, read, write, or study (59 percent); and met a friend or coworker (30 percent).

- **Information literacy outcomes:** Respondents found what they were looking for by asking a librarian for help (51 percent), using the library catalog (49 percent), and searching the Web (43 percent).

- **Business and career information outcomes:** Respondents explored or started or developed a business (36 percent), developed job-related skills (31 percent), and explored job/careers (28 percent).

- **Basic literacy outcomes:** Respondents became a citizen (42 percent), read to a child or assisted a child to choose a book (36 percent), and managed personal finances better (27 percent).[19]

SUMMARY

The social benefits of impacts of the public library on the local community have been documented by studies conducted in the United States, England, and Australia, among others. As shown in Table 19.2, these benefits may impact an individual in a number of different ways.

Table 19.2. Social Benefit Descriptors

Impact Area	Description
Basic literacy	Personal growth, education, improvement in the quality of life, personal development
Business/career	Economic and personal growth, economic impact, personal development
Information literacy	Personal skills, improvement in the quality of life
Library as place	Commons/community information, community development, community focus, local identity
Local history and genealogy	Local culture
Health and well-being	Personal growth, quality of life
Social cohesion	Social policy
General information	Personal growth, access to information
Empowerment	Equity and social justice, social policy

Yet a number of difficulties arise when attempting to asses the social impact of public libraries, including the following:

- Library initiatives are often not sustained, and "best practices" are not shared

- Increased funding for a broader definition of the role of the library seldom appears.

- The same activity in different libraries will differ in terms of the number of people served OR impacted.

- Tools to demonstrate value are difficult to find and use.

- Most people find it difficult to estimate the impact of the library on their lives.

- It is difficult to draw a causal relationship between the availability of a service and a social impact.

- It is difficult to extrapolate the results from several local studies into the broader picture.

- It is difficult to arrive at an operational definition of a social impact and an appropriate method for gathering useful data so that the method could be replicated across several studies.

- Qualitative data can be difficult and expensive to gather, and the results are often viewed with suspicion.

NOTES

1. Leslie Fitch and Jody Warner. Dividends: The Value of Public Libraries in Canada. *The Bottom Line*, 11 (4), 1998, 158–79.

2. Barbara Debono. Assessing the Social Impact of Public Libraries: What the Literature Is Saying. *Australasian Public Libraries and Information Services*, 15 (2), June 2002, 80–95.

3. J. Cavaye. *Social Capital: A Commentary on Issues, Understanding and Measurement.* Sydney: PASCAL Observatory, 2002.

4. Barbara Debono, Assessing the Social Impact of Public Libraries.

5. Ronald B. McCabe. *Civic Librarianship: Renewing the Social Mission of the Public Library.* London: Scarecrow Press, 2003.

6. Fran Matarasso. *Learning Development: An Introduction to the Social Impact of Public Libraries.* London: British Library Research and Innovation Centre, 1998.

7. J. Eve and Peter Brophy. *The Value and Impact of End User IT Services in Public Libraries.* Manchester, England: Centre for Research in Library & Information Management, 2001.

8. S. Briggs, H. Guldberg, and S. Sivaciyan. *Lane Cove Library—A Life: The Social Role and Economic Benefit of Public Libraries.* Sydney: Library Council of NSW, 1996.

9. Eva Cox, Kathleen Swinbourne, Chris Pip, and Suzanne Laing. *A Safe Place to Go: Libraries and Social Capital.* Sydney: State Library of New South Wales, June 2000. Available at http://www.sl.nsw.gov.au/pls/publications/pdf/safe_place.pdf.

10. Carol Oxley. *Libraries/Building/Communities. The Vital Contribution of Victoria's Public Libraries—A Research Report for the Library Board of Victoria and the Victorian Public Library Network. Executive Summary; Report One: Setting the Scene; Report Two: Logging the Benefits; Report Three: Bridging the Gaps; Report Four: Showcasing the Best.* Sydney: State Library of Sydney, 2005. Available at http://www.slv.vic.gov.au/about/information/publications/policies_reports/plu_lbc.html.

11. Candy Hillenbrand. Public Libraries as Developers of Social Capital. *APLIS*, 18 (1), March 2005, 4–12.

12. See, for example, Evelyn Kerslake and Margaret Kinnel. *The Social Impact of Public Libraries: A Literature Review.* British Library Research and Innovation Centre. London: Community Development Foundation, 1997.

13. Rebecca Linley and Bob Usherwood. *New Measures for the New Library: A Social Audit of Public Libraries.* British Library Research & Innovation Centre Report 89. London: British Library Board, 1998.

14. D. H. Blake, W. C. Frederick, and M. S. Myers. *Social Auditing: Evaluating the Impact of Corporate Programmes.* New York: Praeger, 1976.

15. Janie Percy-Smith. Auditing Social Needs. *Policy and Politics*, 20 (1), 1992, 29–34.

16. Lee Miringoff. *The Public Library: A National Survey.* Poughkeepsie, NY: The Marist College Institute for Public Opinion, 2003. A PowerPoint presentation of the poll's results is available at http://midhudson.org/funding/advocacy/Marist_Poll_2003.ppt.

17. Survey results available at http://www/nyla.org.

18. For more information visit http://www.nysl.sysed.gov/rcols/finalrpt.htm#Appendixb.

19. Keith Curry Lance, Marcia J. Rodney, Nicolle O. Steffen, Suzanne Kaller, Rochelle Logan, Christie M. Koontz, and Dean K. Jue. *Counting on Results: New Tools for Outcome-Based Evaluation of Public Libraries.* Aurora, CO: Bibliographic Center for Research, 2002. See also Nicolle O. Steffen, Keith Curry Lance, and Rochelle Logan. Time to Tell the Whole Story: Outcome-Based Evaluation and the Counting on Results Project. *Public Libraries*, 41 (4), July/August 2002, 222–28; and Nicolle O. Steffen and Keith Curry Lance. Who's Doing What: Outcome-Based Evaluation and Demographics in the Counting on Results Project. *Public Libraries*, 41 (5), September/October 2002, 271–76, 278–79.

20

Communicating the Value of the Library

The library director, the library board members, and the library's senior management team will often find opportunities to share the value of the library with interested stakeholders and community members. Whether in conversations, making a presentation, or communicating in writing, it is best if the library selects a framework for sharing its accomplishments. Among the frameworks that might be employed are

- performance measures,
- the balanced scorecard,
- the performance prism, and
- the three Rs.

PERFORMANCE MEASURES

WHY MEASURE PERFORMANCE?
If you don't measure results, you can't tell success from failure.
If you can't see success, you can't reward it.
If you can't reward success, you're probably rewarding failure.
If you can't see success, you can't learn from it.
If you can't recognize failure, you can't correct it.
If you can demonstrate results, you can win public support.
                                        —David Osborne and Ted Gaebler[1]

The use of performance measures is not an end in itself but rather a means to improve operations and services and for reporting to various stakeholders how much the library is used and how efficiently the library is operating. It is important for the library director and the management team to assist in the process of helping the library's stakeholders define success for the institution. It is also important to recognize that the library cannot be all things to all people and so must focus on what services are provided to meet the needs of specific segments of potential users of the library. Defining success is not a destination but a journey, and the definition of success will change over time as the library meets and exceeds its goals.

It is possible to consider the variety of potential measures as forming a hierarchy (see Figure 20.1). The library can utilize a variety of input, process, output, and outcome or impact performance measures.[2]

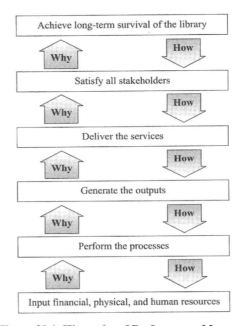

Figure 20.1. Hierarchy of Performance Measures

The key to communicating how effective the library is to its customers is to actively involve the various stakeholders, especially the funding decision makers, in determining what information they would like to know about the library. In particular, asking these individuals what questions about the library they would like answered is very important to have a better understanding of what issues and perspectives are important to them individually and collectively. With this understanding in hand, it is possible to identify a set of performance measures that will have maximum impact in communicating value.

Neil McLean and Clare Wilde have revised and expanded upon the evaluation model originally developed by Orr (see Figure 20.2).[3] This revised model clearly demonstrates the wide variety of measures that can be selected by a library and differentiates the activities in the library that are performed by staff to prepare materials for use (technical processes) from the activities performed by staff that interact with the users of the library (public processes). Remember that a performance measure is simply a quantitative description of a specific process or activity, and the measure requires some context and analysis in order to understand its underlying meaning.

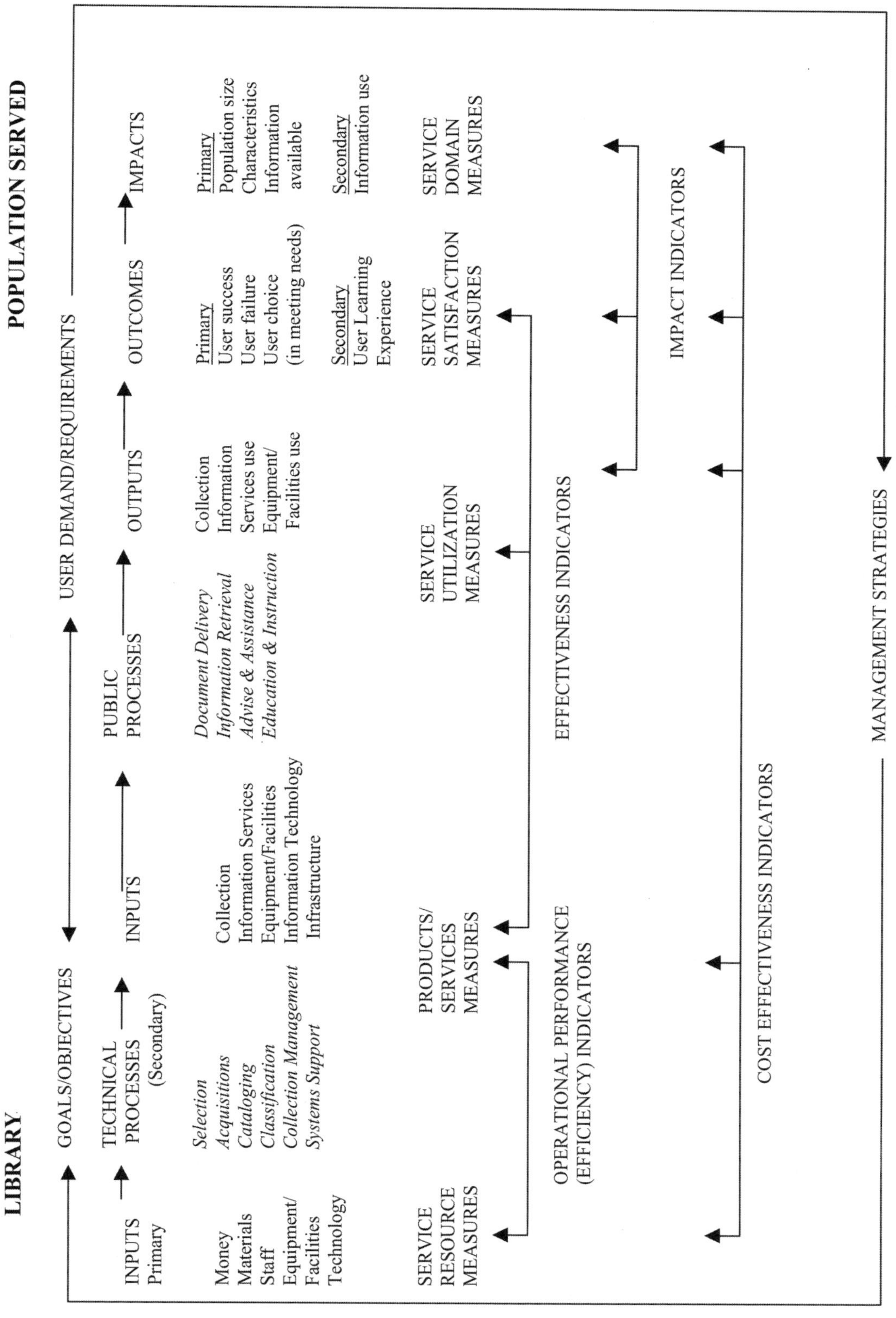

Figure 20.2. Performance Measurement Framework

Ultimately the success of a library director and of the library's budget is a political judgment on the part of the various stakeholders, particularly the funding decision makers and of the citizens themselves (especially if they are called upon to vote for an increased tax levy), about the utility and value of the library to its customers and the larger organizational context.

This is accomplished by first identifying the strategies that the library will be using to deliver the services it has selected as most responsive to the needs of its customers. Then the library has to identify that set of input, process, output, and outcome measures that will reflect the contribution of the library to individuals and to the larger organizational context. But once these have been selected, it is important to ensure that the collection and use of the measures are clearly understood by all library staff members. To achieve the library's vision of the future, goals are set for each measure (usually interim goals are also established). Finally, the performance measures are collected and distributed to all staff members and stakeholders on a quarterly basis. The measures are then discussed in regular library management and staff meetings so that the importance of the measures is clear. Any corrective actions, if any, can then be discussed and planned.

It is also important to select performance measures of activities and services over which the library has complete control. An effective performance measurement system has the following attributes:

- **Clarity of purpose.** The audience for whom the measures are being collected and analyzed is clearly stated. Those in the target audience should readily understand the indicators.

- **Focus.** The measures chosen should reflect the service objectives of the library.

- **Alignment.** The performance measures should be synchronized with the goals and objectives of the library. Too many libraries routinely collect too many statistics and performance measures that then are casually ignored.

- **Balance.** The measures should present a balanced view of the library and its overall performance. Some of the measures should include outcomes and the user perspective. Measures describe different characteristics of performance:

    - *Absolute/relative.* An absolute measure is one that can stand on its own. A relative performance measure is compared to the same measure in other "similar" libraries.

    - *Process/function oriented.* A process measure looks at the various tasks and activities that comprise a functional activity, e.g., cataloging. A functional measure takes a broader view.

    - *Performance or diagnostic.* Some performance measures are designed to measure the achievements of a particular service, while others are gathered to assist in analyzing a process or activity with the goal of improving it.

    - *Objective/subjective.* Objective measures reflect a specific activity, e.g., circulation, while a subjective measure reflects an opinion or observation by a trained professional, e.g., adequacy and depth of a collection, or by customers, e.g., satisfaction surveys. Sometimes objective data are referred to as "hard measures," while subjective data have been called "soft measures."

    - *Direct/indirect.* A direct indicator measures a specific activity (circulation). An indirect indicator provides an estimate for an activity (the number of online catalog searches is used as a surrogate in order to estimate the number of people who used the online catalog, for example, 2.5 searches = 1 person).

- *Leading/lagging.* A leading performance measure provides some advance warning that another activity will increase or decrease. A lagging measure reflects actual performance, e.g., circulation.

- *Social/economic.* Combinations of social and economic outcome measures can be used.

- **Regular refinement.** The performance indicators should be periodically reviewed to ensure that their continued use provides the library with real value. In some cases, a new measure should be introduced and another dropped.

- **Vigorous performance indicators.** Each performance measure should be clearly defined and relevant. The data collected should be unambiguous and not open to manipulation. Readily available statistics, such as the number of Web site hits, are often more dangerous than useful.

The selection, collection, and sharing of performance measures are designed to provide improved services as well as increased accountability by informing all of the library's stakeholders how well the library is actually doing. Among the measures that are reported to stakeholders there should be a balance among input, process (efficiency), output, and outcome measures. The library might want to consider grouping the measures into categories.

For example, Don Mills, director of the Mississauga Public Library in Ontario, Canada, has developed eight categories—the 8 Bs—which are used for planning purposes as well as communicating the library's results to its stakeholders:

- Books—physical and electronic resources
- Bricks—facilities issues
- Bytes—information technology plan
- Bucks—revenue generation (Friends, partnerships, ads)
- Bodies—staff related topics
- Bridges—partnerships
- Boasts—marketing and promotion, celebration of accomplishments
- Board.[4]

These measures are meant to be illustrative rather than prescriptive. Also, it is important to provide some context for each of the measures so that library stakeholders will know whether a market penetration figure, for example, is better than, about the same as, or less than other comparable libraries. In addition, it might be illuminating to provide information about the set of performance measures over the course of the last four or five years so that people will have a better idea of possible trends. Presenting the information in graphical form assists in identifying trends.

THE BALANCED SCORECARD

One approach to communicating value and performance that has taken on an increasingly important role in profit, nonprofit, and governmental agencies is the use of the balanced scorecard.

Responding to the criticisms of the late 1980s that accountants and annual reports provided a narrow, backward-looking or lagging financial perspective and thus were not helpful in helping to understand the overall health and performance of the organization, Robert Kaplan and David Norton suggested through a series of articles and books that the balanced scorecard would provide a broader perspective.[5]

The process of developing a balanced scorecard is based on the premise that all the performance measures that are selected are linked to the strategies that have been selected by the organization. The scorecard approach is based on answering four basic questions, each defining a perspective on the library's value:

- How do customers and stakeholders see the library? (customer perspective)
- What must the library excel at? (internal perspective)
- Can the library continue to improve and create value? (innovation and learning perspective)
- How does the public library look to stakeholders? (financial perspective)

Providing a set of performance measures for each perspective simultaneously lets one see "whether improvements in one area may have been achieved at the expense of another." Using this approach means that the library can consider disparate elements of the competitive agenda, such as becoming more customer orientated, shortening response times, improving collection quality, emphasizing teamwork, and developing totally new services altogether.

Seeing a variety of performance indicators that are focused on the four perspectives allows management to take a broader view. The library does not just pursue circulation, or customer satisfaction, or expenditures on fiction in isolation. Rather, the scorecard provides a vehicle that allows the management team and library staff members to see how their combined actions are reflected in the performance indicators considered as a uniform set.[6] An overview of the balanced scorecard is shown in Figure 20.3.

Customer perspective (users). Customer concerns tend to fall into four categories: time, quality, performance and service, and cost. A variety of customer-focused measures can be employed, including customer satisfaction (although customer satisfaction surveys must be used cautiously in a library setting due to their positively skewed results). The strategies selected by the library should be designed to answer two questions: Who are our customers? What value does the library provide to them?

Internal perspective. Managers need to focus on the critical internal operations that enable them to satisfy customer needs. This part of the scorecard looks at the processes and competencies in which a library must excel. In addition to productivity measures, technological capability, and introduction of new ideas to improve an existing service or introduce a new service might be addressed.

Innovation and learning perspective. This looks at the library's ability to grow, learn, develop, and introduce new services. It focuses on measures such as the quality of the existing infrastructure, organizational culture, and the improvement of library staff member skills. Measures in this perspective are really enablers for the other perspectives. A library will typically identify and create new measures for this perspective.

Financial perspective. In the arena of an academic, public, school, government, or nonprofit library, financial measures such as profitability are not directly relevant. However, regardless of the type of library it can, and must, demonstrate that it makes effective use of the funding that is provided.

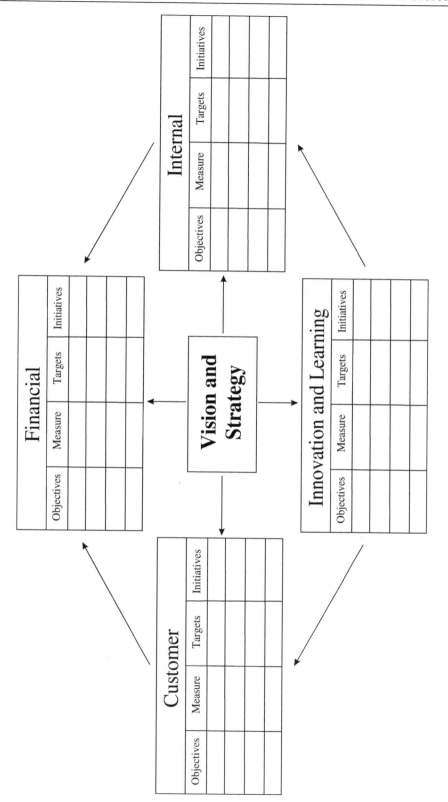

Figure 20.3. The Balanced Scorecard

In the for-profit arena, the assumption is that the innovative perspective (dealing with infrastructure and the quality of staff) will create a more efficient operation (internal perspective). The combination of staff, infrastructure, and internal operations will lead to products and services that will be more appealing to customers. The customers are then going to purchase more products and services, leading to better financial results (financial perspective).

Once measures for each perspective have been identified, the ultimate target and interim goals for each target are selected. One of the challenges is to establish goals that are a bit of a stretch for the library to achieve and yet are based on considering the current performance of the processes used to deliver the results. Arbitrary goals and targets invite fear, frustration, and distortion of the performance measures being collected. One helpful technique is to create process charts that reveal the existing performance.[7]

The resulting scorecard assists a library in translating its vision and strategies by providing a framework that helps communicate the library's strategy through the objectives and measures chosen.

Since traditional measurement systems sprang from the finance function, the performance measurement systems have historically had a control bias. That is, traditional performance measurement systems specify the particular actions they want employees to take and then measure to see whether the employees have in fact taken those actions. In that way, the accounting systems try to control behavior.

The balanced scorecard, on the other hand, puts strategy and vision, not control, at the center. It establishes goals but assumes that people will adopt whatever behavior and take whatever actions are necessary to help achieve those goals. The goal is to minimize the gap that exists between the mission and performance measures. The focus should be on what the library intends to achieve and not the programs and initiatives that are being implemented to achieve the library's vision.

The strength of the balanced scorecard is that the selected performance measures are those, or should be those, that will reflect the strategies embraced by the library. One of the crucial steps is to develop a strategy map that clearly identifies the cause-and-effect relationships of each strategy to the other perspectives.[8] A strategy map is a one-page picture of the library's strategy or strategies that articulates the objectives from the four perspectives. The strategy map thus becomes an anchor with which the library can manage and motivate its staff members.

For example, a library might want to improve the quality and variety of services available to its online customers so that these services will be similar to those received by customers who visit the library. This might require improved technology skill levels for some staff, upgraded technology infrastructures, a change in existing procedures to provide some services, a larger budget allocation for capital expenses, and training. The end result, it is hoped, will be more satisfied online customers. The challenge? Selecting performance measures that reflect the underlying strategy for each perspective. The result will be a series of interconnected objectives and measures flowing through each perspective.

A great many libraries will measure progress in achieving milestones of their annual initiatives. Initiatives should exist to assist the library in achieving its strategic objectives. The initiatives are the means and not the end. Strategy and associated performance measures should focus on what output and outcomes the library intends to achieve, not what programs and initiatives are being implemented.

The balanced scorecard provides a useful framework with a focal point when a library is trying to draw up performance measures for the library. The system is based on the understanding that no *single* measure can focus attention on all the critical areas of the service. And the performance measures that are selected must work together coherently to reflect the achievement of the overall goals of the library.

A Library Scorecard

Robert Kaplan has suggested an alternative scorecard for nonprofit organizations (see Figure 20.4).[9] Rather than using the original balanced scorecard, with its four perspectives created for for-profit firms, a revised balanced scorecard may be more appropriate for academic, public, government, school, and nonprofit libraries. In addition to a reorganized structure, the library balanced scorecard introduces another perspective—*information resources* (see Figure 20.5, p. 340). These information resources are composed of the library's physical collection, the access to electronic databases subscribed to by the library, and resources from other sources, such as libraries through interlibrary loan or a document delivery service.

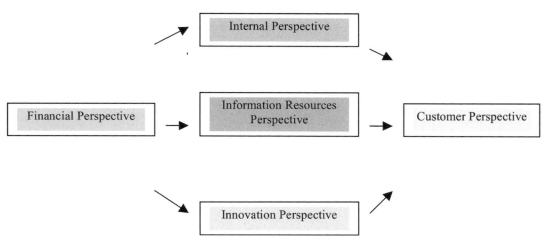

Figure 20.4. The Library Scorecard

The library scorecard model suggests that the financial resources provided to the library are used to provide the information resources, staff (who use a variety of processes and procedures that are measured using the internal perspective) and build the infrastructure and provide staff training. All of these are combined to provide services to users (the customer perspective).

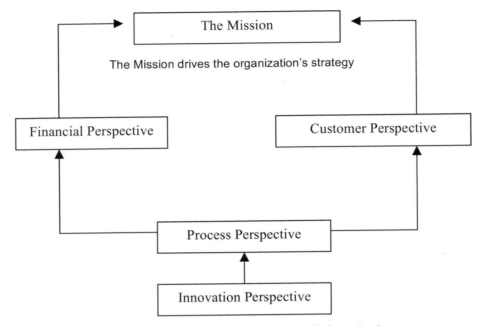

Figure 20.5. Balanced Scorecard for Nonprofit Organizations

PERFORMANCE PRISM

Somewhat similar to the balanced scorecard, the performance prism was developed in England by a team led by Andy Neely and consists of five interrelated perspectives on performance:[10]

- **Stakeholder satisfaction.** Who are our key stakeholders, and what do they want and need?

- **Stakeholder contribution.** What do we want and need from our stakeholders on a reciprocal basis?

- **Strategies.** What strategies do we need to put in place to satisfy the wants and needs of stakeholders while satisfying our own requirements?

- **Processes.** What processes do we need to put in place to enable us to execute our strategies?

- **Capabilities.** What capabilities do we need to put in place to allow us to operate our processes?

These five perspectives provide a broad, comprehensive framework for thinking about organizational performance. Figure 20.6 illustrates these five basic perspectives on performance management.

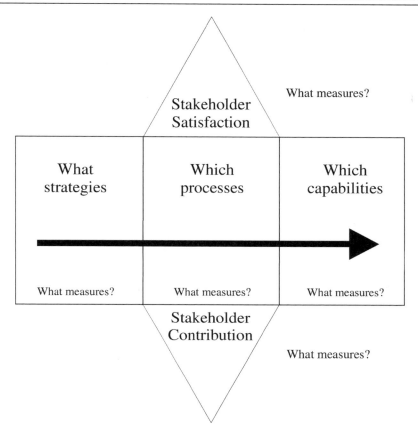

Figure 20.6. The Performance Prism

Compared to the balanced scorecard, the inclusion of the "stakeholder satisfaction" perspective provides a broader view. Stakeholders include funding decision makers, suppliers, and partners as well as customers and employees. Another unique perspective is that of "strategies." This perspective focuses on what strategies are chosen by the library to achieve its vision.

Capabilities are the combination of people, technology, and infrastructure, practices that enable the organization to execute its processes. The obvious question for this perspective is, what are the key capabilities to operate our processes?

The "stakeholder contribution" facet recognizes that not only do various stakeholders make contributions in the form of budgets, support, and other ways. Employees, for example, are looking for a secure place to work with good working conditions, a decent salary, and recognition. In return the organization wants its employees to be responsible when working, offer suggestions, develop their skills, and remain loyal.

The selection of performance measures that are linked to these five perspectives assists the library in managing its resources to better meet the needs of its customers.

THREE Rs OF PERFORMANCE

Yet another potential management tool is three Rs of performance.[11] "This tool provides a balanced approach to performance management by creating a strategic and comprehensive context for decision making (see Figure 20.7).

Reach

(Who? Where?)

Results

(What do we want? Why?)

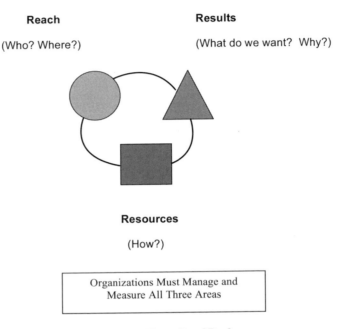

Resources

(How?)

Organizations Must Manage and
Measure All Three Areas

Figure 20.7. The Three Rs of Performance

Resources refer to both the amount of time, money, and energy exerted as well as the type of resources used. Types of resources include capital and people, skill types and competencies required of staff, and the physical and spatial location of resources. It is important to understand the total resources committed to a service, a program, or the entire library system as well as the key characteristics of the resources. Tools such as return on investment (ROI) and net present value (NPV) were developed to optimize resource utilization by maximizing the financial returns.

Reach refers to the breadth and depth of influence over which available resources are spread. Physical (spatial) reach is one dimension, as well as the type of customers the library wishes to reach. For many services and programs, reach goals relate to the number and extent of clients served. Michael Porter, the strategy guru, and others have emphasized that an organization needs to focus on market share. As competition becomes an increasing concern, market share becomes an important indicator of success.

Results refer to the impact on the groups of customers reached by the resources used. Results usually indicate the attainment of a desired outcome for the individual or the larger community being served. Often an organization will focus on service quality as a means to achieve better results. Value has been added when the results are desirable from the customer's perspective. Customers may express themselves by indicating higher levels of satisfaction.

Using a balanced scorecard based on the three Rs of performance, as shown in Figure 20.8, allows a library to better understand the trade-offs inherent in decision making and provide a means for strategic and operational planning while monitoring progress toward achieving specific goals.

Performance Area	Indicators/Measures	Systems
Resources	Investment in core competencies Cost by service offered	Cost accounting
Reach	Clients served by segment Clients served by target population	Client tracking
Results	Service quality Economic benefits Social benefits	Client surveys
Key ratios: Cost per client served Cost per result (service)		

Figure 20.8. Generic Three Rs Scorecard

Because resources, reach, and results are all linked together, the best approach would seem to be to optimize among them in choosing goals and strategies rather than focusing on one of the three Rs. The value of using the three Rs is that they help the top management team of an organization as well as the stakeholders understand the trade-offs associated with a particular decision. Not surprisingly, most organizations focus their efforts on reporting measures concerning resources.

SUMMARY

The value of using a tool such as the balanced scorecard, the performance prism, or the three Rs is that it facilitates the communication process with a variety of stakeholders who are important to the library. In particular, it affords the library director the opportunity of determining what measures are going to be of value to the library's funding decision makers. More important, it provides a vehicle for the library to identify those strategies that it will use to most effectively serve the needs of its customers. Having identified the strategies, the library can then select a set of performance measures to track that are linked to the selected strategies. Performance measures track customer satisfaction and the processes that lead to those results. Thus, it is important for the library to utilize performance measures; what you measure is what you get.[12]

Organizational performance is driven by people and the processes they use to deliver services. Overlaying a new management tool without carefully considering the value and utility of the library's existing organizational structure may mean that all the potential benefits that may arise when using a scorecard will not be achieved. Worse, the existing organizational structure and the traditions embraced by the culture within the library may be setting up a project to implement a scorecard for failure. Thus, it may be necessary to change the existing organizational structure when implementing a scorecard that focuses on outcomes. It is important to remember that scorecards are about providing an overview and balance about the library and not primarily about collecting separate performance measures.

At the conclusion of the strategic planning process, the library director, top management team, and interested stakeholders should be able to answer the following questions:

- What are the mission, vision, and values of the library?

- What is the business of this library, and what is the strategic orientation of the library? Or, what are the strategies being used to reach the library's vision?

- Who are the customers served, and how does the library add value?

- What does the library want to be known for—its reputation?

- What is the nature of the strategy formation process in the library, who participates in it, and where are the strategies documented?

- What are the critical success factors or business drivers for the library?

- How do the library's services and products relate to each of the business drivers?

- Who are the key decision makers for the library?

- What are the service and product priorities of the key stakeholders?

- What are the key stakeholders' perceptions of performance and benefit of the library's services and products?

- What performance measures are used to track the success of the strategies being employed by the library?

- Is the library striving to create a culture of assessment by training staff to use analysis and statistical techniques to solve problems?

- Has the library considered using some form of a balanced scorecard or other management tool to facilitate communicating the value of the library to key stakeholders?

NOTES

1. David Osborne and Ted Gaebler. *Reinventing Government: How the Entrepreneurial Spirit is Transforming the Public Sector*. New York: Addison-Wesley, 1992.

2. Cram, Jennifer. Performance Management, Measurement and Reporting in a Time of Information-centred Change. *The Australian Library Journal*, 45 (3), August 1996, 225–38.

3. Adapted from Neil McLean and Clare Wilde. Evaluating Library Performance: The Search for Relevance. *Australian Academic & Research Libraries*, 22 (3), September 1991, 201.

4. E-mail communication from Don Mills, February 5, 2007.

5. Robert S. Kaplan and David P. Norton. *Strategy Maps: Converting Intangible Assets Into Tangible Outcomes*. Boston: Harvard Business School Press, 2004; Robert S. Kaplan and David P. Norton. *The Strategy-Focused Organization: How Balanced Scorecard Companies Thrive in the New Business Environment*. Boston: Harvard Business School Press, 2001; Robert S. Kaplan and David P. Norton. *The Balanced Scorecard: Translating Strategy Into Action*. Boston: Harvard Business School Press, 1996; Robert S. Kaplan and David P. Norton. The Balanced Scorecard—Measures That Drive Performance. *Harvard Business Review*, January–February 1992, 71–79.

6. Charles Birch. *Future Success: A Balanced Approach to Measuring and Improving Success in Your Organization*. New York: Prentice-Hall, 2000; and Mark Graham Brown. *Winning Score: How to Design and Implement Organizational Scorecards*. Portland, OR: Productivity, 2000.

7. Larry B. Weinstein and Joseph F. Castellano. Benchmarking and Stretch Targets Are Often Adopted to Support the Balanced Scorecard. But Do They Do What Is Necessary to Make the Scorecard Effective? Using Statistical Process Control Might Be More Effective. *CMA Management*, April 2004, 19–22.

8. Robert S. Kaplan and David P. Norton. *Strategy Maps: Converting Intangible Assets into Tangible Outcomes*. Boston: Harvard Business School Press, 2004.

9. Robert S. Kaplan. Strategic Performance Measurement and Management in Nonprofit Organizations. *Nonprofit Management & Leadership*, 11 (3), Spring 2001, 353–70.

10. Andy Neely, Chris Adams, and Mike Kennerley. *The Performance Prism: The Scorecard for Measuring and Managing Business Success*. London: Prentice Hall, 2002;

Andy Neely and Chris Adams. The Performance Prism Perspective. *Journal of Cost Management*, 15 (1), January/February 2001, 7–15; Andy Neely, Chris Adams and Paul Crowe. The Performance Prism in Practice. *Measuring Business Excellence*, 5 (2), 2001, 6–12; and Andy Neely, John Mills, Ken Platts, Mike Gregory, and Huw Richards. Realizing Strategy Through Measurement. *International Journal of Operations & Production Management*, 14 (3), 1994, 140–52.

11. Steve Montague. The Three Rs of Performance: Core Concepts for Planning, Measurement, and Management. Ottawa: Performance Management Network, 1997.

12. K. Nichols. The Crucial Edge of Reinvention: A Primer on Scoping and Measuring for Organizational Change. *Public Administration Quarterly*, 21 (4), 1997, 405–18.

Appendix A:
Raward Library Usability Analysis Tool

Usability Index Checklist	
	Usability Index
	What is the name of the Web site?
	What is the location of the Web site?
	What is the main purpose of the site?
	When was the usability index measured?
Checklist Questions	
Category 1: Finding the Information	
1.1	**Contents**
1.1.1	Does the site include staff contact details?
1.1.2	Are services clearly stated?
1.1.3	Is there a purpose statement?
1.1.4	Does the site have a web interface to the catalogue?
1.2	**Index**
1.2.1	Is an index included?
1.2.2	Are the entries in alphabetical order?
1.2.3	Are secondary and tertiary entries included?
1.3	**Site Map**
1.3.1	Is a site map included?
1.3.2	Are the links in the site map correct?
1.4	**Search Tool**
1.4.1	Is a search tool of the site included?
1.4.2	Choose a topic, e.g., How do I borrow books?; Was it easy to find?
1.5	**Currency of Information**
1.5.1	Is the date of the last update included on every page?
1.5.2	Is new information indicated in some way?

1.5.3	Is there a "What's New" Page?
1.6	**Finding an Answer**
1.6.1	Choose a simple fact: can a user find it in less than 10 minutes?
1.7	**Authority of Information**
1.7.1	Are links to outside resources reliable?
1.7.2	Are links to outside resources appropriate?
1.7.3	Are resources current?
1.8	**Comments Page**
1.8.1	Can comments be made about the site?
1.8.2	Is it possible to get feedback?
1.8.3	Is it possible to ask questions?
1.8.4	Is it possible to get help?
1.9	**Responsibility for Page**
1.9.1	Is it clear who has responsibility for the page?
1.9.2	Are phone, fax, or postal address included on each page?
1.9.3	Are contact details, such as e-mail, included on each page?
Category 2: Understanding the Information	
2.1	**Headings (Choose 2 pages at random)**
2.1.1	Are headings user friendly?
2.1.2	Are headings jargon free?
2.1.3	Are headings intuitive?
2.1.4	Are headings brief and informative?
2.1.5	Are headings within pages labeled correctly?
2.1.6	Do headings stand out on the page?
2.1.7	At least one heading on every page?
2.1.8	Heading levels appropriate to level of detail?
2.1.9	Accurately reflects tasks or information?
2.1.10	Are headings task based?
2.2	**Organization of the Content**
2.2.1	Structure of lists parallel?

2.2.2	Each paragraph has main idea?
2.2.3	Presentation moves from general to specific?
2.2.4	Presentation moves from simple to complex?
2.2.5	Limited to appropriate and necessary topics?
2.2.6	In correct sequence?
2.2.7	Procedures task oriented?
2.3	**Style of Text**
2.3.1	Style conforms to the home institutions desired style?
2.3.2	Active and passive voices used appropriately?
2.3.3	Second person used appropriately?
2.3.4	Present tense predominates?
2.3.5	Reading level acceptable?
2.3.6	One-sentence paragraphs used sparingly?
2.3.7	Sentences simple but not terse?
2.3.8	Is scannability good?
2.3.9	Is text simple, concise, clear?
2.4	**Terminology**
2.4.1	New terms highlighted and defined when first used?
2.4.2	Consistency of terms used?
2.4.3	First occurences of abbreviations follow spelled out words?
2.4.4	Level of technical terms appropriate to audience?
2.5	**Mechanics (Choose 5 pages at random)**
2.5.1	Are spelling, grammar and punctuation correct?
2.5.2	Capitalisation, spelling and punctuation correct?
2.5.3	Acronyms avoided where possible?
Category 3: Supporting User Tasks	
3.1	**Transactional Tasks**
3.1.1	Are reply forms shorter than one page?
3.1.2	Are forms easy to follow?
3.1.3	Is a print equivalent form been made available?

3.2	User Questions
3.2.1	Are Frequently Asked Questions (FAQ) included for the site?
3.2.2	Are Frequently Asked Questions (FAQ) provided at a task level?
3.2.3	Are Help Screens included at a task level?
Category 4: Evaluating the Technical Accuracy	
4.1	**Cross-platform Compatibility:** Does the site view and load equally well in:
4.1.1	Internet Explorer?
4.1.2	Netscape?
4.1.3	On a Windows-based machine?
4.1.4	On a Macintosh?
4.2	**Display and Download Speed (Choose 3 pages at random)**
4.2.1	Home page displays within 10 seconds with a 33.6 modem?
4.2.2	If not, is there feedback indicating the delay?
4.2.3	Is each page size under 70k?
4.2.4	Are graphics under 25k in size?
4.2.5	Are "alt" statements included if graphics are turned off?
4.2.6	If more than 5 graphics on a page, are they 15k or smaller?
4.2.7	Is there visual appeal?
4.2.8	Is there advance notice before downloading large files?
4.2.9	Are thumbnail pictures at least 2.5x5.0 cm?
4.2.10	Do the pages display on an average sized screen?
4.2.11	Does the top level fit on one screen?
4.2.12	If image maps are used are redundant text links provided?
4.3	**HTML Format: (Choose 2 pages at random)**
4.3.1	Is standard HTML code used?
4.3.2	Has metadata been used?
4.3.3	Is the page HTML error free?
4.3.4	Are width and height attributes included on all images?
4.3.5	Are width and height attributes included on all tables?

Category 5: Presenting the Information	
5.1	**Relationship to the Home Institution**
5.1.1	Is their a clear link from the library to the institution's home page?
5.1.2	Is their a clear link to the library from the institution's home page?
5.1.3	Does the library Web site follow the institution's home page?
5.2	**Disability Access**
5.2.1	Does the page provide a text equivalent for every nontext element?
5.2.2	Is information conveyed with color also available without color?
5.2.3	Are documents organized so they may be read without style sheets?
5.3	**Links**
5.3.1	Is there at least one link on every page?
5.3.2	Are links error free?
5.4	**Navigation**
5.4.1	Are there clear navigation tools included on all pages?
5.4.2	Is there Navigation back to home page?
5.4.3	Is there Navigation up and down within a page?
5.5	**Text Format**
5.5.1	Format consistent throughout the site?
5.5.2	Figures and tables aligned correctly?
5.5.3	White space used effectively?
5.5.4	Information presented in readable blocks?
5.5.5	Major topics begin on separate pages?
5.5.6	Are sentences complete within the web screen?
5.6	**Printing?**
5.6.1	Do all the text and graphics print on A4 paper?
[This checklist has 103 questions in total]	
Calculating the Usability Index	
103 x (Total Yes Answers)/(Total Yes and No Answers) x percent	

Appendix B: LibQUAL+ Survey Questions

Please rate the following statements (1 is the lowest, 9 is the highest) by indicating

Minimum—the number that represents the *minimum* level of service that would find acceptable

Desired—the number that represents the level of service that you *personally want*

Perceived—the number that represents the level of service that you *believe* our library currently provides

For each item, you must EITHER rate the item in all three columns OR identify the item as "N/A" (not applicable). Selecting "N/A" will override all other answers.

When it comes to . . .
1) Employees who instill confidence in users
2) Making electronic resources accessible from my home or office
3) Library space that inspires study and learning
4) Giving users individual attention
5) A library Web site enabling me to locate information on my own

When it comes to . . .
6) Employees who are consistently courteous
7) The printed library materials I need for my work
8) Quiet space for individual activities
9) Readiness to respond to users' questions
10) The electronic information resources I need

When it comes to . . .
11) Employees who have the knowledge to answer user questions
12) A comfortable and inviting location
13) Employees who deal with users in a caring fashion
14) Modern equipment that lets me easily access needed information
15) Employees who understand the needs of their users

When it comes to . . .
16) Easy-to-use access tools that allow me to find things on my own
17) A getaway for study, learning or research
18) Willingness to help users
19) Making information easily accessible for independent use
20) Print or electronic journal collections I require for my work

When it comes to . . .
21) Community space for group learning and group study
22) Dependability in handling users' service problems

Author/Title Index

Subject Index

About the Author

JOSEPH R. MATTHEWS is an instructor at the San Jose State University School of Library and Information Science. He is also a consultant specializing in strategic planning, assessment and evaluation of library services, the use of performance measures, and the Library Balanced Scorecard. He lives in Carlsbad, California.